THE NEW AMERICAN MUSICAL

THE NEW AMERICAN MUSICAL

AN ANTHOLOGY FROM THE END OF THE CENTURY

FLOYD COLLINS

RENT

PARADE

THE WILD PARTY

Edited and Introduced by

WILEY HAUSAM

THEATRE COMMUNICATIONS GROUP
NEW YORK 2003

The New American Musical: An Anthology from the End of the Century is published by Theatre Communications Group, 520 8th Avenue, 24th Floor, New York, NY 10018.

This publication is made possible in part with public funds from
the New York State Council on the Arts, a State Agency.

TCG books are exclusively distributed to the book trade by Consortium Book Sales and Distribution, 1045 Westgate Dr., St. Paul, MN 55114.

LIBRARY OF CONGRESS CATALOGING-IN-PUBLICATION DATA

The new American musical : an anthology from the end of the twentieth century /
edited by Wiley Hausam.
p. cm.
Contents: Rent / book, music, and lyrics by Jonathan Larson—Floyd Collins / music and lyrics by Adam Guettel ; book by Tina Landau—Parade / music and lyrics by Jason Robert Brown ; book by Alfred Uhry—The wild party / music and lyrics by Michael John LaChiusa ; book by George C. Wolfe.
ISBN 1-55936-200-6 (pbk. : alk. paper)
Musicals—Librettos. I. Hausam, Wiley.
ML48.N485 2001
782.1'40268—dc21

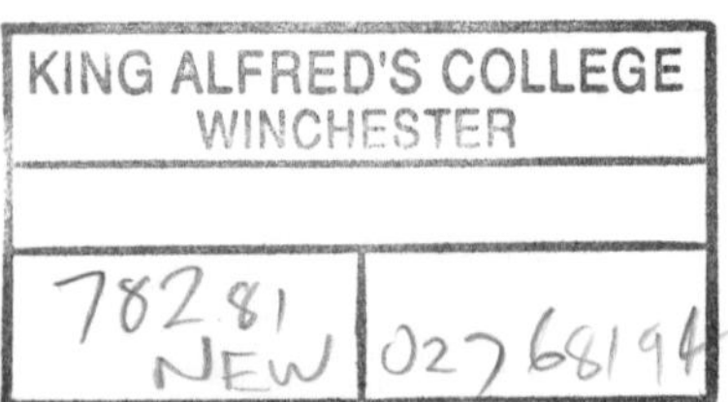

Cover illustration and design by Mark Melnick
Text design and composition by Lisa Govan

First Edition, June 2003

For those in pursuit of
the elusive American musical theater
as a popular art form

But they all qualify, different as they are, for that term "musical comedy" on the grounds of one great unifying factor: they all belong to an art that arises out of American roots, out of our speech, our tempo, our moral attitudes, our way of moving. Out of all this, a new form has been born. Some people claim that it is the forerunner of a new kind of opera; others insist it will never become opera, because it is not art, nor is it meant to be anything but light entertainment. Being a liberal, I can see both sides. We will always have with us the line of gorgeous girls, the star comic and the razzle-dazzle band in the pit.

But there's more in the wind than that. We are in a historical position now similar to that of the popular musical theater in Germany just before Mozart came along. In 1750, the big attraction was what they called the "Singspiel," which was the *Annie Get Your Gun* of its day, star comic and all. This popular form took the leap to a work of art through the genius of Mozart. After all, *The Magic Flute* is a Singspiel; only it's by Mozart.

We are in the same position; all we need is for our Mozart to come along. If and when he does, we surely won't get any *Magic Flute*; what we'll get will be a new form, and perhaps "opera" will be the wrong word for it. There must be a more exciting word for such an exciting event. And this event can happen any second. It's almost as though it is our moment in history, as if there is a historical necessity that gives us such a wealth of creative talent at this precise time.

—LEONARD BERNSTEIN
"American Musical Comedy"
Telecast: October 7, 1956

CONTENTS

Following the text to each musical is production, historical, biographical and rights information.

ACKNOWLEDGMENTS

In the late 1970s I purchased three anthologies of texts to musicals edited by a man named Stanley Richards. Two of them (now out of print as far as I know) were entitled *Great Musicals of the American Theatre*. Every one of those great musicals premiered in the commercial theater on Broadway between 1931 and 1973.

The book and the lyrics of the shows were the heart of these collections. But accompanying the scripts was information about the original productions which was equally absorbing (to an aspiring producer) and important in another way: it helped provide a context for the work. This is what I have attempted to do with this new anthology.

Facts about original productions of theater works are usually neglected and lie scattered about (or are lost), probably because the people who know the facts are too busy making theater to record them. Collecting facts and verifying their accuracy takes a lot of assistance. For this, I offer the following individuals my thanks:

The authors' representatives (agents, attorneys and stock and amateur licensing houses), especially Andrew Boose, William Craver, Deb Hartnett and Charlie Scatamacchia.

The members of each show's original production teams, especially John Corker, Mary Bryant and Don Summa.

The photographers of the original productions, Joan Marcus and Carol Rosegg.

Ben Levit, formerly of the Prince Music Theater, Lynn Moffat at New York Theatre Workshop and Susan Larsen at Playwrights Horizons.

I thank Mark Kelley for suggesting the idea of an anthology to me.

I am grateful to the colleagues who have helped me examine my long and deeply held assumptions about this form: Michael John LaChiusa, Harold Prince, Eric Salzman, George C. Wolfe, the students of Cycle 12 of the Graduate Musical Theater Writing Program at the Tisch School of the Arts, New York University, Sarah Schlesinger and, especially, to Lydia Goehr, for introducing me to a much larger frame of reference. For loyal and understanding friendship during a difficult time, I thank Davis Branco and Fred Hanson. Would that I could still thank my friend, the late Bridget Aschenberg.

I am very grateful to Terry Nemeth of TCG, who was immediately enthusiastic about the idea of this anthology when I brought it to him, and to Kathy Sova who has guided me through the publication process.

My deep thanks go to the composers, lyricists and librettists of the four works contained in this volume.

Wiley Hausam
May 2003

WAY BACK TO PARADISE:

In Search of Today's Great American Musical

The trouble with making predictions is, they're usually wrong.

When conductor/composer Leonard Bernstein made his grand prophecy for the American musical on national television in October 1956 (see preceding epigraph), he was about to begin rehearsals for *Candide,* his mock-operetta based on Voltaire's novel. And he had already been working with director/choreographer Jerome Robbins and librettist Arthur Laurents on and off for seven and a half years on the masterpiece we know as *West Side Story*.

What was Bernstein's prediction? That the Broadway musical was about to begin its ascent from mere light entertainment to a form of lyric theater art on a level with, but somehow different than, opera. The genius who would compose these masterpieces would arrive any moment.

Knowing something about artist egos (I was an artists' representative during my early years in New York), my guess is that Bernstein imagined himself as the American Mozart who would lift Broadway's musical comedy to the level of art. He was not completely wrong. Of course, one masterpiece does not a Mozart make. But that one piece was enormously influential.

For example, *West Side Story* begat Stephen Sondheim (the show's lyricist), who begat, through the artistic influence of his work, the composer/lyricists of the four works represented in this volume: *Floyd Collins, Rent, Parade* and *The Wild Party,* all of which premiered in New York City between 1996 and 2000. What all of these works and authors share is a need to stretch the form and content of the musical to portray our increasingly difficult and complex world, and with tools more broadly expressive than a 32-bar song, a good joke, a chorus line, a happy ending and a lot of spectacular razzle-dazzle.

Even in a collection that contains no work by Sondheim, his work necessarily must be discussed because, for several reasons, the question that hangs over the authors of these musicals is: "How do you follow him?"

Most theater people I know would say Sondheim is the American Mozart who redeemed the promise of the Broadway musical as art after Bernstein and Robbins abandoned it in the 1960s when they returned to their respective worlds of symphony and ballet. The works Sondheim created during the 1970s with his essential co-conceiver, director and producer Hal Prince and, variously, the book writers George Furth, James Goldman, Hugh Wheeler and John Weidman, kept alive (and extended) the tradition begun in 1927 by Jerome Kern and Oscar Hammerstein II with *Show Boat*.

Sondheim's works are notable for their innovations in form, content, tone and musical language while sustaining the excellence of the greatest Broadway composers and lyricists who came before him. What may be less appreciated is that he managed both to uphold songwriting standards and innovate without losing the essence of what audiences think of as the Broadway musical.

Now significantly, with the exception of *A Funny Thing Happened on the Way to the Forum* and *Into the Woods*, his work as a composer/lyricist has never been popular. And it has never made an imprint on the mass culture. There's no doubt, however, that it is artful and has taken its rightful place in the art world. For a new musical to be art without being broadly popular is something relatively new for musicals. It takes the work out of the realm of show business.

Until Sondheim arrived on the scene as a successful composer/lyricist in 1962 with *Forum*, almost all the musicals we still find compelling today (for example, *Show Boat*, *The King and I*, *Guys and Dolls*, *Gypsy* and *Cabaret*) found a broad audience in their time. The notable exceptions are George Gershwin's *Porgy and Bess*, Bernstein's *Candide* and Brecht and Weill's *The Threepenny Opera* (a different kind of special case: *Threepenny* originated in Weimar Germany, was hugely successful all over Europe, and its first New York production was a quick failure).

I don't pretend to understand the link between art and popular acceptance. It's tempting to believe that they cannot co-exist. Yet Shakespeare, Moliere, Dickens, Verdi, Twain, Irving Berlin, Gershwin and Duke Ellington prove that assumption wrong. It's good to be reminded that art and commerce are not necessarily mutually exclusive even though nearly all of today's popular entertainment (devoid of both rich content and a high level of craft) does strongly suggest that. Probably, artful entertainment was always very rare.

Rodgers and Hammerstein pushed the Broadway musical into popular art status in 1943 with *Oklahoma!* Or perhaps it was Hammerstein and Kern in 1927. But since *West Side Story* made its imprint on both Western popular and "high" culture in 1961 (when the film version was released), the musicals that have risen to that very high level have been very few.

An examination of the musical as specifically a popular art form seems important for at least two reasons. First, despite Sondheim's lack of commercial success and mainstream popularity, long runs and large audiences continue to be the measures of success that hang, not just over Broadway, but over the entire musical form. (Three of the pieces in this collection, all but *Rent*, have not been popular). Second, what's at stake here is a tradition that, as recently as 1981, was ranked with modern dance, abstract expressionism and jazz as one of America's great contributions to art. At present, the contemporary musical doesn't seem to belong in this distinguished company.

So what do I mean by the term popular art form? Certainly, it isn't the same thing in 2003 as it was to Bernstein in 1956 or Hammerstein and Kern in 1927. The unanswered, and perhaps unanswerable, questions are: What is a popular art musical today? Is there such a thing? Does the old definition have meaning anymore in our technologized world?

Today on Broadway, theater owners, producers and the press define "popular" as a play or musical that runs long enough to make back its investment (probably ten million dollars in the case of a musical) plus a reasonable profit. If the show plays in a fourteen hundred seat theater at eighty percent of capacity for three years (which is about the amount of time you need to make a profit these days unless you have a runaway smash), that would mean approximately 1.4 million people would have paid to see the show. Let's say that same show is sent on a national tour and another 1.4 million people see it. That show is considered very successful, and yet its total audience is about one percent of the population of the United States.

Only on Broadway would they dream of attaching the word popular to such a tiny percentage. Since *The Jazz Singer* (the first talking and singing movie) was made in 1927 (this was a pivotal year), the technology of mass production has completely transformed the concept of the popular.

Unless a successful new show becomes a successful film, it makes no imprint on our national consciousness. In the rest of the world, other than in England, Australia, Japan and, to a degree, in Germany, a stage show without a film version simply does not exist. Broadway's definition of popularity is of no economic or cultural significance in a capitalist, high-tech, mass-production world.

Now, if that Broadway audience of 1.4 million were composed of America's intellectuals, its wealthy, its power brokers, its most progressive citizens, or even just sophisticated theatergoers, then the small number of the audience might be irrelevant. But by far the largest part of the Broadway audience is none of the above. Mostly, they are middle-aged or aging tourists, many of them from abroad. Many never set foot in a so-called "legitimate" theater except when they're in New York City, which could be two or three times in a lifetime. We welcome them because New York City tourism needs them, but they do not contribute to sustaining a high-quality, adventurous theater.

Representatives of the League of American Theatres and Producers, Broadway's trade organization, might respond that the success of *Cats, Les Miserables* and *The Phantom of the Opera* (all from London in the 1980s), with their long, global lives, completely refutes my point, which is that even hit musicals are not truly popular. My response? First, to be truly popular in the twenty-first century, the work must be successful in an electronic medium. Second, perhaps these musicals can be called popular in the context of live entertainment, but they are not art. To borrow from (and telescope) one of the ideas of World War II–era German critical theorist Theodor Adorno, they are products designed to divert, distract and soothe the largest number of people possible.

"Popular" is a simple term to discuss, as opposed to "Art," a notoriously slippery concept. For example, in 1964 Andy Warhol created an object that looked exactly like the box in which Brillo scouring pads were shipped to stores. He placed it in a gallery, called it art, the art world agreed, and the very idea of art was simultaneously revolutionized and given a serious identity crisis (see philosopher Arthur C. Danto's brilliant analysis in his *The Transfiguration of the Commonplace*). The use of the term is now held hostage to paralyzing theoretical debate or, alternatively, used with complete indiscrimination. Recently, at a conference of philosophers of art, Stanley Cavell, another leading American philosopher, made a passing remark that stayed with me: currently we are experiencing an "inability to distinguish art from life."

His insight triggered my memory of another, written by Neal Gabler, an author who specializes in American culture. He believes we are now unable to distinguish life from entertainment. Combining their ideas with a simple observation about contemporary American life, I assert: we are now unable to distinguish art from entertainment. Since we live in a capitalist, entertainment-centered culture, *all commercially successful entertainment is deemed art*. It seems overstated when you see it in print here.

The point I'm trying to make (one that critics and audiences for musicals won't disagree with but will still unconsciously resist) is that, all cultural indicators to the contrary, a musical doesn't have to be popular to be artistically valuable. What I doubt they'd agree with is, if it aspires to be art today, it's probably more likely to achieve this status if it *isn't* popular. And what's the point of my point? It helps redeem, appropriately, the perceived value of the excellent and intelligent work in this collection.

Only three years into a new millennium, it's already clear that the end of the twentieth century was a special and unusual time for the artful American musical theater. So it may be clarifying, or at least interesting, to look back at the circumstances that preceded it, to give these works a context.

It's a story of decadence and dormancy followed by renewal all of which spanned twenty years, beginning around 1981.

Because of my personal relationship to most of the artists represented here, I'll go out on a limb and write that, in the naive (and I use that term admiringly) way that artists often experience life, these authors intended to make musicals that extended the tradition of *West Side Story* (1957) and Sondheim's *Sweeney Todd* (1979). What do I mean by naive? Well what would make a person who was completely in touch with reality think that there could be more musicals like those two singular masterpieces? Besides naivete, I suppose the answer is youth and arrogance. All those things often go together. And they can help authors create their best work.

In any event, the world changed, and the Broadway musical changed with it, but not without losing the best parts of its essence. Beginning around 1980 or 1981, the popular art musical could no longer survive in the Broadway context because production costs continued to rise, necessitating larger audiences. And there simply wasn't a sophisticated audience that large. In fact, a committed audience for serious musical theater was already shrinking. Perhaps too, the musical was eroded in the audience's minds by the latest technological revolution (cable television, MTV and the personal computer).

Nevertheless, Sondheim's works were still able to get a hearing on Broadway. His exceptionalism was useful to the Broadway establishment; they could point to his artistic genius and mask the sad truth that most new Broadway musicals were declining to a superficiality and banality not seen since the early 1920s.

But the post-Sondheim serious musicals rarely reached Broadway. And of course, if the shows weren't on Broadway, they no longer had any chance at all of being popular. So now what does a young artist do with this concept of popular art musicals so persuasively set forth by Bernstein?

Well maybe he or she just forgets the concept for the time being, and does his or her work (on a smaller scale) and takes it where it's wanted and appreciated. The place where Michael John LaChiusa, Adam Guettel, Jonathan Larson and Jason Robert Brown and their collaborators were wanted was Off-Broadway in New York City by a small group of not-for-profit theaters: Playwrights Horizons, The Public Theater, Lincoln Center Theater, the Music-Theatre Group, the Vineyard Theatre and New York Theatre Workshop. These institutional theaters (with the American Music Theater Festival in Philadelphia and the O'Neill Music Theater Conference in Connecticut) wholeheartedly supported the post-Sondheim generation of writers. Together, these not-for-profit theaters saved serious, new American musical theater by supporting these authors who would transform the art musical's very nature.

After the long artistic drought of the 1980s, the first fruit of renewal was borne in the spring of 1992 when George C. Wolfe and William Finn/James Lapine, with their respective pieces, *Jelly's Last Jam* and *Falsettos*, truly revitalized Broadway. Both shows were full of rage and sorrow (about racism and the AIDS epidemic, respectively) and yet somehow transformed these unconventional emotions (for Broadway) into exemplars of Broadway style, vitality and commercial success without compromising the integrity of their political themes.

On the other hand, some might say that the moment of renewal actually began in 1988 when Julie Taymor made her astonishing and singular *Juan Darien* Off-Broadway with the Music-Theatre Group, or in 1993 when The Public Theater presented the Goodman Theatre of Chicago's production of Jeffrey Lunden and Arthur Perlman's *Wings*. But certainly by the time Michael John LaChiusa's *Hello Again* opened at Lincoln Center Theater in the winter of 1994, the new generation was on its way. (None of these shows moved to Broadway.)

Six years later in the spring of 2000, as LaChiusa and Wolfe's *The Wild Party* opened on Broadway, the fertile moment for the serious, new American musical vanished like a mirage on a desert horizon. The new media industry and the stock market it fueled both crashed. Sondheim turned seventy and, to celebrate, the *New York Times*, in an extended conversation with the Master, pronounced "the new, more urbane Broadway" officially dead. LaChiusa's anthem for star Eartha Kitt ("When It Ends") could not have been more prescient: "So you think the party's gonna last forever / And you'll always fly this high—but that depends. / The higher the high, the harder you're gonna / Crash back down / When it ends."

It's better to remember what was created during the last six years of the century. In order, these were: Wolfe and dancer/choreographer Savion Glover's *Bring in 'Da Noise, Bring in 'Da Funk* (as vital and even more contemporary than *Rent*), Polly Pen's *Bed and Sofa*, Lynn Ahrens and Stephen Flaherty's *Ragtime*, John Cameron Mitchell's *Hedwig and the Angry Inch*, Diedre Murray and Cornelius Eady's *Running Man*, William Finn's *A*

New Brain, Ricky Ian Gordon and Tina Landau's *Dream True*, LaChiusa's *Marie Christine* (for Audra McDonald, the awesome diva and chief proselytizer for this new generation of theater composers), the Richard Nelson/Shaun Davey adaptation of James Joyce's "The Dead" (*James Joyce's The Dead*), and the four pieces in this collection.

(Of these, *Noise/Funk*, *Ragtime*, *James Joyce's The Dead* and *Marie Christine* moved to Broadway. The rest did not. Of the roughly two dozen works developed and produced by the not-for-profit theaters during this time, only *Noise/Funk*, *Rent* and *Hedwig* were commercially successful.)

Viewed as a whole, the works herein form an American landscape that is almost the polar opposite of Rodgers and Hammerstein's interpretation of the 1940s.

Floyd Collins, set mostly in the pitch blackness of a cave in rural Kentucky in 1925, portrays a soul alone with himself while, above ground, the newly born circus of modern media life unconsciously tries to rob Floyd of his human dignity.

Rent is set amidst a gentrification war in New York City's Lower East Side in the mid-1990s. It portrays a community of youthful racial diversity and sexual tolerance brought together, first by the struggle to be an artist in a materialist society, and then by the fight to prevent disease from snuffing out their youthful lives and love.

Parade juxtaposes anti-Semitism and racism against African-Americans in an Atlanta, Georgia, still haunted in 1913 by the ghosts of the Civil War.

And *The Wild Party*, set near Manhattan's Morningside Heights just before the Crash of 1929, observes sensual and spiritual decay, and people desperate to love and be loved but who are pitifully and miserably isolated.

As I suggested earlier, the approximately two dozen musicals developed and produced by the not-for-profit theaters during the 1980s and 1990s transformed the nature of the art musical.

If you remove *West Side Story* and the work of Sondheim from consideration, it seems clear that the essence of a Broadway musical is light, optimistic, stylish, spectacular, saucy, romantic and naive. The traditional musical is a world of escape from harsh realities. It is a wish for Utopia and the late-twentieth-century version of the American Dream, which has devolved merely to a pursuit of happiness through material abundance.

By that definition, which is not complete but I believe still useful, the works in this collection are not musicals at all, and not operas either. They are anti-musicals.

The press never figured this out, trumping up a useless debate about these works: "Are they musicals or are they operas?" Since they are neither, and no third alternative was offered, only one conclusion seemed reasonable: failure. They are either unsuccessful musicals (because they aren't popular and they don't entertain in the conventional manner) or unsuccessful operas (because the drama isn't propelled primarily through the music and the emotional experience isn't the same as in an opera). And this is how three of these fine works were almost completely overlooked.

Sondheim and Prince explored the anti-musical first (which is not surprising given their history of innovation) in 1981, with *Merrily We Roll Along*. Prince has always been a master at combining the truth demanded by art with the entertainment demanded by the Broadway audience.

By cleverly telling the story in reverse, they are able to portray lives of middle-aged disillusionment while retaining the comforting conventions of a classic musical (alternations of song, dance and spoken dialogue, easily memorable songs, tales of youthful romance) in order to *seem* to arrive at the happy ending required by Broadway. But, of course, this apparent happy ending, with three young friends gazing hopefully over Manhattan at the rising dawn (or is it dusk?), is unavoidably ironic: it's actually their promising beginning. Having witnessed their disillusioned, mature selves, we know the show's true ending is not the triumphant end of which they dream. Perhaps this is why, for all of the show's merits, and the half dozen attempts to make it work, it has never really found an audience.

The composers and writers of the new generation have taken the anti-musical several steps further to genuinely confound the expectations, responses and needs of the Broadway musical audience. They have dispensed almost entirely with the two most cherished conventions of the form: the Song (simple in its traditional structure and therefore memorable) and the Happy Ending. Next, entertainment has been made secondary to the political concerns that were the heart of the not-for-profit theaters in the 1980s and 1990s—especially the politics of race, sexual preference and gender. Finally, the mythology of the American Dream, which was merely questioned by Prince and Sondheim, has been indicted by this new generation. Consequently, the work is ironic, skeptical and sometimes disenchanted and disbelieving. When it's funny, it's biting. It leaves teeth marks. Obviously, this is no way to be popular.

Traditional musical theater people don't like either the reality or the idea of an anti-musical. The most valid criticisms are that it is (variously) earnest, ponderous, moralistic or pretentious, that important themes precede full characters in dramatically satisfying conflict. Often, our critics have a point. Those of us in the theater who believe in the power of serious, intelligent lyric theater need to make sure we take ourselves less seriously while holding the work to even higher standards.

But when the authors of an anti-musical get it right, as Brecht and Weill did with their revered *The Threepenny Opera* (1928), indelible impressions become etched in the audience's consciousness. "Mack the Knife," the most unforgettable song in what is probably the original anti-musical, is as corrosive and disturbing today as it ever was.

Similarly unforgettable is the film anti-musical *Dancer in the Dark* (2000). If you haven't seen it, this is the story of a young mother who, in the face of her approaching blindness, finds moments of happiness and strength through escape into such musicals as the Astaire/Rogers and Busby Berkeley films of the 1930s and by acting in a local amateur stage production of *The Sound of Music*. Musicals are the source of the protagonist's faith. Her escape from a brutal, unjust world into song and dance reinforces her naive idealism and belief in human goodness, and this is her undoing. Somehow, director Lars von Trier and songwriter/actress Bjork raise her almost to the level of a tragic heroine.

Essentially, the movie is about the consequences of not living in the real world, and musicals are the polar opposite of the real world. *Dancer in the Dark* seizes on this truth and enlarges it; the film's irony, unusual dramatic structure, idiosyncratic songs and seemingly amateurish approach to traditional musical theater style were welcomed by the imaginative world of independent film. I describe this extraordinary and singular film musical at some length because no stage musical exists that so deeply understands and mines the essence of the musical form (and our contemporary ambivalence toward it) to create powerful drama.

The innovation and intelligence in *Dancer in the Dark* wouldn't be accepted (by audiences or critics) in a stage musical in New York City. Sadly, our community seems no longer open to anything but the most formulaic, old-fashioned "new" musicals. So far, the anti-musical has been welcomed only by the independent film world with its more receptive and forward-thinking aesthetic.

My friend Michael John LaChiusa reminds me that the value of this introduction lies in my testimony because I was there (backstage or in the audience) during rehearsals or early performances of these four shows, and so I am a witness.

Here are moments that are still vivid to me:

Floyd Collins bravely looking his own death in the eye while singing "How Glory Goes." How I had to strain to hold both my breath to keep from sobbing loudly in Playwrights Horizons' first, small theater on West 42nd Street.

The morning after the last dress rehearsal of *Rent* when I received a call from Morgan Jenness, my fellow associate producer at The Public Theater, telling me that Jonathan Larson had died the night before. The unique numbness of sitting in an Off-Broadway theater on East 4th Street under the still unbelievable circumstances while trying to appreciate how the show's fearless sense of protest (against AIDS, homelessness and mindless gentrification) didn't prevent it from finding an audience. I'm convinced that Jonathan's rage at injustice expressed in the show's throbbing vitality is key to its enormous popularity.

The night in November 1998 when we opened Joe's Pub to an ecstatic response: Audra McDonald sang (wondrously) selections from her debut CD *Way Back to Paradise,* devoted to our new generation of composers: Adam (Guettel), Michael John (LaChiusa), Jason (Robert Brown), Ricky Ian Gordon and Jeanine Tesori. All were present in the room and joined her onstage one by one, thereby launching four seasons of a charmed and joyful series devoted to theater songwriters.

The dress rehearsal of *Parade,* with Hal Prince's typically extraordinary production already letter perfect. Leo Frank's trial scene when he leaps up madly from the defense table to sing and dance a prosecution witness's fantasy version of how he seduced and killed little Mary Phagan ("Come Up to My Office"); the boldness and integrity of daring the audience to hate the protagonist whose guilt or innocence is made ambiguous by the musical number.

The hostility that *The Wild Party* created in the press, who decided to pit us against, believe it or not, another terrific version of *The Wild Party* by Andrew Lippa produced at exactly the same time! Apparently, in the history of the New York theater, two new shows based on the same source material had never received their premieres simultaneously, and it was our misfortune to watch the press fall to the occasion. Unfortunately, it was one of those moments when the work couldn't be seen (not even by the critics) because it became obscured by the event that had been created around it.

The lobby of Broadway's Virginia Theatre during previews of *The Wild Party* when Adam Guettel came up to me and said: "I hope it's a big success, because it's important to all of us." He meant Michael John, Jason, George Wolfe, Tina Landau and the rest of our little group. This new generation of composers and librettists knew they had to deliver a good, old-fashioned Broadway hit to prove their worth.

Hal Prince likes to remind us of the critical difference between a flop (a showbiz term) and a failure (an evaluation of artistic worth). *Floyd Collins*, *Parade* and *The Wild Party* were flops, but far from failures. Why weren't they popular? Looking at only the artistic elements, I would have to say that it's as simple as: they were anti-musicals, and the audience and the critics assumed, expected and insisted upon musicals.

It is possible that, unintentionally, this book documents the end of the noble tradition begun by Kern and Hammerstein. If that turns out to be the case, I want to have gone on record: this work is truly excellent; it's just out of synch with the dominant values of our times. A fact to persuade you of the shift in cultural sensibility: not even *West Side Story* has been seen on Broadway since 1980!

As I noted at the beginning of this essay, predictions are foolish. Bernstein was certain of a glorious future that never really arrived. And people have been predicting the imminent death of theater at the hands of an increasingly technologized, mediated society for decades. So far, it hasn't happened. Probably, there will always be theater. But will there be intelligent theater informed by the world's social and political realities? And will there be a significant audience for this kind of theater?

With respect to the lyric theater, the response to these questions should be to commit completely to the restoration of the musical to its youthful vitality and relevance. Bernstein's belief in the enormous and still largely unexplored potential of the form continues to ring true. Admittedly, our chances of regaining the popular art musical are slim. But they are greatest if we seek and implement radical reinvention (onstage, backstage and by developing a sophisticated new audience). Sadly, this is completely opposite to the impulses of the majority working in this field.

It seems likely then that, at least partially because the world has changed so enormously since the musical was invented, we may be forced to choose between commercial and artistic success. If we are, what will we choose? If we choose the path to art does the work created continue to be a musical? And if it isn't, how much should that concern us?

The pursuit of artistic value (with or without commercial success) is my path to a happy ending. I'd like to believe this pursuit will lead to a paradise that may be just over the horizon.

The work in this volume keeps this hope alive in me, and many others, as does the ongoing commitment of these composers, authors and their like-minded colleagues to Bernstein's ideal.

Wiley Hausam
New York City
May 2003

FLOYD COLLINS

Music and Lyrics by Adam Guettel
Book and Additional Lyrics by Tina Landau
Original New York Production Directed by Tina Landau

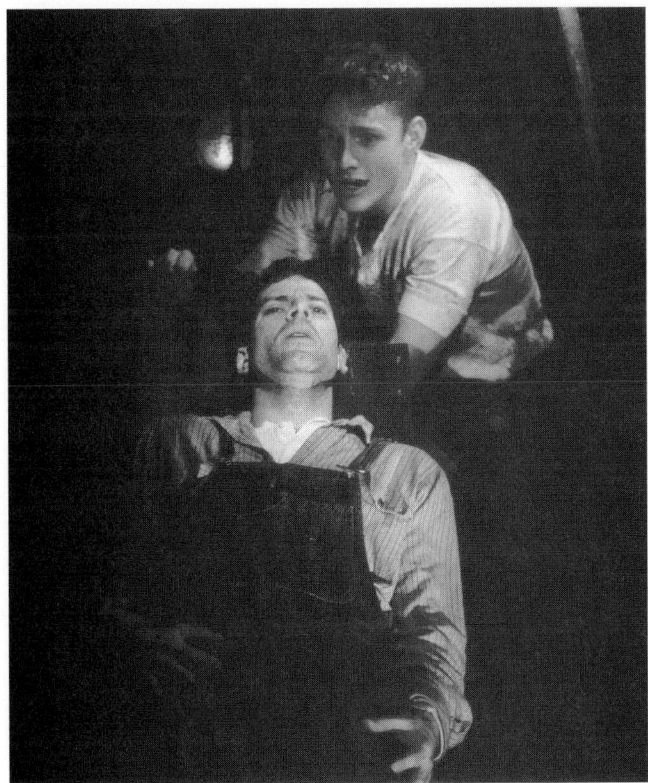

Joan Marcus

Christopher Innvar (Floyd) and Jason Danieley (Homer, top), Playwrights Horizons, 1996.

ADAM GUETTEL:

To my brother, Alec

TINA LANDAU:

For my father, Ely Landau

THE STORY

Near Cave City, Kentucky, in the winter of 1925, a local cave owner and operator, Floyd Collins, was attempting to discover a new cave which would prove his theory that many caves in the region were all part of one, giant underground system. Instead, he became trapped in Sand Cave, one hundred and fifty feet underground. During the next three weeks, one of the most unexpected and disturbing events of American cultural history unfolded on the fields above ground. What began as a small, local rescue attempt soon ballooned into a national crisis demanding outside engineering, dozens of miners, the National Guard and the Red Cross. Because of numerous factors, for days no one could rescue Floyd. One of the few who finally managed to actually reach Collins was Skeets Miller, a cub reporter from the *Louisville Courier-Journal*. He conducted a series of interviews which were relayed to a national press, which went wild, printing numerous front page stories. (Miller won the Pulitzer Prize the following year.) Soon an estimated twenty thousand onlookers arrived from all over America—to help, to get a glimpse of the now heroic Floyd, to exploit the crowd. As the carnival reached its height, Collins was all but forgotten. No one was able to rescue him, and he died trapped underground. Around him swirled the first great media circus of the modern era.

AUTHORS' NOTE

Floyd Collins is based on real events which took place in and around Sand Cave, Kentucky, in 1925. Although we worked to preserve historical accuracy, it was necessary in some cases to take dramatic liberty and combine characters or compress events. We hope that, in the process of translating historical fact into drama, we have respected the integrity of the persons involved and the overall shape of these amazing, true events.

SETTING

The action takes place from January 30–February 16, 1925 on Bee Doyle's farm in Barren County, Kentucky, in and around a small opening in the ground which will later become known as "Sand Cave."

CHARACTERS

(in order of appearance)

JEWELL ESTES	A local teenager
NELLIE COLLINS	Floyd's younger sister
HOMER COLLINS	Floyd's younger brother
MISS JANE	Floyd's stepmother
SKEETS MILLER	A reporter for the *Louisville Courier-Journal*
FLOYD COLLINS	A caver
ED BISHOP	A local caver
BEE DOYLE	Owner of the farm on which Floyd becomes trapped
LEE COLLINS	Floyd's father
H. T. CARMICHAEL	An engineer
CLIFF RONEY	A young filmmaker
DR. HAZLETT	A doctor from Chicago
THREE REPORTERS	
CROWD AT THE CARNIVAL	

A NOTE ON STAGING FROM THE DIRECTOR

Floyd Collins was written to be performed in a spare and fluid space, leaving the physical details of the cave and its surrounds up to the audience's imagination, and allowing for shift of focus and location to occur through movement and light (rather than scenery).

In the original productions, Floyd's trapped position was on a crude, angled slab of wood downstage right. He remained there for the entirety of the piece, except when his dreams allowed him to move freely, as indicated in the text.

The rest of the stage—empty at first except for an expanse of sky—was "above ground." Here, a constructed world grew in the course of the story (all erected by the actors, in character). I placed the entrance to the cave—and later the shaft—upstage left, so that actors could disappear stage left and reappear behind Floyd stage right, creating the sense that they had traveled some distance. This "split-screen" effect was used often, especially in the later scenes involving the shaft (which was defined entirely by a small square of light center stage).

Throughout the piece, characters often remained onstage, in tableau or silhouette, while the focus shifted from above ground to the cave and vice versa. We found that the material most came to life within a setting that was minimal and atmospheric and allowed for such story-telling techniques as jump-cuts, dissolves, flash-backs and continuous simultaneous action.

This is the general approach I had in mind while writing *Floyd*, and what seemed to work well in early productions. Of course, please feel free to try anything else.

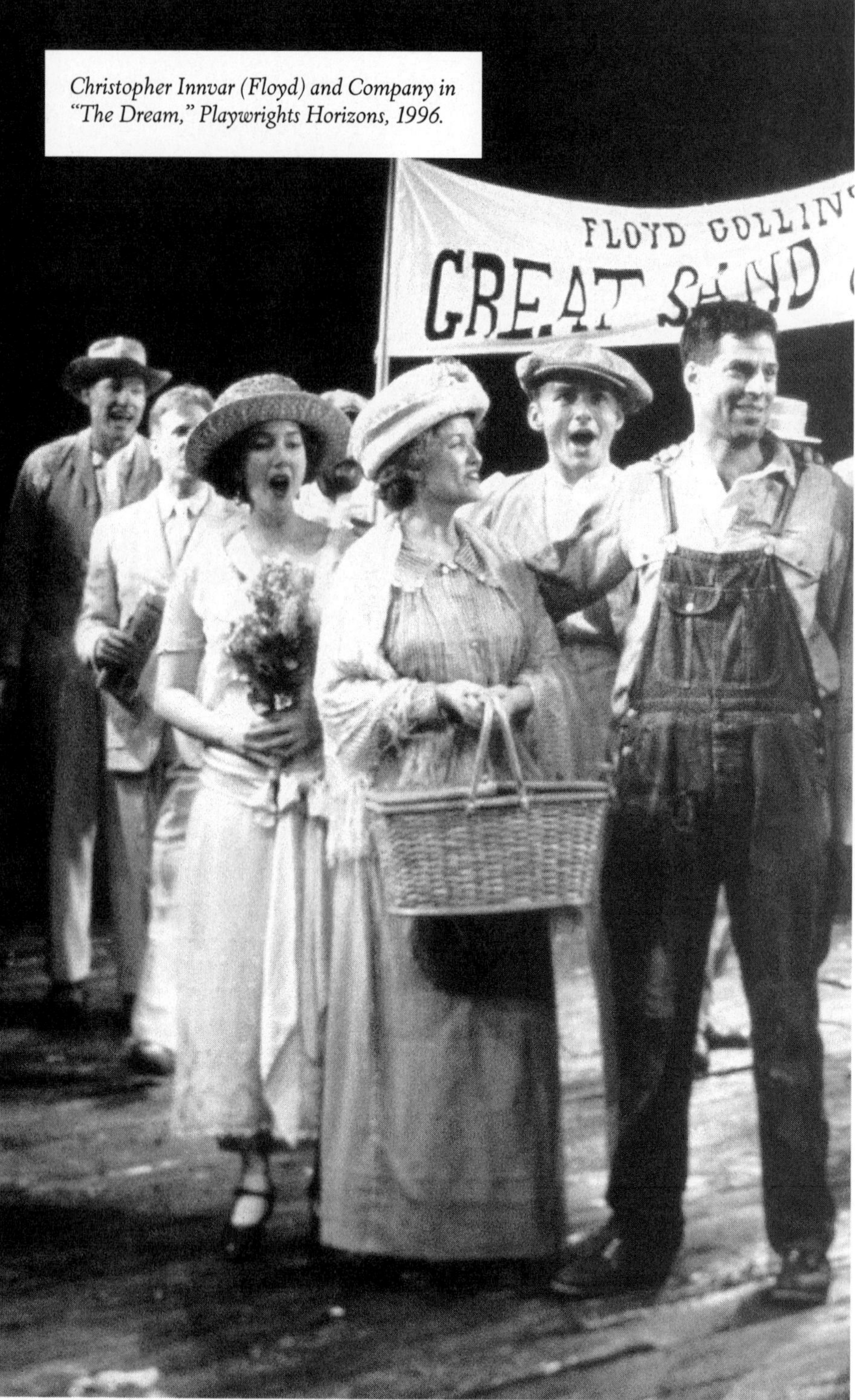

Christopher Innvar (Floyd) and Company in "The Dream," Playwrights Horizons, 1996.

Joan Marcus

MUSICAL SYNOPSIS

Act I

Act II

NOTE: Sung passages are indicated in the text by small caps.

ACT I

Sky. Members of the cast stand in silhouette. Slowly, light fills in.

PROLOGUE

JEWELL:

DEEP IN THE LAND OF THE HOLLOWS AN' CREEKS,
IF'N YOU GIT LOST YOU GIT LOST FER WEEKS;
LISTEN TO THE TALE OF A MAN WHO GOT LOST,
A HUNDRED FEET UNDER THE WINTER FROST.

JEWELL & NELLIE:

NOW, FLOYD WAS A REASONIN' MAN,
HE KNEW WHAT HE WANTED AN' HE HAD A PLAN;
HE WAS JES' AS SMART AS HE WAS BRAVE,
HE WAS GONNA FIND HIM THE PERFECT CAVE.

MISS JANE, NELLIE & HOMER:

EVEN FLOYD KNEW SOMETHIN' WASN'T RIGHT,
HE WAS SUFF'RIN' NIGHTMARES AT NIGHT.

ALL:

BUT HE DIDN'T WORRY 'BOUT WHAT HE DREAMED,
THINGS WAS GOIN' GOOD, OR SO IT SEEMED.
WENT LOOKIN' FER HIS FORTUNE UNDER THE GROUND,

MILLER:

SURE ENOUGH HIS FORTUNE IS WHAT HE FOUND.

(They turn to look at the figure of Floyd Collins, silhouetted against the sky. Floyd carries a battered kerosene lantern and a seventy-two-foot coil of rope slung over his shoulder. He walks toward the cave opening, and the light from the sky starts to disappear. The rest of the cast exits.)

PART ONE: THE CAVE

At the opening of the first passageway, Floyd spots a cricket, gets down on his hands and knees to catch it.

FLOYD: Hey, where ya goin'? Come 'ere! Hello, Mister Cricket. What you got down these passageways? Let's find out if there's a cavern down thar. *(Calling out)* Whooo-ooo-weh!

(Nothing. Floyd's body slumps in disappointment. He watches the cricket crawl up his arm. Then, unexpectedly, he hears a faint echo of his call. He laughs with excitement and takes the cricket off his shoulder.)

Yeah. Ya hear that? Thar's open space somewhere down thar. *(Calling out)* Is she a big 'un?!

(An echo comes back: ". . . Is she a big 'un?!")

My losin' streak is over, boy! Gonna find my treasure underground! This cavern's gonna be the biggest attraction roun' these parts—an' this time folks are gonna pay me to tour her wonders! They'll be tearin' up the mountain!—they'll be campin' in the snow!

IF I FOLLOW THAT SOUND,
I COULD FIND WHAT I'M LOOKIN' FER.
IT COULD BE GLORY CALLIN',
CALLIN' ME.

CALLIN':
"COME ON, BOY! YOU KIN DO IT NOW.
YOU KIN HAVE WHAT YOU DREAM ON."
CALLIN'
AN' COMIN' BACK AN' COMIN' CLEAR;
CALLIN'
IS WHAT I HEAR.

NO MORE PLOWIN' A HARD-SCRABBLE FIELD;
I JES' KNOW, I JES' KNOW IT'S MY LUCKY DAY!

(Floyd starts maneuvering along the passageways, scraping and fighting his way in. At first, he crawls, then eventually slides on his stomach or back.)

All righty, all righty. In we go.

WELCOME, TO FLOYD COLLINS' SAND CAVE!
NAW . . .
WELCOME TO FLOYD COLLINS' *GREAT* SAND CAVE!
NOT FOR THE MEEK; YOU GOTTA BE BRAVE!
NAW . . .
EVERYBODY WELCOME!
A FAMILY TYPE OF THING TO DO.

BALLOONS! POSTCARDS!
GREAT SAND CAVE LANTERNS . . .
AND ROPE? OR SOMETHIN'.
I DUNNO.

YOU GOT YER MAGICAL PASSAGEWAYS,
YOU GOT YER SQUEEZES AN' BENDS;
MY KINGDOM IS OPEN;
COME ONE AN' ALL,
MY TRAVELIN' FRIENDS.

I ALWAYS KNEW YOU'D HEAR MY CALL;
LET ME KNOW THAT YOU HEAR ME NOW . . .

(Singing into the darkness:)

DOH . . .

(And an echo comes back: "Doh . . .")

OH . . .
THERE'S A KIND OF AWE,
YOU CAIN'T CATCH IN A PHOTOGRAPH;
S'LIKE A GIANT JAW,
IT'S CALLIN' ME.

CALLIN':
"COME ON, BOY. YOU KIN FEEL IT NOW.
LIKE YOU AIN'T NEVER FELT AFORE;
AN OPEN DOOR . . ."

So Papa, so you see,
I ain't a crazy cavin' fool, you see!
I always promised to do you right,
An' by the time I get home tonight
All our money worries will be gone;
We will be dreamin' on.

You see, I'll set you up on a valley farm
Where you kin nap under apple trees.
Put up yer feet
Instead of kickin' my ass!

Oh Papa!
Your son's a bi'nessman now!
A so-an'-so! A muck-a-muck!
A real wheeler-dealer!
Gonna do the family proud.

My kingdom is open!
It will amaze and astound.
From all 'cross Kentucky,
They'll come to see what I found.

I always knew that there'd be
Somethin' in the stars fer me.
The stars could be
So fine . . .

(Again calling out:)

Doh-oh-ee-oh . . .

(An echo comes back:)

Ee-oh-oh . . .

(And another echo comes back.)

Gonna follow that sound;
Gonna find what I'm lookin' fer.

THAT'S MY GLORY CALLIN';
IT'S CALLIN' ME.

CALLIN':
"COME ON, BOY! YOU KIN DO IT NOW!
YOU KIN HAVE WHAT YOU DREAM ON."

GLORY,
Ooo . . .
AN' COMIN' CLEAR;
GLORY
IS WHAT I HEAR.

NO MORE PLOWIN' A HARD-SCRABBLE FIELD;
I JES' KNOW, I JES' KNOW IT'S MY LUCKY DAY!

We're so close! "Floyd's a fine boy! He takes after his pa—stubborn as a mule!"

"BUT HE KNOWS HIS OWN MIND!"

I ALWAYS KNEW I'D HEAR
THE SOUND OF VOICES ALL AROUND ME.
THAT'S THE SOUND OF GLORY AFTER ALL;
THAT'S MY CALL!

(He arrives at the top of a narrow chute, no more than two feet high and two feet wide.)

Ah shit. Real squeeze . . . *(He slides through)* Git flat as a board . . . *(He touches a hanging rock)* Ain't nothin' solid here. *(He shimmies through and emerges onto a ledge. He stops short and tries to look down at endless dark space: what must be at least sixty feet of cavern)* Holy . . . *(Pause)* This is it.

(Floyd calls out. This time he receives back not one echo, but two . . . three . . . four . . . from every direction. He ties his rope to a boulder and descends, all the while singing in canon with the echo of his own voice. His lantern creates an eerie tube of light through which he travels. The only sound is Floyd's voice and its reverberation.)

DO-OH-O-DEE-OH . . .

(As Floyd's feet touch ground:)

THERE AIN'T NEVER BEEN ANOTHER MAN IN HERE . . .
NO INDIANS, NO THRILL-SEEKERS,
NO DAMN CRAZY CAVIN' FOOLS!
NOBODY, NOTHIN' 'TIL I FOUND 'ER.

GOD SHOWED HER TO ME FIRST!

(He scrawls his name into the rock floor.)

FLOYD . . .
AND I'M A-CALLIN';
I'M A-CALLIN'!

(He closes his eyes and basks in the feeling of space around him. The music segues.)

TIME TO GIT TO WORK, GIT TO WORK.
COMIN' BACK WITH HOMER AN' ALL THE OTHERS;
GIT A CAVIN' BANKER TO FRONT US THE MONEY.
HEY HEY!

MOVE THE ROCKS, AN' MAKE SOME TRAILS,
AND SMOOTH THE FLOORS, BUILD THE STAIRS.
AN' SET UP SOME BIG SIGNS OUT ON THE ROAD!
THERE'S A TICKET OFFICE, AN' A CURIO SHOP.
AN' REFRESHMENT STAND OPEN SEVEN DAYS A WEEK!

(Floyd starts up the rope. As he climbs, he yodels into space, rejoicing once again in the sound of his own echo.)

OO-EE-YO . . .

(Floyd reaches the top. At the ledge, he leaves the rope tied on the boulder. He thrusts the lantern ahead of him into the crevice.)

All righty, all righty now. Slow an' steady fer the squeeze. Under this damn hangin' rock an' . . .

(The lantern tips over and goes out.)

Damn. Wal, s'only dark. S'happened before. Careful now . . . *(Turns over on his back and inches back through the tunnel, twisting his torso and pressing his feet against the walls and floor of the cave)* In goes the shoulders, 'round goes the hips, git flat as a board, under this hangin' rock an' one final shove oughtta do it—hmf!

(Floyd gives a final, solid kick to turn up into the cubbyhole. The hanging rock breaks loose and falls on his left foot, pinning it down at the ankle.)

Ah—shit. My foot. *(Temper rising)* Pull this sucker out from under this *fool rock*!

(He kicks with his right foot, but more rocks fall and now pin both of his legs.)

My legs! *(Lying on his left side at a forty-five-degree angle, his left cheek resting on the floor, his left arm pinned under his body)* Echh . . . Don't get flurried. S'happened before. Never did worry 'bout gittin' out or nothin'—'cause that jes' ain't your problem. Jes' know caves. Temperature . . . Way they murmur . . .

> If it comes back quick an' paper thin,
> You know what kinda place you're in.
> But if it roll in slow, like thunder,
> You done found a cave a wonder.

Cave a' wonder . . . Always have gotten outta scrapes. Probably 'cause I git into 'em so easy. Lucky.

(Finally collected, Floyd starts digging again. As soon as he does, debris falls and covers his body up to his shoulders. He panics.)

Aaahh! . . . My arms! . . . *(Rising, almost irrational)* Aaaahh! . . . Homer! Aaaahh! . . . How long I gotta lie here with water drippin' in on me?! *(Screams lessening to moans; fast)* Be calm, boy, be calm—oh God, oh God, oh God . . . They'll come for me . . . Might take 'em a day . . . Won't know to look at first . . . They'll think I'm spendin' one of my nights explorin' . . . But Doyle's gonna wonder . . . An' he'll git Homer. That's right, that's right, that's right . . . *(Calling out)* Ho! I'm hung up down here! *(Pause; at first defiant)* Okay, Lord . . . *(Then, negotiating)* Gracious Lord, please make sure they come an' git me. 'Cause I sure gotta take a piss. This thing'll turn out. I jes' know. I'm lucky . . . lucky . . .

(Blackout. The music segues directly into:)

PART TWO: THE RESCUE

Later that day. Several men have gathered outside the cave, including Ed Bishop, descendant of the famous caver Stephen Bishop, and Jewell Estes, a stringy adolescent. Bishop has a coal-oil lantern like Floyd's and has just come out of the cave.

BISHOP *(Huffing and puffing)*: Damn! *(Huff-puff)* Daaaaa-amn!
JEWELL: Wal, is Floyd down thar?
BISHOP: Damn.
JEWELL: Wal?
BISHOP: Doyle was right, he's down thar, but ain't no member of the Bishop clan ever been in a hole like this one here. I'm telling ya—Mammoth Cave is *a hilltop picnic* compared to this. Took my father half a year to git to the end of Great Onyx Cave, but that was a regular slice of *rhubarb pie* next to this one. This here is the meanest, tightest, blackest, wettest, wormiest, clamp-down-on-ya-so-ya-cain't-go-nowhere, suffocatin' sink hole I ever did have the Lord's blessin' to survive! So I know Floyd musta found somethin' or he wouldn't've gone down so deep.
JEWELL: How deep is it?
BISHOP: Wal, I don't rightly know.
JEWELL: Why not?
BISHOP: You through askin' questions, Estes?
LOCALS: Bishop?
BISHOP: All right, all right—wal, I . . . See, I didn't get exactly all the way down to 'im but—
LOCALS *(Simultaneously)*: How come?
JEWELL *(Simultaneously)*: What?
BISHOP: You try fittin' through those squeezes thar! S'all mud an' crumblin' walls.

JEWELL: Wal, my hero!
LOCAL 1: Few too many *hilltop picnics*?
JEWELL: *Rhubarb pies*, I'd say.
BISHOP: Listen, half-pint—

(The land's owner, Bee Doyle, and Lee Collins, Floyd's father, enter. They are followed by Nellie and Miss Jane, Floyd's sister and stepmother, respectively.)

LEE: Mornin' boys.
JEWELL: Mister Collins, sir.
BISHOP: Lee.
LEE: Wal, here we are, I see, once again.
DOYLE: Mornin' fellas. Guess you heard the news.
BISHOP & JEWELL: Mornin' Doyle.
LEE: All right, so who's goin' down to git 'im this time?

(Silence.)

Good mornin' boys! Wake up time! Now who's gonna . . .
BISHOP: I was down thar, Lee. But he's way far under. Must be a hundred an' fifty feet of tight crawlways. I couldn't, uh, fit all the way.
LEE: Jewell, you're small.
JEWELL: Oh yes, sir, I'm ready, sir, gonna go under, sir . . . It's jes' now, I have to, uh . . .
LOCAL 1 *(Aside)*: Slip away like a scairty cat.
LOCAL 2: Meow.
DOYLE: Maybe yer younger boy kin git to him, Lee.
LEE: Homer's been sent fer. We'll see when he gits here.
NELLIE: Homer's gone to buy an automobile.
LEE: Quiet.
JEWELL: Welcome back home, Miss Nellie.
NELLIE: Homer's been savin' seven years to buy an automobile an' take us ridin'. Pardon me. *(Starts to leave)*
LEE: Where are you goin'?
NELLIE: Down under. To git Floyd out.
LEE: You 'have yourself like is proper. A girl got no place here in the first place, let alone yer condition.
NELLIE: That's right Pa, jes' afore I left the 'sylum they said to me, "Now Nellie, don't be goin' spendin' time near no cave openin's with no men folk."

(The men titter. Local 3 enters, confers with Doyle.)

LEE *(Embarrassed)*: Go sit with yer stepmama. 'Scuse my daughter, men—she ain't quite back to herself yet.

(Miss Jane leads Nellie to sit down.)

LOCAL 3 *(At the entrance to the cave)*: Holy be Jesus, will you look at this thing! This ain't no cave, Doyle—this is a little tiny hole in the ground! How the hell's a normal man supposed to scrunch down in thar?

BISHOP: I tol' you.

JEWELL: Wal Floyd ain't no normal man.

LEE: Ain't normal is right . . . how many times I gotta tell him . . . ?

CRAWLIN' ON YOUR HANDS AN' KNEES,
CROWIN' 'BOUT THE CAVE YOU'LL FIND.
CAVIN' NEVER COMES TO NOTHIN',
'TAIN'T WHERE A MAN BELONGS.

STANDIN' ON YOUR OWN TWO FEET,
STRIVIN' TO MAKE SOMETHIN' GROW,
SOMETHIN' THAT'LL COME TO SOMETHIN'.
THAT'S WHERE A MAN BELONGS.

MISS JANE:

DO SOMETHIN' WORTH YOUR WHILE, FLOYD,
WHERE YOU WON'T GIT YOURSELF KILLED.

LEE:

BUT HE'S GOIN' AT IT
HARDER THAN EVER NOW.

MISS JANE:

JUST GOES TO SHOW YA:

LEE & MISS JANE:

REAP WHAT YOU SOW.

LEE: Stubborn as a mule.

DOYLE: Stubborn fer certain—least since his birth mama died.

MISS JANE: But Floyd's always had common sense, Lee. Surely he'll change his ways.

LEE: Common sense!?

He's got the kind of common sense
We could surely live without!
Followin' the wind!
Followin' sink holes,
When he should follow the word.

LEE, MISS JANE & DOYLE:

Word is here on the mountaintop,
'Tain't down there in a worn-out daydream.
It's clear as the sky above
Where a man belongs,
Where a man belongs.

LEE *(Praying with Miss Jane and Nellie)*: I waited patiently fer the Lord an' he inclined unto me an' heard my cry.

BISHOP: You can cry all you want, Lee, but the money ain't up here in *farmin'*—money's down thar in *cavin'*.

Creepin' behind a one-horse plow,
Cryin' over used-up dirt:
Croppin' never comes to nothin',
'Tain't where a man belongs.

BISHOP & JEWELL *(Simultaneously with below)*:

'Splorin' fer somethin' ain't been found,
Spyin' somethin' really big,
Somethin' that'll come to somethin',
That's where a man belongs.

LEE, MISS JANE & NELLIE *(Simultaneously with above)*:

Ah . . .

BISHOP, JEWELL, LOCAL 1 & LOCAL 2:

Do somethin' worth your while, boy;
That's what I'm plannin' to do.

BISHOP:

Gonna find me a cave,
Closer to the road.

LOCAL 1:

'Afore they go to Mammoth Cave,
Folks'll come to me.

JEWELL:

Just goes to show ya:

(For Lee:)

REAP WHAT YOU SOW!

LEE: Jewell Estes, you ain't sowed nothin' but trouble since the day you was born! No common sense!

BISHOP, JEWELL, LOCAL 1 & LOCAL 2:
YOU GOT THE KINDA COMMON SENSE
WE COULD SURELY LIVE WITHOUT.
FARMIN' A RIDGE
AN' CUTTIN' RAIL TIES!

BISHOP:
YOU'LL GET US KILLED THE SLOW WAY.

BISHOP, JEWELL, LOCAL 1 & LOCAL 2 *(Simultaneously with below)*:
MONEY'S DOWN THERE, OH, I JUST KNOW,
'TAIN'T UP HERE IN THE USED-UP DIRT.
MONEY'S DOWN THERE AT THE END OF THIS WIND,
WHERE A MAN BELONGS,
WHERE A MAN BE . . .

LEE, MISS JANE & NELLIE *(Simultaneously with above)*:
AH . . .

LOCAL 1:
GOD HELP YOU IF YOU LIVE IN BARREN COUNTY!

LOCAL 2:
HE WON'T.

LOCAL 1:
LEAST THEY WENT AN' CALLED IT WHAT IT IS!

LOCAL 2:
YES SIR!

DOYLE: Now wait a minute! I have lived here all my life, an' . . .

LOCALS 1 & 2:
FOUR GENERATIONS UP ON FLINT RIDGE,
THE KINDA HERITAGE
I'D JUST AS SOON FORGET!

LOCAL 3 *(To Doyle)*: You're the one cut a deal with Floyd to find a cave on yer land. Warn't fer you he wouldn't be down thar!

LEE: What's this?

DOYLE: I'd been meanin' to tell ya. Floyd could be on to somethin' *lucky* here. If he is, you're set. We're all set.

LEE & MISS JANE:
He's always talkin' 'bout his luck, his glory—

LOCAL 1:
If you live in Barren County,

LEE & MISS JANE:
But there ain't never any luck,

LOCAL 1:
Lord!

LEE & MISS JANE:
Or glory in it.
Spendin' all his time alone.
Underground.

LOCAL 1:
Least they went an' called it what it is.

LEE & MISS JANE:
Diggin' tunnels, puttin' signs on the road.
But no one ever sees 'em.
No one comes.

NELLIE: I do. I go under.

(Everything comes to a halt. Everyone looks at Nellie.)

MISS JANE: Oh Nellie, come here darlin'.

(Beat. Then Nellie breaks away, dances a magical clog dance to Floyd, while the others continue with:)

LEE, MISS JANE & LOCAL 3 *(Simultaneously with below)*:
Crawlin' on your hands and knees,
Crowin' 'bout the cave you'll find.
Cavin'! I say never mind!
'Tain't where a man belongs.

The word is here on the mountaintop,
It ain't there in a worn-out daydream.

THE WORD IS CLEAR AS THE SKY ABOVE.
I JUST KNOW.

BISHOP, JEWELL, DOYLE, LOCAL 1 & LOCAL 2 *(Simultaneously with above)*:

CREEPIN' BEHIND A ONE-HORSE PLOW,
CRYIN' OVER USED-UP DIRT,
CROPPIN' TILL YOU LOSE YER SHIRT,
'TAIN'T WHERE A MAN BELONGS.

MONEY'S DOWN THERE, OH, I JUST KNOW.
'TAIN'T UP HERE IN YER WORN-OUT DIRT.
MONEY'S DOWN THERE AT THE END OF THIS WIND.
I JUST KNOW.

ALL:

IT'S CLEAR AS THE SKY ABOVE
WHERE A MAN BELONGS,
WHERE A MAN BELONGS,
WHERE A MAN BELONGS.

(Homer, Floyd's younger brother, dashes in. He has been running and is all worked-up and out of breath. He is wearing city clothes. He and Nellie see each other, embrace.)

NELLIE: Ho-mer!

HOMER: Nell! Is he out? Where's he at?

NELLIE *(Pointing to the cave)*: He's in thar. Pa won't let me go under.

BISHOP: It's a real chest compressor down thar, Homer.

HOMER: Yeah, well he's gotten out of those afore. Lemme borrow your lantern, Bishop— *(He grabs Bishop's lantern)* An' this moonshine . . . *(Grabs a flask and starts into the cave)*

LEE: Homer, put down that jug.

HOMER: But it's freezin' down under, Pa. This here fire'll keep 'im warm.

LEE: Son—you heard what I tol' you.

(Silence as Homer considers Lee's warning. He takes a look around, grins.)

You testin' my limits, boy?

(Homer darts into the cave.)

You listen to me, boy!

JEWELL: Uh-oh.
LEE: Homer Collins!

(During the following, the men go to Lee and try to calm him down. Eventually, they straggle off, leaving Lee silhouetted against the sky near the cave opening. Miss Jane grabs Nellie.)

MISS JANE: Nellie, I gotta tell ya somethin'. Come here—pretend like we're jes' waitin' quiet now.

NELLIE: What is it?

MISS JANE: Day 'fore last, right 'fore you came home, Pa leaves the house an' Floyd looks out the window makin' sure he's not near. Then he tells me 'bout this hole, how he's been diggin' away rock so as to get down in thar. "For goodness sake, quit goin' in these holes," I said. An' I reminded him how my first husband was caught up under a hill—

NELLIE: An' done died thar.

MISS JANE: Yes, Nellie . . . Done died thar. That's jes' what I reminded 'im of. Your brother was sweet to me, he dried my tears—an' promised he won't go in any dangerous places again after this one. Said it would be his last.

NELLIE: So thar ya go, Miss Jane.

MISS JANE: But then, Nellie, he tol' me 'bout *a dream* he had. "I dreamed I was goin' under," he says, "down . . . an' down . . . Then rocks came a-fallin' fast on me . . . crushin' me, buryin' me alive." I'm scared for him so I tell him so. But he don't listen to my words . . . jes' like he don't listen to his warning dreams.

NELLIE: Aw, Miss Jane, you're gettin' as worked-up as all these men here, all squawkin' and struttin' like roosters with their heads cut off. Ain't no use a-worryin'—

(She pulls her close, whispering:)

Miss Jane—Floyd's got *the luck*. It circles roun' him—he tol' me so. An' my brother ain't the lyin' type. He maybe done tol' you one *bad* dream, Miss Jane, but he done tol' me *hundreds* of *good* ones. He tol' me he'd find a cave with gold at the end of the rainbow—he says to me, "It's gonna turn out jes' like a fair day, Nell." He holds me right in his hands an' says to me:

"LUCKY'S WHAT I AM,
AIN'T NO SUCKLIN' BABY LAMB;

SURE AS HELL DON'T GIVE A DAMN
FER WHAT THEY THINK 'BOUT ME."

MISS JANE: Nellie . . .

NELLIE:

LUCKY, IN HIS WAY,
BUZZIN' IN MY GUT TODAY,
LIKE A CHOIR OF CRICKETS SINGIN',
WE GONNA SELL SOME TICKETS, SINGIN':

HOW'S ABOUT A RADIO?
HOW'S ABOUT A NEW CAR, YA KNOW?
HOW'S ABOUT A VALLEY FARM?
HOW'S ABOUT A BOY ON MY ARM?

GONNA GIT A LITTLE RESPECT,
GONNA HOL' OUR HEADS UP ERECT,
GONNA SHOW 'EM WHAT WE GOT,
SHOW 'EM WHAT WE WILL TAKE
AN' WILL NOT NOW,
AN' WHAT WE GOT NOW
IS A LOT NOW.

MISS JANE: But Nellie darlin' . . .

NELLIE:

NO, NO, DON'T YOU FRET,
I AIN'T TOL' YOU NOTHIN' YET;
WE GON' SING A CAVE DUET
INSIDE A MAGIC DOME.

'CAUSE BEIN' NEAR TO HIM,
I KNOW I'M TRULY LUCKY—
NOW THAT I'VE COME HOME.

MISS JANE: But when dreams talk, Nellie, ya best heed 'em. You listenin' to me? Ya learn to doubt things. Ya don't fool with dreams like that.

NELLIE:

DOUBTIN' NEVER DID US ANY GOOD;
WHY'D YA WANT TO FILL US UP WITH DOUBT?

Doubtin' never did us, no, not one lick of good;
Why don't you jes' help us out, like you should?

Oh, let us dream some . . .

MISS JANE:

Go and dream.

NELLIE:

Let us scheme a cavin' scheme.
If what he says is there is there,
An' God is good an' fair is fair,
We're sitting on a pile of dough
Higher than a grain silo!

MISS JANE:

Think of all the lofty ways,
Think of all the lazy days . . .

NELLIE:

We could take a trip somewhere . . .

MISS JANE:

Anywhere at all, I don't care.

NELLIE:

Git me in a Model A;
I could roll the whole day away now.

MISS JANE:

You don't say now!

NELLIE:

Let's pray now.

NELLIE & MISS JANE:

Good news 'round the bend;
Trouble days is gonna end.

MISS JANE:

Even broken hopes'll mend
'Cause things ain't what they seem.
So lonesome Nellie girl,

NELLIE:

Oh . . .

MISS JANE:

My little pearl, my dreamer:
Dream.

NELLIE:

Oh, how I like to dream . . .

NELLIE & MISS JANE:

'CAUSE I'VE (YOU'VE) COME HOME,
AND I FEEL LUCKY! LUCKY! LUCKY!

(Nellie and Miss Jane remain onstage in silhouette.

Focus shifts to underground, where Floyd hears Homer calling to him through the passageways above.)

HOMER *(Calling)*: Floyd?! Ya down thar, Floyd?!
FLOYD: Homer?
HOMER: Don't see no openin' . . .
FLOYD: Come an' look for a tiny hole jes' o'er my head . . .

(Homer arrives at the chute right above Floyd. He has stripped down and is cut and bruised. He freezes when he views Floyd's situation.)

HOMER: Oh, Jesus.
FLOYD *(Laughing)*: Knew you'd come, Homer. S'only my left foot's got ketched—now help me free my arms, then I'll be able to git outta here.
HOMER: Cain't you help yourself, man?
FLOYD: Cain't you *see* for yourself, man?
HOMER: Cain't see all the way, Floyd.

(Pause. Homer tries to drop down the chute. He struggles to bring his upper body down to Floyd's level. When he can't, he begins to dig around the opening to Floyd.)

But I'll have you outta here quick as lightnin' . . .
FLOYD: Where'd you go off to, Homer?
HOMER: Gone to Louisville—got me a giant surprise, Floyd.
FLOYD: What?
HOMER: Ya cain't tell no one.
FLOYD: Who'm I gonna tell?
HOMER: Got me the Model T!
FLOYD: Yee-hah—'bout time!
HOMER: Fast an' black an' shiny! We're goin' ridin' tomorrow—me, you, an' Nellie. Hell to Pa if he don't want us enjoyin' life none! Was down at the Dixie Garage—that's where Ellis Jones tells me you're hung up . . . An' Mrs. Jones lookin' at me somethin' fine in my new automobile, an' my new city suit with the slick-em in my hair. She's tellin' me I'm lookin' so fine I'm gonna pass for a movie star one day!

FLOYD: 'Fore we go ridin', Homer, I'm a-take you an' Nellie down to see what I found. She's a big 'un, Homer, but I reckon we'd better find ourselves a more invitin' entrance than this one here, huh Homer? Not many folks gonna wanna come down this way I s'pose.

HOMER: Reckon not . . . *(Getting cut by a rock)* Shit!

FLOYD: But we'll find another entrance down below, one leadin' straight to the road . . .

HOMER: Goddammit, Floyd, can't you keep still?! You're wastin' all your energy an' you're makin' the rocks move! Now let me dig 'roun' here an' I'll git you out.

FLOYD: Diggin' thar won't touch 'er, Homer—that's solid limestone thar.

(Homer tries to maneuver in toward Floyd.)

HOMER: Maybe I kin squeeze in over ya . . .

FLOYD: Won't fit, boy. Whole ceiling might come down. Damn rain.

HOMER: All right, all right, Floyd—what then? Cain't you jes' wiggle yer foot an' pull it out? Go on an' try, Floyd—you din't even try.

FLOYD: Whadda ya think I've been tryin' to do all goddamn night—wiggle it *in*?! It ain't no use, kid—I'm tellin' you—

HOMER: But Floyd—

FLOYD: I'm trapped, Homer—don't you get it? Trapped.

(The words fall like lead. Beat.)

HOMER: I ain't never heard you say that afore.

FLOYD: Wal I ain't never felt it afore. Trapped—thar. Trapped—you heard me say it now.

(Silence. Then reality sets in for the first time. Floyd panics.)

Aw, no—I gotta git outta here! Git me out, I wanna git out!

HOMER: Stop it, Floyd. Stop wigglin'—lie still now!

FLOYD: I've been lyin' still fer two days!

HOMER: Shh, Floyd—I'm tellin' ya—

FLOYD: I don't wanna spend another night here.

HOMER: S'okay, Floyd. S'all right now. We spent a night in the first cave you found, 'member? 'Member, Floyd?

FLOYD: No.

HOMER: An' it passed jes' like a blink. Shh. That's right. Stay calm now.

You had jes' found that cave an' we went under an' stayed up all night. Me an' you know how to spend nights in a cave.

FLOYD: It was dark.

HOMER: Yeah, but it was peaceful, Floyd. Shh, that's right. An' when we left that cave, we walked out to the sight of the sun risin', 'member, Floyd? *(Laughs)* Stubborn mule you were. Been searchin' fer weeks fer that breathin' hole. Day an' night, out explorin', musta been two o'clock in the mornin' . . .

The house was quiet,
'Member, Floyd?
We was all snorin'
An' sleepin' real sound.
You came atop the hill, Floyd,
Like a monkey, jes' a-screechin' an' a-leapin' . . .

You crazy loon.

'Member, Floyd? 'Member how ya screamed?
You hollered somethin' 'bout a cave;
In our nightclothes we came a-toddlin' out.
An' Miss Jane in that ol' sleepin' bonnet,
Like a duck, she was waddlin'.
'Member, Floyd? 'Member how she looked?

We was holdin' hands
As you marched us across the field.

Was a whole mess a stars that night.

As we enter in,
The lights of the sky
Die down, like still,
Like cool, like nightfall . . .

We have each other's hands,
We have what we can picture,
That's all we need
To pass the time . . .

FLOYD:

Time inside has a way of flowin' on,

HOMER:

Goin' on a wind,

FLOYD:

It take itself a dive.

HOMER:

Time inside kinda puts me in a mind
Of when Mama was alive . . .

FLOYD & HOMER:

When Mama was alive.

No one even says a word;
We are happy dreamin',
We are. An' before we know it—
Daybreak is on.

HOMER:

That's how it's gonna be;
That I promise.
Long as you remember that,
From nightfall to daybreak,
From sundown to dawn,
I'm stayin' here.

(Floyd starts to fall asleep.)

That's right . . . You rest now. Yer baby brother's gonna git you through the night.

(Homer curls up as best he can, keeping a silent vigil as Floyd sleeps. Above ground, Skeets Miller, a reporter, stands in a pool of light. He speaks directly out, as if to the audience, as he "writes" his story by speaking it.)

MILLER: There are patches of snow on the ground as I stumble through a cornfield in the bleak Kentucky dawn, comma, seven miles from world famous Mammoth Cave, period. It is February 1, comma, 1925, comma, and I am a skinny, red-haired cub reporter for the *Louisville Courier* dash *Journal,* comma, sent to investigate reports that a man named Floyd Collins is trapped in an underground cavern, period.

Hello—

(He turns to Homer, who now sits outside the cave, huddled and shivering. It is the next morning.)

I'm Skeets Miller.

(Homer ignores him.)

I hear you're the brother of the fellow that's trapped in the cave?

HOMER: You a reporter?

MILLER: Yes, I'm from the *Louisville Courier-Journal.* I'm Skeets Miller, hello. I usually write for sports. And obits. Uh, you see, the city editor thought this was another one of those hoaxes put on by you cave owners, so he sent me this time. *(Pause)* Instead of McClane. *(Pause)* Is your brother still alive? *(Silence)* Mr. Collins—do you know if your brother is still alive?

HOMER: Why're you called Skeets?

MILLER: Huh? Oh, yes. *(Giggles)* Well ya see, they say I'm no bigger 'an a mosquito. Skeets—'squito. *(Gesturing to his size)* Me. *(Silence)* Are you going to get him out?

HOMER: If you're so interested, thar's the hole over thar—go see fer yourself.

(He looks at Miller for the first time, cold and stony.)

MILLER: Myself . . . Okay.

(Beat. Suddenly Miller turns, walks briskly to the cave and disappears into the trench.)

HOMER *(Almost a smile)*: Goddamn . . . *(Calling after him)* Go feet first! Hey! Wait a minute, fella—you got no light!

(The scene around Homer comes to life as people burst onstage. Nellie and Miss Jane still sit together on a log or bench. Doyle bounds on with some Locals. Jewell has a guitar and sits with Bishop, a couple of other men are nearby. They are making up songs.)

DOYLE: Hey, Homer! Thar's people arrivin'!

(They confer.)

NELLIE *(Sneaking closer to Jewell)*: Squirt! Hurry! Come here!—

JEWELL: Excuse me, gentlemen. My lady beckons.

(He hands over the guitar to Bishop and goes to Nellie. She takes some sandwiches out of her pockets and hands them to Jewell.)

NELLIE: My stepmama's got a watch on me—quick! Take these sandwiches I made—take 'em into my brother!

JEWELL: Wal don't you go callin' me squirt—

NELLIE: Wal never you mind. The one that gets to my brother's a hero, you know. Wanna be a hero—or a squirt?

MISS JANE *(Interrupting)*: Nellie!
(Shooing Jewell away) Jewell Estes, always asking fer trouble.

(Miss Jane leads Nellie back to the bench.)

JEWELL: Bishop, I am goin' on a mission! I am now goin' under to Floyd!

(H. T. Carmichael, an engineer, enters with a man or two who work for him, carrying survey equipment. He is an imposing and distinct presence, dressed smartly in city clothes. Lee follows him.)

CARMICHAEL: All right, set it up right here—we'll start the survey along this line, going towards the overhang—

HOMER *(Approaching Carmichael)*: Excuse me, sir—this hill ain't made for shaftin'.

LEE: Where're yer manners, son? This here's Mr. Carmichael, come from the Kentucky Rock Asphalt Company *(Stressing the words) to help us.*

HOMER: Pa, Floyd ain't gonna last long enough for a shaft.

LEE: Mr. Carmichael, this here's my youngest boy, Homer.

CARMICHAEL: Pleased to meet you, Homer. H. T. Carmichael—Kentucky Rock *and* Asphalt Company. We're going to foot the bill for the entire rescue operation.

HOMER: Wait—

CARMICHAEL: Now don't you worry, we're not goin' to sink a shaft . . . just yet. I'm only sending for the equipment and men now, but—

HOMER: We best jes' keep on diggin' with our hands—

CARMICHAEL: What I was just explaining to your father here, partner—before you interrupted, that is—is that the best option, for the moment, and the one we really should try first, is to get a harness on him and pull.

HOMER: That wouldn't work. Floyd's foot might be torn off.

CARMICHAEL: And we also might get him out. Besides, it's really not up to you, now is it, son? *(Looking to Lee)* Mr. Collins? Would you like to share your opinion with your boy here?

LEE: Wal, I ain't sure.

CARMICHAEL: You have only two choices as I see it, sir: you can take the chance, and let me try to pull him out, get him safe and sound right at your side again, or you can stand around doing nothing—not *you* of course, Mr. Collins, but *(Gesturing to Bishop, Doyle, etc.)* these men here. Sir, if we don't drag 'im out now, well . . . Your boy might not come out at all.

LEE: Wal, the harness *might* be worth a try.

HOMER: No, Pa!

LEE: It's up to me. An' I say s'worth a try.

CARMICHAEL: Good. You won't be sorry, sir. *(To Homer)* Tough kid.

(Focus returns to Jewell. Bishop and Doyle are listening to his new verse with great amusement.)

JEWELL *(Ad-libbing, as if trying to write it on the spot)*:

DEEP IN THE LAND OF THE HOLLOWS AN' CREEKS,
IF'N YOU GIT LOST, YOU GIT LOST FER WEEKS.

That's the first part I made up, an' in the next part I'm gonna tell about how I took all the sandwiches I brang from Nellie plus some whiskey I'd snuck in! An' all the time he's sayin', "Praised be Jesus for you, Jewell, my best friend. I love you, Jewell, I love you! I know I'll git out now!"

HOMER: An' then he grew wings an' you all flew out together up to heaven.

JEWELL *(Stops playing)*: Say what?

HOMER *(Teasing)*: What'd the walls of them passageways look like as you're goin' down?

JEWELL: Huh?

HOMER: D'ya see all them sandwiches stuffed into them ledges?—

JEWELL: Huh?

HOMER: By all them squirts too scairt to go down under?

(The others laugh at Jewell. Homer walks away.)

JEWELL *(Calling after him)*: You callin' me a "squirt"?!

(Miller explodes out of the cave, stumbling and covered in mud from head to foot. As he crashes downstage, the others on the scene move upstage and remain in a frozen—but active—silhouette. Miller sinks to the ground and lowers his head between his knees.)

MILLER *(Heightened speech; fast, panicked, in the middle of reliving it)*:
I LANDED ON HIM!
THAT THING!
HORRIBLE! WET . . .
SOMETHING, JELLY OR WORMS, OR SOMETHING . . .
MY HAND ON HIM.

GOD! FOR CHRIST SAKE!
HEAD OF HAIR!
NO; OH NO . . .

MOANIN', THIRSTIN', GROANIN'
OR YELPIN' LIKE CROAKIN' . . .

(Pause.)

ALIVE?

(He coughs, is overcome with nausea.)

CHRIST SAKE!
CHATTERING, SO AWFUL COLD.
HELPLESS, ANIMAL AND HOPELESS,

(Pause.)

I THINK . . .
HOPELESS.

(He laughs with relief.)

I AM NOT THERE.
IT IS NOT ME.

(Putting his hand to his pounding heart.)

GET HOLD OVER IT!
IT'S OVER.
YOU'RE OUT.

(Suddenly, Nellie is there, as if appearing out of thin air. She stares down at Miller.)

NELLIE: Hey, mister.

MILLER *(Disoriented)*: Huh?

NELLIE: You saw him, *didn't* ya?

MILLER *(Starting to collect himself and getting up)*: Uh . . . sorry, miss, if you'll excuse me . . .

NELLIE: Is he keepin' company?

MILLER: Company?

NELLIE: With the crickets? Did he tell you?

MILLER: Crickets? . . . Uh . . . I . . . Excuse me, miss, I gotta get my story in. *(Tips his hat and starts to leave)*

NELLIE: Floyd's friends with the crickets down under. Bet thar's a heap you don't know 'bout Floyd you oughtta have in one of them stories of yours.

(Miller stops and turns around.)

Personal thangs . . .

MILLER: Who are you?

NELLIE: Nellie.

MILLER: Nellie?

NELLIE: His sister, Miss Nellie Collins. *(Pause)* He knows more 'bout rocks an' caves an' such as any college boy or professor type. Knows the names of all the stones—taught himself. Everything.

(Miller goes to Nellie.)

See, I know Floyd better 'n anyone, an' he knows me purty good. He came to visit me all the way to Green Haven when I was thar. See I understan' 'im 'cause we think the same thoughts, him an' me. He's always sayin' we're a fine pair 'cause my head's in the clouds an' his is in the dirt. *(Laughs)*

MILLER: What else . . . ?

NELLIE: Well, fer one thing, he's got the Luck—carries it with 'im whenever he goes explorin'. An ol' compass an' he calls it the Luck. Did ya see the Luck, mister?

MILLER: S'mighty dark down there. Hard to see anything.

NELLIE: I bet it's right beautiful. I wanna go, too.

MILLER: Beautiful? No, I wouldn't exactly say . . . Beautiful?

(Suddenly there's a commotion at the site. Carmichael gets the attention of the crowd.)

CARMICHAEL: All right, men, here's the plan. We're going to feed one end of a rope to a harness ring and the other end up the passageway. One man every twenty feet. We'll need a steady line of men. Good balance. If you're smart and strong and not afraid of risking your life to save another's, meet up right here.

(No response.)

Homer, you go and find a harness'll fit your brother. We need a rope 'least a hundred feet long.

(Still no response.)

Don't you people have a rope 'round here?

(Nothing.)

Listen, folks, I know you don't know me—I know I'm an outsider to ya, but I promise—I'm here to help. And with a little cooperation between us, we can have your friend out in no time at all.

(Pause. Still a tentativeness in the crowd.)

HOMER: He's right. I'll be first on the line, 'side a Floyd.

CARMICHAEL: And I'll be determining the order around here, son. Now—who's got down to Collins?

HOMER: He's my brother, an' I'll be first on line—

CARMICHAEL: Well, I heard you couldn't get through the last squeeze, son, so how're ya planning to get the harness on him? Now I need to know, who's got *all the way* down?

(Beat. Miller steps forward.)

MILLER: Me—me have. I mean I have—not me—I.

(Pause.)

CARMICHAEL: Who are you?
MILLER: Uh . . . Call me Miller. I'm small. I . . . reached 'im.
BISHOP: That ain't possible.
HOMER: It's true. I watched 'im.

(Carmichael considers a moment.)

CARMICHAEL: All right—you men with me?
BISHOP & JEWELL: We're with you. Yes sir!

(Carmichael points to Doyle.)

DOYLE: Yeah.
CARMICHAEL: Let's go then.

(Movement.)

HOMER *(Running)*: Find a harness—
MILLER *(To himself)*: I'll get the harness on him!
CARMICHAEL: We're going to pull on the count of three, and you all can take it from me!

(The men rush off in various directions, while Nellie remains silhouetted against the sky, reaching for Floyd. Miss Jane holds her back. Floyd's face is illuminated, alone in the cave.)

FLOYD *(Intimate, quiet)*:

AFTER THIS IS OVER, LORD, WILL THERE BE A GIRL FER ME?
I COULD TRY TO 'HAVE LIKE PROPER COMPANY . . .
AN' SHE'D HAVE BLUE EYES, AN' YELLA HAIR,
ALL FALLIN' DOWN IN RINGS,
AN' SHOULDER BLADES LIKE WINGS.
AH . . . HOW SHE WOULD ATTEND ME,
SOFTLY LIKE A HYMN.

AN' IF SHE KNEW ME,
AN' LET ME BE,
I'D NEVER LET HER GO.
I COULDN'T TELL HER SO,
BUT HOW I WOULD ATTEND HER,
SOFTLY LIKE A HYMN,
ALL DAY LONG AN' ALL OUR LONG DAYS . . .

(Suddenly screaming:)

No-o-o! . . .
MILLER: Stop!
HOMER: Stop!
BISHOP: Stop!
JEWELL: Stop!
DOYLE: Stop!
CARMICHAEL: Stop!

(Inside the cave, Miller is with Floyd, Homer right above them past the final squeeze. The harness is on, the rope attached. Homer is just visible in the shadows, and beyond him a line of men continues up into darkness. At the same time, we can see Carmichael above ground where the other end of the rope extends out of the cave.)

HOMER: We don't got to do it, Floyd. Only if you want us to.
FLOYD: Do it, do it—tear my foot off, tear my leg off—I don't care, Homer, so long as you don't leave me alone again . . . Please, Homer, please—don't leave me alone again . . . *(Pause)* Do it. *Do* it!
HOMER *(Beat; calls out)*: Ready!

(The line of men call up "Ready" until it reaches Carmichael at the top.)

CARMICHAEL: One . . . two . . . three . . . *pull*!

(The tension on the rope tightens; Floyd's body straightens five or six inches.)

FLOYD: No-o-o! . . . Don't do it! No-o-o-o-o . . .
CARMICHAEL *(Bellowing)*: Keep going! Pull! Pull!
FLOYD: Stop! It's pullin' me in two!

HOMER & MILLER: Stop! Stop it!

(Homer starts to pull in the opposite direction, trying to release the pressure on Floyd.)

CARMICHAEL: We've got him! He's caught on a snag! Harder—pull harder, men!

FLOYD *(Gasping)*: Stop them—my back . . . I'm breaking . . . Stop . . . oh God . . .

HOMER *(Screaming full voice)*: Stop it! Stop it! We're killing him! Holy Jesus—stop!

(Echoes of "Stop" overlapping.)

CARMICHAEL *(Overlapping)*: Stop! *(Beat)* And relax.

(The rope falls slack. Silence, except for Floyd's quiet whimpering.)

HOMER *(To himself)*: Oh shit . . . Shit, man . . . Now what? . . . Oh shit . . .

(Above ground, a new Reporter appears with a flourish. Then a second one. As they begin to scope the scene, day turns to night. Under Carmichael's direction, the Locals string up work lights in all directions. Two tents are erected—one for snacks and coffee, the other for first-aid. One by one, the men from the harness line exit the cave, exhausted and frightened. They rest at the makeshift camp. Lee sits alone; Miss Jane approaches him.)

MISS JANE: What're you doin' sittin' thar, s'almost midnight.

LEE: Did I do wrong lettin' them pull on 'im like that?

MISS JANE: You couldn't know. You done what you saw fit.

LEE: Like I always done. But things don't come out like ya 'spect 'em—do they Janie?

(She looks at him.)

The chilrun—I taught 'em best I could. But somethin' not quite right with each an' every one. What did I do wrong? They come from me.

MISS JANE: Shh, my angel. All of us is a bit touched if you look close enough. That makes family. Lee—I love yer family. When I married you, I took yer family to be my own.

When times is hard to endure,
An' the world feels a wilderness,
The times is fer makin' family.

'Tis a wintry wind to be sure,
An' when it won't quit blowin',
The times is fer goin' home.

An' as one sweet soul to another,
You an' I
Are a lullaby
To each other.

Hush, my darlin';
Hush-a-bye, angel.
I'm a-side you heart an' hand.

LEE:

Ain't much bacon in the pan or coffee in the pot,
Runnin' real low on firewood,
But we sure as hell have us some family.

Craziest bunch of fools was ever begot,
But there ain't no figurin' what the Lord plans,
An' I don't want no other man's home.

MISS JANE & LEE:

An' as one sweet soul to another,
A family tries
To sing lullabies
To each other.

Hush, my darlin';
Hush-a-bye, angel.
I'm a-side you heart an' hand.
Right a-side you I will stand;
I will stand
Heart an' hand.

(Flash! A Reporter has sneaked up close to Lee and Miss Jane and shot a photograph. It startles everyone at the site.

The focus shifts to Miller and Floyd in the cave. Miller has been under a long time, and is just now inching himself up off of his digging position over Floyd's body. An unlit light bulb hangs nearby, its wire trailing up into the passageways.)

FLOYD: Hey, fella, d'you write the article 'bout the cavern I done found like I tol' you?

MILLER: Yeah, Floyd. I reported it word for word. There. We're almost down to your ankle.

FLOYD: Did it make it to the Louisville paper? You think Bee Doyle saw it?

MILLER: Front page.

FLOYD: Gotcha, Doyle, I tol' you so!

MILLER: I don't think you understand what's going on up there, Floyd. I'm not even sure I do. You're not going to believe this but—

FLOYD: Try me—come on, jes' try me, fella!

MILLER: Well, your . . . my story was syndicated in over twelve hundred newspapers, Floyd.

FLOYD: Woo-ee! *(Beat)* What's that mean?

MILLER: It means they're reading about you all across the country.

FLOYD: Wal, hot diggedy damn, fella—you're a success!

HOMER *(Offstage; calling)*: Miller! The lights are comin' on!

MILLER: Okay!

(The light bulb turns on, as well as a string of lights that recedes into the darkness.)

FLOYD: Oh yeah, light.

MILLER *(Lifting his pad)*: Floyd, what's it feel like to be . . . to be . . .

FLOYD *(Avoiding it)*: You know, I could have this here cavern ready fer the public in two months maybe. Start advertising fer it now.

MILLER: Is that what goes through your mind?

FLOYD: Damn, my teeth is throbbin' . . . Like to rip 'em out my mouth.

MILLER: Do you want some more milk?

FLOYD *(Attacking him)*: Milk!? . . . Milk!!? What am I supposed to do with milk?!

(Pause. Miller doesn't know what to say, puts down his pad.)

MILLER: Floyd, I should leave you alone now.

FLOYD: Miller!

(Miller stops. Pause.)

It's jes' that . . . I ain't never been one for talkin'—'bout myself most 'specially.

(He strains to look up at Miller, a little spent.)

But go on, git your pad.

(Miller starts to write.)

What do I think about? Nellie, fer one thing. Sometimes I think I hear her comin' down to me . . . but usually jes' the crickets. So I talk with them instead.

(Miller smiles.)

I'm not pullin' yer leg, fella . . . Probably shouldn't use that turn a phrase. They tell me 'bout the world down under. These passageways, how many miles they go on an' on . . . See fella, I got me a hunch that all these caves 'round here are all connected to each other . . . Somehow, down thar, where we cain't yet see it . . . everythin' . . . is jes' part of one giant . . . uh . . .

MILLER: System?

FLOYD: Yeah, that's a good word. One giant system.

MILLER: Floyd—why did you come down here? I mean, why would anyone want to crawl into a tiny little hole, day after day, risking your life . . . ?

FLOYD: It's jes' . . . when I'm under . . . I feel right in my bones. I don't know. Why would anyone want to write words?

MILLER *(Chuckles)*: Good question. I'm not sure I do. Heck, until I got this job a couple months ago, my great aspiration was always to be—now don't laugh, Floyd—a baritone on the operatic stage.

(Beat. Then Floyd bursts out laughing. Miller joins him.)

You're not supposed to laugh.

FLOYD: That'd make the cat laugh. *(Singing operatically)* Tra-la-la-la-la! . . . *(Dwindles away to silence)*

MILLER: Do you believe in fate, Floyd? You know—that there's something you're cut out to be?

FLOYD: Wal, I know I'm lucky, that's one thang fer sure. I've always had the Luck with me.

(Miller writes.)

But suddenly, fella, I'm goin' back an' forth thinkin', How will it end? Will I git out, or . . .

See, it's started occurrin' to me, that maybe . . . maybe . . . I might jes' die.

(Miller stops writing.)

I don't mean someday neither . . . but, you know . . . down here . . . stuck in this . . . in this . . . Why'd ya stop writin'?

MILLER *(Realizing it)*: Uh . . . I don't know. I guess, maybe, there are some things that shouldn't be written about . . . I mean when someone's afraid of . . .

FLOYD: Heck, write about it! Death don't frighten me none! I've faced death plenty a times afore. *(Calling out)* She cain't catch me!

MILLER: I'm afraid sometimes.

FLOYD: Wal . . . *(Shrugs)* I believe in heaven, see. My mama's up thar. *(On the verge of tears for the first time)* But it is long . . . long . . .

(Silence.)

MILLER: Floyd, I promise you, right here and now—I make you an oath that I am going to get you out.

FLOYD *(Smiles)*: Sure, fella.

MILLER: I swear to you—or I'll stay in here with you.

FLOYD: You know, my head's clearer now than at any time since I been here—thanks to yer jabberin'. You go now, Mr. Skeets, an' come back when yer rested.

(Miller starts to leave.)

MILLER: I'm not giving up 'til you're free, Floyd. It's only one more foot till we reach that rock. And I'll be back real soon!

FLOYD *(Calling after him)*: Ain't no hurry! *(Then to himself)* I ain't goin' nowhere.

(Miller is gone.

Incidental music underscores Floyd as he sings to himself:)

DOH-DEE-A-DOHT-N-DOH-DEE

(Suddenly, from above ground, Nellie calls back to him in song:)

NELLIE:

Doh-dee-a-doht-n-doh-dee . . .

FLOYD & NELLIE:

Doh-dee-a-doh

NELLIE:

Wee-dap-pa-da

FLOYD:

Doo-wee-dap-pa-da

NELLIE:

Wee-dap-pa-da-dum
Da-dee-a-da-dum-da-da-ah . . .

FLOYD:

Dee-um-dum-ah . . .

FLOYD & NELLIE:

Welcome home.

FLOYD: I done missed ya, Nell.

(The scene above ground is full of activity: Carmichael, Homer, Miller, the Locals and the Reporters all make various crosses on- and offstage as the urgency and chaos of the rescue increases. Additional planking and barriers are put up at the entrance to the cave. A young man named Cliff Roney approaches Bishop.)

RONEY: Excuse me, do you know where the fella in the cave is?

(In another place, Homer catches up with Miller.)

HOMER: Miller! Did you reach all the way ag'in? I mean, touch him when you took that light down?

MILLER: Yep.

HOMER: I don't see how you do it. I jes' cain't make myself any smaller . . . That last hole thar . . .

MILLER: Homer, I made good progress digging this time. I—

HOMER: How many inches?

MILLER: I don't know—three, four maybe.

HOMER: Wal, which one? Four? Ya think ya made four inches?!

MILLER: I . . . maybe. I—

HOMER: Good goin', fella! With four inches I think I kin git through!

(Roney approaches Homer.)

RONEY: Excuse me, do *you* know where the fella in the cave is?
HOMER: Who are you?
RONEY: Cliff Roney—Louisville Motion Picture Company. Pleased to meet you.
MILLER *(Leaving)*: 'Scuse me.
HOMER: Homer Collins. An' my brother's right down thar. *(Points to the ground)*
RONEY *(Walking away)*: Very funny. *(Suddenly turns back)* Hold it right there—don't move! Yep—that's it all right. I think ya got the look. Anyone ever tell you that?
HOMER: What?
RONEY: The look, the look!
HOMER: The l*u*ck? . . .
RONEY: The *look*. The kind of face that belongs on the silver screen.

(No response.)

Movies? . . . Hollywood? . . .

(No response.)

Homer— *(Putting his arm around him)* I have a feeling we're gonna be good buddies, you and me.
HOMER: Jes' one thang on my mind now, mister—hammer, chisel, an' goin' under ag'in. 'Scuse me.
RONEY: That's three.
HOMER: Huh?
RONEY: *Three* things, Homer. Ya need me, kiddo—saw it right away.

(Dr. Hazlett arrives at the site carrying a medical bag and smoking a cigarette. He spots Lee, who is sitting in a stupor, coughing.)

HAZLETT: How long have you had that cough, sir?
LEE: What's it to you?
HAZLETT: I'm the doctor they sent from Chicago. Put me on an aeroplane. I'm Dr. Hazlett. Are you Lee Collins?
LEE: You here to help us git my boy out?

HAZLETT: Yes—well, I mean, no. Uh . . . You see, Mr. Collins, I didn't receive the proper information in Chicago. I had no idea . . . There's obviously no way I could work down there.

LEE: Why not?

HAZLETT *(Gently)*: You must be kidding. Have you looked down there?

LEE: A hole's a hole.

(Lee struggles to stand up.
Focus shifts to Homer and Miller.)

HOMER: Miller—you know these people? There's some movie fella, and reporters startin' to come from—

MILLER: No, I don't know where they're from. Homer, listen—Carmichael just made an announcement. Now don't fly off the handle, but . . . He's decided to close off the passageways.

HOMER *(Flying off the handle)*: What?! An announcement to who?!

MILLER: He's closing off the cave entrance and says—

HOMER: Oh no he's not! I've had enough of outlanders, Miller. An' I'm goin' under right now to git my brother.

MILLER: But—

HOMER: We're too close to stop now!

(The focus shifts back to Lee and Dr. Hazlett.)

LEE: Doctor, listen—no matter how hard they tugged 'im, if'n his leg ain't gonna move from under that rock . . . maybe we should jes' leave it thar . . . his leg I mean.

HAZLETT: That's what I'm saying, Mr. Collins. Amputation is out of the question.

LEE: Why?

HAZLETT: First of all, no one can get in over him. But even if we could operate, we'd have to include the femur, and the loss of blood would be substantial . . . perhaps deadly.

LEE *(Angered)*: You tellin' me ya cain't do it?

(Miss Jane enters, having heard the upset Lee.)

MISS JANE: Lee, come inside with me now.

HAZLETT: I'm sorry, Mr. Collins. I can only help out up here. I've arranged with the Red Cross to set up—

LEE: Would two hundred dollars change yer mind?
MISS JANE: We don't have that kind of money!
HOMER *(To Nellie)*: If anyone asks after me, don't say nothin'. I'm goin' under. *(Starts away)*
NELLIE: Hey, Homer— *(Nellie hugs him)*
HOMER: Next time I see you, I'll have our brother at my side.

(During the following dialogue, Homer goes inconspicuously to the cave entrance and disappears inside.)

LEE: Five hundred then? I give you five hundred to go down thar.
MISS JANE: 'Scuse us, Doctor. Lee, what's come o'er you? Yer not actin' yerself.
LEE: If we got some money, Janie—jes' some money . . .
MISS JANE: 'Tain't got nothin' to do with money!

(Carmichael enters. Miller follows, trying to speak to him.)

CARMICHAEL: All right, everybody—the cave area is off limits to unauthorized personnel until further notice. Mr. Collins, we've set a tent up for you and your family. Doc, if you'll come with me. Where's that Collins kid? Not now, Miller—go find Homer Collins and get him in the tent . . . Miller!

(Inside the cave, Homer moves down the passageway toward Floyd.)

HOMER: Floyd? . . . Floyd Collins! . . .
FLOYD: That you, Homer?
HOMER: You betcha! An' *this time* I come to git you out!
FLOYD: Whad'ya come for *last time*?!
HOMER: I'm a-comin', I'm a-comin', I'm a comin' . . .
FLOYD: He's a-comin', he's a-comin', he's a-comin' . . . *(As if to someone)* Now scram, y'all—we gotta make room for Homer!

(Homer arrives at the chute above Floyd's head. He stops and peers down.)

HOMER: Who the hell are you talkin' to?
FLOYD: If you could fit yer fat head through that hole, maybe you could find out.

(Homer starts digging at the chute with the chisel and hammer, removing rocks one at a time to enlarge the opening. He works hard, making good progress throughout the rest of the scene.)

HOMER: All right, listen here, Mr. Hole—you ain't so tough you kin—

FLOYD: Who the hell are *you* talkin' to, boy?! Talkin' to crickets one thang—talkin' to holes . . . Wal . . .

(He whistles as if to say, "You've really lost your mind!")

HOMER: Talkin' to 'em's better 'n gettin' trapped in 'em.

FLOYD: Don't smart mouth me, boy, or I'm gonna give you what fer.

HOMER: I'd like to see you try.

FLOYD: Don't make me come up thar. *(Pause; impatiently)* How much longer? Come on, come on! Cain't you do nothin' to help me, Homer?!

HOMER: Quiet, Floyd! You'd think you'd done got swallowed up by quick-sand, way you're hollerin'. You ain't gonna drown or nothin', ya know.

FLOYD: Hey, Homer—what's pink an' green an' flies all over?

(Homer shoots his brother a look. Pause.)

Homer?

(Homer gets an idea, a twinkle in his eye.)

Homer? Ya thar, buddy?

HOMER *(Spoken in rhythm)*:
WHAT'S MADE A STONE BUT'S SOFT LIKE A PILLOW?

FLOYD: That's not what I asked you. What's pink an' green an' flies all over?

HOMER *(Spoken in rhythm)*:
WHAT'S MADE A STONE BUT'S SOFT LIKE A PILLOW?
WHERE YOU KIN LAY ON TOP OR SINK DOWN IN IT?
WHERE YOU KIN GIT UNDERNEATH, BUT IT DON'T CRUSH YOU?

(He sings:)

COME ON, THINK NOW.
YOU BETTER THINK NOW, FLOYD.

GIVE IT SOME THOUGHT, NOW.
IT AIN'T HARD!

YOU KNOW; I KNOW YOU KNOW.
I'M A-HARKENIN' BACK TO A TIME AGO
WHEN A DAY WASN'T DONE IF WE DIDN'T RAISE HELL,
AND THE SUN PUT US UNDER ITS MAGIC SPELL.

Huh? You're a dumb-ass, you know that? You must be the dumbest ass . . .

FLOYD: Shut up! I got it.

HOMER: Wal?

FLOYD: Sand!

HOMER: Sorry.

FLOYD: But its made a stone an' soft like a feather; you kin lay on top or sink down in it—

HOMER: Yeah, but that ain't this riddle an' you ain't got it yet, so keep thinkin', an' use yer *brain* this time.

(Spoken in rhythm:)

WHAT'S MADE A STONE BUT'S SOFT LIKE A PILLOW?

FLOYD: I done tol' you already, Homer. I said, "Sand!" Like "The Great Sand Cave!"

HOMER: An' I said, "Sorry."

(Spoken in rhythm:)

WHAT'S MADE A STONE BUT'S SOFT LIKE A PILLOW?
WHERE YOU KIN FLOAT ON TOP OR DIVE DOWN IN IT?
WHERE YOU KIN SINK UNDERNEATH, BUT IT DON'T CRUSH YOU?

(He sings:)

COME ON, THINK NOW.
YOU BETTER THINK NOW, FLOYD.
GIVE IT SOME THOUGHT, NOW.
IT AIN'T HARD!

YOU KNOW; I KNOW YOU KNOW.
I'M A-HARKENIN' BACK TO A TIME AGO
WHEN YOU'D SAY TO ME, "HOMER, ARE YOU READY?
ARE YOU SET?"
AN' I'D SAY TO YOU, "FLOYD, ARE YOU READY TO GIT WET?"

FLOYD:

I KNOW!
WHAT'S SOFT JES' LIKE A PILLOW,
MADE A ROCK CARVED IN STONE?
THE ANSWER TO THE RIDDLE
SURELY IS THE QUARRY!

FLOYD & HOMER:

THE QUARRY!

(Floyd rises up from his trapped position; he and Homer relive their memory.)

FLOYD:

THE SUN BEATIN' DOWN
ON OUR FACES ALL BLISTERIN' HOT, HOMER.
WE'D RUN OFF ALONE
TO OUR OWN SECRET SPOT, HOMER.
UNDER THE SHADE 'SIDE OUR OL' FISHIN' HOLE,
WE'D EACH HAVE SOME WORMS AN' AN OL' FISHIN' POLE.

HOMER:

WITH SCHOOL FAR AWAY
LIKE IT WARN'T THERE AT ALL, FLOYD.
WE'D HOOK FOR A DAY
AND WE'D SURE AS HELL HAVE US A BALL, FLOYD.
GO FOR A SWIM JES' TO COOL OFF OUR HIDE;
FLOAT ON TOP WITH THE SKY OPEN WIDE!

(They settle back into their positions at the chute, except Homer lies in Floyd's trapped position and Floyd stands above him.)

FLOYD: All right, okay—I got one fer you.

(Spoken in rhythm:)

WHAT'S GOT A TRUNK AN' A TAIL AN' FIFTY LIMBS?

HOMER: Shhh, I'm concentratin' on diggin', Floyd.

FLOYD: You ain't concentratin', you fibber. You jes' a wee bit slow in the head, jes' like you always was, a wee bit slow.

(Spoken in rhythm:)

WHAT'S GOT A TRUNK AN' A TAIL AN' FIFTY LIMBS?
THAT YOU KIN RIDE ALL DAY BUT YOU DON'T GO NOWHERE,
ONLY FRONT TO BACK, TO AN' FRO?

(He sings:)

COME ON, THINK NOW.
YOU BETTER THINK NOW, HOMER.
GIVE IT SOME THOUGHT, NOW.
IT AIN'T HARD!

YOU KNOW; I KNOW YOU KNOW.
I'M A-HARKENIN' BACK TO A TIME AGO
WHEN A DAY DIDN'T PASS THAT YOU COULDN'T CATCH US TRYIN',
RIDIN' HIGH TILL IT FELT LIKE FLYIN'.

HOMER:

I KNOW!
THE ANSWER TO THE RIDDLE—
TRUNK AND A TAIL AND FIFTY LIMBS!—
THE ANSWER TO THE RIDDLE
SURELY IS THE SWING TREE!

FLOYD & HOMER:

THE SWING TREE!

(They both rise again and relive the memory:)

HOMER:

WE'D SHIMMY ON UP
LIKE AN INDIAN HUNTIN' A SQUIRREL, FLOYD.

FLOYD:

DA, DA, DACKY, DICKY, DA . . .
DA, DA, DACKY, DICKY, DICKA.

HOMER:

Up to the crook
Where we could look down on the world, Floyd.

FLOYD:

Da, da, dacky, dicky, da . . .
Da, da, dacky, dicky, dicka.

HOMER:

Out on a limb where that ol' rope was hung,
High 'bove the water, waiting to be swung.

FLOYD:

Da, da, dacky, dicky, da . . .

FLOYD & HOMER:

Da, da, dacky, dicky, dicka.

Slide down the rope
An' my legs start to pump, Homer (Floyd).

HOMER:

Da, da, dacky, dicky, da.

FLOYD:

Da, da, dacky, dicky, dicka.

FLOYD & HOMER:

My heart starts to pound,
An' my head starts to thump, Homer (Floyd).

FLOYD:

Da, da, dacky, dicky, da.

FLOYD & HOMER:

Da, da, dacky, dicky, dicka.

Higher an' higher I'm swingin' along.
We'd git to singin' that ol' swingin' song!

Da, da, dacky, dicky, da . . .
Da, da, dacky, dicky, dicka . . .

FLOYD:

An' when I don't weigh nothin',
Light as air, I let go.
Spinnin' off an' flippin' over;
All that water far below.

An' I open up for my swan dive,
My spread eagle,
My Jesus-on-the-cross!

For Thine is the kingdom and the power and the glory . . .
Forever and ever . . . through the flashing sun . . .
Ever an' ever . . .
Over an' over . . .
Fallin' . . .
Into that black water . . .
An' that rock, stickin' up an' comin' at my face!
That cold, black grave . . . Cold grave . . .

(Spoken) Grave . . .

(Floyd collapses onto the ground. Homer runs to him, then drags him back to his trapped position—the fantasy has ended.)

HOMER: Floyd? Floyd, come on back now . . . It's me, buddy, come to yer rescue. Now you jes' lie there an' rest, Floyd, 'cause I'm about to git you free.

Now, here's the final riddle, Floyd. See if you can answer me this:

(Spoken in rhythm:)

What's strong as a bull an' smart as a fox?
Quick as a hare an' stubborn as a mule,
Kin make like a snake through the tiniest hole,
Kin git hung up fer days an' turn out fine?

(He sings:)

Lookee here, now.
There ain't no two ways about it.
You don't have to worry at all,
We're almost there.

You know; I know you know.
I'm a-harkenin' back to a time ago
When a day didn't end that we didn't help each other,

KINDA LIKE A FRIEND AN' KINDA LIKE A BROTHER.
AN' IT DON'T MATTER NONE IF IT'S ME OR IF IT'S YOU;
THERE AIN'T NO HOLE THAT WE CAN'T PULL THROUGH!

(Homer finally breaks through the hole to Floyd, and drops in beside him.)

FLOYD:
I KNOW!

HOMER:
HOT DAMN!

FLOYD:
YES SIR!

HOMER:
OO-EE!

FLOYD:
IT'S GOOD TO SEE YOU, HOMER!

HOMER:
WE BETTER CLEAN YOU UP
BEFORE THEY TAKE YER PICTURE!

FLOYD:
YOU'S JES' AS UGLY AS YOU EVER WAS!
WHAT TOOK YOU SO DAMN LONG?
TALKIN' TOO MUCH, LIKE YOU ALWAYS ARE.

HOMER:
WHAT'S FAST AN' BLACK AN' SHINY?

FLOYD:
FAST ENOUGH TO MAKE A PANTHER SQUALL?

HOMER:
WHO'S GONNA BE THERE IN IT?

FLOYD:
LOOKIN' FINE AN' SITTIN' TALL—

HOMER:
STRAIGHT TO LOUISVILLE, WHO WILL TEAR?

FLOYD:
FAR AWAY FROM THE TOIL AN' CARE,

HOMER:
WITH MONEY TO BURN,

FLOYD:
ON A HELL OF A SPREE,

HOMER:

Devil to pay,

FLOYD & HOMER:

It's plain to see;
That's an easy one:
That's us!
That's us!

(The two brothers grab each other, rejoicing. Blackout.)

ACT II

PART THREE: THE CARNIVAL

The lights come up on Homer as he crawls out of the cave opening, carrying his hammer and chisel from the preceding scene. Silence. Homer breathes heavily, then collapses on the ground. He tries to stagger to his feet.

RONEY *(Offstage)*: Cut! No, no, no!

(Roney enters carrying his crude motion-picture camera.)

Homer—you gotta make it look *real*.

HOMER *(Nods, looking at ground)*: Uh-uh.

RONEY: That means slow and . . . you know—all excruciatin' . . . and *real*.

HOMER: Huh?

RONEY: It said in the paper that yer back was breakin' and yer hands was bloody. Now I wanna see—

HOMER: I jes' done it like I done it the first time.

RONEY: Homer, Homer, Homer—you cain't jes' feel the pain inside—you gotta *show* it. Here—some nice wet mud ought to do it— *(Smearing dirt on Homer's clothes and face)* make it look *real* real . . . Bingo!

HOMER: Look, Mr. Roney—I'd love to be in one of yer movies one day, but right now, my brother is still trapped, an' I got to get back to the work area, sir. *(He leaves)*

RONEY *(Running after Homer)*: Homer!

(In another place, Doyle, Bishop and Jewell sit reading a newspaper. Miller is in the background, thinking about his next attempt. A Reporter appears, eavesdropping on the Locals from a distance.)

DOYLE *(Reading from newspaper)*: "SKEETS RULES CAVE CITY—PLUCK IS INFECTIOUS. At breakfast this morning, William Burke 'Skeets' Miller was full of plans for the day. One could easily see that he was about to jump off the seat with impatience. And it must be remembered that he had gone to bed at 4:30 this morning and that this was only 7:30." Hell, this Miller guy's makin' us locals look bad. Every time ya turn aroun', he's down under with Floyd an' we're up here, ya know, sittin' on our butts.

BISHOP: I don't think we look so bad.

JEWELL: Yeah.

DOYLE: Wal, I sure wouldn't mind havin' *my* picture in the paper.

JEWELL: Yeah—mine too.

(A second Reporter appears.)

DOYLE: Miller sayin' here, "When I cleared the dirt from my eyes, I could see that the rock couldn't have weighed more than twenty pounds and was shaped like a leg of lamb."

JEWELL: Ah, hogwash!

(A third Reporter appears.)

BISHOP: Biggest leg of lamb *I* ever saw.

JEWELL: A hundred pounds at least—maybe *two* hundred!

DOYLE: Whoa, whoa, whoa—I thought you said it was too dark to see down thar.

JEWELL: Um . . . uh . . . *(A quick lie)* But I could feel it was huge.

(The Reporters descend on the site. Miller finds himself in their midst, thrown off by their information, speed and arrogance.)

REPORTERS:

GET ME NEW YORK CITY!
HELLO, CHICAGO?
COULD YOU PUT ME THROUGH TO BOWLING GREEN?
YOU READY FOR THE LOW-DOWN,
THE REAL STRAIGHT POOP?
HERE COMES THE MOTHER LODE SCOOP.

GET ME BUTTE, MONTANA!
HELLO, SAVANNAH?

COULD YOU PUT ME THROUGH TO ABILENE?
YOU READY FOR THE INFO?
'CAUSE SHE'S A PIP!
I'M MIGHTY GLAD I MADE THE TRIP!

(Spoken in rhythm:)

CAVE CITY, COMMA,
CAPITAL "K," CAPITAL "Y."
FEBRUARY FOUR:

"CAVE MAN UNDERGROUND!"

REPORTER 3:
YOU GOT IT?

REPORTERS 1 & 2:
YEAH.

REPORTERS:
"CAVE MAN UNDERGROUND, IMPRISONED BY ROCK."

REPORTERS 1 & 2:
"CAVE MAN TRAPPED INSIDE A BOULDER."

REPORTER 3: Somewhere in the cold hills of Kentucky, comma, a caver named Floyd Collins lies pinned in a sandy cave by a boulder on his foot, period.

REPORTERS 1 & 3:
"KENTUCKIAN CAUGHT ALONE; COFFIN OF STONE."

REPORTER 2: The Kentuckian is trapped for no one knows how long under a two-ton slab of granite, period.

REPORTERS 2 & 3:
"BURIED WHILE STILL ALIVE."

REPORTER 1: The brave man lies in a coffin of stone, comma, trapped under nearly . . . *(Sings:)*

SEVEN TONS OF ROCK!
IS THAT REMARKABLE?

LOCALS *(Reading newspapers)*:
THAT'S REMARKABLE!

REPORTERS:

Is that remarkable enough?

LOCALS:

Most amazing thing I ever saw!

REPORTERS:

Is it incredible?

LOCALS:

Whoa!

REPORTERS:

I wonder what tomorrow will bring?!

(Homer gathers the Locals.)

HOMER: Doyle, Bishop—I just read in the paper that this Carmichael fella is up for a promotion at his company. Now that starts 'splainin' some of his behavior around here.

(Carmichael is speaking to a Reporter.)

CARMICHAEL: In all modesty, I think it's still up to me to get Collins out. Me and *(A plug)* the men of the Kentucky Rock and Asphalt Company. Thank you. *(Goes to the Locals)* All right, gentlemen . . .

HOMER *(Under his breath)*: I don't see no gentlemen 'roun' here.

CARMICHAEL: Hello, Homer. So we're goin' to start shoring for the rescue shaft.

HOMER *(Jumping to his feet)*: Oh no we're not!

CARMICHAEL *(To Reporters)*: It's all right, boys—he's just a little overwrought.

(Posing with Homer, pretending to smile; under his breath:)

Listen friend, it's under control.

HOMER *(Also forcing a smile for the cameras)*: Under whose control? You don't know what you're doin'.

CARMICHAEL: I'm a licensed engineer and I know exactly what I'm doing.

BISHOP: But you don't know caves.

CARMICHAEL: And you, fella, don't know machines.

(Camera flash. They break the pose.)

Now move out of my way.

MILLER: Mr. Carmichael, I need to speak to you. I have an idea. I want to go down again—with a jack and a crowbar—I think I can pry the rock off his foot.

CARMICHAEL: You're not serious, Miller?

MILLER: We have to try something, and soon, sir. The one thing we can't have happen is for Floyd to lose hope.

REPORTER 1: Floyd's starting to lose hope . . .

REPORTER 2: Lose hope!

REPORTER 3: Lose hope!

MILLER *(Turning, seeing the Reporters)*: What . . . ? Excuse me—I didn't say that Floyd's starting to lose hope—exactly. I said that if we don't—

ALL REPORTERS *(Interrupting)*:

I WANT THE *WALLA WALLA BUGLE*!
THE *PADUCAH TRIBUNE*!
IS THIS THE *MEXICALI TELEGRAM*?
YOU READY FOR THE LOWDOWN,
THE REAL STRAIGHT POOP?
HERE COMES THE MOTHER LODE SCOOP!

I WANT THE *ALAMAGORDA BANNER*!
THE *BOISE GAZETTE*!
GET ME THE *BUMBLEBEE* IN BIRMINGHAM!
YOU READY FOR THE GOODS?
'CAUSE SHE'S READY TO POP!
THIS IS GOING OVER THE TOP!

(Spoken in rhythm:)

CAVE CITY, COMMA,
CAPITAL "K," CAPITAL "Y."
FEBRUARY FIVE:

(They sing:)

"CAVE VICTIM LOSING HOPE."

REPORTER 3:

ACCORDING TO SKEETS MILLER . . .

MILLER:

HUH?

REPORTER 3:

. . . Comma . . .

REPORTERS 1 & 2:

"Cave Victim Crying Out, Asking for Milk."

REPORTER 3:

. . . Collins is quickly slipping into a state of deep despair.

REPORTERS 1 & 3:

"Crying Out in Deep Despair to Tear His Foot Off!"

REPORTER 2: The trapped man was heard to cry out, comma, quotes, "Get me out of here," comma, "even if you have to tear my foot off!" exclamation, close quotes.

REPORTERS 2 & 3:

"Losing Hope and Crying Out in Deep Despair to Hurry."

REPORTER 1: Floyd is reported to be in a state of delirium, conversing with the cave crickets and even begging them to . . .

REPORTERS:

Hurry, hurry,
Hurry, hurry, hurry, hurry,
"*Pull me out!*"

Remarkable?

MILLER: Wait . . .

REPORTERS:

Is that remarkable enough?

MILLER: If you report what you see . . .

REPORTERS:

Is it incredible?

MILLER: Whoa!

REPORTERS & LOCALS:

I wonder what tomorrow will bring?!

(The Reporters go to interview the family members.)

REPORTERS: Nellie! . . . Miss Jane! . . . Homer! . . .
REPORTER 1: Miss Nellie Collins, is it true, ma'am, that you just returned from Green Haven Mental Institution?
NELLIE: Is it true, sir, that you have something in yer front tooth?
REPORTER 1: What? . . . What?
NELLIE: Thar's something on yer tooth.

(Embarrassed, the Reporter checks his teeth as the focus shifts to another area.)

MISS JANE: Lee, thar's a fella jes' arrived from People's Bank. An he's sayin' he wants to help us some with our money trouble.
LEE: Oh, God bless him, Janie. Where is he?
REPORTER 1: God bless him!
REPORTER 2: God bless him!
REPORTER 3: The Collins family is deeply religious!

REPORTERS:
GIMME THE *LACKAWANNA PULPIT*!
THE *PIERRE PICAYUNE*?
IS THIS THE *TALLAHASSEE DEMOCRAT*?
SHARPEN THAT WOODIE,
'CAUSE HERE'S THE DOPE,
CHOCK-FULL OF TRAGEDY AND HOPE!

I'D LIKE THE *PONCA CITY SUN*!
THE *SAGINAW GLOBE*!
PUT ME THROUGH TO THE *ESCANABA FINCH*!
GRAB THAT FEATHER
AND DOUBLE DIP;
THIS BIRD IS READY TO RIP!

"COLLINS FAMILY WAITS AND PRAYS."

CAVE CITY, COMMA, CAPITAL "K," CAPITAL "Y." FEBRUARY SIX:

"NELLIE, JANE, OLD MAN COLLINS, SITTING ON LOG."
REPORTERS 1 & 3:
"THE PICTURE OF THE WEATHERED FAMILY IS TOUCHING."

REPORTER 2: The picture of the old weathered farmer and his bent backwoods wife is a touching one, period.

REPORTERS 2 & 3:
"A VIRGINAL AND COLORFUL EXAMPLE OF THE LIFE."

REPORTER 1: The virginal sister is a colorful example of the folkways and eccentricities of the hillbilly life, period.

REPORTERS *(Spoken in rhythm)*:
REMARKABLY ENOUGH, COMMA,
ALTHOUGH THEY LIVE SUCH SIMPLE LIVES, COMMA,
THE COLLINS FAMILY MANAGES TO OWN A CAR
AND EVEN WEAR SHOES.

BISHOP *(Off-handedly)*: I'm freezin'.

REPORTERS *(Looking at Bishop)*:
WHAT?

(They look at each other.)

HE'S FREE!

MILLER: What the . . . ?

REPORTERS *(Sing)*:
FLOYD COLLINS IS FREE!
DOYLE *(Spoken in rhythm)*:
HOGWASH!
BISHOP *(Spoken in rhythm)*:
AMAZING!
JEWELL *(Spoken in rhythm)*:
BALDERDASH!
REPORTERS *(Sing)*:
HE'S FREE!
FAMILY *(Spoken in rhythm)*:
HOOEY!

MILLER: But I was just with him and he's—

REPORTERS & MILLER *(Sing)*:

NOT FREE!

REPORTERS *(Pouncing on Miller as their next story; spoken in rhythm)*:

"SKEETS MILLER—CELEBRITY HACK!"

ALL *(Sing)*:

I WONDER WHAT TOMORROW WILL BRING?!

REPORTERS *(Spoken in rhythm)*:

GO ON, YA KNOW YER YELLA!
NOW LISTEN, FELLA,
THIS AIN'T NO LITERARY MAGAZINE!

(They sing:)

I ONLY WANT THE GOODIES,
THE MOTHER LODE SCOOP!
I ONLY WANT TO SCOOP—
I ONLY WANT TO SCOOP—
I ONLY WANT TO SCOOP THE POOP!

SCOOP THE POOP!
SCOOP THE POOP!

(Flash pots explode as Miller freezes momentarily in the middle of a hoard of Reporters. Silence as Miller speaks:)

MILLER *(Spoken in rhythm)*:

WHAT . . . HAVE I SET IN MOTION HERE? . . .

(The freeze breaks as Miller looks up, confused, dissociated.)

THIS MORNING THERE WAS A TRAFFIC JAM EXTENDING FOUR MILES FROM BEE DOYLE'S FARM, WITH NOT ONE OF THE THOUSANDS OF AUTOMOBILES MOVING. FROM KANSAS CITY TO NEW YORK CITY, PEOPLE HAVE CLOSED THEIR NEWSPAPERS AND TRAVELED HERE ON HORSEBACK, BY BUGGY, BY BICYCLE, ON FOOT. SOME HAVE COME TO OFFER HELP, WHILE OTHERS ARE HERE, IT SEEMS, TO WATCH, TO SOCIALIZE, OR TO HAWK THEIR WARES. SMALL CONCESSIONS AND COMMISSARIES SEEM TO SPROUT UP HOURLY ON THE HILLSIDE . . .

(Balloons, printed with "Sand Cave," float everywhere. "The Carnival" is a highly expressionistic dance of the circus at Sand Cave from what will turn out to be Floyd's point of view. It portrays the frenzy and the energy of the huge crowd at the site. People from all over the country have arrived. They are engaged in all methods of profiteering and partying. They dance on Floyd's grave. The scene is forceful and surreal, somewhere between clog dancing and Fellini.

The numbered sections in "The Carnival" correspond to places in the musical score. It is important that the dialogue is timed to the music.)

Section 1

REPORTER ON RADIO: We're here, live from Sand Cave with our guest, a Frederick Jordan, who has set up a portable kitchen on a nearby field.

FREDERICK JORDAN: These people is hungry is all I know. We sold out at noon today, but my brother-in-law is comin' with a flatbed tomorrow. Fifteen hundred pounds of meat and produce. Ought to take us through lunch at least.

JEWELL *(Regarding the radio microphone)*: Mister—how does that thing work?

Section 2

CARMICHAEL: Hey! Get off a there!

DOYLE *(Enjoying it)*: Shit, all these folks an' newspaper types come ta see my house an' ta shake my hand! *(Takes a swig of liquor)*

HAWKER 1: Sand Cave balloons—only a nickel!

LEE: Hello, folks—wanna take a tour of the Collins farm? Open ever day. *(Laughs)*

Section 3

HAWKER 1: Sand Cave balloons! . . .

HAWKER 2: Elixirs! . . .

HAWKER 3: Likkerish sticks! . . .

HAWKER 2: Dizziness, the ague! . . .

HAWKER 3: Camp chairs, apple pies, big fat cows! . . .

HAWKER 1: Buy it here! Edgar Allan Poe's . . .

HAWKER 2: "The Pit and the Pendulum!"

Section 3A

LEE: An' here's a picture of my boy Floyd—see? Only a dollar even. *(Laughs again, with the laugh turning into a hacking cough)*

Section 4

(The crowd whistles under:)

MILLER: Today the *Louisville Courier-Journal* sold one hundred thousand papers more than usual. Overnight, Floyd Collins has become the most written about, read about and prayed for individual in the United States.

Section 5

(Floyd, below. He tosses and wriggles, half-conscious, waking as if seeing the nightmare unfolding above him, then drifting off again. Jewell approaches Homer.)

JEWELL: Well, well—what's a big star like you doin' sittin' in the mud like a hog, Collins? Seems like yer whole family is 'bout right losin' their marbles. You got a look-see at yer papa recently?

(No response.)

This here telegram came in today—I dunno know how, but *some*how it ended up right here in my pocket, kin you believe it? Anywise, I took the liberty of openin' it fer ya, figurin' how we're such good buddies an' all.

(Homer reaches for the telegram but Jewell keeps it away. Roney enters and watches.)

Says here they're offerin' you to go sing on the vaudeville stage. 'Magine that, as if yer head ain't swelled up big enough already in these movies.

(Jewell drops the telegram and leaves.)

RONEY *(Picking up the telegram, slapping Homer on the back in congratulations)*: Hey, kid, I knew you got what it takes!

HOMER: Heck, I ain't never even been in a theater.
RONEY: Well, well.

Section 6

(Doyle talks to a crowd.)

DOYLE: I know we all been thinkin' on Floyd an' I ain't one to ask fer charity . . . but I *am* gonna need some help with the damage done here.

(Doyle holds out his hat and several bystanders reach forward, putting money in his hat.)

Thank you, thank you—we'll see your money is put to good use.
LEE: Floyd Collins' onyx!
MISS JANE: Lee—that rock ain't worth nothin'.

Section 7

(Crash! Crash! Crash! The crowd watches as fireworks light up the sky. They "ooh" and "ahh.")

Section 8

(Floyd sings—a jittery, desperate vocalise. A small crowd has gathered around a boxer. Crash! Crash! Crash!)

Section 9

MILLER *(Reading from a newspaper with disbelief)*: "Sparkplug Eddie Bray, champion welterweight fighter, announced today that he would keep in shape by wielding a shovel here at Sand Cave . . ."?

(Nellie watches as Homer is seduced by Roney's plan.)

RONEY: Homer, you gotta make 'em feel sorry for you—that's what they want to see up there. That's what sells: tears—the strain on your family—

must be something awful. When opportunity comes a-knockin', Homer, you get wise. You play your cards right, an' you bring down the house! I'm talkin' new car! Top billing! Private Hollywood estate—an' Mary Pickford for a girlfriend! Before you know it—Homer Collins, matinee idol!

Section 10

(Floyd sings. "The Carnival" reaches a climax.)

Section 11

MILLER: As an estimated thirty thousand visitors make their way to this obscure field in Kentucky, the once-barren farm begins to look more like a country fair— *(Begins to make his way into the cave)* A carnival . . . A dream . . .

(As Miller takes his place behind Floyd, "The Carnival" starts to fade. It eventually becomes an echoey hallucination, receding in Floyd's mind.)

Are you listening, Floyd?
HAWKER 1: Sand Cave balloons—only a nickel!
MILLER: Have you heard anything I've said?
HAWKER 2: Get'cher prayer books!
FLOYD: Yeah, yeah . . . a traffic jam four miles from Bee's farm . . .
MILLER: That's right—
FLOYD: A country fair—
MILLER: Yep.
HAWKERS: Floyd Collins scrapbooks!
FLOYD: A carnival . . . A dream . . .

("The Carnival" is gone. Inside the cave, Miller lies directly on top of Floyd, working around his left foot. Bishop calls from the passageway:)

BISHOP: What's goin' on down thar? It's been two hours an' we're soakin' wet. Carmichael's wantin' to start the shorin'.
FLOYD: Tell Bishop you got the jack an' crowbar set again.
MILLER *(Calling back)*: I got the jack and crowbar set. I'm gonna try again.

(Miller works the crowbar in beside Floyd's foot.)

BISHOP: Hurry, man. Don't forgit we're freezin' here . . .
FLOYD: Okay, Miller, now turn the jackscrew.
MILLER: I'm turning . . . Nothing.
FLOYD: Damn.
BISHOP: What's goin' on down thar? It's cold, Miller.
FLOYD: It's okay, fella. Try it this time with the wooden blocks.

(Miller prepares to repeat the attempt, putting some blocks in place to close up the space.)

BISHOP: Anyone gonna answer me? Is it working?!
MILLER *(Simultaneously, calling)*: Not yet.
FLOYD *(Simultaneously, calling)*: Almost.
BISHOP: Wal, hurry up—how much longer?
MILLER: All right. It's set.
FLOYD: Good.
MILLER: I'm holding 'em in.
FLOYD: Good.
BISHOP: How much longer?
MILLER: I'm turning . . .
FLOYD: Good.
MILLER: Turning . . . Look!
FLOYD: I feel 'er!
MILLER: The jackscrew—she's moving!
FLOYD: I felt it! Keep goin' Miller—turn, turn, turn . . . Keep turnin', fella—it's comin' loose. I feel it!

(The blocks slip and tumble out.)

MILLER: Goddamn it!

(Silence.)

BISHOP: What's happenin' now?
MILLER *(Calling, frustrated)*: You men go on up!
BISHOP: We're staying 'til you get it, Miller. So hurry up—try agin.

(Miller stares into space.)

FLOYD *(Quiet)*: Fella, you git on out of here. You need a rest.
MILLER: I'm sorry . . . really . . . I . . . It's just that I can barely see anymore and . . .

(Above ground, Nellie starts to sing to herself.)

FLOYD: Shhh! Shhh! Listen!
MILLER: What?
FLOYD: I hear 'er.
MILLER *(Listening)*: I don't hear anything. *(Pause)* Just the wind.
FLOYD: You go up top, Miller.
MILLER: All right, Floyd—
FLOYD: But afore you do . . .
MILLER: Yeah?

(Long pause. Miller is still.)

FLOYD: Kiss me good-bye.

(Beat. Tentative and fumbling, Miller leans down and kisses Floyd.)

MILLER: Bye, Floyd.
FLOYD: Bye, Skeets. See you in heaven.

(The sound of distant rumbling begins. Quiet.)

Thar she is agin . . .
BISHOP: Miller? . . .
MILLER: I'm coming, Bishop!
BISHOP: Miller—listen.
FLOYD *(Smiling)*: He hears 'er.
MILLER: Hears . . . *(Listening)* What is that?
FLOYD: Git on out now, fella.
MILLER: But . . . you . . .
FLOYD: I'd hurry if I was you.
BISHOP: Miller . . .
FLOYD: Hurry.
BISHOP: Miller, come on!
MILLER: Floyd, I wish I could—
BISHOP: I'm outta here, Miller!

FLOYD: Move it, fella!
BISHOP: The walls . . .
MILLER: I'm sorry, Floyd. I—
FLOYD: That you, Nellie, come to git me out?
MILLER: I don't want to leave you.
BISHOP: They're cavin' in, Miller!
MILLER: I'll be back, Floyd, I . . .

(The sound of earth falling. Miller disappears up the passageway.)

FLOYD:

DA DA, DACKY DICKY DA—
DA DA, DACKY DICKY DA DA—
DA DA, DACKY DICKY DA—
DA DA, DACKY DICKY DA—

(The cave-in begins. The walls around Floyd begin to shake as the light slowly closes in on his face. The roar becomes deafening. Floyd screams, as the focus abruptly shifts to above ground.)

MILLER *(Fast, panicked)*: Dateline, February seven. A cave-in late tonight has cut Floyd Collins off from the outside world, period. Fortunately, comma, tests show that the trapped man is still alive, period. It seems possible, comma, that the cave-in was caused by too many men being in the tight, unstable passageways, comma, and due to the body heat and the brushing of bodies against wet cave walls . . . Goddamn it!
NELLIE: Mr. Skeets?
MILLER: Huh?

(Miller looks up; Nellie and he are alone onstage. In the background are sounds from "The Carnival.")

NELLIE: Is Floyd . . . all right?
MILLER: Uh . . . Yeah, I think . . . That sound—horrible and . . . I'm sorry, Miss Nellie. I, um . . . Sealed off—he's sealed off . . .
NELLIE: Mr. Skeets—
MILLER: I don't know what else to do!
NELLIE: But *I* do. S'all right, Mr. Skeets. *I* know. *(Calming him)* Thar now. *(Pause)* Mr. Skeets, cave-in don't matter none. You'll see. You rest now, an' I'll be back in a jiffy. *(Goes to the cave entrance)*

MILLER: Wait! Miss Nellie!

(He runs after her.)

You can't . . . You best go on back now to your family.

NELLIE *(Leaning in to whisper)*: I gotta go into the cave. He needs me. S'gettin' time.

MILLER: Miss Nellie, you're not allowed to be here. You know they closed this area off.

NELLIE *(Starting into the cave)*: But the wind . . .

MILLER *(Holding her back)*: You can't go under! It's too dangerous and you couldn't possibly—

NELLIE:

BUT WHY CAN ALL OF YOU GO?
LIKE FIRE! LIKE AIR!
'TAIN'T FAIR
THAT ALL A YOU GO.

YOU MEN, GOIN' UNDER,
ALWAYS SCOOTIN' 'ROUND AN' A-RUNNIN' THINGS,
ALWAYS GOIN' 'ROUND AN' A-RUNNIN' THINGS.
TICK TOCK TICK TOCK, TOCK TICK TOCK!

I'M ACHIN' A-GO . . . PLEASE.
I'M ACHIN' T' SET 'IM FREE.
WHAT'S WRONG WITH ME?
WHAT'S WRONG WITH ME?

MILLER: Shhh, now. You're fine as candy, Miss Nellie. A young gal like you should at least try to enjoy some of the bright lights and colors if you can. Now go along.

(They both look off for a moment. Pause.)

Evenin'.

(Miller makes sure she's on her way out, then leaves. Nellie lingers.)

NELLIE: I'm a-come to you, Floyd—no matter what.

I'M A-WALK YOU THROUGH THE MOUNTAIN
ON A BEARSKIN RUG,
THROUGH THE GREAT HALLS YOU DREAM OF
AN' TELL OF SO OFTEN.
I'M A-KEEP YOU JES' AS WARM
AS A GOOD NIGHT HUG,
AS WE FOLLOW 'LONG THE DIAMONDS
TO THE OUTSIDE.

YOU KIN TAKE ME ON A TOUR
OF THE EMERALD TOWERS,
TO THE SPIRES OF SAPPHIRES
AN' WATERFALLS A CRYSTAL.
WE'LL LAY DOWN TO SLEEP
WITH THE GYPSUM FLOWERS,
AS WE FOLLOW 'LONG THE DIAMONDS
TO THE OUTSIDE.
Ooo . . .

GONNA GIT YOU OUTTA THERE,
TO A LAND A BABIES DANCIN'
WITH A BANJO IN THE AIR.
AN' THE SKY IS ALL LIT UP
WITH LEMONS AND ROSES;
EVERYTHIN' FROM YOUR HEAD TO YOUR TOES IS WARM.
LISTEN TO ME NOW.

I'M A-WALK YOU THROUGH THE MOUNTAIN
ON A BEARSKIN RUG,
THROUGH THE GREAT HALLS YOU DREAM OF
AN' TELL OF SO OFTEN.
I'M A-TAKE YOU BY THE HAND,
AN' WITH A GENTLE TUG,
WE'LL BE GONE—
WE'LL BE LONG GONE—
AS WE FOLLOW 'LONG THE DIAMONDS
TO THE OUTSIDE.
AS WE FOLLOW 'LONG THE DIAMONDS
TO THE OUTSIDE.

(Beat. Then a sudden blast of light from newly erected floodlights in the area. Carmichael bounds on followed by several National Guardsmen, Workers, and a flock of Reporters. Others enter in the course of the scene. Barbed wire is erected and the site takes on an aggressive military atmosphere. Doyle sits to one side, drinking—already drunk—watching.)

CARMICHAEL *(Talking to ten people at once)*: Start the power shovel—Bishop, get the pneumatic drill back down here goddamn it . . . Estes, go help Bishop . . . and I want you to call Frankfort right away and tell them we need at least fifty more Guardsmen . . . Private, get that girl out of here, this is restricted area now . . . We gotta get that canvas up before the rain hits again . . .

REPORTER 1: Mr. Carmichael, is it true that you're having trouble getting the shaft started?

CARMICHAEL: Press conferences will be held every hour on the hour. Until then, press *(Points off)* behind the fence. That includes you, Miller.

MILLER: But I'm part of the rescue team.

CARMICHAEL: Not anymore.

MILLER: But Mr. Carmichael—

CARMICHAEL: We're diggin' my shaft. I don't need you anymore. *(Calling off)* Start 'er up!

(The power shovel begins hauling and droning; the bucket raising and lowering.)

DOYLE *(In drunken memory, as a child)*: Yes sir, Papa, I swear I'll take care of our farm—

HOMER: Carmichael—

NELLIE *(To Homer)*: Shame on you, brother. *(To Guardsman)* Let go of me.

HOMER *(To Nellie)*: What? . . .

NELLIE: Shame on you.

HOMER *(To Nellie, fierce)*: Shame on me what?!

NELLIE: Act the big shot, act the big shot . . .

DOYLE: Keep the cornfields full at harvest *(Bitter)* not trampled on by no machines . . .

HOMER: Carmichael?

DOYLE: No rain turnin' roads to mud pie . . .

(Thunder cracks; it begins to rain. Umbrellas go up around the site.)

Aw, come on . . .

CARMICHAEL: Shit.

DOYLE *(Calling up)*: Lord! What'd I ever do to you?

MISS JANE: Come in the tent, Lee.

LEE *(Pushing her hand off him)*: S'long as my boy's down thar, I'm stayin' out here e'en if it kills me.

HOMER: Carmichael!!

CARMICHAEL *(Whirling on him, fast, as if he might chew him alive)*: You know what, Collins, I've had just about enough of your loud mouth blabberin'. Case you ain't heard the news, *part-ner,* I am now in full command of the rescue operation—courtesy of Brigadier General Denhardt and Governor William J. Field of the Commonwealth of Kentucky! Now what *that* means, *part-ner,* is that I'm gonna finally get your brother out, and what it *also* means is that no one is allowed in this area without my direct approval. Got it?

HOMER: The shaft's no damned good! Shit!

LEE: Watch that mouth, boy!

HOMER: We got to go back in the passageway!

LEE: Homer!

CARMICHAEL: There *is* no more passageway!

HOMER: Thanks to who?! You goddamn military son-of-a-bitch.

CARMICHAEL *(Full of genuine pride; quiet)*: I am the only one 'round here doing anything to get your brother out *(To the Reporters)* for the record. *(To the Guardsmen, referring to Homer)* Now, remove him from the site. And don't allow him back in.

(Several Guardsmen move in to pull Homer away; he fights back. Lee tries to stop Homer but Homer is dragged away by the Guardsmen. Lee collapses and Miss Jane rushes to his side. The commotion freezes in a tableau. Elsewhere, to one side, Homer stands alone. It continues to rain.)

HOMER:

GIT COMFORTABLE, CARMICHAEL;
HUNKER DOWN A WHILE.
TEAR UP BEE DOYLE'S LAND IF YOU LIKE,
SPECIAL CARMICHAEL STYLE.

DO IT LIKE YER BLIND,
LIKE YER SWINGIN' A SHOVEL OR A BIG OL' CHAIN,
LIKE YER MADDER 'AN HELL
AN' RIGHT AS RAIN.

I WAS WRONG;
SEE, I DIDN'T KNOW THAT'S HOW IT'S DONE.
SEE, THAT'S FUNNY;
I DIDN'T KNOW.

GIT COMFORTABLE, OUTLANDER,
STRUT AN' STOMP AROUN',
ACT LIKE YOU WAS BORN RIGHT HERE,
SPROUTED OUTTA THIS GROUN'.

THESE HILLS'LL TAKE YA IN, HECK!
YOU HARNESS-PULLIN', FOOL SHAFT-DIGGIN',
OUTLANDER SPECK OF FLY SHIT ON MY BOOT,
CITY-SLICKIN' SUIT.

I WAS WRONG;
SEE, I DIDN'T KNOW THAT'S HOW IT'S DONE.
SEE, THAT'S FUNNY;
I DIDN'T KNOW.

SEE, I DIDN'T KNOW
THERE'S NO PLACE FOR ME HERE.
I WAS WRONG—
I'M ALL WRONG—
DON'T KNOW WHAT TO DO NO MORE, FLOYD.
FLOYD.
BROTHER MINE.
FLOYD. FLOYD. FLOYD . . .

(Music continues under. The crowd melts away as the focus shifts to Carmichael giving a press conference.)

CARMICHAEL: Well once we have the shaft down far enough, we'll then begin to dig a lateral tunnel right to the victim's side. But, yes, for the time being, we've been forced to abandon the power shovel in that exhaust from its engine was discovered to be drawn into the cave. In addition, dynamite and jackhammers have been abandoned in that they cause danger of collapse. Uh . . . Thank you.

REPORTER 1: Mr. Carmichael, what's that leave then?

DOYLE *(Laughing; to himself)*: Watch 'im say hand tools.

CARMICHAEL: We're hard at work now with teams of men using . . . hand tools.

(At the bottom of the shaft, Jewell and Bishop are both covered in mud and almost unrecognizable. Jewell is shivering and on the verge of tears. Carmichael is seen in silhouette upstage, where he calls into the shaft entrance.)

JEWELL: Cain't feel my hands . . .
BISHOP: Keep that side from bucklin'.
JEWELL: I'm tryin', I'm tryin' . . .
BISHOP: Try harder. Goddamn!—more limestone . . .
CARMICHAEL *(Calling down)*: How're you men doing down there?

(Bishop and Jewell look at each other in silence.)

You need a rest? Next shift's ready if you're fading. *(Pause)* Bishop?
BISHOP *(Calling up)*: It's jes' the water, Carmichael. Must be 'least five inches 'round our ankles.
JEWELL: A foot. Tell 'im a foot.
CARMICHAEL: Well, it's raining cats and dogs up here.

(Pause. The sound of creaking.)

JEWELL *(Quiet; seeing the wall start to go)*: Bishop? . . .
BISHOP: Not now, Estes.
JEWELL: It's the timber, Bishop. She's leanin' . . .

(More creaking sounds, a gradual slide . . . Stillness and quiet for a moment as Jewell and Bishop stare at the shifting walls.)

BISHOP: What the . . . ?
CARMICHAEL: What's going on down there, Bishop?
BISHOP: We've got trouble . . .
JEWELL: Looks like the walls . . . tiltin' . . . Holy . . .
BISHOP *(Calling)*: Bring us up! Hurry up! Bring us up!

(Sound of shaft starting to collapse.)

CARMICHAEL *(Calling out)*: Shaft collapsing! Get those men out of there!

(Lights start to go down on Jewell and Bishop.)

Get the loose rock and dirt scooped out, get new timbers in place! We're going to suspend a platform with cables from above. Clear the site—out of the way, out of the way!

(The stage erupts in chaos as Jewell and Bishop are lifted and the shaft collapses.

When the noise and activity settle: on a deserted corner of field, Miss Jane sits as Lee hunches over, picking up empty soda bottles and sticking them in a sack. Nellie stands off to the side.)

LEE *(Muttering to himself)*: Sixteen . . . seventeen . . . *(Simultaneously with Miss Jane)* Eighteen . . . nineteen . . .

MISS JANE *(Simultaneously with Lee)*: Soda pop bottles, candy wrappers . . . Bee's home's a waterin' place . . . an' a parkin' place too . . .

LEE: An' twenty . . . makes a nickel! *(Starting the next twenty)* One . . . two . . .

(Homer enters.)

HOMER: What's he doin'?

MISS JANE: Jes' tryin' to see after us.

HOMER: I have somethin' to tell y'all.

MISS JANE: What is it?

HOMER: I'm . . . leavin'. *(Haltingly)* I've decided . . . once they git Floyd out . . . to leave . . . here.

(Lee stops in his tracks for a moment, then continues, ignoring Homer.)

LEE: Three . . . four . . .

(Nellie goes to Homer. They look at each other, then hold each other.)

HOMER *(Quiet)*: I'm sorry, Nell . . .

LEE *(Under his breath)*: Good fer nothin' ingrate.

HOMER: Pardon me?

MISS JANE: Homer, don't. Ain't time to.

HOMER: Ain't never time to. *(Pause; again to Lee)* What'd you say?

LEE: Twenty would make a dime!

HOMER *(Gentle; pleading)*: Papa—look at me. Talk to me . . . Please . . .
LEE: Ain't up to us no how, boy.
HOMER: What?
LEE: It's in the hands of the Lord. Praise God. If we go to him on bended knee an' with reverent hearts, he will hear us. *(Praying)* O Lord God, who turned back the tide at Galilee, have pity on yer child imprisoned in yer earth. Give 'im back to us. But if, Lord, it be thy will that he *not* return, then Lord . . .

(Very quietly, Nellie begins singing to herself:)

NELLIE:
Oo-oo . . .

HOMER *(To Lee)*: What're ya sayin'?

NELLIE:
FLOYD? . . .

LEE: . . . then Thy will be done. Amen.

NELLIE:
Oo-oo . . .

HOMER: S'all right by you to watch Floyd die?

NELLIE:
I KIN HEAR YOU, FLOYD.

MISS JANE: Homer . . .

NELLIE:
Oo-oo . . .

LEE *(Indicating Nellie)*: See Nellie, boy. Like you always done. Drove the devil back inside 'er.

NELLIE:
FLOYD . . .

Oo-oo . . .

HOMER: Answer me, Pa. Cain't stand to see none of us make a life fer ourselves—that it?

NELLIE:

I KIN HEAR YOU, FLOYD . . .

LEE: Yer pointin' down to hell, boy.

HOMER *(Sarcastically)*: An' yer goin' to heaven, makin' a buck off our own flesh an' blood?

MISS JANE: Homer, please. Yer pa's not himself.

HOMER *(Simultaneously with Lee)*: Sellin' photographs, makin' flyers . . .

LEE *(Simultaneously with Homer)*: I'm a puttin food in that mouth, an' wood in the stove—runnin' the farm like a man! The farm! The *farm*!!

HOMER: Rocks an' gullies, Pa—that's all we got here.

LEE: 'Stead of you two's—crawlin 'roun' inside of the earth 'stead of on *top* it like God intended! Ain't natural . . .

HOMER: It's always this, Pa—

LEE: Quiet!

HOMER: No! Not this time.

MISS JANE: Homer—

LEE: I says—

HOMER: Jes' killin' us all, slow but sure.

LEE: Yer brother's been lost to the ways of the Lord!

HOMER: Wal I ain't dyin' . . . *(Simultaneously with Lee)* I ain't dyin' here! Ya hear me?

LEE *(Simultaneously with Homer)*: All of ya's—foolish, slothful—with yer automobiles an' yer cavin' ways an' yer loony bins an', "Lee come inside," an,' "Lee do *this*," an' "Lee do *that*." Naggin' woman! What kind of family, eh? What kind?!

HOMER: 'Tain't *our* fault Mama died! *(Years of resentment; with disdain)* An' 'tain't our fault neither that *you* died *with* 'er!

(Suddenly Lee lashes out and slaps Homer, who falls to the ground. Silence. Nellie touches the ground. She sings quietly to Floyd.

The scene slowly shifts . . . Jewell is in the shaft area, with his guitar. It is snowing.)

JEWELL:

DEEP IN THE LAND OF THE HOLLOWS AN' CREEKS,
IF'N YOU GIT LOST YOU GIT LOST FER WEEKS;

LISTEN TO THE TALE OF A MAN WHO GOT LOST
HUNDRED FEET UNDER THE WINTER FROST.

(During the following, time passes. Men sit huddled in groups, playing cards, drinking coffee, sleeping, cutting out hearts for Valentine's Day, and other assorted activities. Homer and Nellie might sit together. The song should be led by Jewell, but the following solo lines can be assigned to any of the three Locals according to the particular strengths of a given cast.)

DOYLE:
NOW FLOYD WAS A REASONIN' MAN,
HE KNEW WHAT HE WANTED AN' HE HAD A PLAN.
HE WAS JES' AS SMART AS HE WAS BRAVE;
HE WAS GONNA FIND HIM THE PERFECT CAVE.

BISHOP:
EVEN FLOYD KNEW SOMETHIN' WASN'T RIGHT,
HE WAS SUFFERIN' NIGHTMARES AT NIGHT.

BISHOP, DOYLE & JEWELL:
BUT HE DIDN'T WORRY 'BOUT WHAT HE DREAMED
THINGS WAS GOIN' GOOD, OR SO IT SEEMED.
WENT LOOKIN' FER HIS FORTUNE UNDER THE GROUND—

(They look at a Reporter who is about to take a photograph.)

SURE ENOUGH HIS FORTUNE IS WHAT HE FOUND.

(Flash.)

MILLER: Wednesday.

JEWELL OR BISHOP:
THE AIR WAS COLD AND THE GROUND WAS WET,
I WAS JUST AS MUDDY AS A MAN COULD GET.
HADN'T ANY LIGHT BUT A LITTLE OIL LANTERN.
GOT YOU IN SO TIGHT THAT YOU KNOW YOU CAN'T TURN BACK.

(Dr. Hazlett approaches Carmichael, who has fallen asleep sitting up. When he gently touches him, Carmichael instantly bolts to his feet, pacing as if trying to figure out what to do, or where he is. Dr. Hazlett tries to calm him.)

SLITHERIN' AROUND ON MY BELLY AND KNEES,
I COULD FEEL MY FINGERTIPS ABOUT TO FREEZE.
I COULD ALMOST SEE WHERE THE PRISONER LAY.
JUST ABOUT TO HOLLER WHEN I HEARD HIM PRAY:

(Sitting alone, Lee cries.)

BISHOP, DOYLE & JEWELL:
"OH MY LORD HAVE MERCY ON MY SOUL,
DON'T LET ME DIE ALONE IN THIS DARK HOLE.
AND WHEN MY SAVIOR IS AT HAND,
I'LL BE SURE TO MEET HIM ON TOP OF THE LAND."

CARMICHAEL *(Walking away from Dr. Hazlett)*: Excuse me.

JEWELL OR BISHOP:
"WON'T GO DIGGIN' 'ROUND IN THE HOLLOWS AND HOLES,
I'M A-LEAVE IT UP TO THE HOGS AND MOLES.
NEVER SET ANOTHER FOOT INSIDE A CAVE,
IF I MAKE IT OUTTA THIS LONESOME GRAVE."

AND THERE HE REMAINS
ALL ALONE IN A COLD KENTUCKY HILLSIDE.

MILLER: Thursday.

(Carmichael, Guardsmen, et al., are at the top of the shaft—sometimes looking down into the hole—working or watching or waiting.)

HOMER:
HE WAS LAYIN' STILL LIKE HE WAS DEAD,
WATER TRICKLIN' DOWN ON TOP HIS HEAD.
SEVEN WHOLE DAYS HE HADN'T HAD A CRUMB,
HIS EYES WERE SUNK AND WEARISOME.
HE SWALLOWED WHAT I HAD RIGHT OUTTA MY HAN',
THEN HE TOOK SOME COFFEE FROM AN OLD TIN CAN.
TOL' 'IM WE WOULD SOON DIG 'IM OUTTA THIS PLACE,
AND A LITTLE SMILE GOES ACROSS HIS FACE.

BISHOP, DOYLE, JEWELL & HOMER:
HE SAID, "BOY, THANK GOD THAT YOU ARE HERE,
NOW I KNOW MY RESCUE IS NEAR.

An' when my time comes to die,
I'll be sure to do it where I can see sky."

CARMICHAEL *(Calling for work duty)*: Doyle.

(Doyle looks at Carmichael, then walks away.)

JEWELL OR BISHOP:
"Won't go diggin' 'round in the hollows and holes,
I'm a-leave it up to the hogs and moles,
Never set another foot inside a cave,
If I make it outta this lonesome grave."

CARMICHAEL: Estes.

(Jewell walks away.)

BISHOP & HOMER:
And there he remains
All alone in a cold Kentucky hillside.

CARMICHAEL: Bishop.

(Bishop walks away.)

HOMER:
And there he remains
All alone in a cold Kentucky hillside.

CARMICHAEL *(Calling after Bishop)*: Look, there's a man trapped down there—and we're gonna keep goin', we're goin' to reach him if it's only me, one shovel, and a hoist operator!

MILLER: Carmichael—I want to go down.

DR. HAZLETT: It's suicide down there, Miller.

MILLER: I want to go down.

(Pause. Carmichael turns to Miller.)

CARMICHAEL: All right. It's you, Miller.

(Miller nods.)

C'mon son, let's start the lateral tunnel.

(Miller and Carmichael walk toward the shaft area as the focus shifts to Floyd.)

FLOYD *(Scrunching his face)*: Crickets, feel yer feelers ticklin' . . . Git! Git! *(Mutters toward his hands)* Hello, worms. You worms kin eat my hands . . .

(He starts coughing. Lights come up on Miller in the shaft, digging. The sounds of the coughing and digging meld together.)

(Suddenly) What . . . ?!

MILLER *(Overlapping Floyd)*: Floyd?!

FLOYD *(Listens with his whole body; quiet)*: D'ya hear somethin', Mr. Cricket? . . .

CARMICHAEL *(Calling from above)*: You okay down there, Miller?

MILLER: Shhh—hold on, Carmichael. I . . . I think I heard something!

FLOYD *(Almost hearing their shouts)*: What?! . . .

MILLER: Floyd?

(Silence. Then Floyd and Carmichael at almost the same time:)

FLOYD: Who is it?! Come an' git me!

CARMICHAEL *(Offstage)*: Is there a problem, Miller?

MILLER: No, there's no problem! I'm gonna start the digging. *(Listening)* Floyd—buddy—are you there?

FLOYD: Nah—'tain't nothin'. *(Falls asleep)*

MILLER: I could have sworn . . . No.

(Some timber falls near him.)

Holy cripes! Floyd?!

(Floyd hears something in his sleep and turns.)

Floyd Collins?!

FLOYD *(Waking violently)*: Huh?! . . . Shhh . . .

MILLER *(Quietly; to himself)*: No . . . jes' listen. No . . . nobody.
FLOYD: No one . . . jes' maggot in my ear.

(During the following there is silence, except for the constant subtle creaking and shifting of the shaft walls and the sliding mud.)

MILLER: Floyd? You once told me you could hear the cave speak. Well, if you can hear her now, then hear my voice inside 'er. *Hang on, Floyd.* Forgive me . . . for turning you into a story. *(Ironically)* Like a real live newspaper man. *(Bangs the rock)* William Burke Miller *(Bang)*, small as a 'squito but full of pluck. *(Bang)* Hang on, Floyd. *(Bang!)* Better than any story we could make up *(Bang!)*, better than all 'em . . . *(Bang!)* Damn hucksters! *(Hurts himself)* Better than all of us!

(Miller bangs up against a piece of shoring. It crumbles and mud starts to slide, giving Miller a fright. He looks up to discover a small crevice.)

A . . . cricket? . . . *(Peers through, straining to see)* Crickets! Tons of . . . Carmichael! Carmichael! The light bulb—I see it . . . We're there . . . We're there!
CARMICHAEL *(Offstage)*: All right—this is it! Let's go, men!
MILLER: Floyd?!
CARMICHAEL *(Offstage)*: We've reached 'im!

(Floyd lies still. Nellie begins singing from off somewhere distant. Floyd gradually comes to; he sings back to her. Nellie's voice gets closer and closer. Floyd looks up, straining to see in the dark, and Nellie is there beside him. She is wearing a beautiful, white summer dress. A dream:)

FLOYD:
    IS IT . . . IS IT REALLY YOU?
NELLIE:
    FLOYD!
FLOYD:
    IS IT . . . IS IT REALLY HAPPENIN'?
NELLIE:
    YES!
FLOYD:
    I DECLARE, I DECLARE, I DECLARE
    I NEVER SAW SUCH BEAUTY AS MY SISTER GIRL.

NELLIE:

No, sir!

FLOYD:

Can it . . . Can it really be true?

NELLIE:

Yes sir!

FLOYD:

Like a . . . like a miracle,
Finally on my feet again!

(Floyd stands up in his place. Nellie gestures for him to come out of the cave.)

NELLIE:

Circlin', circlin', circlin' around!
You got the Luck!

FLOYD:

We both got the Luck!

NELLIE:

Us two we got it!

FLOYD:

Right here!

NELLIE *(Simultaneously)*:

Circlin', circlin' . . .

FLOYD *(Simultaneously)*:

I got ya . . .
Ah . . .

NELLIE & FLOYD:

Welcome home.

(Finally together, they embrace.)

FLOYD: I done missed ya, Nell. Worried 'bout ya at the 'sylum.
NELLIE: But you was right thar a side me, Floyd, jes' like I been with you.

Some people go place to place;
Some people go underground;
Some gotta go crazy like;
I jes' journey in,
An' that is where I've been.

WE ALL GO SOMEWHERE,
AN' THAT'S HOW WE GIT ALONG.
IF FOLKS JES' DON'T UNDERSTAND IT,
WHY, THAT AIN'T NOTHIN' WRONG.

YOU AN' ME, WE FOLLOW A SOUND
THAT IS WHISTLIN' AROUND IN THE AIR.
SINCE MAMA'S GONE, WE HEARD IT CALLIN' . . .

AND IT'S KIND OF RESTFUL,
WHEN YOU SEE THAT YOU'RE NOT ALONE.
WE'RE FINALLY TOGETHER
HERE IN THE UNKNOWN.

WE'RE ALWAYS WOND'RIN' AND WANTIN' TO KNOW
WHY WE ARE WHAT WE ARE.
WE ALWAYS HAVE THE WHISTLIN' QUESTION,
AN' THERE AIN'T NO ANSWER,
BUT ONLY THE ASKIN' FOREVER . . .

(Nellie and Floyd are startled by the sound of a car horn—Aaa-oo-gaa! It's Homer in his shiny black new automobile. He, too, is dressed in white.)

HOMER:
AAA-OO-GAA!

FLOYD: Homer?!

HOMER:
TIME TO GO!

FLOYD: Where're we going?

HOMER:
Y'ALL HOP IN MY SHINY AUTOMOBILE . . .

FLOYD: Hot damn, she's a beauty beaut!

HOMER:
'CAUSE YOU GOTTA BE THERE FOR YOUR OPENING DAY!
HEY, HEY!

FLOYD: What opening day?

HOMER:
WE MOVED THE ROCKS,

FLOYD: We did?!

HOMER:
AN' MADE SOME TRAILS,
HOMER & NELLIE:
AN' SMOOTHED THE FLOORS,
AN' BUILT THE STAIRS.

FLOYD: Hot damn! You must have worked like dogs!

HOMER & NELLIE:
AN' SET UP SOME BIG SIGNS HERE ON THE ROAD!
NELLIE:
THERE'S A TICKET OFFICE,
FLOYD:
AN' A CURIO SHOP?
FLOYD, NELLIE & HOMER:
AN' REFRESHMENT STAND
OPEN SEVEN DAYS A WEEK,
FLOYD & HOMER:
AT THE GREAT SAND CAVE!

(They drive off in the automobile, singing in canon. They arrive at the new Sand Cave. It is a glorious day: yellow sun, blue sky. A crowd is there to welcome and celebrate Floyd. Everyone is beautiful and happy, dressed in various shades of white. Even the balloons are white.)

CROWD *(Simultaneously)*:
THE GREAT SAND CAVE!
FLOYD *(Simultaneously)*:
DA DA DACKY DICKY DA
CROWD:
FLOYD COLLINS!
(Simultaneously) THE GREAT SAND CAVE!
FLOYD *(Simultaneously)*:
DA DA DACKY DICKY DICKA

CROWD:

THE GREATEST CAVER EVER KNOWN!

(Simultaneously) THE GREAT SAND CAVE!

FLOYD *(Simultaneously)*:

DA DA DACKY DICKY DA

CROWD:

FLOYD COLLINS!

(Simultaneously) THE GREAT SAND CAVE!

FLOYD *(Simultaneously)*:

DA DA DACKY DICKY DICKA

CROWD:

THE GREATEST CAVER EVER KNOWN!

(Floyd greets Reporters and Miller; he jokes with his friends, the Locals; he meets Carmichael. Then the Collins family comes together, holding each other in a glorious, loving family portrait.)

FAMILY *(Simultaneously)*:

NO MORE PLOWIN' A HARD SCRABBLE FIELD,

I JES' KNEW IT, I KNEW WE WAS LUCKY.

LEE *(Simultaneously)*:

MY BOY!

MY BOY!

FLOYD:

PAPA!

LISTEN TO THIS! YOU GOTTA HEAR THIS!

NELLIE:

LUCKY . . .

PAPA . . .

LEE & MISS JANE:

MY BOY!

FLOYD, NELLIE & HOMER:

PAPA!

(Floyd raises his hand and everyone immediately falls silent. He goes into his calling position as at the beginning when he first heard the echo. With tremendous anticipation, Floyd leans forward and sings:)

FLOYD:

DOH-YO-EE-OH-OH . . .

(There is an excruciatingly long silence as everyone waits for the echo, but no sounds comes back.)

LEE: No, son. Yer still trapped.

(The dream starts to turn into a nightmare.)

CROWD:

THE GREATEST CAVER EVER KNOWN,
THE GREATEST CAVER EVER KNOWN.

LEE: Jes' left to die . . .

CROWD:

BURIED WITH HIS TREASURE . . .
BURIED WITH HIS TREASURE . . .
BURIED WITH HIS TREASURE . . .

FLOYD:

NO, PA, WHAT YA TALKIN'?
I'M FREE NOW.
IT'S ALL OVER.
THIS HAS GOT TO BE!

(The crowd continues the cacophony as Floyd begins to get pulled away, back toward his place in the cave, as if by a mysterious force. The scene starts to dissolve. As he moves past Nellie, Floyd reaches out and tries to hold on to her, their lyrics becoming intertwined.)

NO, NELLIE.
WHAT'S HAP'NIN'?
PULL ME, HOLD ON TO ME . . .
HOLD ON TO ME . . .
NELLIE?
NO!

(He tries to pull her with him.)

NELLIE:

FLOYD, LET GO . . .
FLOYD, LET GO.

YOU HAVE TO LET GO . . .
YOU HAVE TO LET GO, FLOYD.
OOO . . .
YOU HAVE TO LET GO.
EH-OH . . .
OH . . .

(Floyd is back in his trapped position. Everything else is gone.)

FLOYD: Let go. Let go.

(He awakens. Silence.)

I'm ready now, Lord. I know I warn't no Sunday school mama's boy. But faith is hopin' for somethin', believin' what you can't see.

I HAD FAITH ALL MY LIFE!

I wanna ask you somethin'.

IS IT WARM?
IS IT SOFT AGAINST YOUR FACE?
DO YOU FEEL A KIND A GRACE INSIDE THE BREEZE?
WILL THERE BE TREES?

IS THERE LIGHT?
DOES IT HOVER ON THE GROUND?
DOES IT SHINE FROM ALL AROUND,
OR JES' FROM YOU?

IS IT ENDLESS AND EMPTY,
AN' YOU WANDER ON YOUR OWN?
SLOWLY FORGIT ABOUT
THE FOLKS THAT YOU HAVE KNOWN?

OR DOES RISIN' BREAD FILL UP THE AIR
FROM OPEN KITCHENS EVER'WHERE?
FAMILIAR FACES FAR AS YOU CAN SEE,
LIKE A FAMILY?

(During the following, Floyd slowly starts to sit up.)

Do we live?
Is it like a little town?
Do we get to look back down at who we love?
Are we above?

Are we everywhere?
Are we anywhere at all?
Do we hear a trumpet call us
An' we're by Your side?

Will I want, will I wish
For all the things I should have done:
Longing to finish
What I only just begun?

Or has a shinin' truth been waiting there
For all the questions everywhere?
In a world a-wonderin', suddenly you know;
An' you will always know . . .

Will my mama be there waitin' for me,
Smilin' like the way she does
An' holdin' out her arms,
An' she calls my name?
She will hold me just the same . . .

(Miller appears.)

MILLER: The prisoner's body was wedged in so tightly there was no longer any room at all between his chest and the cave ceiling. A cave cricket perched on his nose, nibbling away at the tip. The doctors believe he died sometime on Friday the 13th, known as Hoodoo Day in Cave Country. The carnival at Sand Cave packed up and went home.

(Miller is gone.)

FLOYD:

Only heaven knows how glory goes,

WHAT EACH OF US WAS MEANT TO BE.
IN THE STARLIGHT, THAT IS WHAT WE ARE.
I CAN SEE SO FAR . . .

(Floyd stands. He walks to the open space, lifts his arms and turns in a slow circle, as if ascending into the light above him. He sings the "Cave Canon" once again. As the light shifts into the sky, Floyd turns and follows it upstage. He walks into the light, into the sky. Just before he disappears, he stops and remains in silhouette. Ever so slowly, the light fades with the last of Floyd's dying echoes . . .

Blackout.)

THE END

DATE OF SCRIPT

June 1999

COPYRIGHT

The following songs have additional lyrics by Tina Landau: "The Carnival"; "Daybreak"; "Family Scene"; "I Landed on Him"; "The Riddle Song"; "Through the Mountain."

PERFORMING RIGHTS

All other inquiries should be addressed to the authors' representatives as follows:

For Adam Guettel: Douglas & Kopelman Artists, Inc., 393 West 49th Street, Suite 5G, New York, NY 10019. Attn: Sarah Douglas. Phone: 212-445-0160. Fax: 212-246-7138.

For Tina Landau: Helen Merrill Ltd., 295 Lafayette Street, Suite 915, New York, NY 10012. Attn: Beth Blickers. Phone: 212-226-5015. Fax: 212-226-5079.

ORIGINAL PRODUCTION

Floyd Collins was commissioned by Philadelphia's American Music Theater Festival (Marjorie Samoff, Producing Director; Ben Levit, Artistic Director; Donna Vidas Powell, Managing Director), which produced the world premiere in 1994.

The work was subsequently redeveloped at Playwrights Horizons (Tim Sanford, Artistic Director; Leslie Marcus, Managing Director; Lynn Landis, General Manager), which gave it its New York premiere on February 9, 1996. *Floyd Collins* played twenty-eight previews and twenty-five performances and closed on March 24, 1996.

Floyd Collins was directed by Tina Landau. The set was designed by James Schuette, costumes by Melina Root, lighting by Scott Zielinski, sound by Dan Moses Schreier, orchestrations by Bruce Coughlin; the production stage manager was Erica Schwartz, the consulting producer was Don Scardino, the casting director was Janet Foster, the production manager was Christopher Boll and the music director/conductor was Ted Sperling. Production photographs were taken by Joan Marcus; the graphic design for the Nonesuch CD was by Barbara de Wilde.

The original cast (in order of appearance) was as follows:

FLOYD COLLINS .... Christopher Innvar
BEE DOYLE .... Stephen Lee Anderson
ED BISHOP .... Rudy Roberson
JEWELL ESTES .... Jesse Lenat
LEE COLLINS .... Don Chastain
MISS JANE .... Cass Morgan
NELLIE COLLINS .... Theresa McCarthy
HOMER COLLINS .... Jason Danieley
SKEETS MILLER .... Martin Moran
H. T. CARMICHAEL .... Michael Mulheren
CLIFF RONEY/REPORTER .... Brian d'Arcy James
DR. HAZLETT/REPORTER .... Matthew Bennett
REPORTER/CON MAN .... James Bohanek

AWARDS

Floyd Collins was awarded the Lucille Lortel Award for Outstanding Musical. An OBIE Award was given to Bruce Coughlin (Orchestrator) and Adam Guettel (Composer) for Music; a Drama Desk Award went to Dan Moses Schreier for Sound Design.

AUDIORECORDING, VIDEORECORDING AND MUSIC PUBLISHING

Original Cast Recording: Nonesuch Records 79434-2. Produced by Tommy Krasker.

Videotaped by the New York Public Library's Theatre on Film and Tape Archive at Playwrights Horizons on March 23, 1996. 124 minutes. Format: 3/4" SP Color. Catalog Number: NCOV 1913. Restricted to qualified researchers. Contact: New York Public Library for the Performing Arts, 40 Lincoln Center Plaza, New York, NY 10023-7498; telephone: 212-870-1642; website: www.nypl.org/research/lpa/lpa.html

Music Publishing: Williamson Music.

ORCHESTRA INSTRUMENTATION

Piano/Keyboards
Violin
Viola/Violin
Bass
Guitar/Banjo
Harmonica
Percussion

MAJOR PRODUCTIONS

A touring production directed by Tina Landau was mounted by three not-for-profit theaters in 1999. It played as follows: Old Globe Theatre, San Diego, California, February 11–March 21, 1999; American Music Theater

Festival (now Prince Music Theater), Philadelphia, Pennsylvania, April 1–17, 1999; the Goodman Theatre, Chicago, Illinois, April 23–June 5, 1999.

The Bridewell Theatre in London, England, presented the musical from July 8–31, 1999. The production was directed by Clive Paget.

BIOGRAPHIES

ADAM GUETTEL (Composer/Lyricist) was born in 1964. His work includes *Love's Fire* with John Guare; *Saturn Returns* (*Myths & Hymns* on Nonesuch); the score for *Arguing the World,* a feature documentary by Joe Dorman; and the score for *Jack.* Four of Mr. Guettel's songs are featured on Audra McDonald's *Way Back to Paradise* (Nonesuch). He is the recipient of the Stephen Sondheim Award (1990), the OBIE Award (1996) and the Lucille Lortel Award (1996) (the latter two for *Floyd Collins*), and the ASCAP New Horizons Award (1997). In May 1999, Mr. Guettel performed a concert evening of his work at New York's Town Hall. His latest musical, *The Light in the Piazza,* premieres at Intiman Theatre in 2003.

Joan Marcus

Adam Guettel and Tina Landau

TINA LANDAU (Director and Librettist) is a writer and director whose original work includes the play *Space,* which premiered at Steppenwolf Theatre Company in Chicago (where she is a company member), and which was subsequently produced at the Mark Taper Forum in Los Angeles and The Joseph Papp Public Theater/New York Shakespeare Festival in New York. Other work which she wrote and directed includes *Dream True* (with composer Ricky Ian Gordon) at the Vineyard Theater, *States of Independence* (also with Gordon) at the Prince Music Theater, and a new project for Disney currently titled *When You Wish.* For En Garde Arts in New York City, she wrote and directed *Stonewall: Night Variations* and directed *Trojan Women: A Love Story* and *Orestes.* Other original work includes *1969 (or Howie Takes a Trip)* at the Humana Festival, *American Vaudeville* (with director Anne Bogart) and *In Twilite* at American Repertory Theatre in Boston. Her directing credits include *The Time of Your Life*; *The Ballad of Little Jo*, a new musical by Mike Reid and Sarah Schlesinger; Charles L. Mee's *Berlin Circle* and *Time to Burn* (all at Steppenwolf Theatre Company). She directed *Saturn Returns* (by Adam Guettel) at The Public Theater/NYSF, and José Rivera's *Cloud Tectonics* and *Marisol*. Ms. Landau is a graduate of Yale College and later attended A.R.T.'s Institute for Advanced Theatre Training at Harvard. She made her Broadway directing debut in 2000 with the revival of Styne, Comden & Green's *Bells Are Ringing*, starring Faith Prince.

AMERICAN MUSIC THEATER FESTIVAL (Producer) Founded in 1984 by producing director Marjorie Samoff and artistic director Eric Salzman as an annual festival, AMTF was solely devoted to musical theater in all its forms, including opera, music drama, musical comedy, experimental work and cabaret. Now under the direction of Samoff, the company was renamed the Prince Music Theater in 1999 in honor of Harold Prince, the great director and board member of the theater. The theater has produced more than eighty works, fifty of which have been world or American premieres. These include *Floyd Collins* and *Band in Berlin*. More than forty Prince Music Theater productions have gone on to open in New York and/or tour nationally and internationally (including three on Broadway and one Off-Broadway). Eighteen productions have been recorded as original cast albums, most recently the three short musicals known as *3hree*.

PLAYWRIGHTS HORIZONS (Producer) Founded more than thirty years ago as a writer's theater, Playwrights Horizons has presented the work of more than three hundred and fifty writers, and has been the recipient of numerous awards and honors. Christopher Durang's *Sister Mary Ignatius Explains It All for You*, A. R. Gurney's *Later Life*, Scott McPherson's *Marvin's Room*, Wendy Wasserstein's *The Heidi Chronicles* and Alfred Uhry's *Driving Miss Daisy* all debuted at Playwrights Horizons. The theater has produced such critically acclaimed musicals as William Finn's *Falsettos*, Stephen Sondheim and James Lapine's *Sunday in the Park with George*, Lynn Ahrens and Stephen Flaherty's *Once on This Island*, Jeanine Tesori and Brian Crawley's *Violet* and *James Joyce's The Dead* by Richard Nelson and Shaun Davey. The theater was founded by Robert Moss. André Bishop was the artistic director from 1981 through 1991. The current artistic director is Tim Sanford.

RENT

Book, Music and Lyrics by Jonathan Larson
Original New York Production Directed by Michael Greif

Joan Marcus

Adam Pascal (Roger) and Daphne Rubin-Vega (Mimi), New York Theatre Workshop, 1996.

"It took my brother Jonnie fifteen years of really hard work to become an overnight sensation. So we'd like to dedicate this to all those who are out there still working in restaurants, driving taxis, doing whatever they have to do to scrape by for their art. Stay true to yourselves and to your dreams and know they can come true."

—Julie Larson,
in accepting the Tony Award for *Rent*,
posthumously on behalf of Jonathan Larson

THE STORY

Broadly following the theme of Puccini's *La Bohème, Rent* is a tale of love and the sense of community shared by young artists. It opens on Christmas Eve with aspiring filmmaker Mark and his struggling songwriter roommate Roger freezing in the loft they share in an industrial building on New York City's Lower East Side. In the empty lot next door, homeless people have established a tent city. Their former roommate Benny, now a budding real estate tycoon (thanks to his wealthy father-in-law), owns both the building and the empty lot. In the flush of his new-found riches he had promised the young artists that they could stay rent-free, but now announces he is going to evict everyone from the lot and erect a cyber-arts studio. Their one-time roommate Tom Collins survives a mugging and falls in love with a transvestite street drummer Angel; both, it turns out, are suffering from AIDS.

Mark's former girlfriend Maureen, with the help of her new lover Joanne, schedules a protest against Benny's plan. At the same time, Roger meets, and is strongly attracted to, downstairs neighbor Mimi, an S&M dancer. Despite her eager interest in him, and his obvious return of those feelings, he is unwilling to commit to any relationship. Maureen's performance generates a riot among the homeless, after which the friends go to celebrate at the Life Café. Roger and Mimi, both HIV-positive, fall deeply in love. Act I (and the party) end when Joanne returns to report that police have padlocked the building and are sweeping the lot.

During the course of the next year, we share the quarreling, on-again, off-again relationship of the lesbian lovers; Mark's struggle against the lure of a well-paying television job; Roger and Mimi's typical lover spats; her battles against addiction when she feels rejected; Benny's attempts to regain acceptance by the group; and, ultimately, the death of Angel. After Angel's funeral on Halloween, Roger leaves for Santa Fe, and Mimi, utterly forsaken, takes to the street to be alone with her eventual illness. Unable to stay away, Roger soon returns, but can't find Mimi until Christmas Eve, when Maureen and Joanne discover her, close to death, and bring her to the loft.

She appears to die as Roger sings the love song he'd written for her, but then comes to life after seeing Angel, who has told her to "turn around and listen to that boy's song." In the finale, the group reaffirms love as the strongest emotion of life, because there is "no day but today."

Rent is based upon the opera *La Bohème* by Giacomo Puccini, and Henri Murger's novel *Scènes de la vie de Bohème*.

CHARACTERS

(in order of appearance)

MARK COHEN	An aspiring filmmaker
ROGER DAVIS	A struggling songwriter with HIV
MARK'S MOM	
TOM COLLINS	Mark and Roger's ex-roommate, recently expelled from MIT, soon to be teaching at NYU
BENJAMIN COFFIN III	Another ex-roommate, a budding real estate tycoon, and Mimi's ex-boyfriend
JOANNE JEFFERSON	Maureen Johnson's girlfriend
ANGEL DUMOTT SCHUNARD	A transvestite street drummer with AIDS
MIMI MARQUEZ	An S & M dancer and a junkie with HIV
MR. & MRS. JEFFERSON	
HOMELESS PEOPLE	
PAUL	Life-support group leader
GORDON, STEVE, ALI, PAM, LISA	Members of the group
SQUEEGEEMAN	
POLICE OFFICERS	
VENDORS	
JUNKIES	
MAUREEN JOHNSON	A performance artist, Joanne's girlfriend, and Mark's ex-girlfriend
RESTAURANT MAN	
MR. GREY	
ALEXI DARLING	A TV producer from *Buzzline*
PASTOR	
ROGER'S MOM	
MIMI'S MOM	

MUSICAL SYNOPSIS

Act I

Act II

NOTE: Sung passages are indicated in the text by small caps.

The Company celebrates the end of Act I with the rousing "La Vie Bohème," New York Theatre Workshop, 1996.

Joan Marcus

ACT I

The audience enters the theatre to discover the curtainless set. The one set piece on stage left is a huge tower that represents:

(A) A totem-pole Christmas tree which stands in an abandoned lot,
(B) A wood stove and a snaky chimney that is the center of the boys' loft apartment and
(C) The steeple of a church in Act II.

There is a wooden-platform loft area on stage right with a railing around it, under which sits "The Band" of five musicians. It has an escape staircase on the upstage side. There is a black, waist-high rail fence downstage left of them.

On stage, once the house is open, crew and band members could and should move about informally, in preparation for the play.

The Lower East Side. Christmas Eve. An industrial loft.

The top floor of what was once a music-publishing factory. Old rock and roll posters hang on the walls. Many posters have Roger's picture on it, advertising gigs at CBGB's and The Pyramid Club.

Roger enters from up left with an electric guitar and crosses to a guitar amp sitting on a chair at center. He casually plugs in and sets levels, then crosses downstage and sits on the table.

After a few beats, the company, led by Mark, enters from all directions and fills the stage. Mark sets up a small tripod and a 16-mm movie camera down center, aimed upstage. He addresses the audience:

MARK: We begin on Christmas Eve with me, Mark, and my roommate, Roger. We live in an industrial loft on the corner of 11th Street and Avenue B. It's the top floor of what was once a music-publishing factory. Old rock and roll posters hang on the walls. They have Roger's picture advertising gigs at CBGB's and The Pyramid Club. We have an illegal wood-burning stove; its exhaust pipe crawls up to a skylight. All of our electrical appliances are plugged into one thick extension cord which snakes its way out a window. Outside, a small tent city has sprung up in the lot next to our building. Inside, it's freezing because we have no heat.

(He turns the camera to Roger.)

Smile!

(He sings:)

DECEMBER 24. NINE P.M.
EASTERN STANDARD TIME
FROM HERE ON IN
I SHOOT WITHOUT A SCRIPT

SEE IF ANYTHING COMES OF IT
INSTEAD OF MY OLD SHIT

FIRST SHOT—ROGER
TUNING HIS FENDER GUITAR
HE HASN'T PLAYED IN A YEAR

ROGER:
THIS WON'T TUNE

MARK:
SO WE HEAR
HE'S JUST COMING BACK
FROM HALF A YEAR OF WITHDRAWAL

ROGER:
ARE YOU TALKING TO ME?

MARK:
NOT AT ALL

ARE YOU READY? HOLD THAT FOCUS— STEADY
TELL THE FOLKS AT HOME WHAT YOU'RE DOING ROGER? . . .

ROGER:
I'M WRITING ONE GREAT—

MARK: The phone rings.

ROGER:

Saved!

MARK *(To audience)*:

We screen
Zoom in on the answering machine!

(An actor sets a telephone on a chair and we see Mark's Mom in a light special.)

MARK & ROGER'S OUTGOING MESSAGE:

"Speak" . . . ("Beeeep!")

MARK'S MOM:

That was a very loud beep
I don't even know if this is working
Mark—Mark—are you there?
Are you screening your calls—it's Mom

We wanted to call and say we love you
And we'll miss you tomorrow
Cindy and the kids are here—send their love
Oh, I hope you like the hotplate

Just don't leave it on dear
When you leave the house

Oh and Mark
We're sorry to hear that Maureen dumped you
I say c'est la vie
So let her be a lesbian
There are other fish in the sea

. . . Love Mom

(Lights fade on Mark's Mom and answering machine.)

MARK:

Tell the folks at home what you're doing Roger? . . .

ROGER:

I'm writing one great song—

MARK: The phone rings.

ROGER:

YESSS!

MARK:

WE SCREEN.

MARK & ROGER'S OUTGOING MESSAGE:

"SPEAK" . . . ("BEEEEP!")

(Lights fade up on the street. The street is the front-door area of the boys' building. A battered public phone is nearby. Tom Collins stands at the phone.)

COLLINS:

"CHESTNUTS ROASTING—"

MARK *(As he picks up phone)*:

COLLINS!

COLLINS:

I'M DOWNSTAIRS.

MARK:

HEY!

COLLINS:

ROGER PICKED UP THE PHONE??

MARK:

NO, IT'S ME.

COLLINS:

THROW DOWN THE KEY.

(Mark pulls out a small leather pouch and drops it off the apron down center as if out a window, just as a weighted leather pouch plops down from "upstairs" and Collins catches it.)

MARK:

A WILD NIGHT IS NOW PRE-ORDAINED

(Two thugs appear above Collins with clubs. They are obviously close to attacking him.)

COLLINS *(Into the phone)*:

I MAY BE DETAINED.

(Thugs beat and kick Collins. Collins falls to the ground as lights fade on him.)

MARK:

WHAT DOES HE MEAN? . . .

(Phone rings again.)

WHAT DO YOU MEAN—DETAINED?

(Lights come up on Benny, on a cell phone.)

BENNY:

HO HO HO

MARK & ROGER:

BENNY! (SHIT!)

BENNY:

DUDES, I'M ON MY WAY

MARK & ROGER:

GREAT! (FUCK!)

BENNY:

I NEED THE RENT

MARK:

WHAT RENT?

BENNY:

THIS PAST YEAR'S RENT WHICH I LET SLIDE

MARK:

LET SLIDE? YOU SAID WE WERE "GOLDEN"

ROGER:

WHEN YOU BOUGHT THE BUILDING

MARK:

WHEN WE WERE ROOMMATES

ROGER:

REMEMBER—YOU LIVED HERE!?

BENNY:

HOW COULD I FORGET?
YOU, ME, COLLINS AND MAUREEN

HOW *IS* THE DRAMA QUEEN?

MARK:

SHE'S PERFORMING TONIGHT

BENNY:

I KNOW.
STILL HER PRODUCTION MANAGER?

MARK:

TWO DAYS AGO I WAS BUMPED

BENNY:

YOU STILL DATING HER?

MARK:

LAST MONTH I WAS DUMPED

ROGER:

SHE'S IN LOVE

BENNY:

SHE'S GOT A NEW MAN

MARK:

WELL—NO

BENNY:

WHAT'S HIS NAME?

MARK & BENNY:

JOANNE

BENNY:

RENT, MY AMIGOS, IS DUE
OR I WILL HAVE TO EVICT YOU
BE THERE IN A FEW.

(Roger defiantly picks out "Musetta's Theme" from Puccini's La Bohème *on the electric guitar. The fuse blows on the amp.)*

MARK: The power blows . . .

(The stage bursts into a flurry of movement and all but Mark and Roger freeze in a group upstage.
Mark and Roger sing:)

HOW DO YOU DOCUMENT REAL LIFE
WHEN REAL LIFE'S GETTING MORE
LIKE FICTION EACH DAY?
HEADLINES—BREADLINES
BLOW MY MIND

AND NOW THIS DEADLINE:
"EVICTION—OR PAY"
RENT

ROGER:

HOW DO YOU WRITE A SONG
WHEN THE CHORDS SOUND WRONG
THOUGH THEY ONCE SOUNDED RIGHT AND RARE?
WHEN THE NOTES ARE SOUR
WHERE IS THE POWER
YOU ONCE HAD TO IGNITE THE AIR?

MARK:

WE'RE HUNGRY AND FROZEN

ROGER:

SOME LIFE THAT WE'VE CHOSEN

MARK & ROGER:

HOW WE GONNA PAY
HOW WE GONNA PAY
HOW WE GONNA PAY
LAST YEAR'S RENT?

MARK:

WE LIGHT CANDLES

ROGER:

HOW DO YOU START A FIRE
WHEN THERE'S NOTHING TO BURN
AND IT FEELS LIKE SOMETHING'S STUCK IN YOUR FLUE?

MARK:

HOW CAN YOU GENERATE HEAT
WHEN YOU CAN'T FEEL YOUR FEET

MARK & ROGER:

AND THEY'RE TURNING BLUE!

MARK:

YOU LIGHT UP A MEAN BLAZE

(Roger grabs one of his own posters.)

ROGER:

WITH POSTERS—

(Mark grabs old manuscripts.)

MARK:

And screenplays

MARK & ROGER:

How we gonna pay
How we gonna pay
How we gonna pay
Last year's rent?

(Lights out on loft, up on phone booth. Joanne Jefferson appears at the pay phone.)

JOANNE:

Don't screen, Maureen
It's me—Joanne
Your substitute production manager
Hey hey hey! (Did you eat?)
Don't change the subject, Maureen
But darling—you haven't eaten all day

You won't throw up
You won't throw up
The digital delay—
Didn't blow up (exactly)
There may have been one teeny tiny spark
You're not calling Mark

(Collins struggles and stands.)

COLLINS:

How do you stay on your feet
When on every street
It's, "Trick or treat?"
(And tonight its "trick")
"Welcome back to town"
I should lie down
Everything's brown
And uh—oh
I feel sick

MARK *(At the window)*:

Where *is* he?

COLLINS:

GETTING DIZZY

(Collins collapses.)

MARK & ROGER:

HOW WE GONNA PAY
HOW WE GONNA PAY
HOW WE GONNA PAY
LAST YEAR'S RENT?

(They stoke the fire. Cross-cut to Benny's Range Rover.)

BENNY *(On cell phone)*:

ALISON BABY—YOU SOUND SAD
I CAN'T BELIEVE THOSE TWO
AFTER EVERYTHING I'VE DONE

EVER SINCE OUR WEDDING
I'M DIRT—THEY'LL SEE
I CAN HELP THEM ALL OUT IN THE LONG RUN

(Lights up on Joanne at the phone, the loft, and Collins on the ground.)

FORCES ARE GATHERING
FORCES ARE GATHERING
CAN'T TURN AWAY
FORCES ARE GATHERING

COLLINS *(Overlapping "Forces are gathering")*:

UGHHHH—
UGHHHH—
UGHHHH—I CAN'T THINK
UGHHHH—
UGHHHH—
UGHHHH—I NEED A DRINK

MARK *(Reading from a script page)*:

"THE MUSIC IGNITES THE NIGHT WITH PASSIONATE FIRE"

JOANNE:

MAUREEN—I'M NOT A THEATER PERSON

ROGER:

"THE NARRATION CRACKLES AND POPS WITH INCENDIARY WIT"

JOANNE:

COULD NEVER BE A THEATER PERSON

COLLINS *(Overlapping "theater person")*:

I CAN'T THINK.

MARK:

ZOOM IN AS THEY BURN THE PAST TO THE GROUND

JOANNE *(Realizing she's been cut off)*:

HELLO?

MARK & ROGER:

AND FEEL THE HEAT OF THE FUTURE'S GLOW

JOANNE:

HELLO?

(The phone rings, Mark picks it up.)

MARK:

HELLO, MAUREEN?
YOUR EQUIPMENT WON'T WORK?
OKAY—ALL RIGHT, I'LL GO!

MARK & HALF THE COMPANY:

HOW DO YOU LEAVE THE PAST BEHIND
WHEN IT KEEPS FINDING WAYS TO GET TO YOUR HEART?
IT REACHES WAY DOWN DEEP AND TEARS YOU INSIDE-OUT
'TIL YOU'RE TORN APART
RENT

ROGER & OTHER HALF OF THE COMPANY:

HOW CAN YOU CONNECT IN AN AGE
WHERE STRANGERS, LANDLORDS, LOVERS
YOUR OWN BLOOD CELLS BETRAY?

ALL:

WHAT BINDS THE FABRIC TOGETHER
WHEN THE RAGING, SHIFTING WINDS OF CHANGE
KEEP RIPPING AWAY?

BENNY:

DRAW A LINE IN THE SAND
AND THEN MAKE A STAND

ROGER:

USE YOUR CAMERA TO SPAR

MARK:

USE YOUR GUITAR

ALL:

WHEN THEY ACT TOUGH—YOU CALL THEIR BLUFF

MARK & ROGER:

WE'RE NOT GONNA PAY

MARK, ROGER & HALF OF THE COMPANY:

WE'RE NOT GONNA PAY

MARK, ROGER & OTHER HALF OF THE COMPANY:

WE'RE NOT GONNA PAY

ALL:

LAST YEAR'S RENT
THIS YEAR'S RENT
NEXT YEAR'S RENT

RENT RENT RENT RENT RENT
WE'RE NOT GONNA PAY RENT

MARK & ROGER:

'CAUSE EVERYTHING IS RENT

(The street, in front of the pay phone. A Homeless Man appears on the right. Across the stage, sitting on the sculpture, is Angel Dumott Schunard with a plastic tub balanced like a drum between his knees.)

A HOMELESS MAN:

CHRISTMAS BELLS ARE RINGING
CHRISTMAS BELLS ARE RINGING
CHRISTMAS BELLS ARE RINGING
SOMEWHERE ELSE!
NOT HERE.

(The Homeless Man exits. Angel drums. He gets a good beat going on the tub. A moan interrupts him. He starts to drum again, then sees Collins limping.

They sing:)

ANGEL:

YOU OKAY, HONEY?

COLLINS:

I'M AFRAID SO

ANGEL:

THEY GET ANY MONEY?

COLLINS:

No
Had none to get—
But they purloined my coat—
Well you missed a sleeve!—Thanks

ANGEL:

Hell it's Christmas eve
I'm Angel

COLLINS:

Angel? . . . Indeed
An angel of the first degree
Friends call me Collins—Tom Collins
Nice tree . . .

ANGEL:

Let's get a Band-Aid for your knee
I'll change, there's a "life support" meeting
At nine-thirty
Yes—this body provides a comfortable home
For the Acquired Immune Deficiency Syndrome

COLLINS:

As does mine

ANGEL:

We'll get along fine
Get you a coat, have a bite
Make a night—I'm flush

COLLINS:

My friends are waiting—

ANGEL:

You're cute when you blush
The more the merry—ho ho ho
And I do not take no.

(They walk off. Lights up on loft.)

ROGER: Where are you going?
MARK: Maureen calls.
ROGER: You're such a sucker.
MARK: I don't suppose you'd like to see her show in the lot tonight? Or come to dinner?
ROGER: Zoom in on my empty wallet.

MARK: Touché. Take your AZT.

CLOSE ON ROGER
HIS GIRLFRIEND APRIL
LEFT A NOTE SAYING: "WE'VE GOT AIDS"
BEFORE SLITTING HER WRISTS IN THE BATHROOM

I'll check up on you later. Change your mind. You have to get out of the house.

(Roger sings:)

ROGER:
I'M WRITING ONE GREAT SONG BEFORE I . . .

ONE SONG
GLORY
ONE SONG
BEFORE I GO
GLORY
ONE SONG TO LEAVE BEHIND

FIND ONE SONG
ONE LAST REFRAIN
GLORY
FROM THE PRETTY BOY FRONT MAN
WHO WASTED OPPORTUNITY

ONE SONG
HE HAD THE WORLD AT HIS FEET
GLORY
IN THE EYES OF A YOUNG GIRL
A YOUNG GIRL
FIND GLORY
BEYOND THE CHEAP COLORED LIGHTS

ONE SONG
BEFORE THE SUN SETS
GLORY—ON ANOTHER EMPTY LIFE
TIME FLIES—TIME DIES

Glory—one blaze of glory
One blaze of glory—glory

Find
Glory
In a song that rings true
Truth like a blazing fire
An eternal flame

Find
One song
A song about love
Glory
From the soul of a young man
A young man

Find
The one song
Before the virus takes hold
Glory
Like a sunset
One song
To redeem this empty life

Time flies
And then—no need to endure anymore
Time dies

(A knock on the "door." It is Mimi.)

The door.

*(He crosses to the "door."
Roger and Mimi sing:)*

What'd you forget?

(Mimi enters, with a candle.)

MIMI:

Got a light?

ROGER:

I know you?—you're—
You're shivering

MIMI:

It's nothing
They turned off my heat
And I'm just a little
Weak on my feet
Would you light my candle?
What are you staring at?

ROGER:

Nothing
Your hair in the moonlight
You look familiar

(He lights her candle. She starts to leave, but stumbles.)

Can you make it?

MIMI:

Just haven't eaten much today
At least the room stopped spinning. Anyway. What?

ROGER:

Nothing
Your smile reminded me of—

MIMI:

I always remind people of—who is she?

ROGER:

She died. Her name was April

(Mimi discreetly blows out candle.)

MIMI:

It's out again
Sorry about your friend
Would you light my candle?

(He lights the candle. They linger, awkwardly.)

ROGER:

Well—

MIMI:

Yeah. Ow!

ROGER:

Oh. The wax—it's—!

MIMI:

Dripping! I like it—between my—

ROGER:

Fingers. I figured . . .
Oh, well. Good night.

(She exits. He starts toward his guitar. Another knock. Roger answers it.)

It blew out again?

MIMI:

No—I think that I dropped my stash

ROGER:

I know I've seen you out and about
When I used to go out
Your candle's out

MIMI:

I'm illin'—I had it when I walked in the door
It was pure—is it on the floor?

ROGER:

The floor?

(She gets down on all fours and starts looking for her stash. She looks back at him. He stares at her.)

MIMI:

They say that I have the best ass below 14th Street
Is it true?

ROGER:

What?

MIMI:

You're staring again

ROGER:

Oh no
I mean you do—have a nice—
I mean—you look familiar

MIMI:

Like your dead girlfriend?

ROGER:

Only when you smiled
But I'm sure I've seen you somewhere else—

MIMI:

Do you go to the Cat Scratch Club?
That's where I work—I dance—help me look

ROGER:

Yes!
They used to tie you up—

MIMI:

It's a living

ROGER:

I didn't recognize you
Without the handcuffs

MIMI:

We could light the candle
Oh won't you light the candle?

(He lights it again.)

ROGER:

Why don't you forget that stuff
You look like you're sixteen

MIMI:

I'm nineteen—but I'm old for my age
I'm just born to be bad

ROGER:

I once was born to be bad
I used to shiver like that

MIMI:

I have no heat—I told you

ROGER:

I used to sweat

MIMI:

I got a cold

ROGER:

Uh-huh
I used to be a junkie

MIMI:

BUT NOW AND THEN I LIKE TO—

ROGER:

UH-HUH

MIMI:

FEEL GOOD

ROGER:

HERE IT—UM—

(He picks up a small object—crack bag.)

MIMI:

WHAT'S THAT?

ROGER:

CANDY BAR WRAPPER

(He puts it behind his back and into his back pocket.)

MIMI:

WE COULD LIGHT THE CANDLE

(He discreetly blows out the candle.)

WHAT'D YOU DO WITH MY CANDLE?

ROGER:

THAT WAS MY LAST MATCH

MIMI:

OUR EYES'LL ADJUST. THANK GOD FOR THE MOON.

ROGER:

MAYBE IT'S NOT THE MOON AT ALL
I HEAR SPIKE LEE'S SHOOTING DOWN THE STREET

MIMI:

BAH-HUMBUG . . . BAH-HUMBUG

(She places her hand under his, pretending to do it by mistake.)

ROGER:

COLD HANDS

MIMI:

YOURS TOO.

Big. Like my father's.
You wanna dance?

ROGER:

With you?

MIMI:

No—with my father

ROGER:

I'm Roger

MIMI:

They call me
They call me Mimi.

(She goes to him, puts her arms around him, reaches into his pocket, nabs the stash and sexily exits.

Scene change. Joanne's loft. In blackout, another phone rings. We see Maureen, in silhouette.)

MAUREEN'S OUTGOING MESSAGE: Hi. You've reached Maureen and Joanne. Leave a message and don't forget "Over the Moon"—my performance, protesting the eviction of the homeless (and artists) from the 11th Street lot. Tonight at midnight in the lot between A and B. Party at Life Café to follow. *(Beep)*

(Singing:)

MR. JEFFERSON:

Well, Joanne—we're off
I tried you at the office
And they said you're stage managing or something

MRS. JEFFERSON:

Remind her that those unwed mothers in Harlem
Need her legal help too

MR. JEFFERSON:

Call Daisy for our itinerary or Alfred at Pound Ridge
Or Eileen at the State Department in a pinch
We'll be at the spa for New Year's
Unless, the senator changes his mind

MRS. JEFFERSON:

The hearings

MR. JEFFERSON:

OH YES—KITTEN
MUMMY'S CONFIRMATION HEARINGS BEGIN ON THE TENTH
WE'LL NEED YOU—ALONE—BY THE SIXTH

MRS. JEFFERSON:

HAROLD!

MR. JEFFERSON:

YOU HEAR THAT?
IT'S THREE WEEKS AWAY
AND SHE'S ALREADY NERVOUS

MRS. JEFFERSON:

I AM NOT!

MR. JEFFERSON:

FOR MUMMY'S SAKE, KITTEN
NO DOC MARTENS THIS TIME AND WEAR A DRESS . . .
OH, AND KITTEN—HAVE A MERRY

MRS. JEFFERSON:

AND A BRA!!

(The loft.)

MARK *(Sings)*:

ENTER TOM COLLINS
COMPUTER GENIUS, TEACHER, VAGABOND ANARCHIST
WHO RAN NAKED THROUGH THE PARTHENON

(Collins holds Angel's drumming tub, now filled with provisions.)

MARK & COLLINS:

BUSTELO—MARLBORO
BANANA BY THE BUNCH
A BOX OF CAPTAIN CRUNCH WILL TASTE SO GOOD

COLLINS:

AND FIREWOOD

MARK:

LOOK—IT'S SANTA CLAUS

COLLINS:

HOLD YOUR APPLAUSE

(Roger enters.)

ROGER:

Oh hi

COLLINS:

"Oh hi," after seven months

ROGER:

Sorry

COLLINS:

This boy could use some Stoli

COLLINS, MARK & ROGER:

Oh holy night

ROGER:

You struck gold at MIT?

COLLINS:

They expelled me for my theory of actual reality
Which I'll soon impart
To the couch potatoes at New York University
Still haven't left the house?

ROGER:

I was waiting for you don't you know

COLLINS:

Well, tonight's the night
Come to the Life Café after Maureen's show

ROGER:

No flow

COLLINS:

Gentlemen, our benefactor on this Christmas Eve
Whose charity is only matched by talent, I believe
A new member of the Alphabet City avant-garde
Angel Dumott Schunard!

(Angel sashays in. He's gorgeously done up in Santa drag. He has twenty-dollar bills in both hands. He sings:)

ANGEL:

Today for you—tomorrow for me
Today for you—tomorrow for me

COLLINS:

And you should hear her beat!

ROGER:

You earned this on the street?

ANGEL:

It was my lucky day today on Avenue A
When a lady in a limousine drove my way
She said, "Dahling—be a dear—haven't slept in a year
I need your help to make my neighbor's yappy dog
Disappear"

"This Akita—Evita—just won't shut up
I believe if you play non-stop that pup
Will breathe its very last high-strung breath
I'm certain that cur will bark itself to death"

Today for you—tomorrow for me
Today for you—tomorrow for me

We agreed on a fee—a thousand-dollar guarantee
Tax-free—and a bonus if I trim her tree
Now who could foretell that it would go so well
But sure as I am here that dog is now in doggy hell

After an hour—Evita—in all her glory
On the window ledge of that twenty-third story
Like Thelma and Louise did when they got the blues
Swan dove into the courtyard of the Gracie Mews

Today for you—tomorrow for me
Today for you—tomorrow for me

(Angel does a fantabulous drum/dance solo.)

Then back to the street where I met my sweet
where he was moanin' and groanin' on the cold concrete
The nurse took him home for some mercurochrome
And I dressed his wounds and got him back on his feet

Singing:
Today for you—tomorrow for me
Today for you—tomorrow for me
Today for you—tomorrow for me
Today for you—tomorrow for me

BENNY *(Entering)*:

JOY TO THE WORLD . . .

HEY YOU BUM—YEAH, YOU, MOVE OVER
GET YOUR ASS OFF THAT RANGE ROVER

MARK: That attitude toward the homeless is exactly what Maureen is protesting tonight. *(To audience; holding camera up to Benny)* Close up: our ex-roommate Benjamin Coffin III who married Alison Grey of the Westport Greys, then bought the building and the lot next door from his father-in-law in hopes of starting a cyber-studio.

(They sing:)

BENNY:

MAUREEN IS PROTESTING
LOSING HER PERFORMANCE SPACE
NOT MY ATTITUDE

ROGER:

WHAT'S HAPPENED TO BENNY
WHAT HAPPENED TO HIS HEART
AND THE IDEALS HE ONCE PURSUED

BENNY:

ANY OWNER OF THE LOT NEXT DOOR
HAS THE RIGHT TO DO WITH IT AS HE PLEASES

COLLINS:

HAPPY BIRTHDAY, JESUS!

BENNY:

THE RENT

MARK:

YOU'RE WASTING YOUR TIME

ROGER:

WE'RE BROKE

MARK:

AND YOU BROKE YOUR WORD—THIS IS ABSURD

BENNY:

THERE IS ONE WAY YOU WON'T HAVE TO PAY

ROGER:

I KNEW IT!

BENNY:

Next door the home of
Cyber Arts you see
And now that the block is re-zoned
Our dream can become a reality

You'll see boys
You'll see boys

A state of the art digital
Virtual interactive studio
I'll forego your rent and on paper guarantee
That you can stay here for free
If you do me one small favor

MARK:

What?

BENNY:

Convince Maureen to cancel her protest

MARK:

Why not just get an injunction and call the cops

BENNY:

I did and they're on standby
But my investors would rather
I handle this quietly

ROGER:

You can't quietly wipe out an entire tent city
Then watch *It's a Wonderful Life* on TV!

BENNY:

You want to produce films?—(and) write songs?
You need somewhere to do it!
It's what we used to dream about
Think twice before you pooh-pooh it

You'll see boys
You'll see boys

You'll see—the beauty of a studio
That lets us do our work and get paid
With condos on the top
Whose rent keeps open our shop

JUST STOP HER PROTEST
AND YOU'LL HAVE IT MADE
YOU'LL SEE—OR YOU'LL PACK.

(Benny exits.)

ANGEL:
THAT BOY COULD USE SOME PROZAC

ROGER:
OR HEAVY DRUGS

MARK:
OR GROUP HUGS

COLLINS:
WHICH REMINDS ME—
WE HAVE A DETOUR TO MAKE TONIGHT
ANYONE WHO WANTS TO CAN COME ALONG

ANGEL:
LIFE SUPPORT'S A GROUP FOR PEOPLE COPING WITH LIFE
WE DON'T HAVE TO STAY TOO LONG

MARK:
FIRST I'VE GOT A PROTEST TO SAVE

ANGEL:
ROGER?

ROGER:
I'M NOT MUCH COMPANY YOU'LL FIND

MARK:
BEHAVE!

ANGEL:
HE'LL CATCH UP LATER—HE'S GOT OTHER THINGS ON HIS MIND
YOU'LL SEE BOYS

MARK & COLLINS:
WE'LL SEE BOYS

ROGER:
LET IT BE BOYS!

COLLINS:
I LIKE BOYS

ANGEL:
BOYS LIKE ME

ALL:
WE'LL SEE.

(The lot. Joanne is reexamining the cable connections for the umpteenth time. Mark and Joanne sing:)

MARK:

AND SO—INTO THE ABYSS
THE LOT. WHERE A SMALL STAGE IS PARTIALLY SET UP

JOANNE:

"LINE IN" . . .
I WENT TO HARVARD FOR THIS . . .

MARK:

CLOSE ON MARK'S NOSE DIVE

JOANNE:

"LINE OUT" . . .

MARK:

WILL HE GET OUT OF HERE ALIVE? . . .

(Joanne notices Mark crossing to her.)

JOANNE:

MARK?

MARK:

HI.

JOANNE:

I TOLD HER NOT TO CALL YOU

MARK:

THAT'S MAUREEN
BUT CAN I HELP SINCE I'M HERE

JOANNE:

I'VE HIRED AN ENGINEER . . .

MARK:

GREAT!
SO, NICE TO HAVE MET YOU

JOANNE:

WAIT!
SHE'S THREE HOURS LATE

THE SAMPLES WON'T DELAY
BUT THE CABLE—

MARK:

THERE'S ANOTHER WAY
SAY SOMETHING—ANYTHING

JOANNE *(Into the mike)*:

TEST—ONE, TWO THREE . . .

MARK:

ANYTHING BUT THAT

JOANNE:

THIS IS WEIRD

MARK:

IT'S WEIRD

JOANNE:

VERY WEIRD

MARK:

FUCKIN' WEIRD

JOANNE:

I'M SO MAD
THAT I DON'T KNOW WHAT TO DO
FIGHTING WITH MICROPHONES
FREEZING DOWN TO MY BONES
AND TO TOP IT ALL OFF
I'M WITH YOU

MARK:

FEEL LIKE GOING INSANE?
GOT A FIRE IN YOUR BRAIN?
AND YOU'RE THINKING OF DRINKING GASOLINE?

JOANNE:

AS A MATTER OF FACT—

MARK:

HONEY, I KNOW THIS ACT
IT'S CALLED THE "TANGO MAUREEN"

THE TANGO MAUREEN
IT'S A DARK, DIZZY
MERRY-GO-ROUND
AS SHE KEEPS YOU DANGLING

JOANNE:

YOU'RE WRONG

MARK:

YOUR HEART SHE IS MANGLING

JOANNE:

IT'S DIFFERENT WITH ME

MARK:

AND YOU TOSS AND YOU TURN
'CAUSE HER COLD EYES CAN BURN
YET YOU YEARN AND YOU CHURN AND REBOUND

JOANNE:

I THINK I KNOW WHAT YOU MEAN

MARK & JOANNE:

THE TANGO MAUREEN

MARK:

HAS SHE EVER
POUTED HER LIPS
AND CALLED YOU "POOKIE?"

JOANNE:

NEVER

MARK:

HAVE YOU EVER DOUBTED A KISS OR TWO?

JOANNE:

THIS IS SPOOKY
DID YOU SWOON
WHEN SHE WALKED THROUGH THE DOOR?

MARK:

EVERY TIME—SO BE CAUTIOUS

JOANNE:

DID SHE MOON OVER OTHER BOYS?—

MARK:

MORE THAN MOON—

JOANNE:

I'M GETTING NAUSEOUS

(They dance. Mark leads.)

MARK: Where'd you learn to tango?

JOANNE: With the French ambassador's daughter in her dorm room at Miss Porter's. And you?

MARK: With Nanette Himmelfarb, the rabbi's daughter, at the Scarsdale Jewish Community Center.

(They switch. Joanne leads.)

It's hard to do this backwards.
JOANNE: You should try it in heels!

SHE CHEATED
MARK:
SHE CHEATED
JOANNE:
MAUREEN CHEATED
MARK:
FUCKIN' CHEATED
JOANNE:
I'M DEFEATED
I SHOULD GIVE UP RIGHT NOW
MARK:
GOTTA LOOK ON THE BRIGHT SIDE
WITH ALL OF YOUR MIGHT
JOANNE:
I'D FALL FOR HER STILL ANYHOW
MARK & JOANNE:
WHEN YOU'RE DANCING HER DANCE
YOU DON'T STAND A CHANCE
HER GRIP OF ROMANCE
MAKES YOU FALL
MARK:
SO YOU THINK, "MIGHT AS WELL"
JOANNE:
"DANCE A TANGO TO HELL"
MARK & JOANNE:
"AT LEAST I'LL HAVE TANGOED AT ALL"

THE TANGO MAUREEN
GOTTA DANCE 'TIL YOUR DIVA IS THROUGH
YOU PRETEND TO BELIEVE HER
'CAUSE IN THE END—YOU CAN'T LEAVE HER

BUT THE END IT WILL COME
STILL YOU HAVE TO PLAY DUMB

'TIL YOU'RE GLUM AND YOU BUM
AND TURN BLUE

MARK:
WHY DO WE LOVE WHEN SHE'S MEAN?

JOANNE:
AND SHE CAN BE SO OBSCENE

MARK:
TRY THE MIKE

JOANNE:
MY MAUREEN . . .

(The word "Maureen" echoes in digital delay land: "een, een, een . . .")

MARK:
PATCHED

JOANNE:
THANKS

MARK:
YOU KNOW—I FEEL GREAT NOW!

JOANNE:
I FEEL LOUSY

(Pay phone rings. Joanne picks it up.)

HI, HONEY, WE'RE . . .
POOKIE?
YOU NEVER CALLED ME POOKIE
FORGET IT
WE'RE PATCHED

(She hangs up, looks at Mark.)

MARK & JOANNE:
THE TANGO MAUREEN!

(Life support group. Paul, the support group leader, sits on the downstage right railing, above, facing upstage. Gordon, one of the members of the group, is standing downstage left, facing the audience. As the group members enter they introduce themselves and form a semi-circle.

Note: the names of the HIV group members, marked with an aster-

isk, should change every night, and should honor actual friends of the company who have died of AIDS.)

STEVE*: Steve
GORDON*: Gordon.
ALI*: Ali.
PAM*: Pam.
LISA*: Lisa.
ANGEL: Hi, I'm Angel.
COLLINS: Tom. Collins.
PAUL: I'm Paul. Let's begin.

ALL *(Singing)*:
THERE'S ONLY US
THERE'S ONLY THIS . . .

(Mark noisily enters.)

MARK:
SORRY . . . EXCUSE ME . . . OOPS
PAUL:
AND YOU ARE?
MARK:
OH—I'M NOT—
I'M JUST HERE TO—
I DON'T HAVE—
I'M HERE WITH—
UM—MARK
MARK—I'M MARK

WELL—THIS IS QUITE AN OPERATION
PAUL:
SIT DOWN MARK
WE'LL CONTINUE THE AFFIRMATION
ALL:
FORGET REGRET OR LIFE IS YOURS TO MISS
GORDON*:
EXCUSE ME PAUL—I'M HAVING A PROBLEM WITH THIS
THIS CREDO—
MY T-CELLS ARE LOW—
I REGRET THAT NEWS, OKAY?

PAUL:

Alright
But Gordon—how do you feel today?

GORDON*:

What do you mean?

PAUL:

How do you feel today?

GORDON*:

Okay

PAUL:

Is that all?

GORDON*:

Best I've felt all year

PAUL:

Then why choose fear?

GORDON*:

I'm a New Yorker!
Fear's my life!

Look—I find some of what you teach suspect
Because I'm used to relying on intellect
But I try to open up to what I don't know

GORDON* & ROGER *(Who sings from his loft)*:

Because reason says I should have died three years ago

ALL:

No other road
No other way
No day but today.

(Mimi's apartment. She sings:)

MIMI:

What's the time?
Well it's gotta be close to midnight
My body's talking to me
It says, "Time for danger"

It says, "I wanna commit a crime
Wanna be the cause of a fight
Wanna put on a tight skirt and flirt with a stranger"

I've had a knack from way back
At breaking the rules once I learn the games
Get up—life's too quick

I know someplace sick
Where this chick'll dance in the flames
We don't need any money
I always get in for free
You can get in, too
If you get in with me

Let's go out tonight
I have to go out tonight
You wanna play?
Let's run away
We won't be back
Before it's Christmas Day
Take me out tonight (meow)

When I get a wink from the doorman
Do you know how lucky you'll be?
That you're on line with the feline of Avenue B

Let's go out tonight
I have to go out tonight
You wanna prowl
Be my night owl?
Well take my hand, we're gonna howl
Out tonight

In the evening I've got to roam
Can't sleep in the city of neon and chrome
Feels too damn much like home
When the Spanish babies cry

So let's find a bar
So dark we forget who we are
Where all the scars from the
Nevers and Maybes die

LET'S GO OUT TONIGHT
HAVE TO GO OUT TONIGHT
YOU'RE SWEET
WANNA HIT THE STREET?
WANNA WAIL AT THE MOON LIKE A CAT IN HEAT?
JUST TAKE ME OUT TONIGHT

(She makes her way to Roger's door and ends the song in front of him.)

PLEASE TAKE ME OUT TONIGHT
DON'T FORSAKE ME—OUT TONIGHT
I'LL LET YOU MAKE ME—OUT TONIGHT
TONIGHT—TONIGHT—TONIGHT

(The loft. Mimi plants a huge kiss on Roger. He recoils. They sing:)

ROGER:

WHO DO YOU THINK YOU ARE?
BARGING IN ON ME AND MY GUITAR
LITTLE GIRL—HEY
THE DOOR IS THAT WAY
YOU BETTER GO YOU KNOW
THE FIRE'S OUT ANYWAY

TAKE THE POWDER—TAKE YOUR CANDLE
YOUR SWEET WHISPER
I JUST CAN'T HANDLE

WELL TAKE YOUR HAIR IN THE MOONLIGHT
YOUR BROWN EYES—GOOD-BYE, GOOD NIGHT

I SHOULD TELL YOU I SHOULD TELL YOU
I SHOULD TELL YOU I SHOULD—NO!

ANOTHER TIME—ANOTHER PLACE
OUR TEMPERATURE WOULD CLIMB
THERE'D BE A LONG EMBRACE
WE'D DO ANOTHER DANCE
IT'D BE ANOTHER PLAY
LOOKING FOR ROMANCE?

Come back another day
Another day

MIMI:

The heart may freeze or it can burn
The pain will ease if I can learn

There is no future
There is no past
I live this moment
As my last

There's only us
There's only this
Forget regret
Or life is yours to miss
No other road
No other way
No day but today

ROGER:

Excuse me if I'm off track
But if you're so wise?
Then tell me—why do you need smack?

Take your needle
Take your fancy prayer
And don't forget
Get the moonlight out of your hair
Long ago—you might've lit up my heart
But the fire's dead—ain't never ever gonna start

Another time—another place
The words would only rhyme
We'd be in outer space
It'd be another song
We'd sing another way
You wanna prove me wrong?
Come back another day
Another day

MIMI:

There's only, "Yes"
Only tonight

We must let go
To know what's right
No other course
No other way
No day but today

(Lights slowly fade up on the support group.)

MIMI & OTHERS:
I can't control
My destiny
I trust my soul
My only goal
Is just—to be

ROGER *(Overlapping "I can't control")*:
Control your temper
She doesn't see
Who says that there's a soul
Just let me be

ALL:
There's only now
There's only here
Give into love
Or live in fear
No other path
No other way
No day but today
No day but today
No day but today
No day but today
No day but today
No day but today

ROGER *(Overlapping "There's only now")*:
Who do you think you are?
Barging in on me and my
Guitar
Little girl, hey
The door is that way
The fire's out anyway
Take your powder

TAKE THE CANDLE
TAKE YOUR BROWN EYES
YOUR PRETTY SMILE
YOUR SILHOUETTE

ANOTHER TIME, ANOTHER PLACE
ANOTHER RHYME, A WARM EMBRACE
ANOTHER DANCE, ANOTHER WAY
ANOTHER CHANCE, ANOTHER DAY

ALL *(Except Roger)*:
NO DAY BUT TODAY.

(Mimi and the support group exit. Roger and one person from the group—Steve—remain.
Various scenes play as the Company sings:)

ROGER:
I'M WRITING ONE GREAT SONG BEFORE I . . .

STEVE*:
WILL I LOSE MY DIGNITY
WILL SOMEONE CARE
WILL I WAKE TOMORROW
FROM THIS NIGHTMARE?

GROUP #1:
WILL I LOSE MY DIGNITY
WILL SOMEONE CARE
WILL I WAKE TOMORROW
FROM THIS NIGHTMARE?

GROUP #2:
WILL I LOSE MY DIGNITY
WILL SOMEONE CARE
WILL I WAKE TOMORROW
FROM THIS NIGHTMARE?

GROUP #3:
WILL I LOSE MY DIGNITY
WILL SOMEONE CARE
WILL I WAKE TOMORROW
FROM THIS NIGHTMARE?

GROUP #4:
WILL I LOSE MY DIGNITY
WILL SOMEONE CARE

WILL I WAKE TOMORROW
FROM THIS NIGHTMARE?

(Roger puts on his coat and exits the loft.
On the street.)

THREE HOMELESS PEOPLE:
CHRISTMAS BELLS ARE RINGING
CHRISTMAS BELLS ARE RINGING
CHRISTMAS BELLS ARE RINGING—
OUT OF TOWN
SANTA FE

SQUEEGEEMAN:
HONEST LIVING, MAN!

(He recoils as if he's almost been run over by a car. The audience hears a car screech.)

FELIZ NAVIDAD!

(Three Police Officers—in full riot gear—enter and approach a Homeless Woman sleeping in a blanket. First Officer pokes her with a nightstick.)

HOMELESS WOMAN:
EVENING, OFFICERS

(Without answering, the First Officer raises his nightstick again.)

MARK *(Pointing his camera)*:
SMILE FOR TED KOPPEL, OFFICER MARTIN!

(The First Officer lowers his stick.)

HOMELESS WOMAN:
AND A MERRY CHRISTMAS TO YOUR FAMILY

POLICE OFFICERS:
RIGHT!!

(The Police Officers exit. Mark films Homeless Woman.)

HOMELESS WOMAN *(To Mark)*:

WHO THE FUCK DO YOU THINK YOU ARE?
I DON'T NEED NO GODDAMN HELP
FROM SOME BLEEDING HEART CAMERAMAN
MY LIFE'S NOT FOR YOU TO
MAKE A NAME FOR YOURSELF ON!

ANGEL:

EASY SUGAR, EASY
HE WAS JUST TRYING TO—

HOMELESS WOMAN:

JUST TRYING TO USE ME TO KILL HIS GUILT
IT'S NOT THAT KIND OF MOVIE, HONEY
LET'S GO—THIS LOT IS FULL OF
MOTHERFUCKING ARTISTS
HEY ARTIST
GOTTA DOLLAR?
I THOUGHT NOT.

(She crosses to down left with another Homeless Person.)

ANGEL:

NEW YORK CITY—

MARK:

UH-HUH

ANGEL:

CENTER OF THE UNIVERSE

COLLINS:

SING IT, GIRL—

ANGEL:

TIMES ARE SHITTY
BUT I'M PRETTY SURE THEY CAN'T GET MUCH WORSE

MARK:

I HEAR YOU

ANGEL:

IT'S A COMFORT TO KNOW
WHEN YOU'RE SINGING THE HIT-THE-ROAD BLUES
THAT ANYWHERE ELSE YOU COULD POSSIBLY GO
AFTER NEW YORK'D BE A PLEASURE CRUISE

COLLINS:

Now you're talking
Well, I'm thwarted by a metaphysic puzzle
And I'm sick of grading papers—that I know
And I'm shouting in my sleep, I need a muzzle
All this misery pays no salary, so
Let's open up a restaurant
In Santa Fe
Oh sunny Santa Fe would be nice
We'll open up a restaurant in Santa Fe
And leave this to the roaches and mice

Oh—oh

ALL:

Oh—

ANGEL:

You teach?

COLLINS:

I teach—computer-age philosophy
But my students would rather watch TV

ANGEL:

America

ALL:

America!

COLLINS:

You're a sensitive aesthete
Brush the sauce onto the meat
You could make the menu sparkle with rhyme
You could drum a gentle drum
I could seat guests as they come
Chatting not about Heidegger, but wine!

COLLINS & THREE HOMELESS PEOPLE *(In shadows)*:

Let's open up a restaurant in Santa Fe

ALL *(Overlapping "Santa Fe")*:

Santa Fe

COLLINS & THREE HOMELESS PEOPLE *(In shadows)*:

Our labors would reap financial gains

ALL:

Gains, gains, gains

COLLINS:

We'll open up a restaurant in Santa Fe

ALL *(Overlapping "Santa Fe")*:

Santa Fe

COLLINS:

And save from devastation our brains

THREE HOMELESS PEOPLE:

Save our brains

COLLINS:

We'll pack up all our junk and fly so far away
Devote ourselves to projects that sell
We'll open up a restaurant in Santa Fe

ALL *(Overlapping "Santa Fe")*:

Santa Fe

COLLINS:

Forget this cold bohemian hell
Oh—

ALL:

Oh—

COLLINS:

Do you know the way to Santa Fe?
You know, tumbleweeds . . . prairie dogs . . .
Yeah.

MARK *(Spoken)*:

I'll see you at the show
I'll try and convince Roger to go.

(Mark exits.)

ANGEL:

Alone at last

COLLINS:

He'll be back—I guarantee

ANGEL:

I've been hearing violins all night

COLLINS:

Anything to do with me?
Are we a thing?

ANGEL:

Darling—we're everything

(Sings:)

Live in my house
I'll be your shelter
Just pay me back
With one thousand kisses
Be my lover and I'll cover you

COLLINS:

Open your door
I'll be your tenant
Don't got much baggage

To lay at your feet
But sweet kisses I've got to spare
I'll be there and I'll cover you

ANGEL & COLLINS:

I think they meant it
When they said you can't buy love
Now I know you can rent it
A new lease you are, my love
On life—be my life

(They do a short dance.)

Just slip me on
I'll be your blanket
Wherever—whatever—I'll be your coat

ANGEL:

You'll be my king
And I'll be your castle

COLLINS:

No you'll be my queen
And I'll be your moat

ANGEL & COLLINS:

I think they meant it
When they said you can't buy love

Now I know you can rent it
A new lease you are, my love
On life

All my life
I've longed to discover
Something as true as this is

COLLINS:
So with a thousand sweet kisses
I'll cover you

ANGEL *(Overlapping "So with a thousand . . .")*:
If you're cold and you're
Lonely

COLLINS:
With a thousand sweet kisses
I'll cover you

ANGEL *(Overlapping "I'll cover you")*:
You've got one nickel only
With a thousand sweet kisses
I'll cover you

COLLINS:
When you're worn out and tired

ANGEL:
With a thousand sweet kisses
I'll cover you

COLLINS:
When your heart has expired

ANGEL & COLLINS:
Oh lover I'll cover you
Oh lover I'll cover you.

(At the pay phone. Joanne sings:)

JOANNE *(On cell phone)*:
Steve—Joanne
The Murget case?
A dismissal!
Great work counselor

(The pay phone rings. She answers it.)

We're okay

Honeybear—wait!
I'm on the other phone

Yes I have the cowbell
We're okay

(Into cell phone:)

So tell them we'll sue
But a settlement will do
Sexual harassment—and civil rights too

Steve, you're great

(Into pay phone:)

No you cut the paper plate
Didja cheat on Mark a lot would you say?
We're okay
Honey, hold on . . .

(Into cell phone:)

Steve . . . hold on . . .

(She presses call waiting button on cellular phone.)

Hello?

Dad—yes
I beeped you
Maureen is coming to mother's hearing
We're okay

(Into pay phone:)

Honeybear—what?
Newt's lesbian sister
I'll tell them

(Into cell phone:)

You heard?

(Into pay phone:)

THEY HEARD
WE'RE OKAY

(Into cell phone:)

AND TO YOU DAD

(She presses call waiting as she sings into pay phone:)

YES—JILL IS THERE?

(Into cell phone:)

STEVE GOTTA—

(Into pay phone:)

JILL WITH THE SHORT BLACK HAIR?
THE CALVIN KLEIN MODEL?

(Into cell phone:)

STEVE GOTTA GO!

(Into pay phone:)

THE MODEL WHO LIVES IN PENTHOUSE A???
WE'RE
WE'RE OKAY

I'M ON MY WAY.

(Various locations. St. Mark's Place. The Company sings:)

FIVE HOMELESS PEOPLE:
CHRISTMAS BELLS ARE RINGING
CHRISTMAS BELLS ARE RINGING
CHRISTMAS BELLS ARE SINGING

ON TV—AT SAKS

SQUEEGEEMAN:

HONEST LIVING, HONEST LIVING
HONEST LIVING, HONEST LIVING
HONEST LIVING, HONEST LIVING

FIVE HOMELESS PEOPLE:

CAN'T YOU SPARE A DIME OR TWO
HERE BUT FOR THE GRACE OF GOD GO YOU
YOU'LL BE MERRY
I'LL BE MERRY
THOUGH MERRY AIN'T IN MY VOCABULARY

NO SLEIGH BELLS
NO SANTA CLAUS
NO YULE LOG
NO TINSEL
NO HOLLY
NO HEARTH
NO

SOLOIST:

"RUDOLPH THE RED-NOSED REINDEER"

FIVE HOMELESS PEOPLE:

"RUDOLPH THE RED-NOSED REINDEER"
NO ROOM AT THE HOLIDAY INN—OH NO

(A few flakes of snow descend.)

AND IT'S BEGINNING TO SNOW

(The bare stage explodes into life! St. Mark's Place on Christmas Eve—an open air bazaar of color, noise, movement.)

VENDORS:

HATS, BATS, SHOES, BOOZE
MOUNTAIN BIKES, POTPOURRI
LEATHER BAGS, GIRLIE MAGS
FORTY-FIVES, AZT

VENDOR #1:

NO ONE'S BUYING
FEEL LIKE CRYING

ALL:

No room at the Holiday Inn—oh no
And it's beginning to snow

(Lights up on one woman, showing off a collection of stolen coats to Collins and Angel.)

VENDOR #2:

How about a fur—
In perfect shape
Owned by an MBA from uptown

I got a tweed
Broken in by a greedy
Broker who went broke
And then broke down

COLLINS:

You don't have to do this

ANGEL:

Hush your mouth, it's Christmas

COLLINS:

I do not deserve you, Angel

Give—give
All you do
Is give

ANGEL *(Overlapping "Give—give")*:

Wait—what's on the floor?
Let's see some more

COLLINS:

Give me some way to show

ANGEL *(Overlapping "Give me some way . . .")*:

No—no—no . . . no.

COLLINS:

How you've touched me so

ANGEL:

Kiss me—it's beginning to snow

(Lights focus on Mark and Roger.)

MARK:

. . . She said, "Would you light my candle"
And she put on a pout
And she wanted you
To take her out tonight?

ROGER:

Right

MARK:

She got you out!

ROGER:

She was more than okay
But I pushed her away
It was bad—I got mad
And I had to get her out of my sight

MARK:

Wait, wait wait—you said she was sweet

ROGER:

Let's go eat—I'll just get fat
It's the one vice left—when you're dead meat

(Mimi enters looking for "the Man.")

There—that's her

MARK:

Maureen?

ROGER:

Mimi!

MARK:

Whoa!

ROGER:

I should go.

MARK & ROGER:

Hey—it's beginning to snow

(The Police Officers, in riot gear, enter.)

POLICE OFFICERS:

"I'm dreaming of a white—right—Christmas"

(The Police Officers exit.)

MIMI & JUNKIES:

FOLLOW THE MAN—FOLLOW THE MAN
WITH HIS POCKETS FULL OF THE JAM
FOLLOW THE MAN—FOLLOW THE MAN
HELP ME OUT, DADDY
IF YOU CAN

GOT ANY D, MAN?

THE MAN:

I'M COOL

MIMI & JUNKIES:

GOT ANY C, MAN?

THE MAN:

I'M COOL

MIMI & JUNKIES:

GOT ANY X?
ANY SMACK?
ANY HORSE?
ANY JUGIE BOOGIE, BOY?
ANY BLOW?

(Roger pulls Mimi aside.)

ROGER:

HEY

MIMI:

HEY

ROGER:

I JUST WANT TO SAY
I'M SORRY FOR THE WAY—

MIMI:

FORGET IT

ROGER:

I BLEW UP
CAN I MAKE IT UP TO YOU?

MIMI:

HOW?

ROGER:

DINNER PARTY?

MIMI:

THAT'LL DO

THE MAN:

HEY LOVER BOY—CUTIE PIE
YOU STEAL MY CLIENT—YOU DIE

ROGER:

YOU DIDN'T MISS ME—YOU WON'T MISS HER
YOU'LL NEVER LACK FOR CUSTOMERS

JUNKIES:

I'M WILLIN'
I'M ILLIN'
I GOTTA GET MY SICKNESS OFF

GOTTA RUN, GOTTA RIDE
GOTTA GUN, GOTTA HIDE—GOTTA GO

THE MAN:

AND IT'S BEGINNING TO SNOW

(Benny enters, talking on his cell phone.)

BENNY:

WE'RE OUT OF LUCK ALISON—
THE PROTEST IS ON

COAT VENDOR:

L.L. BEAN, GEOFFREY BEENE
BURBERRY ZIP-OUT LINING

JUNKIES *(Overlapping "L.L. Bean")*:

GOT ANY C, MAN?
GOT ANY D, MAN?
GOT ANY B, MAN?
GOT ANY CRACK?
GOT ANY X?

COAT VENDOR:

HONEST LIVING—

ROGER:

MARK, THIS IS MIMI—

MARK & MIMI:

HI

ROGER *(To Mark)*:

SHE'LL BE DINING—WITH US

COAT VENDOR:

HERE'S A NEW ARRIVAL

THE MAN:

THAT *IS* AN OUNCE

VENDORS:

HATS, DATS, BATS

COLLINS:

THAT'S MY COAT!

COAT VENDOR:

WE GIVE DISCOUNTS

MARK:

I THINK WE'VE MET

ANGEL:

LET'S GET A BETTER ONE

COLLINS:

IT'S A SHAM

MIMI:

THAT'S WHAT HE SAID

THE MAN:

I *SAID* IT'S A GRAM!

COLLINS:

BUT SHE'S A THIEF!

ANGEL:

BUT SHE BROUGHT US TOGETHER

BENNY:

WHICH INVESTOR IS COMING??

COLLINS:

I'LL TAKE THE LEATHER

BENNY:

YOUR FATHER?—DAMN!

HOMELESS PEOPLE & VENDORS *(Simultaneously with Police Officers and Junkies below)*:

CHRISTMAS BELLS ARE SWINGING
CHRISTMAS BELLS ARE RINGING
CHRISTMAS BELLS ARE SINGING
IN MY DREAMS—NEXT YEAR

(Benny and a Caroler join in.)

HOMELESS PEOPLE, VENDORS, BENNY & CAROLER *(Continuing with groups below)*:

ONCE YOU DONATE YOU CAN GO
CELEBRATE IN TUCKAHOE

You'll feel cherry
I'll feel cheery
Though I don't really know that theory
No bathrobe
No Steuben glass
No cappuccino makers
No pearls, no diamonds
No "chestnuts roasting on an open fire"
"Chestnuts roasting on an open fire"

No room at the Holiday Inn—oh no

POLICE OFFICERS *(Simultaneously with above and below)*:

I'm dreaming of a right Christmas
Just like the ones I used to know
Jingle bells—prison cells
Jingle bells—prison cells

Fa la la la—fa la la la
You have the right to remain
Silent night holy night

Fall on your knees oh night divine
You'll do some time
Fa la la la la
Fa la la la la

JUNKIES *(Simultaneously with groups above)*:

Got any C, man?
Got any D, man?
Got any B, man?
Got any X?—crack?

I'm willin'—I'm illin'
Gotta get my sickness off
C-D help me
Follow the man—follow the man
Follow the man
Jugie boogie—jugie boogie

Follow the man—follow the man
Any crack any X any jugie boogie, boy

ANY BLOW ANY X ANY JUGIE BOOGIE, BOY
GOT ANY D, MAN, GOT ANY C, MAN
GOT ANY CRACK—ANY X—ANY JUGIE BOOGIE?

COAT VENDOR:
TWENTY-FIVE

ANGEL:
FIFTEEN

COAT VENDOR:
TWENTY-FIVE

ANGEL:
FIFTEEN

COAT VENDOR:
TWENTY-FIVE

ANGEL:
FIFTEEN

COAT VENDOR:
NO WAY
TWENTY-FOUR

ANGEL:
FIFTEEN

COAT VENDOR:
TWENTY-FOUR

ANGEL:
FIFTEEN

COAT VENDOR:
TWENTY-FOUR

ANGEL:
FIFTEEN

COAT VENDOR:
NOT TODAY
TWENTY-THREE

ANGEL:
FIFTEEN

COAT VENDOR:
TWENTY-THREE

ANGEL:
FIFTEEN

COAT VENDOR:
TWENTY-THREE

ANGEL:

FIFTEEN
IT'S OLD

COAT VENDOR:

TWENTY-TWO

ANGEL:

FIFTEEN

COAT VENDOR:

TWENTY-ONE

ANGEL:

FIFTEEN

COAT VENDOR:

SEVENTEEN

ANGEL:

FIFTEEN

COAT VENDOR:

FIFTEEN

ANGEL & COAT VENDOR:

SOLD!

MARK & ROGER:

LET'S
GO
TO
THE LOT—MAUREEN'S PERFORMING

MIMI:

WHO'S MAUREEN?

ROGER:

HIS EX

MARK:

BUT I AM OVER HER

ROGER:

LET'S
NOT
HOLD HANDS YET

MIMI:

IS THAT A WARNING?

MARK, ROGER & MIMI:

HE/YOU/I
JUST
NEED(S)

To take it slow
I should tell you I should tell you
I should tell you I should tell you
I should tell you I . . .

ALL:

And it's beginning to
And it's beginning to
And it's beginning to—

(Blackout. We see a headlight come through the up center door. When it reaches downstage, the lights come up. Maureen is there.)

MAUREEN: Joanne, which way to the stage!

ALL:

Snow!!!

*(Blackout.
The lot.)*

MARK: Maureen's performance.

(Maureen is in front of a microphone. She performs "Over the Moon":)

MAUREEN: Last night I had a dream. I found myself in a desert called Cyberland. It was hot. My canteen had sprung a leak and I was thirsty. Out of the abyss walked a cow—Elsie. I asked if she had anything to drink. "I'm forbidden to produce milk," she said. "In Cyberland, we only drink Diet Coke."

(Reverb: "Coke, Coke, Coke . . .")

She said, "Only thing to do is jump over the moon. They've closed everything real down . . . like barns, troughs and performance spaces . . . and replaced it all with lies and rules and virtual life."

(Reverb: "life, life, life . . .")

"But there is a way out."

BACKUPS:

Leap of faith, leap of faith
Leap of faith, leap of faith

MAUREEN: "Only thing to do is jump over the moon. I gotta get out of here! It's like I'm being tied to the hood of a yellow rental truck, packed in with fertilizer and fuel oil, pushed over a cliff by a suicidal Mickey Mouse!—I've gotta gotta gotta gotta gotta gotta gotta gotta gotta gotta find a way . . ." *(Simultaneously with Backups:)*

> "TO JUMP OVER THE MOON
> ONLY THING TO DO IS
> JUMP OVER THE MOON"

BACKUPS *(Simultaneously with Maureen)*:

> LEAP OF FAITH . . . *(Etc.)*

MAUREEN: Then a little bulldog entered. His name (we have learned) was Benny. And although he once had principles, he abandoned them to live as a lap dog to a wealthy daughter of the revolution. One, two, three. "That's bull," Benny said. "Ever since the cat took up the fiddle, that cow's been jumpy. And the dish and spoon were evicted from the table—and eloped . . . She's had trouble with her milk and that moon ever since. Maybe it's a female thing. 'Cause who'd want to leave Cyberland anyway? . . . Walls ain't so bad. The dish and spoon for instance. They were down on their luck—knocked on my doghouse door. I said, 'Not in my backyard, utensils! Go back to China!'" "The only way out—is up," Elsie whispered to me. "A leap of faith. Still thirsty?" "Parched." "Have some milk." "I lowered myself beneath her swollen udder and sucked the sweetest milk I'd ever tasted."

(Maureen makes a slurping, sucking sound.)

"Climb on board," she said. And as a harvest moon rose over Cyberland, we reared back and sprang into a gallop. Leaping out of orbit!!! I awoke singing:

BACKUPS:

> LEAP OF FAITH
> LEAP OF FAITH

MAUREEN:

> ONLY THING TO DO
> ONLY THING TO DO IS JUMP
> ONLY THING TO DO IS JUMP OVER THE MOON
> ONLY THING TO DO IS JUMP OVER THE MOON

OVER THE MOON—OVER THE
MOOOOOOOO
MOOOOOOOO
MOOOOOOOO
MOO WITH ME.

(She encourages the audience to moo with her. She says, "C'mon, sir, moo with me," etc. They do. When the "moos" reach a crescendo, she cuts them off with a big sweep of her arms.)

Thank you.

(Blackout.

Life Café. Down right, the principals are lined up waiting to be seated. Down center is a large table. Down and to the right is a smaller table occupied by Benny and Mr. Grey. The Restaurant Man tries to shoo the friends out.

The Company sings:)

RESTAURANT MAN:
NO PLEASE NO
NOT TONIGHT PLEASE NO
MISTER—CAN'T YOU GO—
NOT TONIGHT—CAN'T HAVE A SCENE

ROGER:
WHAT?

RESTAURANT MAN:
GO, PLEASE GO
YOU—HELLO, SIR—
I SAID NO
IMPORTANT CUSTOMER

MARK:
WHAT AM I—JUST A BLUR?

RESTAURANT MAN:
YOU SIT ALL NIGHT—YOU NEVER BUY!

MARK:
THAT'S A LIE—THAT'S A LIE
I HAD A TEA THE OTHER DAY

RESTAURANT MAN:
YOU COULDN'T PAY.

MARK:

Oh yeah

COLLINS:

Benjamin Coffin III—here?

RESTAURANT MAN:

Oh no!

ALL:

Wine and beer!

MAUREEN:

The enemy of Avenue A
We'll stay

(They sit.)

RESTAURANT MAN:

Oy vey!

COLLINS:

What brings the mogul in his own mind to the Life Café?

BENNY:

I would like to propose a toast
To Maureen's noble try
It went well

MAUREEN:

Go to hell

BENNY:

Was the yuppie scum stomped
Not counting the homeless
How many tickets weren't comped

ROGER:

Why *did* Muffy—

BENNY:

Alison

ROGER:

Miss the show?

BENNY:

There was a death in the family
If you must know

ANGEL:

Who died?

BENNY:

Our Akita

(Beat.)

BENNY, MARK, ANGEL & COLLINS:

Evita

BENNY:

Mimi—I'm surprised
A bright and charming girl like you
Hangs out with these slackers
Who don't adhere to deals

They make fun—yet I'm the one
Attempting to do some good
Or do you really want a neighborhood
Where people piss on your stoop every night?

Bohemia, bohemia's
A fallacy in your head
This is Calcutta
Bohemia's dead

(The bohemians immediately enact a mock funeral—Mark delivering a "eulogy.")

MARK:

Dearly beloved we gather here to say our good-byes

COLLINS & ROGER:

Dies irae—dies illa
Kyrie eleison
Yitgadal V'yitkadesh *(Etc.)*

MARK:

Here she lies
No one knew her worth
The late great daughter of mother earth
On this night when we celebrate the birth
In that little town of Bethlehem
We raise our glass—you bet your ass to—

(Maureen shows hers.)

La vie bohème

ALL:

La vie bohème
La vie bohème
La vie bohème
La vie bohème

(All continue singing on alternate lines:)

MARK:

To days of inspiration,
Playing hooky, making
Something
Out of nothing, the need
To express—
To communicate
To going against the grain
Going insane
Going mad

To loving tension, no pension
To more than one dimension
To starving for attention
Hating convention, hating
Pretension
Not to mention of course

Hating dear old mom and dad
To riding your bike
Midday past the three-
Piece suits—
To fruits—to no absolutes—
To Absolut—to choice—
To the *Village Voice*—
To any passing fad

ALL:

Oooooh . . .

MARK *(Overlapping "Oooooh"):*

To being an us—for once—
Instead of a them—

ALL:

La vie bohème
La vie bohème . . .

(Joanne enters.)

MAUREEN:

Is the equipment in a pyramid?

JOANNE:

It is, Maureen

MAUREEN:

The mixer doesn't have a case
Don't give me that face

(She smacks Joanne's ass as she exits. Mr. Grey reacts.)

MR. GREY:

Ahhemm!

MAUREEN:

Hey mister—she's my sister

RESTAURANT MAN:

So that's five miso soup, four seaweed salad
Three soy burger dinner, two tofu dog platter
And one pasta with meatless balls

A BOY:

Ugh

COLLINS:

It tastes the same

MIMI:

If you close your eyes

RESTAURANT MAN:

And thirteen orders of fries
Is that it here?

ALL:

Wine and beer!

MIMI & ANGEL:

To hand-crafted beers made in local breweries
To yoga, to yogurt, to rice and beans and cheese

To leather, to dildos, to curry vindaloo
To huevos rancheros and Maya Angelou

MAUREEN & COLLINS:

Emotions, devotion, to causing a commotion
Creation, vacation

MARK:

Mucho masturbation

MAUREEN & COLLINS:

Compassion, to fashion, to passion when it's new

COLLINS:

To Sontag

ANGEL:

To Sondheim

FOUR PEOPLE:

To anything taboo

COLLINS & ROGER:

Ginsberg, Dylan, Cunningham and Cage
Lenny Bruce, Langston Hughes

MAUREEN:

To the stage

SOLOIST #1:

To Uta

SOLOIST #2:

To Buddha

FOUR PEOPLE:

Pablo Neruda, too

MARK & MIMI:

Why Dorothy and Toto went over the rainbow
To blow off Auntie Em—la vie bohème

(Joanne returns.)

MAUREEN:

And wipe the speakers off before you pack

JOANNE:

Yes, Maureen

MAUREEN:

Well—hurry back

(Maureen and Joanne kiss. Joanne exits.)

MR. GREY:

Sisters?

MAUREEN:

We're close

(Angel jumps on top of Collins, who's on the table. They kiss.)

ANGEL, COLLINS, MAUREEN & MR. GREY:

Brothers!

ALL:

Bisexuals, trisexuals, homo sapiens,
Carcinogens, hallucinogens, men, Pee Wee Herman
German wine, turpentine, Gertrude Stein
Antonioni, Bertolucci, Kurosawa
Carmina Burana
To apathy, to entropy, to empathy, ecstasy
Vaclav Havel—the Sex Pistols, 8BC,
To no shame—never playing the fame game

COLLINS:

To marijuana

ALL:

To sodomy
It's between God and me
To S&M

(Mr. Grey walks out.)

BENNY:

Waiter . . . waiter . . . waiter

ALL:

La vie bohème

COLLINS: In honor of the death of bohemia an impromptu salon will commence immediately following dinner . . . Mimi Marquez, clad only in bubble wrap, will perform her famous lawn chair, handcuff dance to the sounds of iced tea being stirred.

ROGER: And Mark Cohen will preview his new documentary about his inability to hold an erection on the High Holy Days.

(Roger picks up an electric guitar and starts to tune it.)

MARK: And Maureen Johnson, back from her spectacular one-night engagement at the 11th Street lot, will sing Native American tribal chants backwards through her vocoder, while accompanying herself on the electric cello—which she has never studied.

(At this point, Joanne reenters to see Maureen kiss Mark. Joanne exits. Benny pulls Mimi aside.)

BENNY:

YOUR NEW BOYFRIEND DOESN'T KNOW ABOUT US?

MIMI:

THERE'S NOTHING TO KNOW

BENNY:

DON'T YOU THINK THAT WE SHOULD DISCUSS—

MIMI:

IT WAS THREE MONTHS AGO

BENNY:

HE DOESN'T ACT LIKE HE'S WITH YOU

MIMI:

WE'RE TAKING IT SLOW

BENNY:

WHERE IS HE NOW?

MIMI:

HE'S RIGHT—HMM

BENNY:

UH-HUH

MIMI:

WHERE'D HE GO?

MARK: Roger will attempt to write a bittersweet, evocative song.

(Roger starts to play "Musetta's Theme.")

That doesn't remind us of "Musetta's Waltz."

COLLINS: Angel Dumott Schunard will model the latest fall fashions from Paris while accompanying herself on the ten-gallon plastic pickle tub.

ANGEL: And Collins will recount his exploits as an anarchist—including the tale of his successful reprogramming of the MIT virtual reality equipment to self-destruct, as it broadcast the words:

ALL: "Actual reality—ACT UP—Fight AIDS!"

BENNY: Check!!

(Benny exits. Lights on Mimi and Roger.)

MIMI:

EXCUSE ME—DID I DO SOMETHING WRONG?
I GET INVITED—THEN IGNORED—ALL NIGHT LONG

ROGER:

I'VE BEEN TRYING—I'M NOT LYING
NO ONE'S PERFECT. I'VE GOT BAGGAGE

MIMI:

LIFE'S TOO SHORT—BABE—TIME IS FLYING
I'M LOOKING FOR BAGGAGE THAT GOES WITH MINE

ROGER:

I SHOULD TELL YOU—

MIMI:

I'VE GOT BAGGAGE, TOO

ROGER:

I SHOULD TELL YOU—

ROGER & MIMI:

BAGGAGE—WINE—

OTHERS:

AND BEER!

(Several beepers go off. Each person turns off their own.)

MIMI:

AZT BREAK

(Mimi, Angel, waiter, techno girl and Collins take pills.)

ROGER:

YOU?

MIMI:

ME. YOU?

ROGER:

MIMI . . .

(Sings:)

I should tell you I'm a disaster
I forget how to begin it

MIMI *(Sings)*:
Let's just make this part go faster
I have yet—to be in it
I should tell you

ROGER:
I should tell you

MIMI:
I should tell you

ROGER:
I should tell you

MIMI:
I should tell I blew the candle out
Just to get back in

ROGER:
I'd forgotten how to smile
Until your candle burned my skin

MIMI:
I should tell you

ROGER:
I should tell you

MIMI:
I should tell you

ROGER & MIMI:
I should tell

Well, here we go
Now we—

MIMI:
Oh no

ROGER:
I know—this something is
Here goes—

MIMI:
Here goes

ROGER:
Guess so
It's starting to—
Who knows—

MIMI:

Who knows

ROGER & MIMI:

Who knows where
Who goes there
Who knows
Here goes

Trusting desire—starting to learn
Walking through fire without a burn
Clinging—a shoulder, a leap begins
Stinging and older, asleep on pins

So here we go
Now we—

ROGER:

Oh no

MIMI:

I know

ROGER:

Oh no

ROGER & MIMI:

Who knows where—who goes there

Here goes—here goes
Here goes—here goes
Here goes—here goes.

(Roger and Mimi exit. Joanne reenters, obviously steamed. Maureen and Joanne sing:)

MAUREEN:

Are we packed?

JOANNE:

Yes and by next week
I want you to be

MAUREEN:

Pookie?

JOANNE:

And you should see
They've padlocked your building

AND THEY'RE RIOTING ON AVENUE B
BENNY CALLED THE COPS

MAUREEN:

THAT FUCK

JOANNE:

THEY DON'T KNOW WHAT THEY'RE DOING
THE COPS ARE SWEEPING THE LOT
BUT NO ONE'S LEAVING
THEY'RE SITTING THERE, MOOING!

ALL:

YEAH!!!

(Pandemonium in the restaurant.)

TO DANCE!

A GIRL:

NO WAY TO MAKE A LIVING, MASOCHISM, PAIN, PERFECTION
MUSCLE SPASM, CHIROPRACTORS, SHORT CAREERS, EATING
DISORDERS

ALL:

FILM

MARK:

ADVENTURE, TEDIUM, NO FAMILY, BORING LOCATIONS
DARK ROOMS, PERFECT FACES, EGOS, MONEY, HOLLYWOOD AND
SLEAZE

ALL:

MUSIC

ANGEL:

FOOD OF LOVE, EMOTION, MATHEMATICS, ISOLATION, RHYTHM,
POWER, FEELING, HARMONY, AND
HEAVY COMPETITION

ALL:

ANARCHY

COLLINS & MAUREEN:

REVOLUTION, JUSTICE, SCREAMING FOR SOLUTIONS
FORCING CHANGES, RISK, AND DANGER, MAKING NOISE AND
MAKING PLEAS

ALL:

TO FAGGOTS, LEZZIES, DYKES, CROSS-DRESSERS TOO

MAUREEN:

TO ME

MARK:

To me

COLLINS & ANGEL:

To me

ALL:

To you, and you and you, you and you
To people living with, living with, living with
Not dying from disease

Let he among us without sin
Be the first to condemn

La vie bohème
La vie bohème
La vie bohème . . .

MARK *(Simultaneously with the Company below)*:

Anyone out of the mainstream
Is anyone *in* the mainstream?
Anyone alive—with a sex drive

ALL *(Simultaneously with Mark)*:

La vie bohème
La vie bohème
La vie bohème . . .

MARK:

Tear down the wall
Aren't we all
The opposite of war isn't peace . . .
It's creation

ALL:

La vie bohème . . .

MARK: The riot continues. The Christmas tree goes up in flames. The snow dances. Oblivious, Mimi and Roger share a small, lovely kiss.

ALL: Viva la vie bohème!

ACT II

The Company enters from all directions again and forms a line across the apron of the stage. They sing:

THE COMPANY:

FIVE HUNDRED TWENTY-FIVE THOUSAND
SIX HUNDRED MINUTES
FIVE HUNDRED TWENTY-FIVE THOUSAND
MOMENTS SO DEAR
FIVE HUNDRED TWENTY-FIVE THOUSAND
SIX HUNDRED MINUTES
HOW DO YOU MEASURE—MEASURE A YEAR?

IN DAYLIGHTS—IN SUNSETS
IN MIDNIGHTS—IN CUPS OF COFFEE
IN INCHES—IN MILES
IN LAUGHTER—IN STRIFE

IN—FIVE HUNDRED TWENTY-FIVE THOUSAND
SIX HUNDRED MINUTES
HOW DO YOU MEASURE
A YEAR IN THE LIFE?

HOW ABOUT LOVE?
HOW ABOUT LOVE?
HOW ABOUT LOVE?
MEASURE IN LOVE

SEASONS OF LOVE
SEASONS OF LOVE

SOLOIST #1:

Five hundred twenty-five thousand
Six hundred minutes
Five hundred twenty-five thousand
Journeys to plan

Five hundred twenty-five thousand
Six hundred minutes
How do you measure the life
Of a woman or a man?

SOLOIST #2:

In truths that she learned
Or in times that he cried
In bridges he burned
Or the way that she died

ALL:

It's time now—to sing out
Though the story never ends
Let's celebrate
Remember a year in the life of friends

Remember the love

	SOLOIST #1:
Remember the love	You got to, you got to
Remember the love	Remember the gifts from
Measure in love	Up above.

SOLOIST #1:

Measure, measure your life in lo . . .

	SOLOIST #2:
Seasons of love	Lo . . .
Seasons of love . . .	. . . ve . . .

(New Year's Eve. The street. One table is on its end and serves as the "door.")

MARK *(Carrying mock door)*: Pan to the padlocked door. New Year's rocking eve. The breaking-back-into-the-building party . . .

(Roger and Mimi try in vain to pry off a "padlock" from the "door." They're happy. They sing:)

MIMI:

How long 'til next year?

ROGER:

Three and a half minutes . . .

MIMI:

I'm giving up my vices
I'm going back—back to school
Eviction or not
This week's been so hot
That long as I've got you
I know I'll be cool

I couldn't crack the love code, dear
'Til you made the lock on my heart explode
It's gonna be a happy new year
A happy new year

(Mark enters the scene.)

MARK:

Coast is clear
You're supposed to be working
That's for midnight
Where are they?
There isn't much time

MIMI:

Maybe they're dressing
I mean what does one wear that's apropos
For a party—that's also a crime?

(Maureen enters, wearing a skintight "cat burglar" suit, and holding a bag of potato chips.)

MAUREEN:

Chips, anyone?

MARK:

You can take the girl out of Hicksville
But you can't take the Hicksville out of the girl

MAUREEN:

My riot got you on TV
I deserve a royalty

MIMI:

Be nice you two
Or no god-awful champagne

MAUREEN:

Don't mind if I do
No luck?

ROGER:

Bolted plywood, padlocked with a chain
A total dead end

MAUREEN *(Takes out a cell phone and dials)*:

Just like my ex-girlfriend

(On cell phone:)

Honey? . . .
I know you're there . . .
Please pick up the phone
Are you okay?

It's not funny
It's not fair
How can I atone?
Are you okay?

I lose control
But I can learn to behave
Give me one more chance
Let me be your slave

I'll kiss your Doc Martens
Let me kiss your Doc Martens
Your every wish I will obey

(Joanne enters.)

JOANNE:

That might be okay
Down girl
Heel . . . stay

I did a bit of research
With my friends at Legal Aid
Technically, you're squatters
There's hope
But just in case

(She whips out . . .)

MARK & JOANNE:
Rope?
MARK *(Pointing off)*:
We can hoist a line—
JOANNE:
To the fire escape—
MARK:
And tie off at
MARK & JOANNE:
That bench!
MAUREEN:
I can't take them as chums
JOANNE:
Start hoisting . . . wench

(Mark, Joanne and Maureen exit. Roger and Mimi laugh in each other's arms.)

ROGER:
I think I should be laughing
Yet I forget
Forget how to begin

I'm feeling something inside
And yet I still can't decide
If I should hide
Or make a wide open grin

Last week I wanted just to disappear
My life was dust
But now it just may be a happy new year
A happy new year

(Collins and Angel enter. Collins, in full black, carries a bottle of champagne. Angel is in a blond wig, plastic shower-curtain dress and calf-high, pink, high-heeled boots.)

COLLINS:

BOND—JAMES BOND

ANGEL:

AND PUSSY GALORE—IN PERSON

MIMI:

PUSSY—YOU CAME PREPARED

ANGEL:

I WAS A BOY SCOUT ONCE
AND A BROWNIE
'TIL SOME BRAT GOT SCARED

COLLINS *(To Mimi)*:

AHA! MONEYPENNY—MY MARTINI!

MIMI:

WILL BAD CHAMPAGNE DO?

ROGER:

THAT'S SHAKEN—NOT STIRRED

COLLINS:

PUSSY—THE BOLTS

(Collins takes a swig as Angel retrieves a small blowtorch.)

ANGEL:

JUST SAY THE WORD!

(Angel turns on the torch. Lights go to black.)

MIMI:

TWO MINUTES LEFT TO EXECUTE OUR PLAN

COLLINS:

WHERE'S EVERYONE ELSE?

ROGER:

PLAYING SPIDERMAN

(Mark, Joanne and Maureen appear upstage center.)

MARK:

IRONIC CLOSE UP: TIGHT

(Angel turns off the torch.
Light up on Mark's Mom, holding up a phone.)

On the phone machine's red light
Once the boho boys are gone
The power mysteriously comes on *(Beep)*

MARK'S MOM *(On chair)*:
Mark, it's the Wicked Witch of the West
Your mother
Happy New Year from Scarsdale
We're all impressed that the riot footage
Made the *Nightly News*
Even your father says *Mazel Tov*
Honey—call him
Love, Mom *(Beep)*

(Mark's Mom, stepping off chair, passes the phone to Alexi Darling.)

ALEXI DARLING *(On chair)*:
Mark Cohen
Alexi Darling from *Buzzline*

MARK: Oh, that show's so sleazy.

ALEXI DARLING:
Your footage of the riots A-one
Feature segment—network—deal time
I'm sending you a contract
Ker-ching—ker-ching
Marky give us a call
970-4301
Or at home try 863-6754
Or—my cell phone at 919-763-0090
Or—you can e-mail me
At darling alexi newscom dot net
Or—you can page me at—

(Beeeep!)

MAUREEN:
I think we need an agent!

MARK:

We?

JOANNE:

That's selling out

MARK:

But it's nice to dream

MAUREEN:

Yeah—it's network TV
And it's all thanks to me

MARK:

Somehow I think I smell
The whiff of a scheme

JOANNE:

Me, too

MAUREEN:

We can plan another protest

JOANNE:

We?!

MAUREEN:

This time you can shoot from the start . . .

(To Mark:)

You'll direct

(To front:)

Starring me!

(Lights shift back to downstairs.)

MIMI:

5,4,3 . . .

ANGEL:

Open sesame!!

(The door falls away, revealing Mark, Joanne and Maureen.)

ALL:

Happy New Year

HAPPY NEW YEAR
HAPPY NEW . . . .

(Benny enters.)

BENNY:
I SEE THAT YOU'VE BEATEN ME TO THE PUNCH
ROGER:
HOW DID YOU KNOW WE'D BE HERE?
BENNY:
I HAD A HUNCH
MARK:
YOU'RE NOT MAD?
BENNY:
I'M HERE TO END THIS WAR
IT'S A SHAME YOU WENT AND DESTROYED THE DOOR
MIMI:
WHY ALL THE SUDDEN THE BIG ABOUT-FACE?
BENNY:
THE CREDIT IS YOURS
YOU MADE A GOOD CASE
ROGER:
WHAT CASE?
BENNY:
MIMI CAME TO SEE ME
AND SHE HAD MUCH TO SAY
MIMI:
THAT'S NOT HOW YOU PUT IT AT ALL YESTERDAY
BENNY:
I COULDN'T STOP THINKING ABOUT THE WHOLE MESS
MARK—YOU MIGHT WANT THIS ON FILM

(Mark picks up his camera.)

MARK:
I GUESS
BENNY *(Formally)*:
I REGRET THE
UNLUCKY CIRCUMSTANCES
OF THE PAST SEVEN DAYS

ROGER:

Circumstances?
You padlocked our door

BENNY:

And it's with great pleasure
On behalf of Cyberarts
That I hand you this key

(He hands Roger the key.)

ANGEL:

Golf claps

(They oblige.)

MARK:

I had no juice in my battery

BENNY:

Reshoot

ROGER *(Returns key to Benny)*:

I see—this is a photo opportunity

MAUREEN:

The benevolent god
Ushers the poor artists back to their flat
Were you planning on taking down the barbed wire
From the lot, too?

ROGER:

Anything but that!

BENNY:

Clearing the lot was a safety concern
We break ground this month
But you can return

MAUREEN:

That's why you're here with people you hate
Instead of with Muffy at Muffy's estate

BENNY:

I'd honestly rather be with you tonight
Than in Westport—

ROGER:

Spare us, old sport, the sound bite

BENNY:

Mimi—since your ways are so seductive

MIMI:

You came on to me!

BENNY:

Persuade him not to be so counterproductive

ROGER:

Liar!

BENNY:

Why not tell them what you wore to my place?

MIMI:

I was on my way to work

BENNY:

Black leather and lace!
My desk was a mess
(I think I'm) still sore

MIMI:

'Cause I kicked him and told him I wasn't his whore!

BENNY:

Does your boyfriend know
Who your last boyfriend was?

ROGER:

I'm not her boyfriend
I don't care what she does

ANGEL:

People! Is this any way to start a new year?
Have compassion
Benny just lost his cat

BENNY:

My dog—but I appreciate that

ANGEL:

My cat had a fall
And I went through hell

BENNY:

It's like losing a—
How did you know that she fell?

(Collins hands Benny a glass of champagne.)

COLLINS:

Champagne?

BENNY:

Don't mind if I do

To dogs

ALL BUT BENNY:

No Benny—to you!

ANGEL:

Let's make a resolution

MIMI:

I'll drink to that

COLLINS:

Let's always stay friends

JOANNE:

Though we may have our disputes

MAUREEN:

This family tree's got deep roots

MARK:

Friendship is thicker than blood

ROGER:

That depends

MIMI:

Depends on trust

ROGER:

Depends on true devotion

JOANNE:

Depends on love

MARK *(To Roger)*:

Depends on not denying emotion

ROGER:

Perhaps

ALL:

It's gonna be a happy new year

ROGER:

I guess

ALL:

It's gonna be a happy new year

ROGER:

You're right

(Angel brings Roger to Mimi. Angel and the others move away from them.)

ANGEL:

It's gonna be a happy new year

ROGER & MIMI:

I'm sorry

ROGER:

Coming?

MIMI:

In a minute—I'm fine—go

(He kisses her and exits. The Man appears.)

THE MAN:

Well, well, well. What have we here?

(He moves to Mimi.)

It's gonna be a happy new year
There, there . . . *(Etc.)*

(Fade out.
Light up on Mark.)

MARK: Valentine's Day . . . Pan across the empty lot. Roger's down at Mimi's where he's been for almost two months now, although he keeps talking about selling his guitar and heading out of town. Still jealous of Benny . . . God knows where Collins and Angel are . . . Could be that new shantytown near the river or a suite at the Plaza . . . Maureen and Joanne are rehearsing.

(Joanne's loft.)

JOANNE:

I said—once more *from the top*!!!

MAUREEN:

I said no!!!

MARK: That is if they're speaking this week . . . Me? I'm here. Nowhere.

(Lights remain on Maureen and Joanne.)

JOANNE: The line is, "Cyberarts and its corporate sponsor, Grey Communications, wish to mitigate the Christmas Eve Riots . . ." What is so difficult . . .

MAUREEN: It just doesn't roll off my tongue. I like my version.

JOANNE: You—dressed as a groundhog—to protest the ground-breaking . . .

MAUREEN: It's a metaphor!

JOANNE: It's . . . less than brilliant.

MAUREEN: That's it, Miss Ivy League!

JOANNE: What?

MAUREEN: Ever since New Year's I haven't said boo. I let *you* direct. I didn't pierce my nipples because it grossed *you* out. I didn't stay and dance at the Clit Club that night, 'cause *you* wanted to go home . . .

JOANNE: You were flirting with the woman in rubber.

MAUREEN: *That's* what this is about?? There will *always* be women in rubber—FLIRTING WITH ME!! Give me a break.

(She sings:)

EVERY SINGLE DAY
I WALK DOWN THE STREET
I HEAR PEOPLE SAY:
"BABY'S SO SWEET"

EVER SINCE PUBERTY
EVERYBODY STARES AT ME
BOYS—GIRLS
I CAN'T HELP IT BABY

SO BE KIND
AND DON'T LOSE YOUR MIND
JUST REMEMBER THAT I'M YOUR BABY

TAKE ME FOR WHAT I AM
WHO I WAS MEANT TO BE
AND IF YOU GIVE A DAMN
TAKE ME BABY OR LEAVE ME
TAKE ME BABY OR LEAVE ME

A TIGER IN A CAGE
CAN NEVER SEE THE SUN

This diva needs her stage
Baby—let's have fun!

You are the one I choose
Folks'd kill to fill your shoes
You love the limelight, too, now baby

So be mine or don't waste my time
Cryin': "Honeybear—are you still my baby?"

Take me for what I am
Who I was meant to be
And if you give a damn
Take me baby or leave me

No way—can I be what I'm not
But hey—don't you want your girl hot!
Don't fight—don't lose your head
'Cause every night—who's in your bed? Who?
Who's in your bed?

(She pouts in Joanne's direction.)

Kiss, pookie.

JOANNE: It won't work.
I look before I leap
I love margins and discipline
I make lists in my sleep
Baby what's my sin?

Never quit—I follow through
I hate mess—but I love you
What to do
With my impromptu baby

So be wise
'Cause this girl satisfies
You've got a prize who don't compromise
You're one lucky baby
Take me for what I am

MAUREEN:

A CONTROL FREAK

JOANNE:

WHO I WAS MEANT TO BE

MAUREEN:

A SNOB—YET OVER ATTENTIVE

JOANNE:

AND IF YOU GIVE A DAMN

MAUREEN:

A LOVABLE, DROLL GEEK

JOANNE:

TAKE ME BABY OR LEAVE ME

MAUREEN:

AND ANAL RETENTIVE!

MAUREEN & JOANNE:

THAT'S IT!

JOANNE:

THE STRAW THAT BREAKS MY BACK

MAUREEN & JOANNE:

I QUIT

JOANNE:

UNLESS YOU TAKE IT BACK

MAUREEN & JOANNE:

WOMEN

MAUREEN:

WHAT IS IT ABOUT THEM?

MAUREEN & JOANNE:

CAN'T LIVE
WITH THEM—
OR WITHOUT THEM!

TAKE ME FOR WHAT I AM
WHO I WAS MEANT TO BE
AND IF YOU GIVE A DAMN
THEN YOU'LL TAKE ME BABY OR LEAVE ME
TAKE ME BABY
OR LEAVE ME

GUESS I'M LEAVIN'
I'M GONE!

(They both sit. The Company sings:)

COMPANY:

IN DIAPERS—REPORT CARDS
IN SPOKED WHEELS—IN SPEEDING TICKETS
IN CONTRACTS—DOLLARS
IN FUNERALS—IN BIRTHS

IN—FIVE HUNDRED TWENTY-FIVE THOUSAND
SIX HUNDRED MINUTES
HOW DO YOU FIGURE
A LAST YEAR ON EARTH?

FIGURE IN LOVE
FIGURE IN LOVE
FIGURE IN LOVE
MEASURE IN LOVE
SEASONS OF LOVE
SEASONS OF LOVE.

(Mimi's apartment. Beds are seen downstage. One is a hospital bed, occupied by Angel. Roger sits on another. Joanne is on another. Mimi approaches Roger, in a hurry.)

ROGER: Where *were* you?
MIMI: I'm sorry, I'm late . . .
ROGER *(Interrupting)*: I know. You lost your keys. No, you went for a walk; you had to help your mother. *(As he picks up the guitar)* How's Benny? I'm working upstairs tonight.
MIMI: Wait . . .

I SHOULD TELL YOU
I SHOULD . . .

Never mind . . .

ROGER:

HAPPY SPRING.

(He exits. She reveals a just-purchased stash bag and angrily flings it across the room.

As Mimi sings, a stylized "musical beds" is choreographed around her. During the bridge of the song, Collins carries Angel from the hospital bed and Roger takes his place. By the end of the song, Joanne and Maureen are reunited, as are Roger and Mimi. Collins and Angel lie down together.)

MIMI:

WITHOUT YOU
THE GROUND THAWS
THE RAIN FALLS
THE GRASS GROWS

WITHOUT YOU
THE SEEDS ROOT
THE FLOWERS BLOOM
THE CHILDREN PLAY

THE STARS GLEAM
THE POETS DREAM
THE EAGLES FLY
WITHOUT YOU

THE EARTH TURNS
THE SUN BURNS
BUT I DIE
WITHOUT YOU

WITHOUT YOU
THE BREEZE WARMS
THE GIRL SMILES
THE CLOUD MOVES

WITHOUT YOU
THE TIDES CHANGE
THE BOYS RUN
THE OCEANS CRASH

THE CROWDS ROAR
THE DAYS SOAR

THE BABIES CRY
WITHOUT YOU

THE MOON GLOWS
THE RIVER FLOWS
BUT I DIE
WITHOUT YOU

ROGER:
THE WORLD REVIVES

MIMI:
COLORS RENEW

ROGER & MIMI:
BUT I KNOW BLUE
ONLY BLUE
LONELY BLUE
WITHIN ME, BLUE
WITHOUT YOU

MIMI:
WITHOUT YOU
THE HAND GROPES
THE EAR HEARS
THE PULSE BEATS

ROGER:
WITHOUT YOU
THE EYES GAZE
THE LEGS WALK
THE LUNGS BREATHE

ROGER & MIMI:
THE MIND CHURNS
THE HEART YEARNS
THE TEARS DRY
WITHOUT YOU

LIFE GOES ON
BUT I'M GONE
'CAUSE I DIE

ROGER:
WITHOUT YOU

MIMI:
WITHOUT YOU

ROGER:

Without you

ROGER & MIMI:

Without you.

(The loft. The phone rings.)

MARK & ROGER'S OUTGOING MESSAGE:

"Speak" . . . ("Beeep!")

ALEXI DARLING:

Mark Cohen
Alexi Darling
Labor Day weekend
In East Hampton
On the beach
Just saw Alec Baldwin
Told him you say hi
Just kidding

We still need directors
You still need money
You know you need money
Pick up the phone
Don't be afraid of ker-ching ker-ching

Marky—sell us your soul
Just kidding
We're waiting . . . *(Beep)*

(Various fantasy bed locales. The Company forms two main groups. As the music begins, a group of dancers start a sensual life and death dance, while a group of actors gather around a table center stage to speak words of passion which punctuate the dancing.

The Company sings:)

ROGER, MARK, JOANNE & BENNY:

Hot—hot—hot—sweat—sweet
Wet—wet—wet—red—heat
Hot—hot—hot—sweat—sweet
Wet—wet—wet—red—heat

PLEASE DON'T STOP PLEASE
PLEASE DON'T STOP STOP
STOP STOP STOP DON'T
PLEASE PLEASE PLEASE PLEASE
HOT—HOT—HOT—SWEAT—SWEET
WET—WET—WET—RED—HEAT
STICKY—LICKY—TRICKLE—TICKLE
STEAMY—CREAMY—STROKING—SOAKING

MIMI, COLLINS, MAUREEN & ANGEL:
HOT—HOT—HOT—SWEAT—SWEET
WET—WET—WET—RED—HEAT

COLLINS:
TOUCH!

MAUREEN:
TASTE!

MIMI:
DEEP!

COLLINS:
DARK!

MAUREEN:
KISS!

COLLINS:
BEG!

MIMI:
SLAP!

(Mark throws a sheet overhead. The actors, now on the table, cover themselves with it, while moving to the music, maintaining arm movement from side to side under the sheet.)

MIMI, COLLINS & MAUREEN:
FEAR!

COLLINS:
THICK!

MIMI, COLLINS & MAUREEN:
RED, RED
RED, RED,
RED, RED—PLEASE

MAUREEN:
HARDER!

ANGEL:

FASTER!

MAUREEN:

WETTER!

MIMI:

BASTARD!

COLLINS:

YOU WHORE!

MAUREEN:

YOU CANNIBAL!

MIMI & ANGEL:

MORE!

MAUREEN:

YOU ANIMAL!

MIMI, COLLINS & MAUREEN:

FLUID NO FLUID NO CONTACT YES NO CONTACT

ALL:

FIRE FIRE BURN—BURN YES!
NO LATEX RUBBER RUBBER
FIRE LATEX RUBBER LATEX BUMMER LOVER BUMMER.

(The music explodes into a fevered rhythmic heat as Angel is revealed in a lone spotlight, dancing wildly. He sings:)

ANGEL:

TAKE ME
TAKE ME
TAKE ME . . .
TAKE ME
TAKE ME

TODAY FOR YOU
TOMORROW FOR ME
TODAY ME
TOMORROW YOU
TOMORROW YOU
LOVE
YOU
LOVE YOU
LOVE

I LOVE
YOU I LOVE
YOU!

TAKE ME
TAKE ME
I LOVE YOU.

(The music dies as Angel vanishes.)

ROGER'S VOICE:
UMM
JOANNE'S VOICE:
WAIT!
MIMI'S VOICE:
SLIPPED!
COLLINS'S VOICE:
SHIT!
JOANNE'S VOICE:
OW!
ROGER'S VOICE:
WHERE'D IT GO?
MIMI'S VOICE:
SAFE!
COLLINS'S VOICE:
DAMN!
MAUREEN'S VOICE:
I THINK I MISSED—DON'T GET PISSED
ALL BUT COLLINS:
IT WAS BAD FOR ME—WAS IT BAD FOR YOU?
JOANNE:
IT'S OVER
MAUREEN:
IT'S OVER
ROGER:
IT'S OVER
MIMI:
IT'S OVER
COLLINS:
IT'S OVER.

(A church. Music begins.)

MIMI: Angel was one of my closest friends. It's right that it's Halloween, because it was her favorite holiday. I knew we'd hit it off the moment we met—that skinhead was bothering her and she said she was more of a man than he'd ever be and more of a woman than he'd ever get . . .

MARK: . . . and that time he walked up to this group of tourists—and they were petrified because, A—they were obviously lost, and B—had probably never spoken to a drag queen before in their lives . . . and he . . . *She* just offered to escort them out of Alphabet City . . . And then she let them take a picture with her—and then she said she'd help 'em find the Circle Line . . .

MAUREEN: . . . so much more original than any of us—You'd find an old tablecloth on the street and make a dress—and next year, sure enough—they'd be mass-producing them at the Gap! You always said how lucky you were that we were all friends—but it was us, baby, who were the lucky ones.

COLLINS:

LIVE IN MY HOUSE
I'LL BE YOUR SHELTER
JUST PAY ME BACK WITH ONE THOUSAND KISSES
BE MY LOVER
AND I'LL COVER YOU

OPEN YOUR DOOR—I'LL BE YOUR TENANT
DON'T GOT MUCH BAGGAGE
TO LAY AT YOUR FEET
BUT SWEET KISSES I'VE GOT TO SPARE
I'LL BE THERE—I'LL COVER YOU

I THINK THEY MEANT IT
WHEN THEY SAID YOU CAN'T BUY LOVE
NOW I KNOW YOU CAN RENT IT
A NEW LEASE YOU ARE, MY LOVE, ON LIFE

ALL MY LIFE
I'VE LONGED TO DISCOVER
SOMETHING AS TRUE
AS THIS IS

SOLOIST:

So with a thousand sweet kisses
I'll cover you

COLLINS:

If you're cold and you're lonely

2 SOLOISTS:

With a thousand sweet kisses
I'll cover you

COLLINS:

You've got one nickel only

3 SOLOISTS:

With a thousand sweet kisses
I'll cover you

COLLINS:

When you're worn out and tired

3 SOLOISTS:

With a thousand sweet kisses
I'll cover you

COLLINS:

When your heart has expired

COLLINS, SOLOISTS & CHOIR:

Five hundred twenty-five thousand six hundred minutes
Five hundred twenty-five thousand moments so dear
Five hundred twenty-five thousand six hundred minutes
Five hundred twenty-five thousand six hundred—
Measure a year
Oh lover I'll cover you
Oh lover I'll cover you

COLLINS & THE COMPANY:

Oh lover
I'll cover you
Oh lover

COLLINS:

I'll cover you

THE COMPANY:

Five hundred twenty-five thousand six hundred minutes
Five hundred twenty-five thousand
Seasons of love

COLLINS:

I will cover you.

(Outside the church. Mark is on a pay phone.)

MARK: Hi. It's Mark Cohen. Is Alexi there? . . . No need to bother her. Just let her know I'm running a little late for my appointment . . . I'm at my . . . Yes, I'll still be there . . . Yes, I signed the contract . . . Thanks . . .

(He sings:)

How did we get here?
How the hell . . .
Pan left—close on the steeple of the church

How did I get here?
How the hell . . .
Christmas

Christmas Eve—last year
How could a night so frozen
Be so scalding hot?
How can a morning this mild
Be so raw?

Why are entire years strewn
On the cutting room floor of memory
When single frames from one magic night
Forever flicker in close-up
On the 3-D IMAX of my mind?

That's poetic
That's pathetic

Why did Mimi knock on Roger's door
And Collins choose that phone booth
Back where Angel set up his drums?
Why did Maureen's equipment break down?

Why am I the witness?
And when I capture it on film
Will it mean that it's the end
And I'm alone?

(The friends sing:)

MIMI:

IT'S TRUE YOU SOLD YOUR GUITAR AND BOUGHT A CAR?

ROGER:

IT'S TRUE—I'M LEAVING NOW FOR SANTA FE
IT'S TRUE YOU'RE WITH THIS YUPPIE SCUM?

BENNY:

YOU SAID—YOU'D NEVER SPEAK TO HIM AGAIN

MIMI:

NOT NOW

MAUREEN:

WHO SAID THAT YOU HAVE ANY SAY
IN WHO SHE SAYS THINGS TO AT ALL?

ROGER:

YEAH!

JOANNE:

WHO SAID THAT YOU SHOULD STICK YOUR NOSE IN OTHER PEOPLE'S . . .

MAUREEN:

WHO SAID I WAS TALKING TO YOU?

JOANNE *(Simultaneously with Mark)*:

WE USED TO HAVE THIS FIGHT EACH NIGHT
SHE'D NEVER ADMIT I EXISTED

MARK *(Simultaneously with Joanne)*:

CALM DOWN
EVERYONE PLEASE

MIMI:

HE WAS THE SAME WAY—HE WAS ALWAYS:
"RUN AWAY—HIT THE ROAD
DON'T COMMIT"—YOU'RE FULL OF SHIT

BENNY *(Overlapping "Don't commit")*:

MIMI

JOANNE:

SHE'S IN DENIAL

MIMI:

HE'S IN DENIAL

JOANNE:

DIDN'T GIVE AN INCH
WHEN I GAVE A MILE

MARK *(Overlapping "When I gave")*:

COME ON

MIMI:

I GAVE A MILE

ROGER:

GAVE A MILE TO WHO?

MARK & BENNY:

COME ON GUYS CHILL!

MIMI & JOANNE:

I'D BE HAPPY TO DIE FOR A TASTE
OF WHAT ANGEL HAD
SOMEONE TO LIVE FOR—UNAFRAID
TO SAY I LOVE YOU

ROGER:

ALL YOUR WORDS ARE NICE, MIMI
BUT LOVE'S NOT A THREE-WAY STREET
YOU'LL NEVER SHARE REAL LOVE
UNTIL YOU LOVE YOUR SELF—I SHOULD KNOW

COLLINS:

YOU ALL SAID YOU'D BE COOL TODAY
SO PLEASE—FOR MY SAKE . . .
I CAN'T BELIEVE HE'S GONE

(To Roger:)

I CAN'T BELIEVE YOU'RE GOING
I CAN'T BELIEVE THIS FAMILY MUST DIE
ANGEL HELPED US BELIEVE IN LOVE
I CAN'T BELIEVE YOU DISAGREE

ALL:

I CAN'T BELIEVE THIS IS GOOD-BYE.

(Maureen and Joanne immediately burst into tears and embrace.)

MAUREEN:

POOKIE

JOANNE:

HONEYBEAR

MAUREEN:

I MISSED YOU SO MUCH

JOANNE:

I missed you

MAUREEN:

I missed your smell

JOANNE:

Your mouth
Your—

(Joanne kisses Maureen firmly.)

MAUREEN:

Ow

JOANNE:

What?

MAUREEN:

Nothing, pookie

JOANNE:

No, baby—you said, "Ow"—What?

MAUREEN:

You bit my tongue

JOANNE:

No, I didn't

MAUREEN:

You did—it's bleeding

JOANNE:

No, it isn't

MAUREEN:

I think I should know . . .

JOANNE:

Let me see—

MAUREEN:

She doesn't believe me

JOANNE:

I was only trying to . . .

(They hug and exit. The Pastor from the church enters.)

PASTOR:

Thomas B. Collins?

COLLINS:

Coming.

(The Pastor exits. Collins follows.

Benny stands off to the side as Mimi approaches Roger. Roger turns away. She hesitates before leaving with Benny.)

MARK:

I hear there are great restaurants out West

ROGER:

Some of the best. How could she?

MARK:

How could you let her go?

ROGER:

You just don't know . . . How could we lose Angel?

MARK:

Maybe you'll see why when you stop escaping your pain
At least now if you try—Angel's death won't be in vain

ROGER:

His death is in vain

(Mimi reappears up left, in the shadows. She overhears.)

MARK:

Are you insane?
There's so much to care about
There's me—there's Mimi—

ROGER:

Mimi's got her baggage too

MARK:

So do you

ROGER:

Who are you to tell me what I know, what to do?

MARK:

A friend

ROGER:

But who, Mark, are you?
"Mark has got his work,"
They say, "Mark lives for his work,"
And, "Mark's in love with his work"
Mark hides in his work

MARK:

From what?

ROGER:

Facing your failure, facing your loneliness
Facing the fact you live a lie
Yes, you live a lie—tell you why

You're always preaching not to be numb
When that's how you thrive
You pretend to create and observe
When you really detach from feeling alive

MARK:

Perhaps it's because I'm the one of us to survive

ROGER:

Poor baby

MARK:

Mimi still loves Roger
Is Roger really jealous
Or afraid that Mimi's weak

ROGER:

Mimi did look pale

MARK:

Mimi's gotten thin
Mimi's running out of time
Roger's running out the door—

ROGER:

No more! Oh no!
I've gotta go

MARK:

Hey, for somebody who's always been let down,
Who's heading out of town?

ROGER:

For someone who longs for a community of his own,
Who's with his camera, alone?

(Roger takes a step to go, then stops, turns.)

I'll call
I hate the Fall

(Roger turns to go. He discovers Mimi, who has entered.)

YOU HEARD?

MIMI:

EVERY WORD

YOU DON'T WANT BAGGAGE WITHOUT LIFETIME GUARANTEES
YOU DON'T WANT TO WATCH ME DIE?
I JUST CAME TO SAY
GOOD-BYE, LOVE
GOOD-BYE, LOVE
CAME TO SAY GOOD-BYE, LOVE, GOOD-BYE

JUST CAME TO SAY
GOOD-BYE LOVE
GOOD-BYE LOVE
GOOD-BYE LOVE, GOOD-BYE

ROGER *(Overlapping "Just came to say")*:

GLORY
ONE BLAZE OF
GLORY
I HAVE TO FIND

(He exits. Benny returns. Mimi steps away.)

MIMI:

PLEASE DON'T TOUCH ME
UNDERSTAND
I'M SCARED
I NEED TO GO AWAY

MARK:

I KNOW A PLACE—A CLINIC

BENNY:

A REHAB?

MIMI:

MAYBE—COULD YOU?

BENNY:

I'LL PAY

MIMI:

Good-bye love
Good-bye love
Came to say good-bye, love, good-bye

Just came to say
Good-bye love
Good-bye love
Good-bye love

Hello—disease

(She runs off. After a beat, Collins quickly enters with the Pastor behind him.)

PASTOR:

Off the premises now
We give no handouts here!

MARK:

What happened to "rest in peace"?

PASTOR:

Off the premises, queer!

COLLINS:

That's no way to send a boy
To meet his maker
They had to know
We couldn't pay the undertaker

(Pastor starts to exit.)

BENNY:

Don't you worry 'bout him. Hey, I'll take care of it.

(Pastor acknowledges Benny and exits.)

MARK:

Must be nice to have money

COLLINS & BENNY:

No shit

COLLINS:

I THINK IT'S ONLY FAIR TO TELL YOU
YOU JUST PAID FOR THE FUNERAL
OF THE PERSON WHO KILLED YOUR DOG

BENNY:

I KNOW
I ALWAYS HATED THAT DOG!
LET'S PAY HIM OFF
AND THEN GET DRUNK

MARK:

I CAN'T—I HAVE A MEETING

COLLINS & BENNY:

PUNK! LET'S GO!

(Collins and Benny exit.)

MARK *(Imagining)*: "Hi. Mark Cohen here for *Buzzline* . . . Back to you, Alexi. Coming up next: "Vampire Welfare Queens Who Are Compulsive Bowlers." OH MY GOD, WHAT AM I DOING?

(He sings:)

DON'T BREATHE TOO DEEP
DON'T THINK ALL DAY
DIVE INTO WORK
DRIVE THE OTHER WAY
THAT DRIP OF HURT
THAT PINT OF SHAME
GOES AWAY
JUST PLAY THE GAME

YOU'RE LIVING IN AMERICA
AT THE END OF THE MILLENNIUM
YOU'RE LIVING IN AMERICA
LEAVE YOUR CONSCIENCE AT THE TONE

AND WHEN YOU'RE LIVING IN AMERICA
AT THE END OF THE MILLENNIUM
YOU'RE WHAT YOU OWN

(Lights up on Roger.)

ROGER:

The filmmaker cannot see

MARK:

And the songwriter cannot hear

ROGER:

Yet I see Mimi everywhere

MARK:

Angel's voice is in my ear

ROGER:

Just tighten those shoulders

MARK:

Just clench your jaw 'til you frown

ROGER:

Just don't let go

MARK & ROGER:

Or you may drown

You're living in America
At the end of the millennium
You're living in America
Where it's like the twilight zone

And when you're living in America
At the end of the millennium
You're what you own

So I own not a notion
I escape and ape content
I don't own emotion—I rent

MARK:

What was it about that night?

ROGER *(Overlapping "night")*:

What was it about that night?

MARK & ROGER:

Connection—in an isolating age

MARK:

For once the shadows gave way to light

ROGER *(Overlapping "light")*:

For once the shadows gave way to light

MARK & ROGER:

For once I didn't disengage

(Mark goes to pay phone and dials.)

MARK:

Angel—I hear you—I hear it
I see it—I see it
My film!

ROGER:

Mimi I see you—I see it
I hear it—I hear it
My song!

MARK *(Simultaneously)*:

Alexi—Mark
Call me a hypocrite
I need to finish my own film

ROGER *(Simultaneously)*:

One song—glory
Mimi
Your eyes

MARK:

I quit!

MARK & ROGER:

Dying in America
At the end of the millennium
We're dying in America
To come into our own

And when you're dying in America
At the end of the millennium
You're not alone

I'm not alone
I'm not alone.

(Blackout.
Once again the phone rings.)

MARK & ROGER'S OUTGOING MESSAGE:

"Speak" . . . ("Beeep!")

ROGER'S MOM:

Roger
This is your mother
Roger, honey I don't get these postcards
"Moving to Santa Fe"
"Back in New York"
"Starting a rock band"
Roger, where *are* you?? Please call

MIMI'S MOM *(Simultaneously with Roger's Mom)*:

Mimi, chica, donde estas?
Tu mama esta llamando
Donde estas Mimi call

MR. JEFFERSON *(Simultaneously with Mimi's Mom)*:

Kitten—wherever are you—call

MARK'S MOM *(Simultaneously with Mr. Jefferson)*:

Mark—are you there—are you there
I don't know if he's there
We're all here wishing you were here, too—
Where are you Mark are you there are you where are you
Mark—are you there—are you there
I don't know if please call your mother.

(The lot and the loft.
The Company sings:)

SEVEN HOMELESS PEOPLE:

Christmas bells are ringing
Christmas bells are ringing
Christmas bells are ringing

How time flies
When compassion dies

No stockings
No candy canes
No gingerbread
No safety net
No loose change
No change no

ONE HOMELESS MAN:

"Santy Claus is coming"

SEVEN HOMELESS PEOPLE:

'Cause Santy Claus ain't coming

No room at the Holiday Inn—again
Well, maybe next year—
Or—when

(Lights shift back to the loft. A small projector sits on a milk crate, which sits on a dolly.)

MARK:

December 24, ten p.m. Eastern Standard Time
I can't believe a year went by so fast
Time to see—what we have—time to see
Turn the projector on

(A rough title credit: "Today 4 U: Proof Positive," appears, then a shot of Roger tuning his guitar last Christmas.)

First shot Roger
With the Fender guitar he just got out of hock
When he sold the car
That took him away and back

ROGER:

I found my song

MARK:

He found his song
If he could just find Mimi

ROGER:

I tried—you know I tried

(Mark's image appears on the screen.)

MARK:

Fade in on Mark
Who's still in the dark

ROGER:

But he's got great footage

MARK:

Which he's cut together

ROGER:

To screen tonight

(Benny's image appears on screen.)

MARK:

In honor of Benny's wife

ROGER:

Muffy

MARK:

Alison
Pulling Benny out of the East Village location

(The projector blows the fuse. Blackout.)

ROGER: Then again. Maybe we won't screen it tonight.
MARK: I wonder how Alison found out about Mimi?
ROGER: Maybe a little bird told her.

(Collins enters in the dark, with twenty-dollar bills.)

COLLINS: Or an Angel.

(Lights fade up.)

I had a little hunch that you could use a little 'flow

ROGER:

Tutoring again?

COLLINS:

Negative

MARK:

Back at NYU?

COLLINS:

No, no, no
I rewired the ATM at the Food Emporium
To provide an honorarium to anyone with the code

MARK & ROGER:

The code—
Well? . . .

COLLINS:

A-n-g-e-l

YET ROBIN HOODING ISN'T THE SOLUTION
THE POWERS THAT BE MUST BE UNDERMINED WHERE THEY DWELL
IN A SMALL, EXCLUSIVE GOURMET INSTITUTION
WHERE WE OVERCHARGE THE WEALTHY CLIENTELE

MARK, ROGER & COLLINS:
WE'LL OPEN UP A RESTAURANT IN SANTA FE
WITH A PRIVATE CORNER BANQUETTE, IN THE BACK
WE'LL MAKE IT YET, WE'LL SOMEHOW GET TO SANTA FE

ROGER:
BUT YOU'D MISS NEW YORK BEFORE YOU COULD UNPACK

MARK, ROGER & COLLINS:
OHH—

(Maureen and Joanne enter carrying Mimi.)

MAUREEN:
MARK! ROGER! ANYONE—HELP!

MARK:
MAUREEN?

MAUREEN:
IT'S MIMI—WE CAN'T GET HER UP THE STAIRS

ROGER:
NO!

(They enter the loft.)

MAUREEN:
SHE WAS HUDDLED IN THE PARK IN THE DARK
AND SHE WAS FREEZING
AND BEGGED TO COME HERE

ROGER:
OVER HERE
OH, GOD—

(They lay her down on the table.)

MIMI:
"GOT A LIGHT—I KNOW YOU—YOU'RE SHIVERING . . ."

JOANNE:
SHE'S BEEN LIVING ON THE STREET

ROGER:

We need some heat

MIMI:

I'm shivering

MARK:

We can buy some wood and something to eat

COLLINS:

I'm afraid she needs more than heat

MIMI:

I heard that

MAUREEN:

Collins will call for a doctor, honey

MIMI:

Don't waste your money on Mimi, me, me

COLLINS:

Hello—911?
I'm on hold

MIMI:

Cold . . . cold . . . would you light my candle

ROGER:

Yes—we'll, oh God—find a candle

MIMI:

I should tell you
I should tell you

ROGER:

I should tell you
I should tell you

MIMI:

I should tell you
Benny wasn't any—

ROGER:

Shhh—I know

I should tell you why I left
It wasn't 'cause I didn't—

MIMI:

I know
I should tell you

ROGER:

I should tell you

MIMI *(Whispering)*:
I SHOULD TELL YOU
I LOVE YOU—

(She fades.)

ROGER:
WHO DO YOU THINK YOU ARE?
LEAVING ME ALONE WITH MY GUITAR *(She stirs)*
HOLD ON THERE'S SOMETHING YOU SHOULD HEAR
IT ISN'T MUCH BUT IT TOOK ALL YEAR

(He begins playing acoustic guitar at her bedside.)

YOUR EYES
AS WE SAID OUR GOOD-BYES
CAN'T GET THEM OUT OF MY MIND
AND I FIND I CAN'T HIDE FROM

YOUR EYES
THE ONES THAT TOOK ME BY SURPRISE
THE NIGHT YOU CAME INTO MY LIFE
WHERE THERE'S MOONLIGHT
I SEE YOUR EYES

(Band takes over.)

HOW'D I LET YOU SLIP AWAY
WHEN I'M LONGING SO TO HOLD YOU?
NOW I'D DIE FOR ONE MORE DAY
'CAUSE THERE'S SOMETHING I SHOULD HAVE TOLD YOU
YES THERE'S SOMETHING I SHOULD HAVE TOLD YOU

WHEN I LOOKED INTO YOUR EYES
WHY DOES DISTANCE MAKE US WISE?
YOU WERE THE SONG ALL ALONG
AND BEFORE THE SONG DIES

I SHOULD TELL YOU I SHOULD TELL YOU
I HAVE ALWAYS LOVED YOU
YOU CAN SEE IT IN MY EYES

(We hear "Musetta's Theme," played correctly and passionately. Mimi's head falls to the side and her arm drops limply off the edge of the table.)

MIMI!

(Suddenly, Mimi's hand regains movement. She's alive!)

MIMI: I jumped over the moon!!
ROGER: What?
MIMI: A leap of Mooooooooooooooo—
JOANNE: She's back!
MIMI: I was in a tunnel. Heading for this warm, white light . . .
MAUREEN: Oh my God!
MIMI: And I swear Angel was there and she looked *good*! And she said, "Turn around girlfriend—and listen to that boy's song . . ."

COLLINS:
SHE'S DRENCHED
MAUREEN:
HER FEVER'S BREAKING
MARK:
THERE IS NO FUTURE—THERE IS NO PAST
ROGER:
THANK GOD THIS MOMENT'S NOT THE LAST
ROGER & MIMI:
THERE'S ONLY US
THERE'S ONLY THIS
FORGET REGRET OR LIFE IS YOURS TO MISS
ALL:
NO OTHER ROAD NO OTHER WAY
NO DAY BUT TODAY

(As the finale grows, the entire company makes its way onto the stage.)

WOMEN:
I CAN'T CONTROL
MY DESTINY
I TRUST MY SOUL
MY ONLY GOAL
IS JUST TO BE

MEN *(Overlapping "I can't control")*:

WILL I LOSE MY DIGNITY
WILL SOMEONE CARE
WILL I WAKE TOMORROW
FROM THIS NIGHTMARE

(Mark's film resumes along with two more films projecting on the back wall: "SCENES FROM RENT.")

WOMEN *(Simultaneously with Men below)*:

WITHOUT YOU
THE HAND GROPES
THE EAR HEARS
THE PULSE BEATS
LIFE GOES ON
BUT I'M GONE
'CAUSE I DIE
WITHOUT YOU
I DIE WITHOUT YOU
I DIE WITHOUT YOU
I DIE WITHOUT YOU
I DIE WITHOUT YOU
I DIE WITHOUT YOU

MEN *(Simultaneously with Women above)*:

THERE'S ONLY NOW
THERE'S ONLY HERE
GIVE IN TO LOVE
OR LIVE IN FEAR
NO OTHER PATH
NO OTHER WAY
NO DAY BUT TODAY
NO DAY BUT TODAY
NO DAY BUT TODAY
NO DAY BUT TODAY
NO DAY BUT TODAY
NO DAY BUT TODAY
NO DAY BUT TODAY.

THE END

DATE OF SCRIPT

April 1996

COPYRIGHT

PERFORMING RIGHTS

All inquiries, including stock and amateur rights, should be addressed to the author's representative as follows:

Writers & Artists Agency, 19 West 44th Street, Suite 1000, New York, NY 10036. Attn: William Craver. Phone: 212-391-1112. Fax: 212-575-6397.

ORIGINAL PRODUCTION

Rent was originally produced Off-Broadway by New York Theatre Workshop where it received its world premiere on January 26, 1996. It received twenty-five previews and twenty-six performances there. Subsequently, it transferred to Broadway where it began previews on April 16, 1996 at the Nederlander Theatre. It opened on April 29 and, at this writing, is still playing there.

Rent was produced on Broadway by Jeffrey Seller, Kevin McCollum, Allan S. Gordon and New York Theatre Workshop (James C. Nicola, Artistic Director; Nancy Kassak Diekmann, Managing Director). *Rent* was directed by Michael Greif. The set was designed by Paul Clay, costumes by

Angela Wendt, lighting by Blake Burba, sound by Kurt Fischer, original concept and additional lyrics by Billy Aronson, musical arrangements by Steve Skinner, music supervision and additional arrangements by Tim Weil, choreography by Marlies Yearby, dramaturgy by Lynn M. Thomson, technical supervision by Unitech Productions, Inc., general management by Emanuel Azenberg and John Corker; the production stage manager was John Vivian, the press representatives were Richard Kornberg and Don Summa and casting was by Bernard Telsey Casting. Production photographs were taken by Joan Marcus; the graphic design was by Spot Design.

The original cast (in order of appearance) was as follows:

ROGER DAVIS . . . . Adam Pascal
MARK COHEN . . . . Anthony Rapp
TOM COLLINS . . . . Jesse L. Martin
BENJAMIN COFFIN III . . . . Taye Diggs
JOANNE JEFFERSON . . . . Fredi Walker
ANGEL DUMOTT SCHUNARD . . . . Wilson Jermaine Heredia
MIMI MARQUEZ . . . . Daphne Rubin-Vega
MAUREEN JOHNSON . . . . Idina Menzel
MARK'S MOM, ALLISON AND OTHERS . . . . Kristen Lee Kelly
MR. JEFFERSON, SOLOIST #2, CAROLER,
A PASTOR AND OTHERS . . . . Byron Utley
MRS. JEFFERSON, SOLOIST #1,
WOMAN WITH BAGS AND OTHERS . . . . Gwen Stewart
GORDON, THE MAN,
MR. GREY AND OTHERS . . . . Timothy Britten Parker
STEVE, MAN WITH SQUEEGEE,
A WAITER AND OTHERS . . . . Gilles Chiasson
PAUL, A COP AND OTHERS . . . . Rodney Hicks
ALEXI DARLING, ROGER'S MOM AND OTHERS . . . . Aiko Nakasone

UNDERSTUDIES: Yassmin Alers, Darius de Haas, Shelley Dickinson, David Driver, Mark Setlock, Simone

AWARDS

Rent received (all in 1996) the Pulitzer Prize for Drama and Tony Awards for Best Musical, Best Score (Jonathan Larson), Best Book (Jonathan Larson) and Best Featured Actor in a Musical (Wilson Jermaine Heredia). It received the New York Drama Critics Circle Award for Best Musical, and Drama Desk Awards for Outstanding Musical, Outstanding Music (Jonathan Larson), Outstanding Lyrics (Jonathan Larson), Outstanding Book, (Jonathan Larson), Outstanding Featured Actor in a Musical (Wilson Jermaine Heredia) and Outstanding Arrangements (Steve Skinner). It was awarded the Outer Critics Circle Award for Best Off-Broadway Musical; the Drama League Award for Best Musical; Theatre World Awards for Outstanding New Talent (Adam Pascal, Daphne Rubin-Vega); and OBIE Awards for Outstanding Book, Music and Lyrics (Jonathan Larson), Outstanding Direction (Michael Greif) and Outstanding Ensemble Performance.

AUDIORECORDING, VIDEORECORDING AND MUSIC PUBLISHING

Original Cast Recording: Dreamworks Records DRMD2-50003. Produced by Arif Mardin. This recording has been certified Platinum by the RIAA.

Videotaped by the New York Public Library's Theatre on Film and Tape Archive at New York Theatre Workshop on March 28, 1996. 141 minutes. Format: 3/4" SP Color. Catalog Number: NCOV 1915. Restricted to qualified researchers. Contact: New York Public Library for the Performing Arts, 40 Lincoln Center Plaza, New York, NY 10023-7498; telephone: 212-870-1642; website: www.nypl.org/research/lpa/lpa.html

Vocal Selections: Hal Leonard Corporation.

ORCHESTRA INSTRUMENTATION

Piano/Synthesizers/Egg
Bass
Guitars
Drums/Percussion
Hammond B-3/Synthesizers/Guitars

PUBLICATION

Rent by Jonathan Larson. The libretto and complete story of the making of the show. Rob Weisbach Books, William Morrow & Company, New York, 1997.

MAJOR PRODUCTIONS

Rent continues to play to worldwide critical acclaim in New York and on tour in the U.S. and Canada. Other productions include: London, Toronto, Australia, Ireland, Germany, Italy, Scandinavia, Holland, Brazil, Mexico, Spain, Japan, Philippines and Korea. Future productions include a national tour of the U.K., as well as productions in Argentina, Portugal, South Africa, Singapore and Switzerland.

BIOGRAPHIES

Jonathan Larson

JONATHAN LARSON (Author, Composer, Lyricist) was born in 1960. For his musical *Rent,* he won the 1996 Pulitzer Prize in Drama as well as Tony Awards for Best Original Score and Best Book of a Musical. In 1994, *Rent* won the Richard Rodgers Development Award and twice received the Gilman & Gonzalez-Falla Theatre Foundation's Commendation Award. In 1989, he was granted the Stephen Sondheim Award from American Music Theater Festival, where he contributed to the musical *Sitting on the Edge of the Future*. In 1988, he won the Richard Rodgers Development Grant for his rock musical, *Superbia*. In 1995, he wrote the score for *J. P. Morgan Saves the Nation,* which was presented by En Garde Arts in 1995. Mr. Larson performed his rock monologue *Tick . . . Tick . . . BOOM!* at Second Stage Theatre, The Village Gate and New York Theatre Workshop. In addition to scoring and songwriting for *Sesame Street,* he created music for a number of children's book-cassettes, including Steven Spielberg's *An American Tail* and *The Land Before Time*. Other film scores include work for *Rolling Stone* magazine publisher, Jann Wenner. He conceived, directed and wrote four original songs for *Away We Go!*, a musical video for children. Mr. Larson died unexpectedly of an aortic aneurysm on January 25, 1996, ten days before his thirty-sixth birthday and one day before the first performance of *Rent* at New York Theatre Workshop.

MICHAEL GREIF (Director) received 1996 Tony and Drama Desk nominations as well as the OBIE Award for his direction of *Rent*. As artistic director of La Jolla Playhouse (1995–1999) he directed Tennessee Williams's *Sweet Bird of Youth*, Jessica Hagedorn's *Dogeaters*, Charlayne Woodard's *Pretty Fire*, Diana Son's *Boy*, Randy Newman's *Faust*, Tony Kushner's *Slavs!*, Neal Bell's adaptation of *Therese Raquin* and Joe Orton's *What the Butler Saw*. As artistic associate at The Joseph Papp Public Theater/New York Shakespeare Festival (1989–1992), he directed Sophie Treadwell's *Machinal* (OBIE Award), Tony Kushner's *Bright Room Called Day*, Connie Congdon's *Casanova*, José Rivera's *Marisol* and Shakespeare's *Pericles*. Regionally, he has directed at Center Stage, Trinity Repertory Company, Williamstown Theatre Festival, the Goodman Theatre and the Mark Taper Forum. He is currently an artistic associate at New York Theatre Workshop, where he helped develop and directed the studio and Off-Broadway productions of *Rent*.

NEW YORK THEARE WORKSHOP (Producer) Since its founding in 1979, New York Theatre Workshop has emerged as a leading voice in the world of Off-Broadway and in the theatre community at large. NYTW remains steadfast to its founding vision and commitment to nurture both emerging and established theater artists, working together with an ever-growing community of artists and audience members to encourage risk, promote collaboration and stimulate experimentation with theatrical forms. Under the direction of James C. Nicola, NYTW inaugurated its new theater at 79 East 4th Street in the spring of 1993 with its award-winning productions of Caryl Churchill's *Owners* and *Traps*. Among the many extraordinary plays developed or premiered at NYTW are Tony Kushner's *Angels in America*, *Slavs!* and *Homebody/Kabul*; Doug Wright's *Quills*; Paul Rudnick's *The Most Fabulous Story Ever Told* and Claudia Shear's *Blown Sideways Through Life* and *Dirty Blonde*. In 1991, NYTW received the OBIE Award for Sustained Achievement.

PARADE

Music and Lyrics by Jason Robert Brown
Book by Alfred Uhry
Co-Conceived by Harold Prince
Original New York Production Directed by Harold Prince

Joan Marcus

Brent Carver (Leo) and Carolee Carmello (Lucille), Lincoln Center Theater, 1998.

JASON ROBERT BROWN:

To Irving Brown
and the memory of Jack Hollday

ALFRED UHRY:

To Harold Prince

THE STORY

In Atlanta, Georgia, on Confederate Memorial Day (April 26, 1913) a young factory worker, Mary Phagan, is murdered during a patriotic celebration. Leo Frank, her boss, is accused of the crime. Leo, Jewish and from Brooklyn, is uncomfortable in the South and with his southern wife, Lucille. Public sentiment is stirred up against him by the press and ambitious politicians, and Leo is convicted of the crime. During a two-year struggle to save his life, he and Lucille come to realize how much they love one another.

CHARACTERS

(in order of appearance)

YOUNG SOLDIER	In the Confederate Army, in 1862
OLD SOLDIER	The same soldier, in 1913
AIDE	
ASSISTANT	
LUCILLE FRANK	Leo Frank's wife; in her middle twenties, Jewish, southern, deferential and well-mannered
LEO FRANK	Manager of Atlanta's National Pencil Factory; somewhat older than Lucille, a Jewish Yankee, reserved and a bit stiff
HUGH DORSEY	District Attorney, in his forties
GOVERNOR SLATON	Governor of Georgia
SALLY SLATON	His wife
FRANKIE EPPS	Sixteen, with the air of a know-it-all
MARY PHAGAN	An employee in the pencil factory, almost fourteen
J. N. STARNES	Police officer
OFFICER IVEY	Police officer
NEWT LEE	Janitor in the factory; a black man of fifty or so
MRS. PHAGAN	Mary's mother
LIZZIE PHAGAN	Mrs. Phagan's sister
FLOYD MACDANIEL	Proprietor of MacDaniel's Saloon
BRITT CRAIG	Reporter at the *Atlanta Georgian*, middle twenties
MOURNERS	
TOM WATSON	Publisher and editor of the *Jeffersonian*
RILEY	The Slatons' black chauffeur
PRISON GUARD	

LUTHER Z. ROSSER	Leo Frank's lawyer
JIM CONLEY	Worker in the factory, black, late twenties
FIDDLIN' JOHN	A fiddler in front of the Atlanta courthouse
JUDGE ROAN	Elderly southern gentleman, unwell
NURSE	Judge Roan's caretaker
FOREMAN	
JURORS	
PSYCHIATRIST	
IOLA STOVER	Mary's co-worker at the factory
MONTEEN	Another girl at the factory
ESSIE	Another girl at the factory
ANGELA	A black citizen
A CHAIN GANG	Black men
MR. PEAVY	Guard, State Prison Farm at Milledgeville
CITIZENS	

MUSICAL SYNOPSIS

Act I

Act II

NOTE: Sung passages are indicated in the text by small caps.

"The Dream of Atlanta": The Confederate Memorial Day Parade, Lincoln Center Theater, 1998.

Joan Marcus

ACT I

SCENE 1

Military drums, in the distance. Then an explosive clang from the orchestra and the lights rise on a verdant field in the small town of Marietta, Georgia, twenty miles from Atlanta. A picturesque and glorious field, with beautiful red hills far off behind it. There is also a large, full oak tree occupying much of stage left. This is a significant tree, and a significant field in our play, but we will not see Marietta again until the second to last scene.

The year is 1862. A Confederate Young Soldier stands alone in the field, facing us. He is newly enlisted, his uniform is crisp, his pack is full. He stands still, and sings:

YOUNG SOLDIER:

Farewell, my Lila—
I'll write every evening.
I've carved our names
In the trunk of this tree.
Farewell, my Lila—
I miss you already,
And dream of the day
When I'll hold you again
In a home safe from fear,
When the Southland is free.

I go to fight for these old hills behind me,
These Old Red Hills of Home.
I go to fight for these old hills remind me
Of a way of life that's pure—
Of the truth that must endure—

In a town called Marietta
In the Old Red Hills of Home.

Pray on this day as I journey beyond them,
These Old Red Hills of Home:
Let all the blood of the North spill upon them
'Til they've paid for what they've wrought,
Taken back the lies they've taught,
And there's peace in Marietta
And we're safe again in Georgia
In the land where Honor lives and breathes—
The Old Red Hills of Home!

Farewell, my Lila. Farewell . . .

(There is a burst of military drums as a crowd of Townspeople emerges from both wings running into place to observe a parade. Mingling, they turn their backs on the audience.

Lights bump up to reveal Peachtree Street in Atlanta, Georgia. It is April 26, 1913—fifty-one years later, and the town is out and about, busy in preparations for the Confederate Memorial Day Parade. The sun is not shining—it is a decidedly overcast day, but nothing stops Atlanta from its business. This is the heart of industrial Georgia, and this frenetic city is as far removed as possible from the gentility of Marietta and the antebellum South. In the distance, we hear a Marching Band as the Confederate Memorial Day Parade approaches offstage.

A fussy male Aide and his female Assistant in 1913 attire enter. They block our view of the Young Soldier.)

AIDE: Captain! Captain! This way, sir. We're assigned to take care of you until the parade starts.

(No answer.)

ASSISTANT: I guess he's hard of hearing. I wonder how he lost that leg?
AIDE: I said we're supposed to escort—

(They move and we see an Old Soldier wearing a tattered uniform and a peg in place of his right leg. This is the Young Soldier, fifty-one years later.)

OLD SOLDIER: Quit hollering. I'm old—not deaf.
AIDE: Your men from the fifty-fifth will be ridin' on their own float in the parade!
OLD SOLDIER: Me and my boys marched into Chickamauga fifty years ago and we'll march down Peachtree Street today.
AIDE: I guess they can march. But you are ridin' in the parade!
OLD SOLDIER *(To Assistant)*: Quit hovering!

(The Aide and his Assistant head offstage.)

LOOK THERE, MY LILA,
THEY CALL ME TO TELL IT,
THE LIVES THAT WE LED
WHEN THE SOUTHLAND WAS FREE.

(During the following, a parade passes upstage out of view of the audience. All that we can see are masses of Confederate flags, the tops of musical instruments, an occasional baton flying in the air, the top of a float or two, dignitaries standing in an open car, maybe the top of a carriage with celebrants, a child or two on someone's shoulders. The entire panoply of a parade as seen from the viewpoint of someone standing five deep in a crowd.

The Old Soldier rises and sings:)

WE GAVE OUR LIVES FOR THE OLD HILLS OF GEORGIA,
THE OLD RED HILLS OF HOME.
NOT MUCH SURVIVES OF THE OLD HILLS OF GEORGIA,
BUT I CLOSE MY EYES AND HEAR
ALL THE TREASURES WE HELD DEAR

(Simultaneously with the Townsmen:)

THE RUSHING OF THE CHATAHOOCHIE,
THE RUSTLIN' IN THE WIND,
AND MAMA IN THE KITCHEN SINGIN',
AND ME AND LILA SWINGIN' IN A TREE.

TOWNSMEN *(Simultaneously with the Old Soldier)*:
THE TALL PINES AND THE RED CLAY,
THE BLUE SKIES AND THE DOGWOOD TREES.
A MAN CAN GROW HIS COTTON
AND HIS CROPS!

OLD SOLDIER & TOWNSMEN:

Oh, I hear it calling, calling,

TOWNSMEN:

Still!

OLD SOLDIER:

And I would gladly give
My good right leg again!
Again!

(The Old Soldier is ushered offstage by the Aide. The parade continues.)

ALL TOWNSPEOPLE:

Again!

God bless the sight
Of the old hills of Georgia,
The Old Red Hills of Home!
(Kneel down to)
Praise those who'd fight
For the old hills of Georgia!
For those proud and valiant men,
We'll sing "Dixie" once again—
For the men of Marietta

For the fathers of Atlanta
Who gave everything for Georgia
And the Old Red Hills of Home!

TOWNSMEN:

For the brothers
of Cobb County
For the patriarchs

(While the Townspeople sing out their last note a cappella, the crowds part in the center and freeze. Lights down.)

SCENE 2

Lights up. We are in the bedroom of Leo and Lucille Frank—decorated with stodgy, heavy furniture.

Lucille, middle twenties, is seated at her vanity, trying to put up her hair, an elaborate procedure involving dexterity, which she doesn't have much of, and many hairpins. She is the quintessential southern wife, deferential and well-mannered. Leo, some years older, comes into the room. He is reserved, a bit stiff—wearing thick glasses, a three-piece suit, tie, watch chain across his chest, etc.

LUCILLE: Leo!
LEO: What?
LUCILLE: Are you goin' to work?
LEO: Of course.
LUCILLE *(Disappointed)*: Oh. I thought . . .
LEO: What?
LUCILLE: Well, I was hopin' we could go and have a picnic in Piedmont Park this afternoon.
LEO: What?
LUCILLE: Did you forget? Today is Confederate Memorial Day.
LEO: Confederate Memorial Day is asinine. Why would anyone want to celebrate losing a war?
LUCILLE: Heavens, Leo! If Georgia is so asinine, why did you move here in the first place?
LEO: You know why. Your uncle offered me a good job. I should have realized it pays so well because you have to live in Atlanta to do it!
LUCILLE *(Flirting)*: I guess that's what I get for marryin' a Yankee.
LEO *(Not flirting)*: You dropped a pin.
LUCILLE: Minnie will get it when she cleans up.

(This irritates him. He picks up the hairpin and puts it on the vanity.)

I was just sure today would be a day off.
LEO: Not for the superintendent.
LUCILLE: Superintendent! Honestly, the way you slave yourself down there, a person'd think you owned that old pencil factory.
LEO: Don't be such a *meshuggeneh*!
LUCILLE: Why do you use words like that?
LEO: Because they're Jewish words and I'm Jewish.
LUCILLE: Well, I am, too, but it doesn't mean I have to speak a foreign language!
LEO: For the life of me, I can't understand how God created you people Jewish and southern at the same time.
LUCILLE: Well, Confederate Memorial Day is a holiday in this part of the world whether you like it or not. May I plan a picnic for the Fourth of July, or will you be working then too?

LEO: Lucille, we've gone through all this. I work hard because I am trying to build us up enough of a nest egg so we can . . . well, you know what I mean— *(Stops, embarrassed)*

LUCILLE *(Teasing him)*: Procreate. It's not a dirty word, Leo. It's all over the Bible. So we can procreate.

LEO: I'll be home for dinner.

LUCILLE: Are you blushing? I swear, I think you are!

LEO: You dropped another pin.

(He leaves. She doesn't pick up the pin, and goes on with her hair. Lights down.)

SCENE 3

Lights up. The Townspeople who have been framing the scene, close in. They continue to observe the Confederate Memorial Day Parade.

11:30. The parade is going strong. The Townspeople sing the city anthem:

TOWNSPEOPLE:

EVER MORE LIVES THE DREAM OF ATLANTA,
EVER MORE HER ETERNAL PRIDE!
STRONG AND SURE IS THE DREAM OF ATLANTA
WHEN HER BROTHERS ARE UNIFIED!
AND THE SOUND OF HER VOICE IS CLEARER
WHEN HER PEOPLE ARE PROUD AND FREE!
NOT A STAR TO THE SKY COULD BE NEARER
THAN MY HEART IS, ATLANTA, TO THEE!

(A man—Dorsey—stands on a parade float and silences the crowd.)

DORSEY: Ladies and gentlemen, I give you the most popular man in Georgia, our governor, the Honorable John Slaton!

(The crowd cheers as John Slaton arrives on the float, accompanied by his wife, Sally Slaton, and the Old Soldier. Slaton speaks into a period microphone, blasting over the crowd:)

SLATON: Today we honor those who honored us fifty-some years ago. Those who gave life and limb for Georgia and suffered unimaginable degradation. But never defeat. The men of Georgia and the women of Georgia have never been defeated . . .

(At this point, we see Leo making his way awkwardly through the crowd. He moves as if he is terrified of bumping into anyone on this very crowded street. Slaton continues silently, as Leo sings:)

LEO:

I GO TO BED AT NIGHT
HOPING WHEN I WAKE
THIS WILL ALL BE GONE
LIKE IT WAS JUST A DREAM
AND I'LL BE HOME AGAIN,
BACK AGAIN IN BROOKLYN.
BACK WITH PEOPLE WHO LOOK LIKE I DO,
AND TALK LIKE I DO,
AND THINK LIKE I DO,
BUT THEN
THE SUN RISES IN ATLANTA AGAIN . . .

SLATON: They have risen from the ashes of war with honor and courage and strength!

LEO:

THESE PEOPLE MAKE ME TENSE.
I LIVE IN FEAR THEY'LL START A CONVERSATION.
THESE PEOPLE MAKE NO SENSE:
THEY TALK AND I JUST STARE AND SHUT MY MOUTH.
IT'S LIKE A FOREIGN LAND.
I DIDN'T UNDERSTAND
THAT BEING SOUTHERN'S NOT JUST BEING IN THE SOUTH.
WHEN I LOOK OUT ON ALL THIS,
HOW CAN I CALL THIS HOME?

SLATON: I am proud to be a Georgian on this day!

LEO:

THESE MEN BELONG IN ZOOS,

ASSORTED SPECTATORS *(Overlapping with Leo)*:

EXCUSE ME! SORRY! GET YOUR SOUVENIRS!
WATCH YOUR STEP, SIR!

LEO:

IT'S LIKE THEY NEVER JOINED CIVILIZATION.

ASSORTED SPECTATORS *(Overlapping "It's like they never joined")*:

WHERE'S THE FELLA WITH THE BEER!
MAMA, THAT MAN PUSHED ME!
LUCINDA! HEY NOW, FELLA!

LEO *(Overlapping "Lucinda!")*:

THE JEWS ARE NOT LIKE JEWS—
I THOUGHT THAT JEWS WERE JEWS,
BUT I WAS WRONG.

ASSORTED SPECTATORS:

YOU GOT BALLOONS? I WANT ONE!
SETTLE DOWN . . . I NEVER IN MY LIFE!
I'LL TAKE A BEER!
THAT SLATON'S HANDSOME . . .

LEO:

I THOUGHT I WOULD BE FINE,
BUT FOUR YEARS DOWN THE LINE,
WITH EV'RY WORD IT'S VERY CLEAR
I DON'T BELONG:

ASSORTED SPECTATORS:

LA LA LA LA IN THE LAND O' COTTON . . .

LEO:

I DON'T CUSS, I DON'T DRAWL,
SO HOW CAN I CALL THIS HOME?

SLATON: Proud that our state is growing and building!

LEO:

HOME CALLS, AND I'M FREE OF THE SOUTHERN BREEZE,
FREE OF MAGNOLIA TREES AND ENDLESS SUNSHINE!
EVERMORE LIVES THE DREAM OF ATLANTA,
BUT NOT MINE!
NOT MINE.

ENSEMBLE:

WE STAND TOGETHER
IN THE GREAT STATE OF GEORGIA!

LEO:

A YANKEE WITH A COLLEGE EDUCATION
WHO BY HIS OWN DESIGN

Is trapped inside the land
That Time forgot!

ENSEMBLE:

Strong and proud!

LEO:

I'm trapped inside this life
And trapped beside a wife
Who would prefer that I'd say,
"Howdy!," not "Shalom!"

(Simultaneously with Ensemble:)

Well, I'm sorry, Lucille,
But I feel what I feel
And this place is surreal,
So how can I call this home?

ENSEMBLE I *(Simultaneously with Leo and Ensemble II)*:

God bless the sight
Of the old hills of Georgia!
The Old Red Hills of
Old Red Hills of Home!

ENSEMBLE II *(Simultaneously with Leo and Ensemble I)*:

Ever more lives the dream of Atlanta,
Ever more her eternal
Old Red Hills of Home!

(Leo disappears off left, on his way to his office, as Slaton's float moves off right.

The crowd parts again to reveal Frankie Epps, sixteen, with close-cropped blond hair and the air of a know-it-all, standing on the corner with a book, waiting for the streetcar. He hums a popular vaudeville tune as he waits.

The streetcar lurches onto the stage, with Mary Phagan as one of the passengers. Mary is almost fourteen, and dressed to beat the band in a fancy white dress with a lavender sash and matching parasol. This scene is played throughout with the exuberance and innocence of healthy flirting, teenage style.

Frankie continues humming stupidly, as he looks for a seat on the streetcar. He is showily nonchalant as he takes a seat next to Mary. She pretends not to notice.

Bouncy ragtime romp.)

FRANKIE: Well, hey sunshine!
MARY: Sunshine? Looks like rain to me.
FRANKIE *(Pulling on her hair ribbon)*: Not in here, it don't.
MARY: Why, Frankie Epps! Quit that, you hear?
FRANKIE: What? I ain't doin' anything! *(Pulls her hair ribbon again. Sings:)*

I'M GONNA GO TO THE PICTURE SHOW.
THERE'S A MOVIE I'VE GOT TO SEE.
YOU KNOW THE ONE CALLED "THE SILVER GUN"?
WELL, I BEEN WATCHIN' SINCE CHAPTER THREE!
I CAN'T WAIT— IT'S AT EIGHT,
AND I WAS WONDERIN' IF YOU'RE FREE . . .

MARY:

GO ON, GO ON, GO ON, GO ON.
YOU KNOW MY MAMA'D NEVER LET ME TILL I TURN SIXTEEN.
GO ON, GO ON, GO ON, GO ON.
BESIDES, I ONLY GO TO PICTURES THAT I HAVEN'T SEEN.

FRANKIE: When do you turn sixteen?
MARY: Two years from next June.
FRANKIE: Too bad about your mama.
MARY: Too bad for you.

(She gets up and crosses to a seat on the other side of the streetcar. Frankie yells to no one in particular:)

FRANKIE:

I KNOW A SPOT NEAR MCCONNACH'S LOT
WHERE YOU CAN SEE THE PARADE REAL CLEAR.

(Mary laughs derisively. Frankie moves a little closer.)

I GOT A BOOK—WANNA TAKE A LOOK?—
CALLED *THE THIEF AND THE BRIGADIER.*

(He holds out the book. She looks at him like he's crazy. He stands over her and extends a piece of chewing gum.)

I GOT GUM—YOU WANT SOME?

MARY:

I HAVEN'T CHEWED GUM FOR A YEAR.

(He sits resignedly next to her.)

FRANKIE:

Go on, go on, go on, go on.
I bet your mama'd let me take you to the picture show.

MARY:

Go on, go on, go on, go on.
I guess you weren't really listenin' when I said, "No!"
Why not ask Iola Stover?
Her mama lets her do whatever she wants.

FRANKIE:

I was hopin' I could go with you.

MARY:

Go on, ask Iola Stover—
Her mama lets her see whoever she wants.

FRANKIE:

Well, maybe I will.

MARY:

I hope you do.

(She stands up as the streetcar lurches to a halt.)

FRANKIE: Where you goin'?
MARY: To the factory. I didn't get my pay this week.
FRANKIE: Okay. I'll see you around.
MARY: At the picture show.
FRANKIE: What? I thought your mama wouldn't let you.
MARY: She will with Essie and Betty Jean. Just not with you!
FRANKIE: Bye, sunshine!

(She swats at him with her parasol and sashays off the streetcar. He skats stupidly to himself as he looks off after her. The streetcar lurches on.)

(De, de, de, de, de, de, de, de, de, de . . .)
Go on, go on, go on, go on . . .

(Spots someone in the crowd) Why, Iola! You goin' to the pictures tonight?

(Lights down as the crowd closes in.)

SCENE 4

Lights up on Townspeople watching the parade. They sing:

TOWNSPEOPLE:

EVER MORE LIVES THE DREAM OF ATLANTA,
EVER MORE HER ETERNAL PRIDE!
STRONG AND SURE IS THE DREAM OF ATLANTA
WHEN HER BROTHERS ARE UNIFIED!

(The crowd continues singing as it separates, revealing the National Pencil Factory, upper level, second floor.

Leo Frank's office. Leo is sitting at his desk, the account book open in front of him, a large yellow legal pad next to that, and an adding machine that he seldom touches. He sings:)

LEO:

TWENTY-EIGHT BOXES OF CAPS
AT FOUR DOLLARS THE GROSS—
THIS IS WRONG, THIS IS WRONG,
I CAN FIX THIS—WAIT.
NINE MORE BOXES IN BACK,
TWENTY-EIGHT MINUS NINE,
AND THEN THIRTY-ONE GIRLS ON THE LINE . . .

(A portion of the crowd moves, and we see Lucille, still at her mirror, still with her hairpins. She sings about the first time she met Leo, while he continues his work, scribbling and erasing, occasionally distracted by the parade outside, and by thoughts of his earlier conversation with Lucille.)

LUCILLE *(Simultaneously with Leo below)*:

SUIT AND A TIE . . .
TERRIBLY QUIET . . .
QUITE A WELL-PAID POSITION.
"GO ON, LUCILLE . . .
BRING HIM HIS COFFEE . . ."

LEO *(Simultaneously with Lucille)*:

TIMES SIX, ONE EIGHTY-SIX . . .
DIVIDE . . . SEVEN SIXTY . . .
GOD—ALL THE NOISE, AND ON *YONTIFF* YET . . .

Four cents a girl for the week . . .
At ten cents an hour . . .

LUCILLE:

Straight from New York, Lucille!
Isn't he smart, Lucille?

Mama, he's comin' around today—
Mama, he's at the door!
Mama, I don't know what I should say . . .
"Well, what are you waitin' for, Lucille?"
What am I waiting for?

LEO:

This is wrong, this is wrong, it's an eight, not a six . . .

LUCILLE:

House and a maid;
Two sets of china—
Everything I was wishin'—
New winter coat;
Real ermine collar—
Who would have known, Lucille?
Married so well, Lucille?

How can he want me, so plain, so prim?
How can he be so sure?
Don't I wish I could be sure like him?
Like Leo?

LEO:

Yes, Lucille, I am building a life for us . . .

LUCILLE:

For Leo?

LEO:

No, Lucille, we cannot have a picnic . . .

LUCILLE:

Didn't my wishes come true for me
The day he walked through the door?
Isn't he all that I knew he'd be?
Brilliant and filled with humility?
Loyal and stable as any tree?
So why do I wait for more?
What am I waiting for?

LEO:

Twenty-three cartons of leads
At two sixty a gross—
This is wrong, this is wrong,
I can fix this . . .

(Mary appears silently at the office door. Leo doesn't see or hear her.)

MARY: Hey.

(Leo drops his pen, startled. He looks up.)

LEO: Yes?
MARY: I came for my pay.
LEO: Name?
MARY: Mary Phagan.

(He goes to the payroll book, looks her up.)

LEO: I don't see it here. Employee number?
MARY: Five oh seven.

(He looks that up.)

LEO: Ah. Not Fagin as in Dickens. Phagan as in phalanx.

(He chuckles at his little joke. She just stands there, as he counts out the money in coins, puts it in a little envelope and records it in his ledger.)

Twelve hours, ten cents an hour. One dollar and twenty cents. Here you are.
MARY: Thank you, sir.

(He nods, goes back to his bookkeeping. She walks toward the door, then turns. The drums of the parade are becoming audible through the window.)

Mr. Frank?

(He finishes a sum at his ledger, looks up.)

LEO: What is it?

MARY: Happy Memorial Day.

(Lights linger on Mary and Leo, he at his desk, she in her finery at the door. Neither moves. Lights down.)

TOWNSPEOPLE *(Singing from offstage)*:
NOT A STAR TO THE SKY COULD BE NEARER
THAN MY HEART IS, ATLANTA, TO THEE!

(We see dimly the street level front entrance of the factory, featuring an impressive staircase leading to the second floor and Leo's office. Under the staircase, Jim Conley, a black janitor, is asleep while his broom sits idly beside him. Blackout.)

SCENE 5

In the dark, the shrill sound of an insistently loud doorbell. It rings, then rings again. Then a third time.

Lights up on the Frank residence. Lucille, in a wrapper and her hair not fixed, comes to the door. It is very early in the morning. She opens the door. Two men—Starnes and Ivey—are on the doorstep.

STARNES: This the residence of a Leo M. Frank?
LUCILLE: Why, yes it is. Is something the matter?
IVEY: Is Mr. Frank at home, ma'am?
LUCILLE: Yes.
STARNES: Could we speak to him, please?
LUCILLE *(Calling)*: Leo! Leo!

(Leo enters. He has hastily put on trousers and is buttoning his shirt. He sees the two men and his hands tremble with the shirt buttons.)

STARNES: Leo M. Frank?
LEO: Yes. What's happened?
STARNES: J. N. Starnes, Atlanta Police Department. This is Officer Ivey.
IVEY: We're gonna need you to get on your shoes and come with us, Mr. Frank.
LEO *(Becoming more agitated)*: Oh, God! Has something happened at the factory?

IVEY: Just get your shoes, please.

LEO: I will, I—Oh God! I need to have my coffee. I'll be with you gentlemen in a minute, soon as I have my—has there been a fire? Tell me, just tell me! It is a fire, isn't it?

LUCILLE: Leo, Leo. *(Lays a calming hand on his arm and speaks to the policemen)* The coffee is almost ready.

STARNES: A tragedy has occurred. We don't have time for coffee.

LEO *(Horrified)*: A tragedy? What? Is somebody dead? Is somebody dead?

(Starnes and Ivey exchange looks. Blackout.)

SCENE 6

Lights up on Newt Lee, a dignified black man of fifty or so. The density of light suggests a grill light at a police station, but the location is not specific. His hands and feet are chained. As a single note repeats insistently in the bass, Newt addresses the audience, singing:

NEWT LEE:

I AM TRYIN' TO REMEMBER . . .
I WAS CHECKIN' ROUN' THE FACT'RY,
AND I WENT INTO THE BASEMENT,
DOWN THE STAIRS INTO THE BASEMENT,
AND I SHINE MY LIGHT AROUND HERE,
IN THE CORNERS AND THE CEILING,
AND I'M 'BOUT TO CHECK THE WASHROOM
WHEN THE LIGHT, IT KINDA CATCHES
ON THIS PILE OF RAGS IN THE MIDDLE OF THE ROOM . . .

(Lights up on the factory basement and we see a body covered with a dirty cloth. Starnes and Ivey bring in Leo, who is very nervous. Starnes whips the cloth off the body.)

LEO *(Trembling, nearly fainting)*: Oh my God! Oh my God! Oh my God!

STARNES: Do you know who this is, Mr. Frank?

LEO: Oh God! It's the little girl I paid yesterday. She came up to my office.

IVEY: Can you give us her name, sir?

LEO *(Extremely emotional)*: I—I—I can't think! Farrell? No. Oh God! Faley? Phagan! The name is Phagan—P-H-A-G-A-N.

STARNES *(Writing it down)*: Phagan.

NEWT:

I AIN'T SEEN NO PILE O' RAGS THERE BEFORE,
So I GO OVER AND I KICK IT,
AND I SHINE DOWN MY LIGHT AND LORD,
LORD, AIN'T NO PILE OF RAGS AT ALL . . .

LEO: Will this be in the newspapers?

IVEY: Does that bother you, sir?

LEO: Well, of course it bothers me! How does it look for the company to have a child killed in our basement?

STARNES: Was she killed in the basement, Mr. Frank?

LEO: I would assume so, I—who did it? Do you know who did it yet?

(No response from the detectives.)

NEWT:

THIS SMALL WHITE BODY
WITH HER TONGUE STICKIN' OUT,
THIS PRETTY LITTLE CHILD
WITH HER EYES WIDE OPEN . . .

LEO: Oh no. You don't think it was my night watchman?

(No answer.)

Newt? Newt Lee? You think it was Newt?

(Silence.)

NEWT:

So I RAN TO THE PHONE
AND I CALLED MR. FRANK,
BUT THE PHONE KEP' RINGIN',
So I CALLED Y'ALL TO HELP ME—
MR. FRANK, HE DIDN'T ANSWER . . .
AND THAT'S ALL I CAN REMEMBER.

LEO: Oh God! Oh my God! You think—you think—that's absurd! It's preposterous. I was at home all night! I didn't even know this child.

I only remembered her name because she was in my office yesterday. How could you possibly— *(Panicked, he starts taking off his clothes, tearing at them, the jacket, the shirt, the undershirt, the trousers, opening the union suit as he speaks)* Look! Look! No marks on me! Where are the scratches? Where are the bruises? Look! Nothing! I want you to write that down. Look at me! What do you see? Nothing!

IVEY: Put your clothes on, Mr. Frank.

LEO: Can I go home now and have my breakfast?

IVEY: No, sir, I'm 'fraid you can't do that.

(Meanwhile, Mrs. Phagan enters, walking toward the factory down Peachtree Street with her sister Lizzie in tow. Mrs. Phagan is a pretty but faded country woman in her early thirties.)

MRS. PHAGAN:

I DO NOT HAVE TIME TO GO PARADIN' THROUGH
THE ENTIRE STATE OF GEORGIA LOOKIN' FOR THAT GIRL.
I'VE GOT HALF A MIND TO . . .
HURRY UP, LIZZIE.

STARNES: Wanna give us the name of a lawyer we can contact for you, Mr. Frank?

LEO *(Badly shaken)*: Oh God! Rosenblatt. Nathan Rosenblatt.

IVEY: Nathan Rosenblatt.

(They start to lead Leo out of the basement. As they do, Mrs. Phagan approaches the street door of the factory where a young rookie Policeman stands guard.)

MRS. PHAGAN: 'Scuse me.

POLICEMAN: Yes, ma'am?

MRS. PHAGAN: I'm hopin' you can he'p me.

POLICEMAN: Yes, ma'am.

MRS. PHAGAN: Well, my daughter didn't come home las' night.

POLICEMAN: Can I have your name please, ma'am?

(Blackout.)

SCENE 7

Lights up. It is dawn and we are at the street door of MacDaniel's Saloon on Pryor Street. The sun rises during the following scene, ending with the extinguishing of the street lamp on the corner.

MacDaniel, the proprietor, opens the door and heaves a young man out into the street. This is Britt Craig, middle twenties, inebriated, disheveled and still good-looking and absolutely charming.

MACDANIEL: Out.
CRAIG: Why you doin' this?
MACDANIEL: Because I'm closed.
CRAIG: Closed? On Saturday night?
MACDANIEL: You're a reporter, Craig. Keep up. It's Sunday morning.

(Craig looks.)

CRAIG: I'll be damned. I love you, Floyd. *(Moves to embrace him)*
MACDANIEL: Out.

(MacDaniel goes inside, slams the door. Craig is on the street. He looks around, starts walking. He sings:)

CRAIG:

Big News!
Another week goes by in Atlanta!
Another fascinating, scintillating, stimulating,
spirit-stirring week!
Big News!
Another Sunday comes to Atlanta!
Another week of news so thrilling
That your average city newshound
Wants to take a flying jump into the creek!

You got a kitten up a tree?
Well, come to me! And I'll see
It makes it on the front page!
The mayor's mother broke her toe?
They gotta know!
Stop the press—it's a mess!

It's the scandal of the age!!
Hell, it's Big News!
Another shock to rock Atlanta!
Another information feast
From the gateway to the whole Southeast!

Look! In the mines and the mills
And the Mexican hills, they got stories to tell.
Look! Now Ohio's afloat.
Soon the women will vote and we'll all go to Hell.
Look! Now that Wilson is in
And old Taft didn't win, Hell, they're comin' to blows!
Look! The Titanic went down,
But I'm stuck in this town with my thumb up my nose

And that's Big News!
Another stir-crazy freak in Atlaaaaanta.
The Board of Estimate's approved a new street! (Yippee!)
They're building churches out of high-grade concrete!
(Looka that!)
They say the rain'll give a break from the heat!
It's a scoop! It's a twist!
It's a reason to exist!
Pray to Heaven, Pray to Zeus!
There's a genius on the loose!

And that's really really really Big News!
You never saw such things in Atlanta!
Another brilliant mind deceased
In the gateway to the whole Southeast!!

What a town!

(Craig collapses into a garbage can and disappears. In a moment, Starnes and Ivey appear. They see Craig and hoist him out of the garbage can.)

STARNES: Craig, what the Hell are you doin' in there?
CRAIG *(Eyes closed)*: Coverin' the police beat.
STARNES: Well, maybe we got somethin' for you.

(In a flash Craig gets himself completely together, tie straight, hair combed, sober and sharp-eyed—the consummate reporter. He is now in the municipal building with a knot of other Reporters.

Hugh Dorsey, the District Attorney, appears and the Reporters shout questions. Dorsey is in his forties—intense, driven—a man on the way up. He holds up a hand for silence, gets it, speaks:)

DORSEY: Chief of Police Starnes has informed me that he is holding two men for further questioning regarding the murder of little Mary Phagan. They are *(Consults a piece of paper)* Ludie Newton Lee—

REPORTER: How do you spell that?

DORSEY: Negro, employed as night watchman at the National Pencil Company, where the murder took place; and Leo Max Frankel, Caucasian, formerly of Brooklyn, New York, employed as superintendent of same. Make that Frank, not Frankel.

(A din of questions from the Reporters. Again, Dorsey's hand goes up. Silence.)

Rest assured, the killer of this child will not roam free. I am on my way to church now, to pray for her soul. I imagine everybody in Atlanta wants to do the same thing.

(He turns to go, refusing to answer any questions. Craig catches up with him.)

CRAIG: Mr. Dorsey, Mr. Dorsey? . . .

DORSEY: What is it, Mr. Craig?

CRAIG: This Frank fella—now he was that little girl's boss, right?

DORSEY: I made my statement, Mr. Craig. I'm in a hurry.

CRAIG: But you wouldn't be holdin' a well-off man like that unless you had a damn good reason.

DORSEY: As I said, nothin' further at this time.

(Dorsey leaves. Craig watches him go, bemused. The lights shift.)

SCENE 8

We are in Leo Frank's cell at Fulton Tower. Leo is in the same clothes we saw him in before. A Guard enters with a tray of food. Leo sniffs it.

Offstage, we hear the sound of Mourners.

MOURNERS *(Singing)*:

THERE IS A FOUNTAIN FILLED WITH BLOOD
DRAWN FROM IMMANUEL'S VEINS,
AND SINNERS PLUNGED BENEATH THAT FLOOD
LOSE ALL THEIR GUILTY STAINS,
LOSE ALL THEIR GUILTY STAINS,
LOSE ALL THEIR GUILTY STAINS . . .

LEO: What's this?
GUARD: Your dinner.
LEO: You expect me to eat this?

(The Guard shrugs.)

I have had nothing in my stomach since last night. Not even coffee. For your information, I am under a physician's care. I have an extremely delicate stomach. I am required to eat regular meals at regular times and I do not eat grease. This is all grease. Take it away.

(The Guard takes it back.)

Bring me an apple and some coffee.

(The Guard snorts out a laugh and turns to go.)

GUARD: Uh-huh. Got you some company, Leo.

(The Guard beckons and Lucille enters. The Guard lets her in the cell, locks the door and leaves.)

LUCILLE: Leo.
LEO: What?
LUCILLE: How are you?
LEO: How do you think?

LUCILLE: I wish you wouldn't act so ugly to the guard.
LEO: Ridiculous.
LUCILLE: He's only doin' his job, honey.
LEO: Fine. He doesn't matter. Nathan will have me out of here by tonight.
LUCILLE: Well, I brought these just in case.

(She hands him a package which he opens to find toilet articles, change of underwear, etc.)

LEO: I won't be needing them.
LUCILLE: Better safe than sorry.
LEO: Safe? You think I'm safe? Are you out of your mind? Do you have eyes in your head? Look at me! I have never committed an illegal act in all my life and here I am locked up in a jailhouse, Lucille! Look where they expect me to go to the toilet! Did you see that plate of pig fat and corn bread I was supposed to eat? Do you have any idea of what spending the night here would be like?
LUCILLE: I just wanted you to be comfortable.
LEO: Well I'm not. I'm not comfortable and I'm not safe and I'm mighty sorry.
LUCILLE: Leo—

(She moves to touch him, He jerks away.)

LEO: Go on home, Lucille. *(Calls out)* Guard!

(Music underscore. The sound of Mourners offstage returns:)

MOURNERS:

THERE IS A FOUNTAIN FILLED WITH BLOOD
DRAWN FROM IMMANUEL'S VEINS . . .

LEO *(To Lucille)*: I'll be there by supper time.

MOURNERS:

AND SINNERS PLUNGED BENEATH THAT FLOOD
LOSE ALL THEIR GUILTY STAINS . . .

(The Guard appears.)

LEO: Let my wife out.

(The Guard opens the cell door. Lucille hesitates, looks at Leo. He looks away. She leaves. Alone, Leo picks up the clean shirt out of the package she has left. He is very frightened. The lights shift abruptly.)

SCENE 9

We are in the governor's office. Slaton is addressing Dorsey.

SLATON: Ugly business, Hughie.
DORSEY: Sure is, Jack.

(Slaton shoots him a sharp look.)

I mean, Governor Slaton.

SLATON: Good people of Georgia been raisin' Hell about children bein' forced to work in fact'ries. Now they're gonna read in their newspapers about a thirteen-year-old girl fastening erasers to pencil caps—two hundred caps an hour, ten hours a day, six days a week. And not only that, she got herself killed doin' it! Know who they're gonna blame?

DORSEY: Well certainly not you, Governor!

SLATON: Damn right they'll blame me. And you. And ev'rybody else holdin' public office. We gotta get to the bottom of this one fast.

DORSEY: Well, they're holdin' two suspects over yonder at the Fulton Tower.

SLATON: Good for them. It's up to you to convict one of 'em.

DORSEY: Done.

SLATON: Done my ass! You got a lousy conviction record, Hughie. How long you think they're gonna keep you in office if you let this one wriggle off the hook?

(Lights down.)

SCENE 10

Lights up on the Marietta Baptist Church. Mary Phagan's funeral has just ended. The minister leads the pallbearers carrying a small white coffin on their shoulders. Frankie is one of the pallbearers. Mrs. Phagan and Lizzie follow the coffin with assorted relatives, simple country people, plus Slaton, Sally and their black chauffeur, Riley. At the tail end of the line—among the other Mourners—we see Tom Watson.

The Mourners sing:

MOURNERS:

THERE IS A FOUNTAIN FILLED WITH BLOOD
DRAWN FROM IMMANUEL'S VEINS,
AND SINNERS PLUNGED BENEATH THAT FLOOD
LOSE ALL THEIR GUILTY STAINS,
LOSE ALL THEIR GUILTY STAINS,
LOSE ALL THEIR GUILTY STAINS;
AND SINNERS PLUNGED BENEATH THAT FLOOD
LOSE ALL THEIR GUILTY STAINS.

(Simultaneously with Craig below:)

THE DYING THIEF REJOICED TO SEE
THAT FOUNTAIN IN HIS DAY,
AND THERE MAY I, THOUGH VILE AS HE,
WASH ALL MY SINS AWAY,
WASH ALL MY SINS AWAY,
WASH ALL MY SINS AWAY;
AND THERE MAY I, THOUGH VILE AS HE,
WASH ALL MY SINS AWAY.

(Craig is on the scene, covering the funeral.)

CRAIG *(Simultaneously with Mourners above)*: The simple white coffin was carried by two of Mary's cousins and two of her young friends. Several more friends volunteered to serve as pallbearers, but they were deemed too small to shoulder the burden, light as it was. Recent heavy rains made the north Georgia red clay soil glow with the burnished brilliance of a spring campfire, as Mary Phagan, two months shy of fourteen, was laid to her final rest.

(Frankie stands, white-lipped, grim—a very different boy than we saw on the streetcar. Craig sees him and heads over.)

FRANKIE *(To himself)*:

GOD FORGIVE ME WHAT I THINK.
GOD FORGIVE ME WHAT I WISH RIGHT NOW.

CRAIG: You must've known Mary pretty well.
FRANKIE: Yes, sir, I did.
CRAIG: This must be a mighty hard day for you.

FRANKIE:

DID YOU EVER HEAR HER LAUGH?
WHEN SHE LAUGHED, YOU SWORE YOU'D NEVER CRY AGAIN.
DID YOU EVER SEE HER SMILE?
HER SMILE WAS LIKE A GLASS OF LEMONADE.
AND SHE SAID FUNNY THINGS,
AND SHE WORE PRETTY DRESSES,
AND SHE LIKED TO SEE THE PICTURES AT THE VFW HALL,
AND SHE LOVED RIDIN' SWINGS,
AND SHE LIKED COTTON CANDY,
BUT I THINK SHE LIKED THE PICTURES BEST OF ALL . . .

NO, IT DON'T MAKE SENSE TO ME
THAT SHE WON'T BE AROUND.
NO, IT DON'T MAKE SENSE TO ME
TO PUT HER IN THE COLD AND LONELY GROUND.
AND NO, IT DON'T MAKE SENSE
THE WAY THE WORLD CAN LET YOU FALL—
I SWEAR IT DON'T MAKE SENSE TO ME AT ALL.

(Frankie fights manfully to keep his composure.)

MOURNERS & CHILDREN:

NO, IT DON'T MAKE SENSE TO ME
THAT SHE WILL NOT BE THERE.

FRANKIE:

WHEN SHE LAUGHED, YOU SWORE YOU'D NEVER CRY AGAIN.

MOURNERS & CHILDREN:

NO, IT DON'T MAKE SENSE TO ME.

LIZZIE:

SHE LOVED WHEN I TIED RIBBONS IN HER HAIR.

ALL *(Except Craig)*:

AND NO, IT DON'T MAKE SENSE,
THE WAY THE SUN CAN STILL BURN DOWN.
NO, IT DON'T MAKE SENSE TO ME . . .

FRANKIE:

God forgive me what I think.

(Craig claps a consoling arm around Frankie's shoulder.)

CRAIG: Tell me, son, got any idea who it was?

(Frankie regains his composure.)

FRANKIE:

God forgive me what I wish right now.
I don't know the coward's name.
I don't know the bastard's face.
But I swear right now to God:
He ain't never gonna git away with what he done to Mary!
Let him quiver in his boots!
Let him run until he bleeds!
I won't rest until I know
He's burning in the ragin' fires of Hell forevermore!

MOURNERS:

There is a fountain filled with blood
Drawn from Immanuel's veins . . .

FRANKIE:

God forgive me what I think.

MOURNERS:

And sinners plunged beneath that flood
Lose all their guilty stains.

FRANKIE:

God forgive me what I wish right now . . .

(Craig continues to watch the Mourners and Frankie move away from the grave.

Watson calls to Slaton:)

WATSON: Governor Slaton!
SLATON *(Frosty; looking at his wife)*: Mr. Watson.
WATSON: A tragic meeting, sir.
SLATON: It surely is.
WATSON: I presume this is Mrs. Slaton?

(Sally nods.)

Tom Watson, publisher and editor-in-chief of the *Jeffersonian*, at your service, ma'am.

SALLY *(With distaste)*: I know all about the *Jeffersonian*, Mr. Watson.

WATSON: Then you know my paper speaks for every right-thinking Christian voter in this state.

SALLY: That's not exactly what—

SLATON: If you'll excuse us now, we have to—

WATSON: The filthy Anti-Christ who did this deed must face his righteous maker! *(His attention goes to the coffin)* I'd like to be alone with Miss Mary now, if you don't mind.

(Watson kneels by the coffin. The Slatons walk away.)

SLATON: That man is a buffoon.

SALLY: That man is dangerous.

SLATON *(To his chauffeur)*: Riley, bring the car around.

RILEY: Yassuh.

(Music underscore. Dorsey, who has been standing nearby, registers all of this and then walks into the next scene.)

SCENE 11

The lights shift, and Newt, shackled hand and foot, is being led across the stage by Ivey to a questioning room at the Fulton County Jail, where Dorsey waits for him. Despite the shackles and the time spent in jail, Newt maintains his dignity. Dorsey is his gentle, fair-minded self, but the following interrogation is ominous nonetheless. Starnes watches from a chair on the side.

DORSEY: Well, hey, Newt! How you feelin' this morning?

NEWT LEE *(Wary)*: All right, thank ya. *(And he remembers to add)* Suh.

DORSEY: Did they give you your coffee yet?

(Newt shakes his head no.)

Well, Hell's bells! Take mine.

(He hands Newt his own cup. Newt looks to Ivey for an okay. Ivey nods. Newt drinks the coffee.)

I b'lieve you have somethin' to say to me, Newt.

(Newt slowly shakes his head no again.)

It was an accident, wadn't it? It was really her fault.

(Newt keeps shaking his head no.)

She looked right at you and she smiled. You were standin' so close and she smelled so sweet.

(Newt continues denying, possibly even saying/singing no.)

You are a man, Newt, after all—a red-blooded man and so am I and so is Ivey and we all know what it feels like to be right up next to a sweet-smellin' girl, near enough to feel that hot breath on your face—

(As Newt starts to speak, Watson begins humming.)

NEWT *(Intoning/repeating to himself)*: I am the resurrection and the life: he that believeth in me, though he were dead, yet shall he live. And whosoever liveth and believeth in me shall never die. I am the resurrection and the life: he that believeth in me . . .

DORSEY *(Simultaneously with Newt)*: I been there, Newt. It's part of bein' a man. You had to touch her, didn't you? You had to smell that skin. I know. I understand. You could tell how much she wanted it. You can tell me, Newt! You helped her slide down her drawers!

(Newt is silenced by Dorsey's intensity. Dorsey stands silently over Newt for a moment, then turns to Starnes.)

. . . Ah, let him go. Hangin' another Nigra ain't enough this time. We gotta do better. Get him out of here!

(Dorsey and Newt continue in half light, but our focus is now drawn to Watson, who is singing with growing passion:)

WATSON:

Sleep, sleep, little angel,
Fear not the sound of drums.
Sleep, sleep, little angel.
Never you cry—
Justice is nigh!
Soon Armageddon comes.

(The lights shift back to the questioning room.)

DORSEY: It was Leo Frank murdered that little girl!
STARNES: You sure about that?
DORSEY: Jesus Christ on a stick! Of course, I'm sure.

(He sings:)

It's in his hands:
See how he rubs 'em both together
Like he's tryin' to get 'em clean?
It's in his eyes:
Wonder why he stares at the floor
And won't look you straight in the face?
Somethin' ain't right.
I can tell, somethin' ain't right.
I can see it in his eyes, boys.

IVEY: But we got no evidence.

DORSEY:

You want evidence? Look at those clothes and that big fancy talk!
You want evidence? Look at him sweatin' from every pore!
Can't you see him just standin' there watchin' that little girl bleed?
He smells of it.
He stinks of it.
What more do you need?

STARNES: An eyewitness wouldn't be bad.

DORSEY: That's right. So get the Hell outta here and go find one!

(Blackout.)

SCENE 12

Lights up on Craig, at his typewriter at the Atlanta Georgian *office. He sings:*

CRAIG:

Big News! My savior has arrived!
My intuition's never been so strong!
Big News! My career has been revived—
All I needed was a snippy, pissy Yankee all along!
Take this superstitious city, add one little Jew from
 Brooklyn
Plus a college education and a mousy little wife,
And Big News! Real Big News!
That poor sucker saved my life!

So give 'im fangs, give 'im horns,
Give 'im scaly, hairy palms!
Have 'im droolin' out the corner of his mouth!
He's a master of disguise!
Check them bug-out, creepy eyes!
Sure, that fella's here to rape the whole damned South!
They'll be bangin' down my door,
Yellin', "More, Craig! More!
Call for justice! We need justice!
Beat the bastard!
Kill the bum!"
Big News! Real Big News!
My savior has finally come!

(Lights up on the Fulton Tower. Leo is in his cell, sitting on his cot, reading a newspaper. He is now wearing a prison uniform. A lot of the wind seems to have gone out of his sails. He seems much more vulnerable without the three-piece suit, the watch chain and the tightly tied necktie. He throws the newspaper to the floor in disgust.)

GUARD: Leo, you ol' dog! You really knock up this little high school girl in Lithonia like it says here? She's sure got herself a sweet pair of knockers—least in the picture there.

LEO: I wouldn't know.

GUARD: Anything you say, nooky hound. Lawyer's here to see you.

(The Guard disappears. Leo straightens up a little bit. The Guard returns with Luther Z. Rosser—an unkempt whale of a man with stains on his jacket, a rumpled shirt, frayed collar, etc.)

ROSSER *(With a firm handshake and a clap on the back)*: Hidey there, Leo! Luther Rosser.

LEO: You're not my lawyer.

ROSSER: Not yet.

LEO: Where's Nathan Rosenblatt?

ROSSER: He's the one sent me.

LEO: Why isn't he here?

ROSSER: 'Cause he knows I'll represent you better. A drunk shouldn't defend another drunk. A Jew shouldn't defend another Jew. Makes sense, don't it? Can you see without those specs?

LEO: No.

ROSSER: Get rid of 'em anyway.

LEO: Why?

ROSSER: Because you look like a goddamn chicken hawk blinkin' at me behind those things. And that hair. Who cut it? An undertaker? Problem is you don't look a lot like a real person, Leo. No wonder everybody thinks you tore into that little girl.

LEO: Now just a minute!

ROSSER: You wanna walk outta here?

LEO: Of course.

ROSSER: Then act more like a good ol' boy.

LEO: Be specific.

ROSSER: Okay. Don't say things like specific. How long you been married?

LEO: Two years.

ROSSER: Mmm. No kids. Too bad. She pregnant?

LEO: Of course not.

ROSSER: What do you mean of course not? You got a pecker, don't you? Maybe I can arrange you a conjugal visit and you can get somethin' goin'.

LEO: That's none of your business.

ROSSER: Everything you do is my business. You piss, puke, fart or spit nickels, I wanna know about it. Leo. Leo. God, I wish your name was Billy or Jimmy Jo or somethin' like that. You don't happen to have a nickname, do you?
LEO: Yes. Nooky hound.

(Rosser laughs. Leo smiles.
Focus shifts to Craig's office. A prim Atlanta Man steps forward from the Ensemble. A spotlight picks him out. Craig circles around him.)

CRAIG:
According to reports obtained exclusively by this reporter,
Prosecutor Dorsey has the villain in his sights.
A highly ranking unnamed source in this investigation tells me
Leo Frank's the only likely culprit in this case.
Anyone with any information on the suspect, Leo Frank,
Should contact this reporter care of the *Atlanta Georgian.*

MAN:
I saw this little kid—
Said, "Look what Leo did!"
And then she run and hid . . .

CRAIG:
Go on, go on, go on, go on now!

(Another spotlight on the other side of the stage lights up—a young Pretty Girl steps forward. Craig and several other Reporters circle around her.)

PRETTY GIRL:
He sat down next to me—
His hand went on my knee—
I had to shake it free!

REPORTERS:
Go on, go on, go on, go on now!

ANOTHER MAN *(Simultaneously with Woman below)*:
I say it idn't fair!
I saw his books, I swear—
That man's a millionaire!

WOMAN *(Simultaneously with Another Man)*:

HE LIKES 'EM YOUNG AND SMALL—
GOT NEKKID PICTURES ALL
PINNED TO HIS OFFICE WALL!

REPORTERS:

GO ON, GO ON, GO ON, GO ON NOW!

(Lights up on Dorsey's office. We see Jim Conley, black, in his late twenties—muscular, self-assured, quick-witted, and dressed in torn, well-worn hand-me-downs. He manages to be charming, even sexy in a dangerous way.)

DORSEY: Jim Conley, your job here at the factory is sweeper, that right?

CONLEY: I prefer "cleaning supervisor" if you don't mind.

DORSEY: Cleaning supervisor, then. Now tell me, Jim, did you notice anything unusual about Mr. Frank?

CONLEY *(Wringing his hands)*: He done himself like this all the time.

DORSEY: Unh-hunh. Anything else?

CONLEY: Well, let me think . . .

DORSEY: Did you ever see him bring any of the factory girls into his private office?

CONLEY: Girls in his office?

(Lights shift to Craig's office. He is surrounded by the Ensemble.)

REPORTERS:

Ooooo . . .

MAN:

HE HAS A KID, YOU KNOW.

ANOTHER MAN *(Overlapping "a kid")*:

MY BROTHER SAYS HE KNOWS.

PSYCHIATRIST *(Overlapping "says he knows")*:

I'VE WATCHED HIM FOR A WHILE.

REPORTERS:

Ooooo . . .

MAN *(Overlapping "for a while")*:

KNOCKED UP SOME STUDENT SO

ANOTHER MAN *(Overlapping "some student")*:

WHEREVER LEO GOES

PSYCHIATRIST *(Overlapping "Leo goes")*:

BEHIND THAT CREEPY SMILE

REPORTERS:

Ooooo . . .

MAN *(Overlapping "creepy smile")*:

He paid to make her go.

ANOTHER MAN *(Overlapping "her go")*:

He carries Mary's clothes!

PSYCHIATRIST *(Overlapping "clothes")*:

The classic pedophile!

ALL THREE MEN:

I know it, yes,
I seen it, yes!
I know it, yes,
I seen it, yes!

MEN & ENSEMBLE:

I know it, yes,
I seen it, yes!
I know it, yes!
I seen it, yes!

REPORTERS *(Overlapping "The classic pedophile")*:

Ooooo . . .
Go on! (Go on!)
Go on! (Go on!)
Go on! (Go on!)
Go on! (Go on!)
Go on! (Go on!)
Go on! (Go on!)
Go on! Go on!
Go on, now!

(We are back in Leo's cell.)

ROSSER: We're gonna hafta get some of your mama's recipes for the ladies' page, long as they ain't too Yankee-fied or peculiar. Potato salad, that's always a good one. Jews do eat potato salad, don't they?

LEO: May I be honest with you?

ROSSER: You gotta be.

LEO: I don't like you. In fact, I dislike you intensely.

ROSSER: You know, I'm getting a feeling about you, Leo. And when I get a feeling, I work up a strategy. And when I work up a strategy I win. Every goddamn time. You don't like me? Fine. I don't like you either, but I swear to God and Jesus and everybody else that I'm gonna win this case and send you home.

LEO: You're growing on me.

(They shake hands.
Back to Craig.)

CRAIG:

LOOK! YOU JUST SCRIBBLE IT DOWN AND IT COVERS THE TOWN LIKE MOLASSES OR MUD!
LOOK! FOR US DRUNKEN OL' BUMS, OPPORTUNITY COMES IN A MAGICAL FLOOD!
LOOK! YOU MIGHT NEVER BE SURE IF YOUR MOTIVES ARE PURE, BUT YOUR PROFITS ARE CLEAR!
LOOK! YOU WERE DOWN AND DEPRESSED, NOW YOU'RE RIDIN' THE CREST OF THE SCOOP OF THE YEAR!

(We are back in Dorsey's office.)

CONLEY: Girls in his office?

DORSEY: Jim, I got a piece of paper here says you spent a little time on the chain gang.

CONLEY: That right?

DORSEY: Twice, according to this. Drunk and disorderly behavior.

CONLEY: Well, I tend to over-celebrate holidays.

DORSEY: And the second time it says here you were out with the road gang and you just up and disappeared.

CONLEY: Well, you know, my term was just about up.

DORSEY: Really? I think you had a few more months to serve. You know what that makes you, don't you?

CONLEY: Lucky.

DORSEY: I was going to say an escaped convict. Now, what should we do about that?

CONLEY: What was that you asked me about Mr. Frank?

(He and Dorsey exchange smiles.)

REPORTERS I & ENSEMBLE I *(Simultaneously with Reporters II)*:

ACCORDIN' TO REPORTS OBTAINED EX-
CLUSIVELY BY THIS REPORTER,
MR. LEO FRANK HAS BEEN IN-

DICTED ON THE CHARGE OF MURDER!
PROSECUTOR DORSEY STATES THE
TRIAL WILL BEGIN IN THE
ATLANTA COUNTY COURTHOUSE
ONLY ONE MONTH FROM TODAY!

REPORTERS II *(Simultaneously with Reporters I)* & ENSEMBLE II *(Echoing Reporters II)*:

EXTRA! EXTRA! LEO FRANK INDICTED!
TRIAL SET FOR A MONTH FROM NOW!
PROSECUTOR DORSEY WILL
TRY THE CASE HIMSELF, HE SAYS!
LUTHER ROSSER WILL REPRESENT
MR. FRANK IN THE FIGHT OF HIS LIFE!
DORSEY PROMISES SURPRISE WITNESSES
AND A QUICK FINISH!

REPORTERS & ENSEMBLES:

MRS. FRANK, THE SUSPECT'S WIFE,
HAS STILL NOT SPOKEN TO REPORTERS!
WHAT'S THE WORD FROM MRS. FRANK?
WHAT'S THE WORD FROM MRS. FRANK?
MRS. FRANK! MRS. FRANK!

SCENE 13

The Reporters are outside the Frank house now, whirling and spinning. Lucille is revealed in the center of the craziness, carrying a wicker hamper. The Reporters are asking questions all at once. Lucille shakes her head no—she's not going to say anything and tries to get through. In the process, the hamper is upset and the contents fall to the ground. This is too much for her.

LUCILLE: Let me alone! Please! Let me alone!

(She fights back her tears and anger, kneels to pick up the contents of the basket. The Reporters scatter.)

CRAIG: Let's leave the lady alone!

(Craig feigns leaving, then when the others are gone, he returns, helps Lucille retrieve her things.)

I hope there isn't much damage, ma'am.

(Lucille does not respond to his presence.)

No. Don't be afraid. I just came back to help.

LUCILLE: I have nothing to say.

CRAIG *(Looking at a jar)*: Watermelon pickles! That's one of my mama's specialties.

(She continues repacking the hamper. He assists.)

And deviled eggs! You're a good cook.

LUCILLE: Not really.

CRAIG : Oh yes! This nose knows all.

(She does not respond.)

I can only imagine how difficult it must be for you, Miz Frank. All these stories about your husband comin' out ev'ry day.

(Without facing him, Lucille sings:)

LUCILLE:

You don't know this man.
You don't know a thing.
You come here with these horrifying stories,
These contemptible conceits,
And you think you understand how a man's heart beats
And you don't know a thing.

(Now she turns and looks at Craig.)

You don't know this man.
You don't even try.
When a man writes his mother every Sunday,
Pays his bills before they're due,
Works so hard to feed his family—
There's your murderer for you—
And you stand here spitting words
That you know aren't true,

THEN YOU DON'T KNOW THIS MAN.
I DON'T THINK YOU COULD.
YOU DON'T HAVE THE RIGHT TO KNOW
A MAN THAT WISE AND GOOD—
HE IS A DECENT MAN!
HE IS AN HONEST MAN!
AND YOU DON'T KNOW . . .
AND YOU NEVER WILL.
NOT FROM ME, NOT FROM ANYONE WHO KNOWS HIM—
NOT A MORSEL, NOT A CRUMB, NOT A CLUE.

CRAIG: You're sayin' he's decent, you're sayin' he's honest, but you're not sayin' he's innocent.

(She addresses him directly:)

LUCILLE:
I HAVE NOTHING MORE TO SAY TO YOU.

(She picks up her basket and walks past him. He watches her, his pad and pencil still out—perhaps she will turn around? But she doesn't. Lights down.)

SCENE 14

A visitor's room in Fulton Jail. A table, two chairs, and an eighteen-inch partition separates the prisoner from the visitor. During the meeting, the Guard stands upstage behind the partition, preventing Lucille from handing Leo the basket of food.

LEO: Did you pay the bill to Jacob's Drug Store this month?
LUCILLE: It just came yesterday.
LEO: We don't want people thinking we can't pay our bills.
LUCILLE: I'll tend to it this evening.
LEO: I don't know why they won't let me have my checkbook!
LUCILLE: It must be against the law.
LEO: Ridiculous! What kind of sense does that make?
LUCILLE: I told you I'll tend to the bill this evening.
LEO: Don't forget.

LUCILLE: I put a jar of watermelon pickles in with your dinner.

LEO: And did the life insurance bill come? It should've by now.

LUCILLE: No, not yet.

LEO: Well, pay it the second it comes. I'm sure they're just looking for a chance to drop us.

LUCILLE *(Ill at ease)*: Leo, I think I'm going to visit Aunt Miriam in Savannah.

LEO: I see. When?

LUCILLE: I'm not sure. A week or two.

LEO: Well, just be back when the trial starts.

LUCILLE: That's why I'm going, Leo.

LEO: What?

LUCILLE: The trial. I—I don't think I can stand it.

LEO: Well you have to stand it! How will it look if you run out of town?

LUCILLE: I don't want everybody staring at me when they say all those awful things about you in the courtroom.

LEO: That's absurd, Lucille. It's all just a bunch of lies and nonsense. Anyway, they'll be staring at me, not you.

LUCILLE: And the mother of that poor little girl! I don't want to see her!

LEO: I don't like the way you're talking.

LUCILLE: I'm just telling you how I feel, Leo.

LEO: You have to be there!

LUCILLE: I'll be here tomorrow with your dinner. *(Starts to go)*

LEO: Lucille!

(She turns.)

LUCILLE: What is it?

LEO: You have to be there!

(The lights fade out as she goes.)

SCENE 15

We hear the sound of a country fiddle playing feverishly. Lights up outside the Atlanta courthouse. At first, we only see the violin player, Fiddlin' John, who stands on a crate and plays. Eventually, we see that the courthouse steps are full of people, jabbering and straining to look into the courthouse windows.

Music begins. The Ensemble sings:

FIDDLIN' JOHN:

PEOPLE OF ATLANTA STAND TOGETHER ON THIS DAY!

(And now Watson rises up from the crowd, waving his newspaper in the air.)

WATSON:

I HAVE COME TO ATLANTA WITH A MESSAGE FROM THE LORD!

FIDDLIN' JOHN:

PEOPLE OF ATLANTA
SWEAR THAT SOMEONE'S GONNA PAY!

WATSON:

I HAVE COME
TO SEE THE DEVIL
GET HIS JUST
AND TRUE REWARD!

ENSEMBLE I *(Variously; overlapping Fiddlin' John and Tom Watson)*:

JIMMY!
WHAT'S HE GONNA SAY?
HEY, GET AWAY FROM THAT WINDOW!
JIMMY!
WELL!
WE'RE GONNA SEE 'IM GET HIS JUST
AND TRUE REWARD!

ENSEMBLE II *(Variously, overlapping "Say? Hey")*:

LOOKA THIS! WAIT!
BOY YOU BETTER MOVE!
I SEE 'IM ON THE WAY!
YES!
GONNA SEE HIM GET HIS JUST
AND TRUE REWARD!

(The interior of the old courtroom has now come into view. The windows of the courtroom are opened wide because of the heat. Big electric fans are placed strategically, but seem to do little good. Many of those in attendance wave handheld fans throughout. The courtroom is packed to the gills with onlookers: the whole range of citizenry—businessmen, elegantly dressed women, simple country people, etc. One gets the feeling that every single person in the state of Georgia is at this courthouse.

We see two black women cleaning the courtroom. One mops the floor; one brings a tray with a pitcher of water and glass to the judge's stand.

In the courtroom are Craig and a knot of Reporters, Mrs. Phagan and her family, and Dorsey with Starnes and Ivey at the prosecution table. One chair remains conspicuously empty—it is meant for Lucille, who has not arrived.

Judge Roan, an unwell and elderly southern gentleman, is pushed on in a wheelchair by his Nurse.

Watson passes his newspapers to the crowd while Fiddlin' John sings:)

FIDDLIN' JOHN:

PEOPLE OF ATLANTA,
BETTER BOW YOUR HEADS IN SHAME . . .

THREE WOMEN:

AMEN!

FIDDLIN' JOHN:

THERE'S A MAN WHO CAME
AND SPIT ON YOUR FINE CITY'S NAME!

SEVERAL MEN:

LEMME AT 'IM!

CROWD:

WATCH OUT!

FIDDLIN' JOHN:

PEOPLE OF ATLANTA,
ALL ARE VICTIMS OF THIS CRIME!
IT IS TIME NOW!

WATSON:

IT IS TIME NOW!

CROWD:

IT IS TIME NOW!

WATSON:

IT IS TIME . . .

(Leo is brought into the courtroom, manacled, by guards. Rosser comes in from the street in a rumpled white suit. He waves to the crowd like a man running for office.)

ROSSER *(To various people)*: Hey! Hey now! Good to see ya! Hey there, Mr. Craig! You write somethin' nice down about Leo's tie. His sweet ol' mama sent it to him for good luck.

LEO: She did not!

(Rosser joins Leo at the defense table. Leo looks at him in disbelief in the face of this lie.)

ROSSER: Stay with me, Leo. *(Looks around)* Where's your better half?
LEO: I wish I knew!
STARNES: All rise.

(The whole courtroom stands as Judge Roan painfully makes his way to the bench.)

LEO: My God! That judge!
ROSSER: Not much we can do about that.
JUDGE ROAN: Mr. Dorsey . . .

(They take their seats. Judge Roan bangs his gavel and Dorsey rises. The doors open and Lucille enters the courtroom quietly. The crowd begins murmuring. Rosser calls to her:)

ROSSER: Miz Frank!

(She makes her way to the empty chair, eyes demurely cast down. She does not look at Leo as she takes her seat. Dorsey waits patiently. Judge Roan motions for him to continue.)

JUDGE ROAN: Get on with it, Mr. Dorsey.
DORSEY: Your Honor, gentlemen of the jury, and good people of Georgia *(Sings)*:

THERE IS A FARMHOUSE IN MARIETTA,
KINDA BATTERED AND FORLORN,
AND IN THAT FARMHOUSE, FOURTEEN YEARS AGO,
A GIRL NAMED MARY WAS BORN.

AND SHE WOULD DANCE IN FIELDS OF COTTON,
SHE HAD A TREE WHERE SHE COULD PLAY,
BUT WHEN HER DADDY DIED TWO YEARS AGO,
MARY AND HER MAMA MOVED AWAY.

IT'S ONLY TWENTY MILES FROM MARIETTA
TO A FACT'RY IN THE CENTER OF THIS TOWN,

And twenty miles was all it took
To strike that sweet girl down.

People of Atlanta fought for freedom to their graves,
And now their city is a fact'ry and their children are its slaves.
People of Atlanta swing their city gates wide,
And look at what you've wrought!

(He points to Leo as he says it, and Leo shrinks from the glare. The crowd outside jeers, and the crowd inside echoes the response. Judge Roan bangs his gavel for silence.

Now Dorsey turns to the witness stand, which is suddenly occupied by Frankie, dressed in the same sharp clothes he wore when we first saw him.)

So, Frankie, you say you rode downtown with Mary on the English Avenue streetcar?

FRANKIE: Yes, sir. Mornin' of the Memorial Day Parade.

DORSEY: And can you tell us what happened?

FRANKIE: Well, she wanted to go to the picture show real bad and I promised I'd take her after the parade. But first she was goin' to the factory to pick up her pay.

DORSEY: And did she get off?

FRANKIE: No, sir. Not right then.

DORSEY: Tell us what happened, Frankie.

FRANKIE: Well, she got up to go and she looked funny. And I said—

(Mary enters in her parade finery, as before. The stage is lit moodily through the electric fans which whirl above the courtroom.)

Somethin' wrong, Mary?

MARY: Mr. Frank.

FRANKIE: Mr. Frank what?

MARY: Looks at me.

FRANKIE: Looks at you? Everybody looks at you.

MARY: Not like Mr. Frank.

FRANKIE: What does he do?

MARY:

He calls my name,
I turn my head,

HE GOT NO WORDS TO SAY.
HIS EYES GET BIG,
MY FACE GETS RED,
AND I WANT TO RUN AWAY,
AND HE LOOKS . . .
AND I WAIT . . .
AND HE SMILES . . .

FRANKIE: You better tell on him.
MARY: Tell who? He's the boss.
FRANKIE: He do the other girls that way?
MARY: I guess. Some of 'em.
FRANKIE: What say I come over there and break his face?
MARY: Go on. You'll miss the parade. I'll see you over to the picture show.
FRANKIE: Well, at least let me come with you to get your pay.
MARY: Save me a seat!

(She disappears. Frankie returns to the courtroom.)

FRANKIE: And that was the last time I ever saw her. *(Looks over at Leo, knots his fist)* I wish I had come over there and broke your damn face!

(Reaction in the courtroom. Dorsey puts an arm on Frankie to calm him. Leo looks nervously at Rosser, who is smiling broadly. Rosser slowly rises to his feet.)

ENSEMBLE I:
THAT'S RIGHT!
YOU TELL 'IM, FRANKIE!
WHAT'S HE GONNA SAY, NOW?
WHAT'S HE . . .
ENSEMBLE II *(Overlapping "You tell 'im")*:
THAT'S RIGHT!
THAT BOY . . .
WHAT'S HE GONNA SAY, NOW?
WATSON *(Simultaneously with Ensemble I)*:
PROOF!
IT IS PROOF
THAT THE LORD HAS SET
BEFORE US!

ROSSER *(Simultaneously with Ensemble I)*: Now, Your Honor, I'm 'fraid I got to object here. I—

(Judge Roan limply bangs his gavel. Leo has not met Frankie's gaze, looking straight ahead, stone-faced.)

DORSEY *(To Rosser)*: Your witness.
ROSSER: Nothing at this time, Your Honor.
LEO *(Sotto voce)*: What?! Do something! He's lying!
ROSSER: Forget about him. I got us a strategy.
LEO: What is it?
ROSSER: Stay with me now.

(Leo bristles, purses his lips angrily, looks to Lucille for agreement. She looks away. Suddenly, Iola Stover, one of Mary's co-workers at the factory, appears on the witness stand.)

DORSEY: Iola Stover, will you describe for the court Mr. Leo Frank's manner in the factory?

IOLA:

HE'LL CALL MY NAME.
I'LL TURN MY HEAD.
HE GOT NO WORDS TO SAY.
HIS EYES GET BIG,
MY FACE GETS RED,
AND I WANT TO RUN AWAY.

(And now, from behind the judge's stand, two other girls from the factory—Essie and Monteen—stand up and begin singing simultaneously with Iola.)

I'LL FEEL HIS BREATH
BACK OF MY NECK.
HIS HAND AGAINST MY CHAIR.
I'LL PUNCH THE CLOCK,
PICK UP MY CHECK,
IT SEEMS LIKE HE'S ALWAYS THERE.

ESSIE & MONTEEN *(Simultaneously with Iola)*:

HE'LL CALL MY NAME.
I'LL TURN MY HEAD.

He got no words to say.
His eyes get big,
My face gets red,
And I want to run away.

IOLA & ESSIE *(Simultaneously with Monteen)*:
I'm in the hall
And then he's there,
He passes much too close.
I change my clothes,
Put up my hair,

MONTEEN *(Simultaneously with Iola & Essie)*:
I'm in the lounge,
I turn around,
He passes much too close.
I eat my lunch,
I hear a sound,

IOLA, ESSIE & MONTEEN:
And somehow, I'm sure he knows—
And I turn,
And he smiles,
And he says:

(Now, Leo joins them, exactly the suave and slithery philanderer the girls are describing.)

LEO:
Why don'tcha come up to my office?
Got a couple o' things you might like to see.
Why don'tcha come up to my office,
About two-fifteen 'til a quarter to three?
If you could maybe swing by, honey,
Well, you know it'd be okay with me
If you came, if you came, if you came,
If you came to my office.

(He goes to each of the girls in turn, dancing slyly in front of them.)

Why don'tcha come up to my office?
I got a bottle o' wine and the cork ain't popped!
Why don'tcha come up to my office,
Where it's nice and cool when the blinds are dropped?

If you could maybe swing by, honey,
We'll pretend that bad ol' clock has stopped
If you came, if you came, if you came,
If you came to my office.

I know this new dance that they're doin' in Manhattan.
I'll get you dancin' like you never done before!
And I'll give you things that they sent me from
Manhattan,
And if you like, well, I got more—
Hell, I got more!

(And now he's at the top of his form, flirting, seducing and dancing up a storm.)

Come on and come up to my office,
I got a fine fried chicken and biscuits for two!
Come on and come up to my office,
We got lots of things that we both can do!
Just take a break and swing by, honey—
No one has to know but me and you
That you came, that you came, that you came, that you
came,
When you came, when you came, when you came, when
you came,
If you came, if you came, if you came, if you came,
So come on! Come on!
Come on!
Come on!
Come on!
Why don'tcha come up and come on and come up to my . . .
Why don'tcha come up and come on and come up to my . . .
Why don'tcha come up and come on and come up?
Come on and come up?
Come on and come up?
Come on and come up?
Come up and come on . . .

(And Leo continues dancing, while the girls, in fear, stare straight forward, avoiding his glance.)

IOLA, ESSIE & MONTEEN:

He calls my name.
I turn my head.
He got no words to say . . .
His eyes get big,
My face gets red,
And I want to run away.

(And now Leo is still. He stares at Iola, rubbing his hands slowly together. The other girls take their seats.)

And he looks,
And I wait,

IOLA:

And . . . he smiles.

(Leo sits at the defense table, still facing forward—Lucille is in her chair behind him, each in their own light.)

LEO: She's lying!

ROSSER: Sit down, Leo. And shut up. I'm not just sittin' on my ass here. I'm workin' out a strategy. We're gonna be fine.

LEO: Tell me!

ROSSER: When it's time, I will.

LEO: Somebody told them to say all that. They were coached. They were coached!

(Back outside the courthouse.)

FIDDLIN' JOHN & TOWNSMAN:

People of Atlanta,
Hear the bells of Judgment chime!

WATSON:

It is time now!

TOWNSPEOPLE:

It is time now!

WATSON:

It is time . . .

(In the courtroom we see Newt uneasily come to the stand and be sworn in.)

DORSEY: Newt, I'm asking you to tell us how Mr. Frank acted.
NEWT *(Nervous)*: Acted?
DORSEY: Around the girls.

NEWT:

I AM TRYING TO REMEMBER . . .

DORSEY: He ever look at those girls sorta funny like?
ROSSER: Objection! Leading the witness!
JUDGE ROAN: Objection sustained.
DORSEY: I'll rephrase that. You ever see Mr. Frank anywhere near where the girls changed their clothes?

NEWT:

WELL, I SEEN HIM BY THE DOORWAY . . .
WHEN THE GIRLS WAS IN THERE CHANGIN' . . .

DORSEY: The ladies' private dressing room. And what was he doin'?

NEWT:

SEE, THE WAY THAT I REMEMBER,
HE WAS LOOKIN' THROUGH THE DOORWAY,
AND THE GIRLS WAS IN THERE DRESSIN',
AND I GUESS THAT HE WAS SWEATIN' . . .
I MEAN THE MAN WAS ALWAYS . . .

DORSEY: That'll be all. Thank you, Newt.
NEWT: But Mr. Dorsey . . .
DORSEY: That'll be all, Newt! Thank you!
LEO: He was coached, too! They're all being coached.
ROSSER: Easy now, Leo. We're gonna be fine.

(Leo stands, incensed.)

LEO: Shame! Shame on you, Newt! . . .

(The crowd reacts. Judge Roan bangs his gavel for order. Lucille has cast her eyes downward, and when Leo turns to meet her glance, he is ashamed. He lowers himself back into his chair.)

ROSSER: Leo, just shut the Hell up.

(Mrs. Phagan has arrived on the witness stand, where Dorsey is gently handling her.)

DORSEY: Mrs. Phagan, can you describe for us, please ma'am, the outfit your daughter Mary wore to town last Memorial Day?

MRS. PHAGAN: Yes, sir, I can. It was her Easter Sunday outfit—the little lavender cotton pongee dress I made her and a straw hat with a parasol to match, and white stockings and her party shoes.

(Dorsey pulls out a small pile of torn, ruined clothes, and holds them up.)

DORSEY: Would these be the clothes?

(The courtroom erupts. Dorsey waves the clothes above his head.)

This befouled and filthy rag used to be a dress—

(Gradually, as Dorsey continues, the noise fades away and the courtroom lights dim. A pinpoint picks up Mrs. Phagan, who sings:)

MRS. PHAGAN *(Simultaneously with Dorsey below)*:

MY CHILD WILL FORGIVE ME
FOR RAISIN' HER POOR,
AND FOR TAKIN' HER OUT OF THE SCHOOL.
MY CHILD WILL FORGIVE ME
FOR NOT DOIN' MORE
TO PROTECT HER FROM MEN
WHO ARE CRUEL,
AND MY CHILD WILL FORGIVE ME
FOR CLOSIN' MY EYES
TO THE DANGERS OF GROWING TOO FAST.
MY CHILD WILL FORGIVE ME
WITH TEARS IN HER EYES
WHEN WE'RE REUNITED AT LAST.

DORSEY *(Simultaneously with Mrs. Phagan, his voice disappearing)*: The dress a proud and happy little girl wore to church on Easter Sunday. This cloth that was found around Mary's throat was torn from her underclothing and placed over her mouth for a gag while Leo Frank tiptoed back to his office for the cord with which to strangle her. When she did not yield to his lust that was not that of other men, he struck her. They say he had no marks on his person—she had no time to inflict marks! Ladies and gentlemen . . .

MRS. PHAGAN *(Simultaneously with Dorsey below)*:
MY CHILD WILL BE SAFE
IN THE ARMS OF THE LORD,
AND AS PURE AS THE DAY OF HER BIRTH.
MY CHILD WILL BE COZIED
AND BLESSED AND ADORED
AS SHE NEVER COULD BE HERE ON EARTH.
AND MY CHILD WILL BE WATCHIN' ME,
GIVIN' ME FAITH
IN A FUTURE THAT'S GOLDEN AND NEW.
MY MARY WILL TEACH ME
TO OPEN MY HEART,

DORSEY *(Simultaneously with Mrs. Phagan, his voice disappearing further)*: Mrs. Phagan, isn't it true that you lost your husband two years ago? And because of that you lost your farm? And you and Mary moved to Atlanta? And you had to take your baby out of school and put her to work at the National Pencil Company. She shoulda been in sixth grade! She shoulda been playin' with her friends!

(Courtroom lights brighten.)

MRS. PHAGAN:
AND SO I FORGIVE YOU,
JEW.

(She sings the word right to Leo, who is shaken.)

DORSEY: That's all, Your Honor.
JUDGE ROAN: You may step down, ma'am.
DORSEY *(Dramatically)*: Bring in Jim Conley!

(The great doors to the courtroom open and Conley enters. He presents a far different picture from the ragtag vagrant we saw previously in

Dorsey's office. Conley has on a well-tailored summer suit, and a neat shirt and tie which he wears well. He walks to the stand slowly, sort of like a runway model, exuding healthy strength and masculinity. He is sworn in, while the Crowd outside sings again:)

CROWD:

LEMME SEE! WATCH OUT!
WHO'S JIM . . .
JIM CONLEY?
WAIT A MINUTE!
LORD, 'NOTHER NIGGER . . .
WATCH OUT! LOOKA THIS!
WHAT'S HE GONNA SAY?
WHAT'S HE GONNA SAY?
WATCH OUT! LOOK! JIMMY!
NOW WAIT A MINUTE!
HE'S NO GOOD—
NO DAMN GOOD . . .
WHO'S THIS? WHAT'S HE DOIN'?
HE'S ASKIN' HIM A QUESTION!
WHAT'S HE GONNA SAY?

WHAT'S HE GONNA SAY?
WHY THEY GONNA . . .
CALL THAT . . .
. . . MAN?

WHAT'S HE GONNA SAY ABOUT . . . ?

OH!
WILL YA LOOKA THAT?

PUTTIN' ON AIRS!
SLICK AS AN ONION!
WHAT'S HE GONNA DO?
WHAT'S HE GONNA SAY?

CONLEY:

HE TOL' ME TO WATCH THE DOOR,
"WATCH THE DOOR"—THAT'S WHAT HE SAID.
THAT'S WHAT HE SAID—I SHOULD MAKE SURE
NO ONE CAME AND INTERRUPTED.
I'D SAY ONCE OR TWICE A MONTH,
HE'D TELL ME, "JIM, YOU WATCH THE DOOR—
I GOT A LADY COMIN'. I GOT A LADY COMIN'."
LIKE I SAID, ONCE OR TWICE A MONTH,
THERE'D BE A LADY COME TO CALL
AND HE'D SAY, "JIM, YOU WATCH THE DOOR,"
THAT'S WHAT HE SAID.

And once, I remember it was two ladies. Another time, there was a black gentleman, I believe he said he was from Chicago . . .

ROSSER: Objection!

JUDGE ROAN: Mr. Dorsey, will you instruct your witness to answer only the questions put to him?

DORSEY: Jim, do you understand the man?
CONLEY: Yes, sir.
DORSEY: All right, then. Jim, will you tell us about the mornin' of April 26?
CONLEY: The day of the parade.

He tol' me to watch the door.
"Watch the door," that's what he said.
That's what he said. "I got a girl,
She'll be comin' up to see me,
She's a very pretty girl,"
He said. "Don't let me catch you lookin' at
Miss Mary Perkins."
That's what he called her, I think,
"Miss Mary Perkins."
So when this Mary came to call
I kep' my eyes down to the floor
'Cause Mr. Frank said not to look,
That's what he said.

Well, next thing, Mr. Frank is yellin' somethin', so I run upstairs, and I open the door, and Mr. Frank looks up.

He said, "We were playin' a game!
Playin' a game!" That's what he said.
That's what he said. And little Mary's
Kinda crumpled in the corner.
He said, "You don't understand—
She didn't want to play the game,
And so I went and hit her—
You see, I had to hit her."
He tol' me I should go and look,
He said she's actin' like she's sick,
And I said, "Lawd, that chil' is dead!"
That's what I said!

And he said, "No! No!
It ain't my fault that girl is dead!"
He said, "No! No!"
That's what he said.

CROWD:

THAT'S WHAT HE SAID!

CONLEY:

HE SAID, "NO! NO!"
AND HIS EYES WERE WILD AND HIS FACE WAS RED.
HE SAID, "NO!"
"NO!"

CROWD *(Overlapping)*:

NO!
NO!

CONLEY:

THAT'S WHAT HE SAID!

CROWD:

THAT'S WHAT HE SAID, THAT'S WHAT HE,
WHAT HE SAID, HE SAID THAT'S,
THAT'S WHAT HE SAID . . .

CONLEY:

HE SAID, "GOTTA GET HER OUT—
LET'S GET HER OUT!" THAT'S WHAT HE SAID.

CROWD:

THAT'S WHAT HE SAID!

CONLEY:

AND SO I FOUND ME
THIS OL' GUNNY SACK AND WRAPPED 'ER.
HE SAID, "YOU'RE A GOOD BOY, JIM—
I KNOW YOU WON'T TELL NO ONE NOTHIN'—
HERE'S A HUNDRED DOLLARS!"

CROWD:

NO! IT CAN'T BE TRUE!

CONLEY:

I GOT A HUNDRED DOLLARS

CROWD:

GOD! WHAT CAN WE DO?

CONLEY:

AND SO I PUT HER ON MY BACK.
WE TOOK THE ELEVATOR DOWN.
HE SAID, "JUS' THROW HER ON THE GROUND!"
THAT'S WHAT HE SAID.

CROWD:

THAT'S WHAT HE SAID.

CONLEY:

Yes, he said,
"No!"
"No!"

CROWD *(Overlapping)*:

No!
No!

CONLEY:

"There ain't no reason I should hang!"
He said, "No!"
"No!"

CROWD *(Overlapping)*:

No!
No!

CONLEY:

That's what he said!

CROWD:

That's what he said!

CONLEY:

He said, "No!"
"No!"

CROWD *(Overlapping)*:

No!
No!

CONLEY:

"There ain't no reason I should hang—
You got money in your pocket and there's plenty more o' that—
I got wealthy friends an' fam'ly, and a wife who's dumb and fat—
I got rich folks out in Brooklyn if I need somewheres to go
And these stupid rednecks never gonna
Know!"

CROWD *(Overlapping)*:

Hang 'im!

CONLEY:

"No!"

CROWD:

Hang 'im!

CONLEY *(Simultaneously with Crowd below)*:

"IT AIN'T MY FAULT THAT GIRL IS DEAD!"
HE SAID, "NO!"
"NO!"
THAT'S WHAT HE SAID!
HE SAID, "NO!"
"NO!"

CROWD *(Simultaneously with Conley above)*:

HANG THE JEW!
HANG 'IM!
HANG 'IM!
MAKE 'IM PAY!
GET 'IM!
NOW!

CONLEY:

AND HIS EYES WERE WILD AND HIS FACE WAS RED
HE SAID, "NO!"

(As this sequence gathers momentum, the overhead fans turn ever more quickly—maddeningly—casting more and more shadow onto the set.)

LEO:

NO!

CROWD *(Overlapping "No!")*:

HANG 'IM!
HANG 'IM!
HANG 'IM! YEAH!
HANG THE KILLER!

FIDDLIN' JOHN *(Overlapping "Hang the killer!")*:

HANG THE KILLER!
PEOPLE OF ATLANTA!

CROWD *(Overlapping "People of Atlanta!")*:

KILL 'IM!
JEW! KILL 'IM!

MAN *(Overlapping "Jew! Kill 'im!")*:

PEOPLE OF ATLANTA!

FIDDLIN' JOHN:

RAISE YOUR VOICES!

CROWD *(Overlapping "Raise your voices!")*:
HANG 'IM!
GET 'IM!
YES!

FRANKIE, MAN & FIDDLIN' JOHN:
RAISE YOUR VOICES HIGH!

CROWD *(Overlapping "Raise your voices high!")*:
MAKE 'IM PAY!
BASTARD! YEAH!
TAKE 'IM DOWN!
KILL 'IM! GET 'IM!

MAN *(Overlapping "Kill 'im!")*:
FOR MARY!

CROWD:
NAIL 'IM! NOW!
HANG 'IM! HANG 'IM!

FIDDLIN' JOHN, FRANKIE, MAN & LIZZIE *(Overlapping "Hang 'im!)*:
HIGH!!

CROWD:
HANG 'IM! HANG 'IM!
HANG 'IM!

FIDDLIN' JOHN, FRANKIE, MAN & LIZZIE *(Overlapping "Hang 'im!)*:
HIGH!!

ROSSER: Objection! Goddammit, objection!

(Judge Roan bangs his gavel, but the strain is wearing on him. The atmosphere is tense.)

JUDGE ROAN: Watch your mouth, sir! As you are well aware, the laws of the state of Georgia do not allow the defendant in a murder trial to testify in his own behalf, but said defendant is allowed to make a statement. Does your client wish to make such a statement at this time, Mr. Rosser?

LEO: No.

ROSSER: Yes, Your Honor. He does.

LEO: What?

ROSSER: This is it. Get up on there.

LEO: I'm not prepared.

ROSSER: I know. That's my strategy.

JUDGE: Proceed.

(Leo looks at Rosser and, with all the dignity he can muster, goes to the witness stand.

Leo waits until the room is completely still and begins to sing, simply, addressing the whole room, but paying special attention to Lucille. For the first time, we see Leo with all his pretensions and affectations stripped away.)

LEO:

IT'S HARD TO SPEAK MY HEART.
I'M NOT A MAN WHO BARES HIS SOUL.
I LET THE MOMENT PASS ME BY—
I STAY WHERE I AM IN CONTROL.
I HIDE BEHIND MY WORK,
SAFE AND SURE OF WHAT TO SAY . . .
I KNOW I MUST SEEM HARD,
I KNOW I MUST SEEM COLD.

I NEVER TOUCHED THAT GIRL—
YOU THINK I'D HURT A CHILD YET?
I'D HARDLY SEEN HER FACE BEFORE—
I SWEAR—I SWORE WE'D BARELY MET.
THESE PEOPLE TRY TO SCARE YOU
WITH THINGS I'VE NEVER SAID.
I KNOW IT MAKES NO SENSE.
I SWEAR I DON'T KNOW WHY . . .

YOU SEE ME AS I AM—YOU CAN'T BELIEVE I'D LIE—
YOU CAN'T BELIEVE I'D DO THESE DEEDS—
A LITTLE MAN WHO'S SCARED AND BLIND,
TOO LOST TO FIND THE WORDS HE NEEDS.
I NEVER TOUCHED THAT CHILD—
GOD—I NEVER RAISED MY HAND!
I STAND BEFORE YOU NOW . . .
INCREDIBLY AFRAID.
I PRAY YOU UNDERSTAND.

(There is a silence. Lucille and Leo lock eyes—she knows he is innocent. Throughout the next exchange, they do not move their eyes from each other.)

JUDGE ROAN: Mr. Rosser.

(Rosser rises and addresses the jury.)

ROSSER: Gentlemen. I have just taken the biggest gamble of my entire career. I forced Leo Frank to speak to you without warning. I did not coach him or rehearse him. Why would I do such a dangerous thing? Because I knew you would recognize the simon-pure truth when you heard it. Gentlemen, look Leo Frank in the eye. Look hard. Don't be afraid of what you see. Because it is the truth and Leo Frank is innocent.

JUDGE ROAN: Mr. Dorsey.

(Dorsey rises to begin his summation:)

DORSEY *(Simultaneously with Ensemble below)*: This angel met her end on the concrete floor of the sweatshop where she toiled away her childhood fastening erasers to pencil caps for ten pennies an hour. She died a noble death without a splotch or blemish upon her. *(Again holds up her bloody clothes above his head)* Your Honor, I've done my duty. I have no apologies to make. There will be but one verdict: GUILTY! GUILTY! GUILTY!

ENSEMBLE *(Singing simultaneously with Dorsey's speech above)*:

BLESS THIS DAY IN THE OLD HILLS OF
GEORGIA
THE OLD RED HILLS OF HOME.
ALL SINNERS PAY IN THE OLD HILLS OF
GEORGIA
LET US FINISH WHAT'S BEGUN
AND LET JESUS' WILL BE DONE!

(Time has passed and Judge Roan turns to the jury.)

JUDGE ROAN: Gentlemen of the jury, have you reached a verdict?

FOREMAN: Yes we have, Your Honor.

JUDGE ROAN: How say you?

FOREMAN: Guilty.

(The crowd lets out a collective exclamation of joy and relief.)

JUDGE ROAN: So say you all?
FOREMAN: Yes, Your Honor.
JUDGE ROAN: Poll the jury, Bailiff.
FOREMAN: Guilty.

(The noon bells start to chime in sync with the repeated word "Guilty." In the street outside the courthouse, the crowd begins to cakewalk.)

JUROR 1: Guilty.
JUROR 2: Guilty.
JUROR 3: Guilty.
JUROR 4: Guilty.

(By now a large portion of the crowd is dancing wildly. The jury box recedes upstage as Leo's cell appears center stage. Leo and Lucille hear the celebration from the street outside.)

JUROR 5: Guilty.

(Leo looks at her as the voices drone on and the bells chime. She reaches out her hand to touch his face. He embraces her.)

JUROR 6: Guilty.
JUROR 7: Guilty.

(The eerie music is replaced by an exultant celebratory cakewalk. And this, for the first time, is heard by Leo and Lucille. They embrace each other, terrified.

Curtain.)

ACT II

SCENE 1

The Confederate Memorial Day Parade. One year later. We hear snare drums. Upstage, behind a scrim, we see Judge Roan's face.

JUDGE ROAN: It is hereby adjudged that the appeal of Leo Max Frank for a new trial be rejected. It is further adjudged and ordered that on the twenty-eighth day of May, nineteen and fourteen, said defendant shall be hanged by the neck until he is dead, and may God have mercy on his soul.

(He bangs his gavel and, in silhouette, we see the parade from Act I, but a little slower than the first time. Discordant. Craig is standing, watching the parade. He turns to us and sings:)

CRAIG:

Now, Leo runs back and forth,
While they're screamin' up North how it just isn't fair.
Wow, they been treatin' this match
Like the latest dispatch from the Dreyfus Affair.

(We see Leo in a dim light in his cell, poring over an enormous book, Legal Statutes of the State of Georgia, 1910.*)*

LEO: Legal procedures and terms . . . Act of God. Affidavit. Alias. Alibi. Appeal . . . Appeal. *(Thumbs past some pages)*

CRAIG:

See? Mary's dead for a year,
But the temperature here's just as hot as before . . .

LEO: The appellant can only ask for a writ of certiorari in such circumstances as—certiorari, writ of certiorari . . .

(The lights black out on Leo. At the same time, downstage, we see two black people: Riley and Angela. He is polishing shoes, she is ironing the wash.)

CRAIG:

GEE—WOULDN'T TAKE SUCH A LOT
FOR THE OPENING SHOT OF A NEW CIVIL WAR!

(Craig exits, perhaps waving a Confederate flag.

As the parade fades away, Riley and Angela polish and iron, parrying between them in a curiously jocular, almost benign manner:)

RILEY:

YOU HEAR A RUMBLIN' AND A ROLLIN'?
IT'S COMIN' DOWN FROM THE NORTH.
IT'S COMIN' UP THROUGH THE GROUND,
AND IT'S A FUNNY OL' SOUND,
'CAUSE IT'S A RUMBLIN' AND A ROLLIN'!

ANGELA:

AND I BET I KNOW WHY—
SEE 'EM ON THE TRAIN,
SEE 'EM ON THE BUS—
THEY NEVER CARED MUCH ABOUT FOLKS LIKE US!

RILEY:

BUT NOW THEY'RE GONNA PAY ATTENTION.
SURE THEY GONNA ASK, "WHY? WHY? WHY?"

ANGELA:

THEY GONNA SAY, "I DON'T KNOW WHAT, I DON'T KNOW HOW!"

RILEY & ANGELA:

WELL, THEY'RE GONNA FIND OUT NOW.
THEY'RE GONNA PAY ATTENTION.

RILEY:

THEY'RE GONNA YELL, "SET THAT MAN FREE!"

(We see Newt carrying his lantern through the factory, making his rounds.)

NEWT:

WELL, THEY SURE AIN'T TALKIN' 'BOUT ME.

RILEY, ANGELA & NEWT:

Now there's a rumblin' and a rollin'.
Here comes the Yankee brigade!

NEWT:

They gonna come through this town—
We better keep our heads down—

RILEY & NEWT:

We better start mumblin' and a-shufflin'.

RILEY, ANGELA & NEWT:

We better polish our smiles.

(The light from Newt's lantern has fallen on Conley, lying on his cot in the factory basement.)

CONLEY:

Old Black Joe at your service,
Won't do nothin' that'll make you nervous.
Won't do nothin' worth a look or a mention

RILEY, ANGELA, NEWT & CONLEY:

And they won't never pay attention!

CONLEY:

They'll never say, "My, my, my!"

RILEY:

They gonna say, "Bring me my boots!"

ANGELA:

"Bring me my tea!"

NEWT:

I betcha thought the slaves were free . . .

ANGELA:

Mister Frank, good for you.
Lotta folks comin' to get you through.
Mister Frank, ain't that grand?
Lotta folks comin' to take a stand.
Mister Frank, knock on wood,
Ain't gonna do you no goddamn good!

CONLEY:

I can tell you this, as a matter of fact,
That the local hotels wouldn't be so packed
If a little black girl had gotten attacked.

RILEY, ANGELA & NEWT:

Go on, go on, go on, go on . . .

RILEY:

THEY COMIN', THEY COMIN' NOW, YESSIRREE!

NEWT:

'CAUSE A WHITE MAN GONNA GET HUNG, YOU SEE.

RILEY, NEWT & CONLEY:

THERE'S A BLACK MAN SWINGIN' IN EV'RY TREE

RILEY, ANGELA, NEWT & CONLEY:

BUT THEY DON'T NEVER PAY ATTENTION!

ANGELA:

OH, NO . . .

CONLEY:

HELL!

RILEY, ANGELA, NEWT & CONLEY:

THEY NEVER SAY, "WHY? WHY? WHY?"

RILEY:

BUT IF A YANKEE BOY FLIES . . .

CONLEY:

SURPRISE!

RILEY & ANGELA:

SURPRISE!

NEWT:

SURPRISE!

RILEY, ANGELA, NEWT & CONLEY:

THEY GONNA PAY ATTENTION!
THEY GONNA YELL, "SET THAT MAN FREE!"

CONLEY *(Singing a snatch of "Camptown Races" as he goes back to his nap)*:

DE DE DE DE DE DE DE
DE DE, DE DE
DE DE DE DE DE DE DE
DE DE DE DE DE.

RILEY, ANGELA & NEWT:

OH, THERE'S GONNA BE A RUMBLIN' AND A ROLLIN', YEAH . . .
THERE'S GONNA BE A RUMBLIN' AND A ROLLIN', YEAH . . .
OH, THERE'S GONNA BE A RUMBLIN' AND A ROLLIN', YEAH . . .
THERE'S GONNA BE A RUMBLIN' AND A ROLLIN', YEAH . . .

(Newt goes off with his lantern. Riley goes back to shining his shoes, and Angela hums as the lights fade on them.

Bustling with energy, Rosser crosses the stage into Leo's cell.)

ROSSER: Hey, Leo!

LEO *(Reading and paying no attention)*: Demurrer, deposition, evidence . . .

ROSSER: Hell of a time gettin' here through that parade.

LEO: What parade?

ROSSER: Time's passin', boy! It's Memorial Day again.

LEO: My least favorite holiday.

ROSSER: Well, I got good news!

LEO: Habeas corpus. Indictment.

ROSSER: I'm fixin' to file another appeal.

LEO: Incompetence.

ROSSER: What in hell are you doin'?

LEO: I asked Lucille to get me these law books from the library.

ROSSER: Now, listen here. You just leave all the legal doo-wacka-doo to me.

LEO: And what'll you do when they reject this appeal like they did the first one?

ROSSER: Who says they will?

LEO: You know what? I'm all those evil things Hugh Dorsey keeps saying I am. I'm a Yankee and I'm college educated and I have an extensive vocabulary. Oh, and I'm a Jew of course! And you know what Jews are, don't you? Smart! *(Goes back to the law book)* Malice. Mandamus. Quo Warranto. Statute of Limitations. Subpoena.

ROSSER: Stay with me, Leo.

LEO: And do what? End up on the wrong end of a rope? Here. Get this to that Craig fellow at the newspaper. *(Hands Rosser a stack of letters)* And this one goes to Mr. Adolph Ochs at the *New York Times*. And this one is to the Chief Justice of the Supreme Court.

ROSSER: Have you lost your mind completely?

LEO: While you were sitting in that courtroom developing that brilliant strategy of yours, Hugh Dorsey was getting away with murder. My murder! I read in this book that the prosecution in a murder case carries the burden of proof. He proved nothing. I was railroaded by redneck savages and people need to know that.

(The Guard has entered the cell to take Leo to the visitors' room. Leo reflexively puts out his hands and the Guard handcuffs him as the scene continues.)

ROSSER: Come on, Leo. People know everything there is to know about your case.

LEO: I don't mean southern people. I mean real people.
Oh, and one more thing.
ROSSER: What's that?
LEO: You're fired.

(The Guard leads Leo out of the cell, leaving Rosser sitting, bemused, on the bed. Lights up on Craig.)

CRAIG:

LOOK—NOT A CLOUD IN THE SKY!
LOOK AT THE TIME RUSHIN' BY!
HELL! WHY COMPLAIN ANYMORE?
I'VE BEEN BLESSED WITH A STORY
THAT JUST DOESN'T DIE!

SCENE 2

Leo's cell. The Guard enters with Lucille.

LUCILLE: Thank you, Mr. Turner.
GUARD: Welcome, ma'am.

(He watches for a moment, then leaves.)

LUCILLE: Hey, honey.
LEO *(Still writing)*: Hey, honey.
LUCILLE: How are you today?
LEO: Not bad.
LUCILLE: I brought you *The Official State of Georgia Legislative Law Review* journals.
LEO: . . . 1907, 1908. Good. Thank you.
LUCILLE: I couldn't cook this morning.
LEO: Something the matter with the stove?
LUCILLE: No. I was busy.
LEO: Doing what?
LUCILLE: I had an appointment with that Mr. Craig.
LEO: You were talking to a reporter?
LUCILLE: Yes.
LEO: I thought we decided you wouldn't do that.

LUCILLE: You decided it, Leo. I didn't. And anyway, Mr. Craig turns out to have a very sympathetic ear.

LEO: Oh God! What did you say?

LUCILLE: Well, he asked me how you are and I said fine, and, in fact, very hopeful because you were busy writing up a documented statement that proves all the evidence given against you at the trial was false.

LEO: You shouldn't have told him that! Now everyone will know!

LUCILLE: Were you planning to keep it a secret?

LEO: I was planning to release it when I'm finished writing it. Don't talk to any more reporters. *(Goes back to work)*

LUCILLE: I can help you, Leo. They're gonna hang you in six weeks unless we do everything that's in our powers to do.

LEO *(Putting down his pencil)*: I know you mean well, honey. I really do. And I appreciate it.

LUCILLE: But keep my stupid mouth shut. Of course, Leo. You're right. Like you always are.

(She sings:)

DO IT ALONE, LEO—DO IT ALL BY YOURSELF.
YOU'RE THE ONLY ONE WHO MATTERS AFTER ALL.
DO IT ALONE, LEO—WHY SHOULD IT BOTHER ME?
I'M JUST GOOD FOR STANDING IN THE SHADOWS
AND STARING AT THE WALLS, LEO.
FIGHT THEM, STRONG AND PROUD—
PRAY YOUR VOICE IS LOUD,
LOUD ENOUGH TO MAKE IT THROUGH THAT DOOR.
WHAT ON EARTH HAVE I BEEN WORRIED FOR?
SOON I WON'T BE WORRIED ANYMORE.

LEO: Why are you doing this?

LUCILLE:

NO, DO IT ALONE, LEO—NOW THERE'S THE RIGHT IDEA:
MAKE ME FEEL AS USELESS AS YOU ALWAYS HAVE.
DO IT ALONE, LEO—WHAT COULD A WOMAN DO?
AFTER ALL, SO MANY PEOPLE LOVE YOU,
THEY'RE DANCING IN THE STREETS, LEO.
ONLY YOU KNOW HOW
TO CHANGE THE FUTURE NOW—

No one knows the pain you're going through—
No one else is suffering but you.

I could be a quiet little girl
And cook your little meal,
And swallow all I feel,
And bow to your command;
Or I could start to scream
Across the whole damned South
And never shut my mouth
Until they understand.

But I can't do it alone, Leo.
Look at me now, Leo.
I can be more . . .
I can bring you home, Leo.
We can bring you home, Leo.
I want you to come home.

(Leo is speechless, locked in his head. Lucille puts her arms around him as the lights fade.)

SCENE 3

One week later. Lights up on the ballroom of the governor's mansion. A tea dance is in progress. A small orchestra is playing the latest dance craze (the Grizzly Bear or the Turkey Trot or some such thing). Party hacks, campaign contributors, etc., mingle and dance with their wives. Dorsey is among the guests. Waiters pass trays of champagne. Craig is off to the side, bored to tears, also hitting the champagne.

In the center of the party is Governor Slaton. He is dancing with his wife Sally. Everyone at the party is watching them dance.

Dorsey is leaning against the banquet table with a cocktail in his hand. Rosser approaches, drink in hand—he's well on the way to being hammered.

ROSSER: Hey, boy!
WAITER: Yassuh?
ROSSER: What's in this?
WAITER: Tea.

ROSSER: Unh-hunh. I was afraid of that.

(Rosser pours a healthy shot from his flask into a punch cup and ladles a tiny bit of tea on top of it. He spots Dorsey.)

DORSEY: Afternoon, Luther.

ROSSER: Hugh Dorsey, you ol' faker! You had that jury so bamboozled they couldn't tell a tit from a telephone pole.

DORSEY: Leo Frank was guilty, Luther. All I did was prove it.

ROSSER: You know damn well Leo Frank couldn't even manage to step on a red ant at a Sunday School picnic!

DORSEY: Sore loser, Luther?

ROSSER: Guilty conscience, Hugh?

DORSEY: No, sir. Not a bit.

(The orchestra finishes one song and the dancers applaud. Instantly, the orchestra strikes up another tune.

Watson emerges suddenly from the crowd, severe and intense. He claps Dorsey's hand.)

WATSON: You are the savior of the Southland, Mr. Dorsey.

DORSEY *(Wanting to get away from him)*: Mr. Watson.

WATSON: The *Jeffersonian* supports you one thousand percent.

DORSEY: Appreciate that, sir.

WATSON: I'm sure you've seen my editorial extolling your virtues in this week's issue?

(He hands Dorsey a newspaper and quotes from memory as Dorsey reads.)

"And Hugh Dorsey was not fooled by the slippery Jew's oily demeanor. He took one look at Leo Frank's bulging satyr eyes and protruding sensual lips and nailed him for the pervert sodomite he is."

ROSSER: Don't let me keep you from your fan club, Hugh. *(Takes a swig from his flask and totters away toward Craig)*

WATSON: And next week I have a piece entitled "Jesus Was Not a Jew." I'll mail you a copy.

DORSEY: You do that, but you'll have to excuse me now, because I need to—

WATSON: I don't think you understand, sir!

DORSEY: Understand?

WATSON: The *Jeffersonian* and I are going to make you the governor of Georgia.

DORSEY: But, Mr. Watson, Georgia already has a governor. *(To Craig and Rosser)* Nutty as a fruit cake!

SLATON *(Singing into Sally's ear)*:

DON'T YA THINK THAT'S PRETTY MUSIC?
THOSE FELLAS SURE CAN PLAY.
THAT BEAT WAS REALLY MADE FOR DANCIN'.
YES, MA'AM, THAT'S PRETTY MUSIC.
I COULD DANCE THE NIGHT AWAY.
YOU CAN HEAR THAT SONG'S SO SWEET AND TRUE,
BUT TRUTH TO TELL, NOT HALF AS SWEET AS YOU.

(Slaton and Sally come off the floor, headed toward Dorsey, who breaks off from Watson to talk to them.)

DORSEY: Afternoon, Governor! I swear, Miss Sally, you could pass for eighteen years old.

SALLY: Hugh Dorsey—sincere as ever!

DORSEY: Yes, ma'am, I am.

SLATON: Lotta mail comin' in about the Frank trial, Hughie. People aren't so happy.

DORSEY: Well, I wouldn't pay much mind to it. Jews lettin' off steam.

SLATON: Not just Jews. Aldermen, mayors, governor of Maine, governor of Illinois, governor of Oregon. Thomas Edison, Henry Ford.

DORSEY: Yankees. Jewish money in back of 'em.

SLATON: I doubt if Jewish money is in back of Henry Ford.

SALLY: Jack, shouldn't you be dancing with some of these ladies?

SLATON: Of course. Excuse me.

(Slaton approaches a contributor's wife and starts to dance with her. He is very graceful as he steps her around the room.)

DORSEY *(Watching)*: Looks like your husband's a regular dancin' fool.

SALLY: That's not the term I'd pick.

DORSEY: My apologies. May I have this dance?

SALLY: No, sir. You may not.

(Sally walks away. Slaton's partner is a little stiff and nervous.)

SLATON:

DON'T YOU THINK THAT'S PRETTY MUSIC?
THIS SONG SURE MAKES YOU SMILE.
SHAME YOU DON'T VISIT HERE MORE OFTEN.
YES, MA'AM, THAT'S PRETTY MUSIC—
JUST LISTEN FOR A WHILE—
IF YOUR FEET WON'T FOLLOW YOUR COMMANDS,
JUST PUT YOURSELF IN GOV'NOR SLATON'S HANDS.

(Slaton returns the lady to her place and, smiling broadly, grabs another woman and takes her for a turn. This partner is quite a dancer.

By now, there is a queue of sorts forming, all ladies hoping to dance with Slaton. One of these ladies is not like the others—dressed severely and looking very uncomfortable—Lucille.)

THAT'S IT! THAT'S RIGHT!
I FOUND MYSELF A PARTNER WHO KNOWS MY STYLE!
THAT'S IT! THAT'S RIGHT!
A BEAUTIFUL LADY TO DANCE A WHILE!
SEEMS YOU KNOW WHAT I NEED,
I'LL EVEN TAKE YOUR LEAD—
WE'RE DANCIN', YES INDEED!
YOU'RE SO LIGHT ON YOUR FEET, WE COULD DANCE FOR A MILE!

SO DON'TCHA STOP THAT PRETTY MUSIC!
SURE MAKES ME FEEL ALIVE!
IF I CAN DANCE WITH YOU TODAY,
WHO CARES WHAT ALL THOSE FOLKS'LL SAY?
YOUR HUSBAND'S FINE, IT'S TRUE,
BUT I'M THE LUCKY GUY WHO GETS TO DANCE WITH YOU,
SO TURN THAT ANKLE AND LET THE MUSIC PLAY!

(And he gracefully deposits her and picks up the next lady. They swing out on to the floor—she's a little clumsy, he's smooth and flowing. Lucille is the next in line—she is becoming more and more nervous.

And now Slaton deposits his partner. He offers his arm to Lucille, and they start to dance.)

SLATON: Hello.
LUCILLE: Hello.

SLATON: Do we know each other, ma'am?
LUCILLE: No.
SLATON: How do you do? My name is Jack Slaton.
LUCILLE: My name is Lucille Frank.
SLATON: Well hey, Miss Frank. Or is it Mrs.? Couldn't possibly be. You look far too young to be married.
LUCILLE: It is Mrs. Mrs. Frank. Mrs. Leo Frank.

(Everything stops. Craig, Watson and Dorsey take special notice.)

I have to talk to you, Governor.
SLATON: I see. Well, Mrs. Frank, as you can see, Miss Sally and I are entertaining guests just now and I can hardly . . .
LUCILLE: I have to talk to you.

(A pause. Sally cues the band to keep playing. Then Slaton reluctantly leads Lucille off the floor. Dorsey watches this scene from a distance. Watson stands to his side.)

CRAIG *(Passing Lucille, as he heads off to refill his glass)*: Hello, Miz Frank.

(The band starts up a new tune. Slaton and Lucille are in a corner of the ballroom, Slaton trying to attract as little attention as possible.)

SLATON *(A bit patronizing)*: I can imagine how difficult all this must be for you, Miz Frank.
LUCILLE: Thank you.
SLATON: And I surely do wish it lay within my power to relieve some of your anguish, but, as you must realize—
LUCILLE: It does.
SLATON: I beg your pardon?
LUCILLE: It does lie within your power. You're the governor!
SLATON: Well, my goodness! Listen to that!

(He holds his arms out to dance. She hesitates.)

Surely you don't plan on lettin' a perfectly good one-step go by the wayside.
LUCILLE: I didn't come here to dance, sir.
SLATON: I know, but the music is so—

(He tries to take her in his arms.)

LUCILLE *(Voice rising)*: No! No more dancing! You have to reopen the case!

SLATON *(Polite but firm)*: You'll have to excuse me now.

(He moves to greet a middle-aged country couple nearby. After a moment, Lucille follows and stands nearby.)

Hey, Roy! Helen! How're the plans for that hospital wing comin'?

MIDDLE-AGED MAN: Real good, thanks to you.

WIFE: And ev'rybody in Valdosta says hey.

SLATON: I'm mighty glad to hear that, because Valdosta is—

LUCILLE: You're a smart man. You're trained as a lawyer.

SLATON: Miz Frank! Please! *(Returns his attention to the couple)* Valdosta's always been like a second home to me.

LUCILLE *(Still at it)*: Don't you have at least one small question about the way my husband's trial was conducted?

SLATON *(His patience at an end)*: Your husband was tried and found guilty by a jury of his peers, ma'am, and that's good enough for me. *(Turns to go)*

LUCILLE: Then you are either a fool or a coward.

(That stops him. He turns back to her. She storms out.)

SALLY: I thought this was supposed to be a party.

(Sally approaches Slaton, somewhat protectively, and offers her hand to dance. Slaton takes her hand and they go on the floor, where the two-step continues.

The two-step seems to pick up speed, and is abruptly stopped by a chord in the orchestra which tears the two-step in half. Blackout.)

SCENE 4

One week later. Judge Roan is onstage in a wheelchair, wheeled by an irritatingly ingratiating Nurse. He is very frail now, a blanket drawn across his lap.

NURSE: You comfortable now, Judge Roan, honey? Here's the pen and writin' paper you were askin' for. I'm gonna go on and tidy your bedclothes for you, sugar. *(Starts off)* Back in a jiffy.

JUDGE ROAN: Don't make it such a jiffy.

(She is gone. He begins to write a letter. He sings:)

I HAVE HEARD THEM IN THE STREET, GOV'NOR.
"JUSTICE! WE HAVE JUSTICE!"
THROUGH THESE OLD AND TIRED WALLS.
CALLING THROUGH THE AUTUMN NIGHTS
THAT STILL MORE BLOOD MUST FLOW
AND I DECLARED IT SO.

AND MAYBE I WAS WRONG.
MAYBE WHAT WAS "OBVIOUS" THEN
WOULD NOT HAVE BEEN FOR LONG,
BUT I WOULD NOT DELAY.

AND MAYBE I WAS RIGHT—
MAYBE I'M AFRAID THAT IN A
HIGHER JUDGE'S SIGHT,
I WON'T KNOW WHAT TO SAY . . .
SO BEFORE I LEAVE THIS WORLD BEHIND,
I HAVE TO SPEAK MY MIND.

WITH HATRED IN THE AIR,
HOW IS ANY MAN TO KNOW
WHAT IS OR ISN'T FAIR.
I LEFT IT UP TO FATE.
IT NOW MAY BE TOO LATE . . .
THEY'LL BE CALLING OUT TO YOU, GOV'NOR.
YOU WILL KNOW WHAT'S RIGHT TO DO.

(We hear a phone ringing. The lights fade slowly on Judge Roan. In the darkness, the phone rings again.)

SCENE 5

The Guard at the Fulton Tower picks up the phone in his office on the second tier of the prison.

GUARD: Hello. Evenin', ma'am. What? No, ma'am, you know I can't do that. Well, all right. Yes, ma'am. Yes, I surely will.

(He hangs up the phone and speaks to Leo, who is in his first-tier cell.)

Hey Leo.

LEO *(Jumping up)*: What is it? What's the matter?

GUARD: Message from your wife.

LEO: Oh God! What happened?

GUARD: She says to tell you that you know who is going to reexamine you know what.

(It is as if Leo has been struck by a thunderbolt.)

LEO: Say that again.

GUARD: You know who is going to reexamine you know what.

LEO: Oh my Lord! Oh my Lord! Thank you! Thank you! You know who "you know who" is?

GUARD: Can't say I do.

LEO: Then you don't know what you know what is.

GUARD: No.

LEO: Oh, my sweet Lucille! How did you ever manage it? *(To Guard)* You don't know what any of this means!

(He sings:)

IT MEANS CANCEL ALL YOUR PARTIES.
FORGET YOUR BIG PARADE.

GUARD: Settle down.

LEO:

IT MEANS THE CROWDS WILL NOT BE CHEERING,
SO DESPITE WHAT YOU'VE BEEN HEARING,
YOU CAN LAY DOWN YOUR SPADE.

GUARD: Leo, hush up!

LEO:

IT MEANS MY MOTHER CAN STOP CRYING,
MY RABBI'S EULOGY CAN WAIT.
IT MEANS THAT DORSEY CAN STOP BEAMING,
AND MY COUSIN CAN STOP DREAMING
OF HIS PORTION OF MY ESTATE.

GUARD: It's past midnight! *(Disappears)*

LEO:

IT MEANS, NO! THIS ISN'T OVER!
NO, THE DATE'S NOT SET!
NO, I WON'T WAKE UP TOMORROW
DROWNING IN MY SWEAT!
IT MEANS I'VE GOT THE GREATEST PARTNER
ANY MAN CAN GET!
IT MEANS I'LL NEVER EVER EVER
UNDERESTIMATE THAT WOMAN,
'CAUSE THIS IS NOT OVER YET!

(He is jumping klutzily around the cell.)

TELL MY UNCLE NOT TO WORRY!
TELL THE REAPER NOT TO HURRY!
MAKE THE HANGMAN STOP HIS DRUMMING
'CAUSE I'M COMING INTO TOWN TO WIN THE DAY!
SOMEHOW I HAVEN'T, WITH MY SCHEMING,
SCREWED THINGS UP BEYOND REDEEMING,
AND WE'RE FINALLY ON OUR WAY!

AND NO, THIS ISN'T OVER!
HELL, IT'S JUST BEGUN!
HAIL THE RESURRECTION OF
THE SOUTH'S LEAST FAV'RITE SON!
IT MEANS I MADE A VOW FOR BETTER:
TWO IS BETTER THAN ONE!
IT MEANS THE JOURNEY AHEAD MAY BE SHORTER;
I MIGHT REACH THE END OF MY ROPE;
BUT SUDDENLY, LOUD AS A MORTAR,
THERE IS HOPE!

(And now we see Lucille, at her writing table.)

FINALLY, HOPE!

LUCILLE:

YES, LEO, THERE IS HOPE!

LEO:

And no, this isn't over!
No, we aren't through!

LUCILLE:

No, this isn't over!
We are fin'lly on our way!

LEO:

No, there's still a million things
That you and I can do!

LUCILLE:

I will speak for you, Leo

LEO:

And I would never have believed it:

LEO & LUCILLE:

The things I see in you!

LEO:

It means a man who isn't guilty
Doesn't have to walk the plank!
It means the gallows still are vacant
And we've got my wife to thank!
It means

LEO & LUCILLE:

You shouldn't underestimate
Lucille and Leo Frank!
'Cause this is not over yet!

LUCILLE:

You see? You see?

LEO:

Yes, I see . . .

LEO *(Simultaneously with Lucille below)*:

Yes, dear, it's wonderful . . .
Listen, now listen, Lucille . . .

LUCILLE *(Simultaneously with Leo above)*:

See how I did what I promised?
It's just like I said to you
Yes, I'm listening . . .

LEO:

Tell him to talk to those factory girls
Make sure he gets the truth . . .

LUCILLE *(Echoing)*:

TALK TO THOSE FACTORY GIRLS,
MAKE SURE HE GETS THE TRUTH . . .

SCENE 6

Lights up on Iola Stover. She sings:

IOLA:

HE'D CALL MY NAME,
I'D TURN MY HEAD,
HE GOT NO WORDS TO SAY.
HIS EYES'D GET BIG,
MY FACE GET RED,
AND I'D WANT TO RUN AWAY.

(We now see Slaton is with her, as well as Monteen and Essie. Lucille enters the scene and sits next to Slaton, watching.)

I'D FEEL HIS BREATH
BACK OF MY NECK,
HIS HAND AGAINST MY CHAIR . . .

ESSIE & MONTEEN *(Simultaneously with Iola above)*:

HE'D CALL MY NAME,
I'D TURN MY HEAD.
HE GOT NO WORDS TO SAY . . .

(Slaton interrupts:)

SLATON: Just a moment. Just a moment here. Let me get this straight. You're sayin' Mr. Frank made you feel uncomfortable.

IOLA: Oh yes, sir. All the time.

LUCILLE *(To Slaton)*: All the time? What does that mean?

SLATON: When, for instance?

IOLA: I'll tell you, one morning back before Christmas, me and Mary was in the ladies' changin' room and he came right in.

SLATON: Without knocking?

IOLA: Yes, sir.

LUCILLE: There's no door to that ladies' room—just a curtain. Go see for yourself.
SLATON: That right, Iola?
IOLA: I reckon.

(Mary is at work with Iola. They are both in work pinafores.)

MARY: No! It's true! I swear! Lonnie Mann is sweet on Monteen!

(The girls all giggle.)

LEO *(Offstage, behind the "curtain")*: Is somebody in there?
MARY *(Suppressing a giggle)*: Yes, sir. Me and Iola.

(Leo comes through the curtain wearing his normal vest, tie, etc. He is tight-lipped.)

LEO: Your break was over ten minutes ago.
MARY: Iola took sick.

(Monteen giggles.)

LEO: She looks all right to me.
IOLA: I'm a little better now.

(By now all the girls are suppressing hysterics.)

LEO: Then go back to work, please. Mr. Montag doesn't pay you to dawdle away the day.

(Mary walks past him, through the "curtain." He looks at her disapprovingly as she exits.)

LUCILLE: Did he touch you?
IOLA: Not exactly.
SLATON: Then he didn't touch you.
LUCILLE: Did he touch any of you?
SLATON: He ever touch any of you? The truth.

(There is no answer.)

I see. Now you all testified that Mr. Frank tried to get you to come to his office.

(The girls look at one another. No one speaks.)

Who did that happen to?

MONTEEN: Well, Hattie Hoover said that Corinthia Wilson told her that . . .

SLATON: He asked this Corinthia Wilson to his office?

ESSIE: Yes, sir.

LUCILLE: Then why didn't she testify?

IOLA *(Uncomfortable)*: She wouldn't.

SLATON: Why not?

ESSIE: She said it never happened.

MONTEEN: And Mr. Dorsey said it didn't matter anyway, long as we . . .

(Iola pokes her. She stops talking.)

SLATON: As long as you what?

IOLA: All told the same thing.

ESSIE: The truth.

SLATON: But you just said the truth was that Mr. Frank never asked any of you to come to his office.

(The girls are silent.)

Did Mr. Dorsey coach you on what to say?

(The girls look at one another. No answer.)

You need any more from these young ladies, Miz Frank?

LUCILLE: I don't think so.

SLATON: I don't think so either.

(Slaton and the girls disappear, and Lucille is once again communicating with Leo.)

LUCILLE:

LEO, IT'S JUST LIKE YOU SAID . . .

LEO:

DARLING, IT'S WONDERFUL . . .

LUCILLE:

Leo, I still can't believe . . .

LEO:

Yes, and I know it, but
Listen, we both have to hurry.
The gov'nor will not be in office
Forever . . .

LUCILLE *(Overlapping "Listen, we both . . .")*:

Leo, we're doing it—
Look, I am hurrying!
I wasn't born yesterday!

LEO:

Go to the fact'ry and find Newt Lee
Make sure he tells the truth!

LUCILLE *(Overlapping "Make sure he tells the truth!")*:

Tell him to find Newt . . .
Leo, I still can't believe it . . .

LEO:

I know . . .
Hurry!

LUCILLE:

I know!
Make sure he tells the truth . . .

(Lights up on Newt. Slaton sits across from him. Lucille is next to Slaton.)

NEWT: The truth? I always tell the truth. Like I said on that stand, Mr. Frank looked at those ladies funny.

LUCILLE: Newt!

NEWT: But Mr. Dorsey wouldn't let me finish. I was gonna say Mr. Frank looked at everybody funny. He's a funny-lookin' man. Beg pardon, ma'am, but it's true. And the least little thing'll set him off.

(He sings:)

I drop a broom,
Switch off the fans,
You see his face get red.
He'd start to sweat,
He'd rub his hands,
His eyes poppin' out his head.

But he never *acted* any funnier with those ladies than he did with anybody else, and I woulda said so, but Mr. Dorsey, he didn't let me. Cut me right off. And Mr. Frank's lawyer, well he didn't ask me anything at all.

(Slaton looks at Lucille, who is thrilled at the progress they're making. Slaton and Newt disappear. Lights rise on Leo and Lucille.)

LEO & LUCILLE:
No, this isn't over!

LEO:
Not while I have you.

LUCILLE:
It's exactly what I hoped . . .

LEO:
Not while ev'ry dream we had
Is somehow coming true!
I mean it's past all comprehending:
Look what you can do!

LUCILLE *(Simultaneously with Leo above)*:
I will speak for you, Leo!
Look what I can do!

LEO:
God, I was such a stupid fool
To think I'd do it all without you,
But this is not over . . .

(We hear a rough, heavy sound—a rhythmic beating noise going on. And we hear the voice of a black man, with a call-and-response chorus of black men singing with him. The scene continues over the singing:)

MAN & MALE CHORUS *(Offstage)*:
Hunh!
Hunh!
Hunh!
Hunh!

Yeah . . . (Yeah . . .)
Hey yeah . . . (Hey yeah . . .)

(Lights up on Slaton and Lucille.)

LUCILLE: Surely you have enough proof by now.
SLATON: Miz Frank, I can't make a decision as important as this one just because you want me to. I need more.
LUCILLE: Well, I'm going with you.
SLATON: No, ma'am, you are not.
LUCILLE: I insist.
SLATON: This is no place to take a lady.

(She shoots him a severe look.)

Not even you. But I'll try not to behave like a fool or a coward.

SCENE 7

We see Conley on a Chain Gang with several other men, breaking rocks. It is outside in the Georgia sun. It's oppressively hot. They sing:

CONLEY & CHAIN GANG:

YEAH . . . (YEAH . . .)
HEY YEAH . . . (HEY YEAH . . .)

I HEAR THE THUNDER ROLLIN'. (YEAH . . .)
IT'S BEHIND THAT WALL. (YEAH . . .)
WE GONNA ROLL LIKE THUNDER.
I'M GONNA TASTE THE MORNIN'
AND FEEL THE RAIN FALL. (FEEL THE RAIN FALL . . .)
YEAH . . . (YEAH . . .)
HEY YEAH . . . (YEAH . . .)

I'M GONNA RISE LIKE SUNSHINE, (YEAH . . .)
IF I SEE HER TURN (YEAH . . .)
I'M GONNA RISE LIKE SUNSHINE,
I'M GONNA SET DOWN ON HER,
AND FEEL THE SUN BURN . . . (FEEL THE SUN BURN . . .)
YEAH . . . (YEAH . . .)
HEY YEAH . . . . (HEY YEAH . . .)

(Two Guards approach. One of them unlocks Conley's chains as the other one cuffs his hands behind his back.)

GUARD 1: Hey Jim, got you a visitor, boy.
CONLEY: Female?
GUARD 2: You wish.
CONLEY: You know it.

(Slaton approaches. Conley regards him coolly.)

SLATON: Hello, Jim.
CONLEY: You who I think you are?
SLATON: Guess so.
CONLEY: All right, then.
SLATON: Coupla questions for you.
CONLEY: You want some water? *(To the Guards)* Bring the gov'nor some water.
SLATON: No thank you.
CONLEY: We fixin' to talk 'bout that mess with Mr. Frank.
SLATON: Yes.
CONLEY: I'm already doin' a year as an accessory. What more y'all want?
SLATON: A little of your time.

(Conley laughs.)

GUARD 2 *(To the Chain Gang)*: What are you girls looking at?

CONLEY *(To the Chain Gang)*:
YEAH . . .
CHAIN GANG *(Never looking at him)*:
YEAH . . .

CONLEY *(Back to Slaton)*: Then I got a little something to say. I made a little mistake up there on the witness stand.
SLATON: That so?
CONLEY: I said I found that dead little white girl with her head towards Alabama Street and her feet towards Hunter Street. That was wrong. She was layin' the other way around. *(Abruptly, to the men:)*

YEAH . . .

CHAIN GANG:

YEAH . . .

SLATON: And that was in the workroom—on the second floor?
CONLEY: Everything else was just like I said it at the courthouse.
SLATON: Well, then I'm a little confused.
CONLEY: Why's that?
SLATON: Well, when they found the body in the basement, coroner's report says there was sawdust in the mouth and the lungs.

CONLEY *(To the men again)*:

YEAH . . .

CHAIN GANG:

YEAH . . .

SLATON: Got any idea what that means?

CONLEY *(Looking right at Slaton with crazy eyes)*:

YEAH YEAH YEAH YEAH . . .

CHAIN GANG:

YEAH . . .

SLATON: Means she had to be breathin' in the basement, because there isn't any sawdust on the second floor. Means she was alive when you carried her into the basement.
CONLEY: Then she musta come back to life, 'cause she was dead as last Christmas Eve when Mr. Frank showed me the body. *(Turns to the men)*

GONNA ROLL LIKE THUNDER . . .

(This time a Guard pulls him to a straight position—a little too hard. Slaton shoots the Guard a look.)

SLATON: Coroner's report raises questions about your story, wouldn't you say?
CONLEY: That coroner—he the one that's blind?
SLATON: That's right.
CONLEY: Mmm. Plenty o' lint on the second floor. Might not a been sawdust in that little girl's mouth—coulda been lint, and how'd he know the difference? I guess lint and sawdust feel the same to a blind man.
SLATON: He's got forty-five years of experience.

CONLEY: That so? You can *try* and prove that in court, I imagine. *(Sudden and abrupt)* You ever been on the chain gang, Gov'nor?
SLATON *(Remaining very cool)*: Not yet.

CONLEY:
You ever break these rocks on the chain gang?
Get yourself thinkin', Gov'nor—
How you wanna have a good time!
Yeah . . .
CHAIN GANG:
Yeah . . .

SLATON *(To the Guards)*: I'm through with him.

(He walks off as the Guards put Conley back into the chains and uncuff his hands. Conley shakes out his hands as he sings:)

CONLEY:
Now Mr. Frank he had a good time!
Man knows how to have a good time!
Yeah!
CHAIN GANG:
Yeah!
CONLEY & CHAIN GANG:
Yeah! (Yeah!)
I get a high fever! (Yeah . . .)
When I hear her call! (Yeah . . .)
She gonna cool my fever— (Yeah . . .)
I gonna take that woman! (Yeah . . .)
We gonna ride like lightnin'. (Yeah . . .)
We gonna roll, roll, roll like thunder
And feel the rain fall . . . (Feel the rain fall . . .)
Yeah . . . (Yeah . . .)
Hey yeah . . . (Hey yeah . . .)

(They continue singing as the lights fade.)

SCENE 8

Lights up on the governor's mansion. Slaton is finishing getting dressed. Sally enters, ready to go out.

SALLY: You ready, Governor?
SLATON: As I'll ever be.
SALLY: Then let's go.

(He helps her with her coat.)

SLATON: Turns out you married a jackass, Miss Sally.
SALLY: Is that supposed to be news to me?
SLATON: All those fine plans. Senator and Mrs. Slaton. Maybe President and Mrs. Slaton. Looks like I'm fixin' to lose us all that.
SALLY: Well I'll tell you what. I'd a whole lot rather be wife to a fine ex-governor than first lady to a chicken.
SLATON: Is that so?
SALLY: Yes it is.
SLATON: I think you're as big a jackass as I am.
SALLY: We'd really better go.
SLATON: Yes, ma'am.

(She takes his arm. They proceed to the gallows. Music begins, ominously. Slaton addresses the crowd, Watson's singing overlaps throughout.)

I have an announcement to make: Leo Frank is no longer a prisoner in the Fulton Tower. At five o'clock this morning, he was removed to another prison location, which will not be disclosed at this time.

WATSON:

WILL YOU WALK WITH YOUR HEAD HELD HIGH?

SLATON: Two thousand years ago, another governor washed his hands and turned a Jew over to a mob. Ever since then, that governor's name has been a curse.

WATSON:

OR MOVE ASIDE WHEN THEY'RE PASSIN' YOU BY?

SLATON: If today another Jew went to his grave because I failed to do my duty, I would all my life find his blood on my hands.

WATSON:

WILL YOU RUN WHEN THE FIRES ARE FANNED?

SLATON: I have reviewed all the evidence in the case of the state of Georgia against Leo Frank, and I have decided to commute his sentence from the death penalty to imprisonment for life.

WATSON:

AND WHERE WILL YOU STAND WHEN THE FLOOD COMES?

You have betrayed the South, John Slaton, and you will reap the consequences!

(Starnes and Ivey grab Watson as he approaches Slaton.)

SLATON: Let him go.

(Slaton continues speaking as Watson begins to climb the scaffold.)

WATSON:

WILL YOU RIDE BY THE SIDE OF GOD
OR WILL YOU HIDE IN THE SOIL AND THE SOD?
WILL YOU FIGHT FOR THE SOUL OF YOUR LAND?
WELL, WHERE WILL YOU STAND WHEN THE FLOOD COMES?

SLATON: All I wish now is that the people of Georgia withhold judgment until they have given calm and careful consideration to the statement I have prepared on the case. I am sure that my action has been the right one, the just one and the one all patriotic Georgians will agree with. Of course I care for the public approbation, but should I have failed to commute Frank I would have been guilty, as I see it, of murder. I can plow and hoe and live in obscurity if necessary, but I could not afford *not* to commute him. It was a plain case of duty as I saw it, and I believe the people will realize that this was my only course.

(Slaton stops speaking as he realizes Watson is facing him on the stairs to the scaffold.)

WATSON:

WHERE WILL YOU STAND WHEN THE FLOOD COMES?

(The stairs separate from the scaffolding. Dorsey enters, heading for Slaton. Craig runs after him.)

CRAIG: Care to comment, Mr. Dorsey?

DORSEY: I was not a part of the governor's decision, Mr. Craig. I'm as surprised as you are.

(A small group has gathered around Watson now, and they join him singing.)

WATSON & ENSEMBLE:

WILL YOU BEG FOR THE JEW'S REWARD
OR WALK WITH US AT THE SIDE OF THE LORD?
PUT YOUR SOUL IN THE DEVIL'S HAND?
WELL, WHERE WILL YOU STAND WHEN THE FLOOD COMES?

(Watson directly addresses Dorsey:)

WATSON:

WHERE WILL YOU STAND?

DORSEY *(To Slaton)*: You wanted a conviction, Jack. I gave you a conviction.

WATSON: Where will you stand?

SLATON: I wanted justice, Hughie.

WATSON & ENSEMBLE:

WHERE WILL YOU STAND?

(Dorsey stands, staring at Slaton, then turns, with fire in his eyes, to face Watson.)

DORSEY: With you, Mr. Watson. I'll be proud to stand with you.

WATSON: God bless the next governor of Georgia!

(Singing, Dorsey begins climbing the stairs to join Watson.)

DORSEY:

Yes, I see through the fog and dust,
So let the mob do whatever they must.
Slaton jumps at the Jew's command—

DORSEY & WATSON:

Well, where will you stand when the flood comes?
Where will you stand?

(And now the whole company has gathered on stage, among them Mrs. Phagan, Frankie and Fiddlin' John, who saws away.)

ALL EXCEPT CRAIG, SLATON & SALLY: Where will you stand?

(Craig steps forward.)

CRAIG: And the news spread like wildfire. An angry crowd marched north on Peachtree Street toward the governor's mansion yelling, "Hang the Yankee lover!"

(Upstage, a torchlight parade passes behind the rear windows.)

ALL EXCEPT CRAIG, SLATON & SALLY:

See them laugh when an angel dies!
See them tell all their Jew-loving lies!
But they'll run on the Judgment Day!
Someone's gonna pay when the flood comes!

See the blood as a city grieves!
See the stain that the Jew-money leaves!
Traitors won't keep the mobs at bay!
Someone's gonna pay when the flood comes!

CRAIG: Windows were smashed in Jewish stores. Jacob Seligman, a clothier, was beaten and left for dead.

WATSON *(Simultaneously with Mrs. Phagan)*:

Mary, Mary, the angel child—
Still your name and your soul are defiled.
Thank God you can't hear the things they say—

MRS. PHAGAN *(Simultaneously with Watson)*:

MARY, MARY,
THE ANGEL CHILD . . .
MY CHILD!

WATSON:

BUT SOMEONE'S GONNA PAY!

DORSEY & WATSON:

SOMEONE'S GONNA PAY!

ALL EXCEPT CRAIG, SLATON & SALLY:

SOMEONE'S GONNA PAY!

(In the ensuing chaos, Slaton and Sally are rushed off the platform and run off the stage. The torches blaze onstage, illuminating Dorsey and Watson as they ascend the platform and lead the furious crowd.)

GEORGIA, HOME OF THE STRONG AND SURE,
FIGHT LIKE HELL FOR THE LAND OF THE PURE!
TEACH THE TRAITOR TO RUN AWAY!

GEORGIA, HOME OF THE STRONG AND SURE,
FIGHT LIKE HELL FOR THE LAND OF THE PURE!
TEACH THE TRAITOR TO RUN AWAY!

GEORGIA, HOME OF THE STRONG AND SURE,
FIGHT LIKE HELL FOR THE LAND OF THE PURE!
TEACH THE TRAITOR TO RUN AWAY!
SOMEONE'S GOTTA PAY!
SOMEONE'S GOTTA PAY WHEN THE FLOOD COMES!

(Blackout.)

SCENE 9

Silence. Then the sound of birds. Lights up on the interior of the state prison farm at Milledgeville—a minimum security prison. Peavy, the armed guard, sits at his desk. Leo is reading in his cell. He is dressed in prison-farm work clothes—rough shirt, overalls. Somehow, he looks comfortable in his own skin for the first time.

Lucille enters, carrying a large picnic hamper. She is flushed, excited, radiant—almost like a bride.

LEO: Lucille! Hey!
LUCILLE: Hey!

(They are very glad to see one another.)

(To Peavy) Hey, Mr. Peavy! I know I'm a little early, but it seemed silly to sit down there at the train station and twiddle my thumbs.
PEAVY: Oh, 'sall right, I reckon. Don'tcha think, Leo?
LEO *(Smiling)*: I reckon.

(Peavy unlocks the cell door, lets Lucille in, then re-locks. Leo and Lucille do not touch, but clearly they want to. They are suddenly shy with one another.)

That a new outfit?
LUCILLE: Yes.
LEO: It's very becoming.
LUCILLE: Thank you, kind sir.

(He sits on his cot. She begins unpacking her hamper, setting out a car robe, a shoebox filled with sandwiches, a mason jar with iced tea, utensils, their china.)

PEAVY: Well, this sure is a new one on me. Warden ain't allowed nothin' like it since I been on this prison farm, and that's twenty-four years.
LUCILLE: You don't say.

(Leo and Lucille exchange grins. Clearly, Peavy is a third wheel here. Lucille continues setting out food, produces flowers which she places in a milk bottle, etc.)

PEAVY: Wish my wife'd do all that for me.
LUCILLE: Your wife gets to eat with you ev'ry day. This will be the first meal Leo and I have shared in over two years.

(Leo watches as she continues to unpack the hamper.)

LEO: You're a wonder, Lucille.
LUCILLE: Am I?
LEO *(With deep emotion)*: You know you are.

(She notices his neck.)

LUCILLE: What's that?
LEO: Nothing.

(She undoes the top of his shirt, sees a bandaged wound.)

LUCILLE: That's not nothing.
LEO: Well, it's all better now.
LUCILLE: Is that why they wouldn't let me visit the last two weeks?
PEAVY: Had him in the infirmary.
LUCILLE: What happened?
LEO: I had a little accident.
PEAVY: Crazy fool Billy Creen come at him in the shower room with a razor.
LUCILLE: Oh, no!
PEAVY: Yes, ma'am. Teeniney bit deeper, nurse said, and we'd a lost him for sure.
LUCILLE: My God! Leo!
LEO: I'm fine. It's almost completely healed!

(He rebuttons his shirt, ties one of the napkins she has set out around his neck, and changes the subject.)

(Sotto voce) How did you get the warden to let us do this?
LUCILLE: I got his daughter a job in Atlanta—clerking at Jacob's Drug Store.
LEO *(Indicating Peavy)*: Did you bribe him, too?
LUCILLE: Not yet.

(Looking in the hamper.)

Oh my! Mr. Peavy!
PEAVY: Yassum?
LUCILLE: Could you do me a favor?

(He comes over to them. She pulls a bottle of whiskey out of the hamper.)

My neighbor lady insisted on stickin' this in the lunch basket. And neither Mr. Frank nor I care for it. Could you think of anyone who might have use of it?

PEAVY: I s'pose I might could.

LUCILLE: Well, thank you so much.

PEAVY: Glad ta be of help, ma'am.

(She hands him the bottle through the bars. Peavy takes the bottle, goes back to sit by his post, which suddenly becomes "a great oak tree." He disappears behind the tree.

Leo and Lucille are now alone. She has finished unpacking her hamper—it is quite a display. Leo watches, sitting on his cot.)

LEO: What is all this?

LUCILLE: Oh, just a little picnic out in the country.

LEO: The country?

LUCILLE: Of course. Isn't this the softest patch of grass you ever saw? And see those flowers all over the meadow? I wonder what they are.

LEO *(In the fantasy with her)*: I think they're called Black-eyed Susans.

LUCILLE: Black-eyed Susans, of course.

(The jail has disappeared. They are in the country on a perfect August afternoon.)

LEO: This is our wedding china.

LUCILLE: Naturally. This is a momentous occasion.

LEO: Yes. Yes it is.

LUCILLE: I've never seen you with a suntan.

LEO: Well, I'm a farm boy now. Probably the only Jewish farm boy in the South.

LUCILLE: It's very becoming.

LEO: Thank you.

LUCILLE: You can plant us a vegetable garden when you come home.

LEO: Okay. *(Falls silent)*

LUCILLE: You are coming home, Leo. It's only a matter of time now.

LEO: Well—

LUCILLE: No. It's goin' to happen. As soon as the fuss dies down, you'll be pardoned completely. I'm sure of it!

LEO: Lucille?

LUCILLE: What?

LEO: How did I get so lucky?
LUCILLE: Lucky? I would hardly call these last two years lucky.

(Leo sings:)

LEO:

I WILL NEVER UNDERSTAND
WHAT I DID TO DESERVE YOU,
OR HOW TO BE THE MAN
THAT I'M SUPPOSED TO BE.
I WILL NEVER UNDERSTAND
IF I LIVE A THOUSAND LIFETIMES
WHY YOU DID THE THINGS YOU DID FOR ME.

JUST LOOK AT YOU—
HOW COULD I NOT BE IN LOVE WITH YOU?
WHAT KIND OF FOOL COULD HAVE TAKEN YOU
FOR GRANTED FOR SO LONG?

ALL THE WASTED TIME,
ALL THE MILLION HOURS,
PUSHING YOU AWAY,
BUILDING UP MY WALL;
ALL THE DAYS GONE BY
TO GLARE, TO POUT, TO PUSH YOU OUT,
AND I NEVER KNEW ANYTHING AT ALL . . .
I NEVER KNEW ANYTHING AT ALL.

LUCILLE:

I WILL NEVER UNDERSTAND
HOW ALL THE WORLD MISJUDGED YOU
WHEN I HAVE ALWAYS KNOWN
HOW LUCKY I MUST BE.
I WILL NEVER UNDERSTAND
HOW I KEPT FROM GOING CRAZY
JUST WAITING THERE TILL YOU CAME HOME TO ME.
NOW LOOK AT ME,
NOW THAT YOU'RE FINALLY HERE WITH ME—
NOW THAT I KNOW I WAS RIGHT TO WAIT
AND EVERYONE ELSE WAS SO WRONG
FOR SO LONG . . .
ALL THE WASTED TIME . . .

LEO:

ALL THE WASTED TIME . . .

LUCILLE:

ALL THE MILLION HOURS.
YEARS ON TOP OF YEARS.
STILL TOO PROUD TO CRAWL—
ALL THE DAYS GONE BY.
TO FEEL THAT I DON'T SATISFY.
AND I NEVER KNEW ANYTHING AT ALL.
I NEVER KNEW ANYTHING AT ALL . . .

LEO:

ALL THE WASTED TIME . . .

LUCILLE:

ALL THE WASTED TIME . . .

LEO:

ALL THE MILLION HOURS.

LEO & LUCILLE:

LEAVES TOO HIGH TO TOUCH,
ROOTS TOO STRONG TO FALL.
ALL THE DAYS GONE BY.
TO NEVER SHOW I LOVED YOU SO.
AND I NEVER KNEW ANYTHING AT ALL.

LEO:

I NEVER KNEW ANYTHING
AT ALL . . .

(He clutches her to him, and they kiss. She leans her head back and he lowers her to the ground—the tree begins to cast a shadow over them—a long, beautiful shadow in greens and golds, and as they make love, the shadow grows and envelops the whole stage. We are transported into the clouds.

In the darkness, Peavy speaks:)

PEAVY: Got to go, ma'am. Gettin' dark.

(Slowly the lights come up. Leo and Lucille are back in the cell, together on the cot, both partly dressed.)

LUCILLE: All right, Mr. Peavy. I'll be right out. *(Puts on the rest of her clothes)*
LEO: So how do we bribe the warden to let us do this again?

LUCILLE: We won't have to, silly. You'll be home.
LEO: I love you.
LUCILLE: I love you, too.

(She stands up, puts on her hat with her pins. Peavy enters, unlocks the cell, lets her out, and locks the door again.)

See you Sunday.
LEO: See you Sunday.

(She touches his cheek and exits with Peavy. Leo lies down on his cot. Lights down.)

SCENE 10

We become aware of what seems to be a line of automobile headlights coming toward us in the dark. We hear a snare drum rattling on in the distance. Leo is asleep in his prison cell. The guard, Peavy, sits at a desk just outside. He is also asleep.

Music underscore. Three men enter quietly—their faces are covered. One of the men knocks out Peavy and breaks the light bulb over his desk. They proceed to unlock the cell and shake Leo awake. He sits up.)

LEO: What is it?
MAN 1: You're comin' with us, Mr. Frank.
LEO *(Half asleep)*: What? What?
MAN 2: Get up.

(They rip off the blanket and drag Leo from the cot. He is wearing a cotton nightshirt embroidered with his initials.)

LEO: Let me put on my pants!
MAN 3: You don't need no pants where you're goin'.

(They take him by his arms, legs and hair, and carry him away. We see the parade of cars—now taillights—move away in the darkness. A brief interlude in the orchestra, and then back to the snare drum.

The first light of morning breaks at an oak tree. A table is placed beneath a low hanging limb. A burlap sack is also in view. Leo is led onstage by his captors. His hands are manacled. He is barefoot and wears only his nightshirt—not even his glasses.

The men remove the kerchiefs from their faces—they are the Old Soldier, Starnes, Ivey, a Guard [not Peavy] and, finally, Frankie.)

OLD SOLDIER: Mr. Frank, do you understand why we've brought you here?

(Leo is silent.)

Mr. Frank?

GUARD: Answer him. *(He shoves Leo)*

LEO *(Stoic and with great dignity)*: I understand.

STARNES: Good. Gettin' light—let's hurry.

(A knotted length of rope is taken from the burlap sack and tied over the branch—the noose end hangs over the table.)

OLD SOLDIER: We are fixin' to carry out the verdict rendered upon you by the state of Georgia. Do you have anything to say?

LEO: What I've always said. I am innocent.

FRANKIE: Now that's a damn lie!

(He goes for Leo, violently, but is stopped by the others.)

OLD SOLDIER: Easy, friend. It's almost over.

(Leo is led toward the table.)

LEO: Just a moment.

IVEY: What is it?

STARNES: Jesus! Time's a-wastin' here!

OLD SOLDIER: What is it, Mr. Frank?

LEO: I'm not wearing—I have on no—I'll be exposed when you put me up there. Please. Can I be covered?

OLD SOLDIER: Take that croaker sack yonder.

(Frankie refuses. The Guard gets the sack and ties it around Leo's waist.)

GUARD: I sure wish we didn't have to do this.

IVEY: Maybe if he confesses we could—you know—just take him on back to prison.

FRANKIE: No!
OLD SOLDIER: We're here to carry out the law.
IVEY: That's what I'm sayin'. If he'd a' confessed it in the courtroom and said he was sorry and all, I b'lieve he'd a got himself a life sentence.
GUARD: I b'lieve he woulda.
STARNES: Buncha pansies!
FRANKIE: Jesus!
IVEY: We'll drive you back to that farm. Looked like a nice place. And you can live out your days.
GUARD: You only got to say you done it. Say you're sorry.
LEO: I am sorry.
IVEY: You see? You see?
LEO: It's a tragedy that lovely little girl had to die.
GUARD: And you wish you hadn't done it, don'tcha?
LEO: I'm afraid I've had to give up wishing.
OLD SOLDIER: Just tell us, sir. That's all we ask.
LEO: All right. I will. I believe God has a plan in all this. And I believe He chose me for a reason. So all this time I've considered and I've pondered and I've prayed but for the life of me I can't seem to come up with what that reason is. I do know this, though. I haven't gone through the last two years just to stand here now and tell you a bald-faced lie. That is not part of God's plan for me.
IVEY: He didn't do it!
STARNES: Shut up.
OLD SOLDIER: Mr. Frank, for the last time, did you kill Mary Phagan?
LEO: I did not.
STARNES: Let's get this over.
LEO: Wait!
STARNES: Jesus! Now what?
LEO: I want my wedding ring to go to my wife.

(The Old Soldier nods—the Guard slides the ring from Leo's finger—someone else ties a blindfold around his eyes. They lift him to the table and place the noose around his neck.)

OLD SOLDIER: Anything else, Mr. Frank?

(Leo quietly begins singing a prayer in Hebrew—a simple prayer with a simple melody:)

LEO:

SH'MA YISROEL, ADONAI ELOHAINU,
ADONAI ECHOD.
BARUCH SHEYM K'VOD MALCHUSO L'OLAM VA'ED.

(While Leo sings:)

FRANKIE: Mary! This is for you!

(Frankie races forward and kicks the table out from under Leo. Simultaneously, Ivey has broken from the vigilantes and crossed the stage by himself, turning his back on the hanging.

The stage freezes with a spotlight on Leo. No motion. Abruptly, terribly, the lights blackout.

Furious chimes ring. The bells cry out again and again. Finally, the ringing stops.)

SCENE 11

There is the sound of a doorbell. It is weeks later. Lucille, in mourning clothes, opens the door of her house. She seems to possess the same kind of dignity that Leo displayed in the previous scene. Craig is on her doorstep.

LUCILLE: The story is over, Mr. Craig.
CRAIG: I know. I'm back covering the police beat.
LUCILLE: Why have you come?
CRAIG *(Thrusting a little package into her hands)*: Here. Man brought this to the office. Said to get it to you.

(She opens the package, takes out the wedding ring. She says nothing.)

If I can ever be of any service at all, please let me know. Just leave word at the paper—or at MacDaniel's saloon.

(She says nothing.)

I heard you're moving up North.
LUCILLE: No. I'm not leaving home.

CRAIG: But after all this . . .
LUCILLE: I'm a Georgia girl. I will always be.

(Far off in the distance, we see Leo sitting at his desk. Mary comes to the door, startling him.)

MARY: Hey.
LEO *(Looking up)*: Yes?
CRAIG: Well, I'm sorry, ma'am. Sorry for your loss.
LUCILLE: Sorry? That won't do, Mr. Craig.
MARY: I came for my pay.
LEO: Name?
MARY: Mary Phagan.
LUCILLE: You'd better hurry.
CRAIG: What?
LUCILLE: It's Memorial Day. Don't you have a parade to cover?

(Craig nods, leaves. Lucille is alone with the wedding ring, which she turns over and over in her hand.)

LEO: Employee number?
MARY: Five oh seven.

LUCILLE:

LEO, OH, LEO.
I KNOW HE'LL PROTECT YOU
AND DON'T BE AFRAID;
I'LL BE FINE HERE—YOU'LL SEE.

LEO: One dollar and twenty cents. Here you are.
MARY: Thank you, sir.

(Mary takes the envelope and walks toward the door, and then stops and slowly turns.)

LUCILLE:

FAREWELL, MY LEO—
YOU'RE RIGHT HERE BESIDE ME,
YOU'RE HERE BY THE DOOR
AND YOU'RE HOLDING MY ARM

AND YOU'RE STROKING MY HAIR
AND YOU'RE FINALLY . . .

MARY: Mr. Frank?
LEO: What is it?

LUCILLE:
. . . FREE.

MARY: Happy Memorial Day.

(Leo and Mary disappear. In the distance, somewhere, the Confederate Memorial Day Parade is in full swing. We see Frankie.)

FRANKIE:
I GO TO FIGHT FOR THESE OLD HILLS BEHIND ME,
THE OLD RED HILLS OF HOME!
I GO TO FIGHT
FOR THESE HILLS THAT REMIND ME
OF A WAY OF LIFE THAT'S PURE,
OF THE TRUTH THAT WILL ENDURE
IN THE CITY OF ATLANTA,
IN THE OLD RED HILLS OF HOME!

(As Lucille fingers the wedding ring, the parade continues including a float carrying new Governor Dorsey, Watson and the Old Soldier.)

ENSEMBLE:
GOD BLESS THE SIGHT OF THE OLD HILLS OF GEORGIA,
THE OLD RED HILLS OF HOME!
PRAISE THOSE WHO'D FIGHT FOR THE OLD HILLS OF GEORGIA!
FOR THOSE PROUD AND VALIANT MEN,
WE'LL SING "DIXIE" ONCE AGAIN!
FOR THE MEN OF MARIETTA — FOR THE BROTHERS OF COBB COUNTY
FOR THE FATHERS OF ATLANTA — FOR THE PATRIARCHS
WHO GAVE EV'RYTHING FOR GEORGIA
AND THE OLD RED HILLS
OF
HOME!

(Lucille walks across the stage putting the wedding ring on her finger. She turns as though she sees something. A final tableau of the proud citizens of Atlanta.

Blackout.)

THE END

DATE OF SCRIPT

June 2000
(National Tour Version)

COPYRIGHT

PERFORMING RIGHTS

The stock and amateur rights to *Parade* are controlled exclusively by Music Theatre International, 421 West 54th Street, New York, NY 10019, without whose permission no performance of it may be made. Telephone: 212-541-4684. Fax: 212-397-4684. Website: http://www.mtishows.com.

Please note: The purchase, rental or use of these materials does not constitute a license to perform this play. Performance without a license is a violation of United States copyright law and an actionable federal offense.

All other inquiries should be addressed to the authors' representatives as follows:

For Jason Robert Brown: Sendroff & Associates, P.C., 1500 Broadway, Suite 2001, New York, NY 10036. Attn: Mark D. Sendroff, Esq. Phone: 212-840-6400. Fax: 212-840-6401. Email: welcome@sendroff.com.

For Alfred Uhry: Paul Weiss Rifkind Wharton & Garrison LLP, 1285 Avenue of the Americas, 31st Floor, New York, NY 10019. Attn: John Breglio, Esq. Phone: 212-373-3325. Fax: 212-373-2831.

ORIGINAL PRODUCTION

Parade was commissioned and developed by Livent (U.S.) Inc. It received its world premiere at Lincoln Center Theater in New York City, beginning previews on November 12, 1998, opening on December 17, 1998, and closing on February 28, 1999, after playing thirty-nine previews and eighty-four performances.

Parade was produced by Lincoln Center Theater (under the direction of André Bishop and Bernard Gersten), in association with Livent (U.S.) Inc. *Parade* was directed by Harold Prince. The set was designed by Riccardo Hernández, costumes by Judith Dolan, lighting by Howell Binkley, sound by Jonathan Deans, musical supervision and direction by Eric Stern, orchestrations by Don Sebesky and Jason Robert Brown, choreography by Patricia Birch; the assistant choreographer was Rob Ashford, the production supervisor was Clayton Phillips, the assistant to Harold Prince was Brad Rouse, the musical theater associate producer was Ira Weitzman, the general manager was Steven C. Callahan, the production manager was Jeff Hamlin, casting was by Beth Russell and Mark Simon, the director of marketing and special projects was Thomas Cott and the director of development was Hattie K. Jutagir. Production photographs were taken by Joan Marcus; illustration and poster design was by James McMullan.

The original cast (in order of appearance) was as follows:

YOUNG SOLDIER .... Jeff Edgerton
OLD SOLDIER .... Don Chastain
AIDE .... Don Stephenson
ASSISTANT .... Melanie Vaughan
LUCILLE FRANK .... Carolee Carmello
LEO FRANK .... Brent Carver
HUGH DORSEY .... Herndon Lackey
GOVERNOR SLATON .... John Hickok
SALLY SLATON .... Anne Torsiglieri
FRANKIE EPPS .... Kirk McDonald
MARY PHAGAN .... Christy Carlson Romano
IOLA STOVER .... Brooke Sunny Moriber
JIM CONLEY .... Rufus Bonds, Jr.
J. N. STARNES .... Peter Samuel
OFFICER IVEY .... Tad Ingram
NEWT LEE .... Ray Aranha

PRISON GUARD . . . . Randy Redd
MRS. PHAGAN . . . . Jessica Molaskey
LIZZIE PHAGAN . . . . Robin Skye
FLOYD MACDANIEL . . . . J. B. Adams
BRITT CRAIG . . . . Evan Pappas
TOM WATSON . . . . John Leslie Wolfe
ANGELA . . . . Angela Lockett
RILEY . . . . J. C. Montgomery
LUTHER ROSSER . . . . J. B. Adams
FIDDLIN' JOHN . . . . Jeff Edgerton
JUDGE ROAN . . . . Don Chastain
NURSE . . . . Adinah Alexander
MONTEEN . . . . Abbi Hutcherson
ESSIE . . . . Emily Klein
MR. PEAVY . . . . Don Stephenson
ENSEMBLE . . . . Adinah Alexander, Duane Boutte, Diana Brownstone, Thursday Farrar, Will Gartshore, Abbi Hutcherson, Tad Ingram, Emily Klein, Angela Lockett, Megan McGinnis, J. C. Montgomery, Brooke Sunny Moriber, Randy Redd, Joel Robertson, Peter Samuel, Robin Skye, Don Stephenson, Bill Szobody, Anne Torsiglieri, Melanie Vaughan, Wysandria Woolsey

AWARDS

Parade received the New York Drama Critic's Circle Award for Best New Musical. It was nominated for nine Tony Awards, including Best Musical, Best Actor (Brent Carver), Best Actress (Carolee Carmello), Best Direction (Harold Prince), Best Book (Alfred Uhry), Best Original Score (Jason Robert Brown), Best Orchestrations (Don Sebesky), Best Scenic Design (Riccardo Hernandez) and Best Choreography (Patricia Birch). It won two Tony Awards: Best Book (Alfred Uhry) and Best Original Score (Jason Robert Brown). It received four Drama Desk Awards: Outstanding Book for a Musical (Alfred Uhry), Outstanding Original Score for a Musical (Jason Robert Brown), Outstanding Musical and Outstanding Actress (Carolee Carmello).

AUDIORECORDING, VIDEORECORDING AND MUSIC PUBLISHING

Original Cast Recording: BMG/RCA 09026-63378-2. Produced by Jeffrey Lesser.

Videotaped by the New York Public Library's Theatre on Film and Tape Archive at Lincoln Center Theater in the Vivian Beaumont on January 20, 1999. 142 minutes. Format: 3/4" SP Color. Catalog Number: NCOV 2270. Restricted to qualified researchers. Contact: New York Public Library for the Performing Arts, 40 Lincoln Center Plaza, New York, NY 10023-7498; telephone: 212-870-1642; website: www.nypl.org/research/lpa/lpa.html

Vocal Selections: Hal Leonard Corporation.

ORCHESTRA INSTRUMENTATION

Violins (3) (2 doubling on Viola)
Cellos (2)
Bass
Reed 1: Piccolo, Flute, Clarinet, Soprano Saxophone, Alto Saxophone
Reed 2: Flute, Oboe, English Horn, Clarinet, Soprano Saxophone, Alto Saxophone
Reed 3: Flute, Clarinet, Bass Clarinet, Soprano Saxophone, Tenor Saxophone
Reed 4: Clarinet, Bass Clarinet, Bassoon, Tenor Saxophone, Baritone Saxophone
Trumpets (2)
Trombone
French Horns (2)
Tuba
Guitar
Drums/Percussion
Drum Set/Percussion: Bell Tree, Tam-Tam, Brake Drum, Chimes, Suspended Cymbals, Finger Cymbals
Percussion 2: Two Timpani, Vibraphone, Xylophone, Bass Drums & Mounted Cymbal, Glockenspiel, Crotales, Suspended Cymbals, Chimes, Wood Blocks, Cow Bells, Triangles, Harmonium, Brake Drums, Hollow Wooden Box, Shakers, Guiro, Sandpaper Blocks, Tambourine, Mark Tree, Bell Tree, Slapstick
Piano/Synthesizer

MAJOR PRODUCTIONS

A national touring production of *Parade* staged by Harold Prince and produced by Theater of the Stars (Christopher B. Manos, producer) opened in Atlanta, Georgia, on June 13, 2000, and subsequently played the following cities: Memphis, Tennessee; Dallas, Texas; St. Paul, Minnesota; Pittsburgh, Pennsylvania; Green Bay, Wisconsin; Denver, Colorado; Seattle, Washington; and Cleveland, Ohio. The touring production closed on October 30, 2000. The cast included thirty-four actors (twenty male, fourteen female) and two swings.

BIOGRAPHIES

Joan Marcus

Jason Robert Brown

JASON ROBERT BROWN (Composer/Lyricist), born in 1970, received the 1999 Tony Award and Drama Desk Award for Best/Outstanding Original Score for his work on *Parade*. Mr. Brown also conducted the show on its national tour. His first musical, *Songs for a New World*, a theatrical song cycle directed by Daisy Prince, played Off-Broadway at the WPA Theatre in the fall of 1995, and has since been seen in more than one hundred productions in North America and the U.K. Both shows were recorded for RCA Victor. Mr. Brown is the composer and lyricist of the musical, *The Last Five Years*, which was cited as one of *Time* magazine's "10 Best of 2001" and won Drama Desk Awards for Outstanding Music and Outstanding Lyrics. The original cast recording is available on Sh-K-Boom Records. Mr. Brown's scores are published by Hal Leonard Music. Mr. Brown is the winner of the 2002 Kleban Award for Outstanding Lyrics and the 1996 Gilman & Gonzalez-Falla Foundation Award for Musical Theatre. Mr. Brown's songs, including the cabaret standard "Stars and the Moon," have been performed and recorded by Audra McDonald, Betty Buckley, Karen Akers, Renée Fleming, Lauren Kennedy, Philip Quast, Jon Hendricks and many others. He served as the conductor and a contributing composer for *Urban Cowboy: The Musical* on Broadway. He is currently at work on a solo album, featuring his band The Caucasian Rhythm Kings. His work as an arranger and conductor includes William Finn's *A New Brain*, Michael John LaChiusa's *The Petrified*

Prince, Andrew Lippa's *john & jen* and Yoko Ono's *New York Rock,* among others. Mr. Brown studied composition at the Eastman School of Music in Rochester, New York, with Samuel Adler, Christopher Rouse and Joseph Schwantner. He now lives in New York City. Mr. Brown is a member of The Dramatists Guild.

Alfred Uhry

ALFRED UHRY is the only playwright ever to win the "triple crown": the Oscar, the Tony and the Pulitzer Prize. He received a Tony nomination for his book for *The Robber Bridegroom* in 1976. His play *Driving Miss Daisy* won the 1988 Pulitzer Prize, as well as the Outer Critics Circle Award. His screenplay for *Driving Miss Daisy* won the 1989 Academy Award as well as the Writers Guild Award. The film also won the Academy Award for Best Picture that year. Other films include *Mystic Pizza* and *Rich in Love.* His play, *The Last Night of Ballyhoo* won the 1997 Tony Award, as well as the Outer Critics Circle Award and the American Theatre Critics Award. His book for the musical, *Parade* (music and lyrics by Jason Robert Brown, directed by Harold Prince) won the 1999 Tony Award, the Drama Desk Award and the New York Critics Association Award. Two of Mr. Uhry's latest plays received world premieres in 2002: *Without Walls* at Williamstown Theatre Festival and *Edgardo Mine* at Hartford Stage Company. Mr. Uhry serves on the council of The Dramatists Guild and is Board President of Young Playwrights Inc., an organization founded by Stephen Sondheim to nurture young playwrights eighteen years of age or younger.

HAROLD PRINCE (Conceiver, Director) is the recipient of a National Medal of Arts for the year 2000 from President Clinton for a career spanning more than forty years, in which "he changed the nature of the American musical." Before becoming a director, Mr. Prince's productions included *The Pajama Game, West Side Story, Fiddler on the Roof* and *A Funny Thing Happened on the Way to the Forum.* One of the most creative figures in the American theater, Mr. Prince directed the premiere productions of *Cabaret, Company, Follies, Candide, Pacific Overtures, A Little Night Music, Sweeney Todd, Evita, The Phantom of the Opera* and *Parade*. Among the plays he has directed are *The Great God Brown, The Visit, End of the World, Play Memory* and his own play, *Grandchild of Kings*. His opera productions have been seen at the Chicago Lyric, The Metropolitan Opera, New York City Opera, San Francisco Opera, Houston Grand Opera, Dallas Opera, Vienna Staatsoper and the Theater Colon in Buenos Aires. Mr. Prince serves as a trustee for the New York Public Library, and served on the National Council of the Arts of the NEA for six years. He has received twenty Tony Awards. He was a 1994 Kennedy Center Honoree.

LINCOLN CENTER THEATER (Producer) Under the direction of André Bishop and Bernard Gersten, and with productions at their Vivian Beaumont and Mitzi E. Newhouse theaters and other theaters on and Off-Broadway, Lincoln Center Theater has become one of New York City's favorite not-for-profit theaters. With more than eighty productions over eighteen years, LCT's productions include *Contact* (Best Musical Tony Award) by Susan Stroman and John Weidman, *Marie Christine* by Michael John LaChiusa, *Far East* by A. R. Gurney, *A New Brain* by William Finn and James Lapine, *Racing Demon* by David Hare, *Arcadia* by Tom Stoppard, *The Sisters Rosensweig* by Wendy Wasserstein and *Six Degrees of Separation* by John Guare. Revivals include *The House of Blue Leaves, Anything Goes, Our Town, Carousel* and *A Delicate Balance*.

THE WILD PARTY

Music and Lyrics by Michael John LaChiusa
Book by Michael John LaChiusa and George C. Wolfe
Original New York Production Directed by George C. Wolfe

Carol Rosegg

Toni Colette (Queenie) and Yancey Arias (Black), Broadway, 2000.

THE STORY

Just before the Crash in 1929, Queenie and Burrs, two vaudevillians in New York City, throw a party in their apartment, inviting their friends from low-level show business. Queenie's best friend Kate brings a handsome young stranger named Black to the party. Queenie and Black find themselves powerfully attracted to each other and abandon their partners for the evening to explore each other. A madly jealous Burrs reacts and the party comes crashing to an end.

The Wild Party is based on the poem *The Wild Party* by Joseph Moncure March, written in 1928, republished in 1994 with illustrations by Art Spiegelman.

CHARACTERS

(in order of appearance)

QUEENIE	A blonde vaudeville chorine; sexy, not young, not old
BURRS	A blackface performer in vaudeville; Queenie's boyfriend
JACKIE	An upper-class playboy, addicted to excess
MISS MADELAINE TRUE	A famous stripper
SALLY	Madelaine's new girlfriend, a heavy-lidded morphine addict
EDDIE MACKREL	An aging Negro champion of the boxing ring
MAE	Eddie's wife and an ex-chorine; white
NADINE	Mae's fourteen-year-old kid sister
PHIL AND OSCAR D'ARMANO	A "brother act," the epitome of Continental colored
DOLORES	An ageless, eternal, ferocious performer of vaguely Latin origins
GOLD & GOLDBERG	Jewish theatrical producers on the Bowery, looking to move uptown
BLACK	Strikingly handsome, suave, cool man of unknown origin
KATE	Queenie's best friend; a dagger-tongued panther, formerly a chorine, now a would-be star

MUSICAL SYNOPSIS

The Wild Party is performed without an intermission.

NOTE: Sung passages are indicated in the text by small caps.

The Company, Broadway, 2000.

Carol Rosegg

THE VAUDEVILLE

Upon entering the theater, we see an ornate, decaying Victorian proscenium and velvet curtains. With the sound of blaring vaudeville music, the curtains rise and men appear—a motley assortment of shapes and sizes. They all exude a sense of malicious glee as they recount the story of Queenie:

MAN 1 (JACKIE):

QUEENIE WAZZA BLONDE AND HER AGE STOOD STILL
AND SHE DANCED TWICE A DAY IN THE VAUDEVILLE.

MAN 2 (GOLD):

GRAY EYES

MAN 3 (OSCAR):

LIPS LIKE COALS AGLOW:

MAN 4 (EDDIE):

HER FACE WAS A TINTED MASK OF SNOW.

MEN *(Canon)*:

QUEENIE WAZZA BLONDE AND HER AGE STOOD STILL
AND SHE DANCED TWICE A DAY IN THE VAUDEVILLE.

MAN 5 (GOLDBERG):

WHAT HIPS (WHAT HIPS)

MAN 6 (PHIL):

WHAT SHOULDERS

MAN 1 (JACKIE):

WHAT A BACK SHE HAD

MEN:

QUEENIE WAZZA WAZZ—

MAN 3 (OSCAR):

HER LEGS WERE BUILT TO DRIVE MEN MAD . . .

MEN:

MAD . . . MAD . . . MAD . . . MAD . . . MAD . . . MAD! . . .

(A line of Chorines enters, Queenie among them. She is a piece of work. Not young, not old. Sexy but not because of her costume. Her face is powdered white. Queenie and the Chorines strut their stuff. It's a nasty routine.)

CHORINES:

"(A) RRIVERDACCI
APALACHEE!
WOOOOOOOO!"

QUEENIE *(Dry)*: Woo.

ALL:

MEN MEN MEN MEN . . .

MAN 2:

THEY MIGHT BE BLACKGUARDS.

MAN 5:

THEY MIGHT BE CURS.

MAN 1:

THEY MIGHT BE ACTORS.

MAN 4:

SPORTS.

MAN 3 & MAN 6:

CHAUFFEURS.

MAN 1:

SHE NEVER INQUIRED
OF THE MEN SHE DESIRED
'BOUT THEIR SOCIAL STATUS OR WEALTH.

MAN 6:

SHE WAS ONLY CONCERNED ABOUT THEIR HEALTH.

MAN 4:

TRUE (TRUE)
SHE KNEW (SHE KNEW)
THERE WAS LITTLE SHE HADN'T BEEN THROUGH.

MAN 3:

AND SHE LIKED HER LOVERS
VIOLENT AND VICIOUS.

MAN 6:

QUEENIE WAS SEXUALLY AMBITIOUS . . .

(The Company of men and women assembles itself around Queenie: a wicked, jived world of cads and would-be's, lurid lips and hips.)

COMPANY:

QUEENIE WAS SEXUALLY AMBITIOUS, SEXUALLY AMBITIOUS, SEXUALLY—
QUEENIE WAZZA WAZZA WAZZA . . . *(Etc.)*

QUEENIE WAZZA, QUEENIE WAZZA—

QUEENIE WAZZA BLONDE AND HER AGE STOOD STILL
AND SHE DANCED TWICE A DAY IN THE VAUDEVILLE.
SO.
SO.
NOW YOU KNOW.
A FASCINATING WOMAN
AS THEY GO . . .

QUEENIE WAZZA WAZZA WAZZA WAZZA WAZZA—QUEENIE!

(Gunshot. Sirens blare. Visual pandemonium. Curtains fly in. All the women, minus Queenie, sing and dance.)

CHORINES:

QUEENIE WAZZA BLONDE AND HER AGE STOOD STILL
AND SHE DANCED TWICE A DAY IN THE VAUDEVILLE.
SHE LIVED AT PRESENT WITH A MAN NAMED BURRS
WHOSE ACT CAME ON JUST AFTER HERS.

HE WAS COMICAL AS SIN
HE WAS COMICAL AS HELL
A GESTURE, A GRIN
AND THE HOUSE WOULD YELL—

(Burrs, in blackface, comes hurling onstage, as if shot from a cannon, or fleeing from hell. A flurry of intensity that is informed by showbiz razzle-dazzle and a rabid-like fury, buried within. He sings a "pastiche" song from his vaudeville act:)

BURRS *(Coon-shouting, à la Jolson)*:

"MARIE IS TRICKY
SLY AND STICKY.
BRUDDA, YOU WATCH OUT FOR DAT GAL:
SHE GWINA LUB-YA LIKE DERE'S NO TOMORR-AH
BUT COME TOMORR-AH YA GOTS PLENTY OF SORR-AH . . ."

I tole Marie, I said, "I-lub-ya-I-lub-ya-I-lub-ya." She said, "I lub ya too! I'd lub ya to up and die and leaves allah-ya money to me!"

(He does a little dance and then . . .)

"She gwina lub-ya like dere's no tomorr-ah
But come tomorr-ah ya gots plenty of . . ."

I tole Marie, I said, "I-lub-ya-I-lub-ya-I-lub-ya." She said, "I lub ya too! An' da iceman an' da milkman an' da egg man!" Hot-chitza-dee!

(The curtains lift to reveal a painted drop—Queenie and Burrs's shabby-looking bedroom)

CHORINES:

Studio
Bedroom
Bath
Kitchenette
Furnished like a third-act passion set.
Oriental—
Sentimental—
They owed two months on the rental.

Sunday noon
Broiling hot
Queenie woke up
Feeling shot.

The Sunday tabloid
Was well supplied
With

MAE:

Murder!

NADINE:

Rape!

KATE & MADELAINE:

And suicide!

CHORINES:

Queenie woke up
Unsatisfied.

(The Chorines sashay off. Lights reveal Queenie lounging in bed, smoking a cigarette. Burrs sits at the kitchen table, drinking coffee, his face buried in a newspaper. Though the domestic "drama" which unfolds is informed by real emotions, it is performed stylistically as if it were a vaudeville skit.)

QUEENIE:

QUEENIE IS SO . . . *(Yawn)* . . . OH MY.
SHE'S AWFUL AWFUL TIRED.
SHE NEEDS HER CUP OF JAVA
SO QUEENIE CAN GET WIRED.

Burrsie?

QUEENIE IS SO . . . *(Stretches)* . . . AH WELL.
CAN'T LIFT A SINGLE TOE.
HER BLOOD'S AS THICK AS LAVA.
MAMA NEEDS A CUPPA JOE.

Burrsie?

BURRS:

A WOMAN WHO SLEEPS TILL HALF PAST TWO
THEN WAKES UP TIRED.
WHADDYA DO WITH A WOMAN WHO SLEEPS
LIKE THE STONE-DEAF DEAD—
NEEDS A KICK IN THE ASS
OR A SMACK IN THE HEAD—

QUEENIE *(Sharp)*: Burrsie. Pour me a cup of coffee.
BURRS *(Exploding)*: The hell I will, you lazy slut! You think you're the Prince of Wales? Or what?

(Queenie ignores Burrs and begins to scat; a scat which embodies her restlessness, her irritability.)

Well?! Queenie! QUEENIE!

(Burrs joins in the scat and the two vocally "go at it." Just as the vocal intensity is building between them, Burrs grabs Queenie and pulls her onto the bed, kissing her. She breaks free and strikes him in the face. He

charges after her. They dodge each other around the kitchen table until she grabs a knife and lunges at him.

All action, all music, all motion abruptly stop—the vaudeville of their marriage has turned into something dangerous, deadly.)

QUEENIE: You touch me—I'll kill you, you filthy bastard.

(Burrs and Queenie stare each other down, only the blade of the knife between them—two animals ready to kill. And then Burrs begins to smile—an ominous smile that transforms into something warm and seemingly sincere.)

BURRS:

DON'T I KNOW WHAT BABY NEEDS?
OH, I KNOW WHAT BABY NEEDS.
DON'T I KNOW WHAT'S BEST FOR YOU?
SURE I KNOW WHAT'S BEST FOR YOU.
DON'T I KNOW HOW BABY THINKS?
DON'T I UNDERSTAND?
DON'T I KNOW YOU BETTER
THAN THE PALM OF YOUR OWN HAND?
DON'T I KNOW YOU'RE GONNA LOVE
WHAT DADDY HAS GOT PLANNED?
WANNA KNOW WHAT I GOT PLANNED?
GIN.
SKIN.
SIN.
FUN . . .

Howzzabout a wild party?

TONIGHT?

QUEENIE *(Smiles)*:

TONIGHT . . .

(With Queenie's smile, the energy of the vaudeville returns to their marriage.)

PUT OUT THE NEWS WE GOT A HOT PARTY.
PUT OUT THE WORD AND GO AND ORDER THE ICE.

We sure could use a little fun, lover.
When was the last time I wore my "new" backless?
When was the last time you smiled?
When was the last time we had a *real* party?
Wet and wicked, fast-time fun
And wild!

BURRS:

Whaddya mean by fun?

QUEENIE:

You're the clown.
You figure it out.

BURRS:

I think we're due to have a wild party.
The time is right to toss a huge she-bang.
Say me and you we throw a wild party.
We'll round up all the old gang.

QUEENIE:

And maybe some new blood
Will turn up to play ball.

QUEENIE & BURRS:

We could always use new skin.

QUEENIE:

I could always use someone fresh
And tan and thin—

BURRS:

We're outta gin—

QUEENIE:

You in?

BURRS:

I'm in.
Go fix your face we gotta get ready.
Pick out the music that you wanna hear.

QUEENIE & BURRS:

Let's give this place a little life, lover.

QUEENIE:

When was the last time I danced the Black Bottom?

BURRS:

You're not gettin' any younger, my child.

QUEENIE & BURRS:

When was the last time we had a *real* party?

LAST YEAR.
LAST MONTH.
YESTERDAY.
BUT ONE THAT WILL NEVER BE
AS WILD . . .
WILD!

(An olio drop flies in proclaiming: "QUEENIE AND BURRS'S WILD PARTY." Jackie charges in.)

PROMENADE OF GUESTS

Jackie sings:

JACKIE:

DON'T GIMME NO SELTZER
'CUZ I NEED MORE THAN FIZZ:
DON'T GIMME NO WATER
I DON'T KNOW WHAT THAT IS:
DON'T GIMME NO LEMON
AND ASK ME TO SQUEEZE—

(Madelaine enters, Sally in tow.)

MADELAINE:

I'M BEGGIN' YOU PLEASE
DON'T LEMME GO DRY.

(Eddie, Mae and Nadine enter.)

EDDIE, MAE & NADINE:

DON'T GIMME NO GRAPE JUICE
'CUZ THAT DON'T GOT NO STING:
I NEED A CONCOCTION
TO MAKE THE TONGUE-TIED SING:
IT'S TIME TO BE HAPPY,
THE DAY HAS BEEN MOURNED—

GUESTS:

AWRIGHT YOU BEEN WARNED:
DON'T LEMME GO . . .

(Phil and Oscar—the Brothers D'Armano—enter.)

BROTHERS D'ARMANO:

DRY:

GUESTS:

THAT IS THE LAW OF THE LAND.

BROTHERS D'ARMANO:

WE GOTTA BE
DRY:

GUESTS:

ALL DAY WE'VE PLOTTED AND PLANNED

BROTHERS D'ARMANO:

HOW NOT TO BE
DRY:

GUESTS:

AND NOW THE NIGHTTIME IS HERE
AND I WANNA NIGHT I WON'T FORGET
SO YOU GOTTA MAKE MINE WILD 'N' WET.

(Dolores enters.)

DON'T GIMME NO ROOT BEER
'CUZ I NEED MORE THAN FOAM:
DON'T GIMME NO JELL-O
I'D RATHER DIE AT HOME:
DON'T GIMME NO COFFEE

DOLORES:

UNLESS IT'S TIME TO LEAVE—

GUESTS:

POUR ME A CUP
WHEN IT'S TIME TO SOBER UP
BUT TO COME DOWN
I NEED TO GET HIGH—
DON'T LEMME GO DON'T LEMME GO DON'T LEMME GO

PHIL:

DRY—

BROTHERS D'ARMANO:

DRY—

BROTHERS D'ARMANO & JACKIE:

DRY—

GUESTS:

Dry—
Don't lemme go don't lemme go don't lemme go

(Burrs greets his Guests, serving them champagne. The Victrola plays. Burrs greets Jackie: "Perfectly formed of face. Slim elegant, full of grace . . .")

BURRS: Jackie!
JACKIE: Burrs!
BURRS: Debonair as ever!
JACKIE: Can't turn it off!

(Burrs greets Eddie and Mae, who has brought her younger sister Nadine.

Eddie: an aging, ex-champion of the boxing ring. "Aggressive, fast—punishment-proof—each hand held a kick like a mule's hoof."

Mae is a plumper, plainer version of Queenie. Her little sister, Nadine is too excited, too thrilled, and too young to be there.)

BURRS: Eddie!
EDDIE: Burrs!
BURRS: How's it goin', champ?
EDDIE: You know me. Too quick, too smooth and too good lookin'.
NADINE: Mae.
BURRS: Mae! Better for night than for day.
MAE: Shut up, Burrs. Does this dress make me look fat?
EDDIE: Tell her Burrs. She's like an expensive bottle of the best champagne.
MAE: Yeah. Skinny on top and wide below.
NADINE *(Nagging)*: Mae!
MAE: What is it? Oh, Burrs, meet my little sister from Poughkeepsie.
NADINE: I'm Nadine. I'm sixteen.
MAE: Fourteen.
NADINE: I wanna be in the vaudeville. I wanna move to New York and drink bathtub gin. *(To Mae)* Is he anybody famous?
BURRS *(Meeting Jackie again)*: Jackie!
JACKIE *(Going for another drink)*: Burrs!
BURRS: Debonair as ever!
JACKIE: Can't turn it off.

(Dolores, an ageless, eternal, ferocious performer of vaguely Latin origins presents herself. You can tell her anything, just don't call her old.)

DOLORES: Voila!
BURRS: Dolores, you look ravishing.
DOLORES: So I've been told. Burrs, darling. Did I ever tell you about the time I walked through the lobby of The Ritz, completely naked, wearing only a string of pearls?
BURRS: Scandalous!
DOLORES: The scandal would have been if the pearls weren't real. Where's Queenie?
BURRS: Changing.
MADELAINE: Into what? Someone with taste in men?

(Burrs greets Madelaine: "Her body was marvelous / A miracle had fused it: / The whole world had seen it / And a good part had used it." She is accompanied by Sally, a heavy-lidded morphine addict, visually and viscerally opaque.)

BURRS: Look, it's the nearly famous stripper, Madelaine True!
MADELAINE: Burrs meet Sally, a postmodernist.
BURRS: In need of a postmortem.
MADELAINE: Then she shall fit right in.
PHIL: We're here!
OSCAR: We're there!
BROTHERS D'ARMANO: We're everywhere!

(Burrs greets Phil and Oscar D'Armano, a nattily dressed "brother act." They are the epitome of continental colored.)

BURRS: Oscar and Phil! Let's hear it ladies and gentlemen for the Brothers D'Armano! How goes it fellas?
PHIL: Last night we had the most marvelous time at Alelia's
OSCAR: The place was dripping with counts. And no-accounts.
PHIL: All pomp! And a lotta pomade.
BURRS: And you two of course were the cat's meow?
PHIL: What can we say. We're champagne in a jelly jar. A splash of cognac on some collard greens.

BROTHERS D'ARMANO *(Launching into a "pastiche" song)*:
"I THINK WE'RE DUE TO HAVE A BIG PARTY:
THE TIME IS RIGHT TO TOSS A HUGE SHE-BANG! . . ."

BURRS: Jackie!
JACKIE *(Appearing again)*: Burrs!
BURRS: Debonair as ever!

JACKIE *(Taking another drink)*:
CAN'T. TURN. IT. OFF.
ALL:
CAN'T. PUT. IT. DOWN.
CAN'T. GET. ENOUGH.
DON'T LEMME GO—DON'T LEMME GO—DON'T LEMME GO

(During the above, the olio drop has lifted to reveal Queenie and Burrs's apartment; sensual, stylish and cheap. There is a baby grand painted gold, a crushed velvet pouf, fabrics on top of fabrics and candles everywhere. The overall look: Scheherazade from the five and dime.)

GUESTS:
DRY! . . .
DRY! . . .
DRY! . . .
DRY! . . .
DRY! . . .

(Queenie makes her entrance. She looks stunning.)

QUEENIE: Hello kids!
ALL GUESTS: Queenie!

(The Brothers D'Armano sing:)

BROTHERS D'ARMANO:
"WHO'S THE BABY ON MY BEAM?
WHO'S THE KITTY IN MY CREAM?
WHO'S THE HIGHLIGHT OF MY DREAM?
GUESS WHO!"

QUEENIE: Who?

BROTHERS D'ARMANO:
"MY BEAUTIFUL BLONDE! . . ."

QUEENIE: Great song fellas. But next time gimme somethin' hot 'n' syncopatin' 'cause you know me. I like my jazz wild, my liquor strong, and my men . . . hardworking.

(The Guests laugh.)

PHIL: Love the dress.
QUEENIE: As good as I look with it on, I look even better with it off.

(The Guests whoop it up.)

BURRS: You could always make an entrance in your underwear.
QUEENIE: Great idea Burrs. Next party I'll be sure to put some on. Now gimme something with ice to take the sting outta this heat.

(She sings:)

WELCOME TO MY PARTY.
GLAD YOU STUMBLED IN.
WELCOME TO MY PARTY.
(BABY, WHERE'S MY ICE?)
WHO HERE'S UP FOR DANCIN'?
WHO HERE'S NEW?
WELCOME TO MY PARTY.

(To Dolores:)

WHO THE HELL INVITED YOU?

YOU'RE HERE BECAUSE YOU LOVE ME.
DON'T I KNOW IT? YES, I KNOW.
YOU'RE HERE BECAUSE YOU LOVE ME
AND 'CUZ THE BOOZE IS CHEAP
AND THE LOWDOWN'S LOW.

WELCOME TO MY PARTY.
YOU KNOW WHAT I NEED.
QUEENIE'S UP FOR JAZZIN'.
QUEENIE'S UP FOR ANYTHING
TONIGHT!

I NEEDTA GET MY ENGINES SMOKIN'.
I NEED IT BAD AND GOD I NEED IT
MORE.
I NEED A LOTTA FRIENDLY STROKIN'.
THERE AIN'T NO HEAVEN
AND THERE AIN'T NO HELL.
NO TURNIN' BACK.
DADDY LOCK THE DOOR!
WELCOME!

(Queenie dances, charming, seducing, dazzling all. At the end of her dance, she is greeted by Dolores.)

DOLORES: Queenie dear you look delectable. Like a little puff pastry someone's already taken a bite of.

QUEENIE: Awww, Dolores, why don't you do the same and bite me.

(Nadine, who's been mesmerized by Queenie since her entrance, places herself directly in Queenie's path.)

NADINE:

I ALWAYS WANTED TO SEE
THE LIGHTS OF BROADWAY:
I ALWAYS WANTED TO HEAR
THE TRAFFIC ROAR!—

QUEENIE: What's this?

NADINE: I'm Nadine. I'm Mae's little sister from Poughkeepsie. I'm sixteen.

MAE: Fourteen

NADINE: I wanna be in the vaudeville. I wanna be a blonde. Can I have a sip?

(Queenie gives her the glass. Nadine gulps the liquor down. Queenie takes the glass from her.)

QUEENIE: Whoa! You wanna hang with Queenie?

(Nadine nods excitedly.)

Lesson number one. Never rush liquor or love. *(Sensuously taking a sip)* Mmmm.

(Nadine becomes Queenie, emulating her every move.)

NADINE: Mmmm.

QUEENIE:

The creatures of the night
Have come here to play.
We don't like the light
And we don't need the day.
People like us
Gotta jazz till we drop
'Cuz people like us
We don't know when to stop—

I know how to party.
Show ya how it's done.
I'll teach ya how to party.
Where the hell's my ice?!
You'll remember this one.
Queenie's guarantee.
Welcome to my party.

Wanna get creamed?
Wanna get juiced?
Wanna get wild?
Follow me!
Follow me!
Follow me!

(Queenie and Nadine meet up with Madelaine and Sally, who sits motionless—a functional catatonic. Burrs is making drinks.)

MADELAINE: Queenie you look absolutely delish! If I wasn't so goddamn in love I'd kill Burrs and steal you away. *(To Burrs)* Hit me with a wet one. *(To Nadine)* Hey! Are you an attractive midget or some child? *(Out)* Hell, ya don't know if ya don't ask.

BURRS: So where'd you meet this one?

MADELAINE: If you must know, the gutter. One evening as I was leaving the theater, I came upon this creature, writhing about, practically naked. At first I thought she was ill but then I realized she was making a comment on the gross commercialization of our theater. I was struck by her passion. Her intellect. Her legs. We've been inseparable ever since.

QUEENIE: When was this?

MADELAINE: Two nights ago. And from the moment our eyes met, we knew we were meant to be together.

(She sings:)

I NEED SOMEBODY WITH SPUNK.
I NEED SOMEBODY WITH THE LUST FOR DANGER.
I NEED SOMEBODY WHO LIKES SEX
IMPULSIVELY.
I NEED SOMEONE LIKE ME.
LIKE SALLY.

(Sally starts to nod out.)

Sally! Sally! Sally!

THIS WOMAN HERE INSPIRED HEMINGWAY AND STRAVINSKY
AND THE MAN WHO INVENTED VASELINE.
THIS WOMAN HERE INSPIRES ME TO GENIUS;
TONIGHT I'M BREAKING IN A WHOLE NEW ROUTINE:

(Madelaine performs a portion of her striptease.)

Art is my clothing . . .
Modernism is dead . . .
I made Alice B. Toklas—cry.

WE ALL NEED SOMEONE LIKE THIS.
THIS PERFECT SPECIMEN OF STYLE PLUS SUBSTANCE.
THIS BRILLIANT MIND WHO SEES THE WORLD
THE WAY I DO.

YOU NEED SOMEBODY LIKE YOU.
I GOT SOMEBODY LIKE ME.

(Sally nonchalantly walks away.)

LIKE ME
LIKE ME
LIKE SALLY.

(Calling after Sally) Sally? Sally? Sally?

MAE *(Overlapping, to the other Guests)*: Tell the story. Tell the story. No, I'll tell the story.

(Queenie and Nadine cross to Jackie.)

QUEENIE: Jackie!

JACKIE: Queenie!

QUEENIE: What are you doing here? Waldorf closed?

JACKIE: Born to champagne but doomed to wallow in bathtub gin. And what do we have here?

QUEENIE: Jackie meet Miss Nadine. She wants to be a blonde.

JACKIE: Ahhh, the Modern Age. Everyone wants to either be a blonde or do one.

NADINE: Are you a movie star?

JACKIE: Actually I'm a student of life. I spent many years in Paris studying at the Sore Bum, before realizing my true vocation was to become le connoisseur de leisure, le objet de pleasure, much to the chagrin of my dear ol' dad.

(He sings:)

MY FATHER WAS A BANKER, YEAH,
ALL WEALTH AND CLASS AND GLORY.
HE SHOWED AFFECTION NOW AND THEN
BUT THAT'S ANOTHER STORY.
HE KNOCKED ME DOWN A PEG.
I'M THE PROVERBIAL BAD EGG.
LITTLE JACKIE WAS FORCED TO FUND HIS LONELY WAY
—BUT NO COMPLAINING HERE.

I'M VERSATILE AND PROUD OF IT;
MY GIFT IS BEING DEXTEROUS.
MY DADDY CALLED ME "DEVIL"
BUT I CALL ME "AMBI-SEXTROUS."
I LIKE IT COARSE AND CHEAP.

I'M THE PROVERBIAL BLACK SHEEP.
HOW DO I SURVIVE IT ALL, YOU SAY?
WELL . . .

S'LONG AS I'VE GOT MY NICE LOOKS.
S'LONG AS I'VE GOT MY OWN HAIR.
S'LONG AS I'VE GOT MY RHYTHM.
S'LONG AS I'VE GOT MY CUP FILLED.
S'LONG I SAY, "I LOVE YOU."
I'M BREEZING THROUGH ANOTHER DAY.

(Jackie takes out an elegant case and begins to prepare lines of cocaine. Nadine takes it all in.)

IT'S LUNCH WITH THE FITZGERALDS
THEN IT'S COCKTAILS WITH DOS PASSOS;
THEN OFF TO SUP WITH GERTIE;
THEN A NIGHTCAP AT PICASSO'S;
THE GAY LIFE LEAVES ME GLUM.
(TONIGHT I NEED TO SLUM.)
HOW WILL I SURVIVE IT ALL YOU SAY?

Well . . .

S'LONG AS I, S'LONG AS I, S'LONG AS I, S'LONG AS I
S'LONG AS I'VE GOT A FREE HAND—
S'LONG AS I'VE GOT A CHILLED GLASS—
S'LONG AS I KEEP MY SAILS UP—
S'LONG AS I KEEP MY EYES CLOSED—
S'LONG AS I SAY—

"I LOVE YOU—
AND YOU—
AND YOU—
AND YOU—
AND YOU—
AND YOU!" . . .

. . . I'M BREEZIN' THROUGH ANOTHER DAY! . . .

(Lights reveal the Brothers D'Armano at the piano surrounded by the rest of the Guests. Queenie and Nadine join the Brothers who are, and will be for most of the evening, playing and singing at the piano.)

OSCAR: The Brothers D'Armano have a ticklish treat!
PHIL: A delightful little ditty with a hot new beat.

BROTHERS D'ARMANO:

"UPTOWN
IS LOOKING MORE LIKE
DOWNTOWN
WHICH IS LOOKING MORE LIKE
UPTOWN
EVERYDAY!

BLACK FOLKS
ARE SOUNDING MORE LIKE
WHITE FOLKS
WHO ARE SOUNDING MORE LIKE
BLACK FOLKS
IN EVERY WAY!

PHIL:

MARTHA GRAHAM AND E. B. WHITE
GOT WET WITH ETHEL WATERS

OSCAR:

WHILE LANGSTON HUGHES PRETENDS
HE'S ONE OF MRS. ASTOR'S DAUGHTERS!"

PHIL: Ha!

BROTHERS D'ARMANO:

"UPTOWN
IS LOOKING MORE LIKE
DOWNTOWN
WHICH IS LOOKING MORE LIKE
UPTOWN
EVERYDAY!"

(The Brothers scat and dance. As the Guests applaud, Burrs crosses to Queenie who has separated herself from the Guests.)

BURRS: Looking for someone?

QUEENIE: Kate. She shoulda been here by now.

BURRS: Damnit Queenie! I can't believe you invited Kate—when you two get together, it's broken glass and dead bodies everywhere.

QUEENIE: What's a party without a few casualties. *(Pouty; flirtatious)* More ice for Queenie.

(Burrs sees that Gold and Goldberg have entered the party and moves Queenie out of his way.)

BURRS: 'N' more money for Burrs. *(Enthusiastically)* Mr. Goldoff! Mr. Goldberg! Gentlemen! Glad you could make it. Come on in. Come on in.

BROTHERS D'ARMANO:

"THE REST OF THE WORLD
MAY BE LYNCHING AND KILLING
AND DYING—SO WHAT? C'EST LA VIE!
MANHATTAN'S A BUBBLE
OF REJUVENATIN' JAZZIN'.
WHO CARES ABOUT THE REST OF THE WORLD?

OSCAR:

NOT ME!

PHIL:

NOT ME!

BROTHERS D'ARMANO:

NOT WE!
UPTOWN
IS LOOKING MORE LIKE
DOWNTOWN
WHICH IS LOOKING MORE LIKE
UPTOWN EVERYDAY!

QUEER BONES
ARE ACTING MORE LIKE
STRAIGHT BONES
WHO ARE ACTING MORE LIKE
QUEER BONES
IT'S ALL SO GAY!

OSCAR:

BESSIE SMITH IS LUSTING FOR
A DISH OF DOROTHY PARKER—

PHIL:

While Carl Van Vechten, naughty boy,
Just wants his chocolate darker.

(The Brothers begin to scat. Burrs joins in.)

BROTHERS D'ARMANO:

Uptown!

(Brothers scat.)

Downtown!

(Burrs scats.)

BURRS:

Uptown!

(Brothers scat.)

BROTHERS D'ARMANO:

Downtown!

(Burrs scats. Brothers and Burrs scat.)

BURRS:

White folks!

(Brothers scat.)

BROTHERS D'ARMANO:

Black folks!

(Burrs scat.)

BURRS:

Straight bones!

(Brothers scat.)

BROTHERS D'ARMANO:
QUEER BONES!

(Burrs scats.)

BURRS:
HIGHBROW!
BROTHERS D'ARMANO:
LOWBROW!
BOWERY!
BROTHERS D'ARMANO & BURRS:
BROADWAY!

UPTOWN
IS LOOKING MORE LIKE
DOWNTOWN
WHICH IS LOOKING MORE LIKE
UPTOWN
EVERYDAY!!!"

Yeah!

(At the end of the number, Jackie grabs the Brothers. The Victrola plays a foxtrot as couples begin to dance.)

JACKIE: Bravo, Brothers, bravo! I say piss on all that Victorianism and honor thy father crap! We are all free to love and to lust whenever and whomever we choose.

(Jackie kisses Oscar and dances with Phil.)

MADELAINE: Only Jackie would invoke Queen Victoria to legitimize screwing half of New York City.
QUEENIE: In the end, isn't everything just one big song and dance for sex?
ALL *(Ad-libs)*: Here! Here! Let's hear it for sex!!

(Sally screams.)

MADELAINE: Isn't she brilliant! Ain't love a kick!
DOLORES: Did I ever tell you about the time I was kidnapped by this Argentinean count who showered me with jewels? In the tradition of

the theater, I escaped and made the curtain. And in the tradition of Dolores Montoya, I kept the jewels.

QUEENIE: And in the tradition of Queenie, let's dance.

(Queenie grabs Oscar and begins to dance. The dancing continues as Burrs returns with drinks.)

BURRS: Enjoying the party?

GOLDBERG: Unbelievable!

GOLD: Fantastic!

GOLDBERG: You got your girls wit'cha girls.

GOLD: Your boys wit'cha your boys.

GOLDBERG: Your coloreds wit'cha whites.

BURRS: Your plaids with your stripes! I hope none of this offends you.

GOLD: Are you kidding?

GOLDBERG: We love it!

GOLD: We're having the time of our lives! *(Confidentially)* By the way Burrs, the name's Gold now, not Goldoff.

GOLDBERG: He changes his name and he's no longer a Jew.

GOLD: Of course I'm a Jew! But these are modern times we're living in. Burrs, ya wanna know why the past is called the past?

BURRS: Why?

GOLD: Because it's the past—it's over. It's about taller buildings, faster cars—

GOLDBERG: Jew-less Jews.

GOLD *(Fake laugh)*: Can we not talk about this now?

BURRS: Queenie.

QUEENIE: In a minute.

BURRS *(Agitated; pleasant)*: Oh, Queenie.

QUEENIE: I said in a minute.

BURRS: Gentlemen.

(Burrs goes to Queenie and forcibly dances her away from the other Guests.)

"UPTOWN IS LOOKING MORE LIKE DOWNTOWN
WHICH IS LOOKING MORE LIKE UPTOWN EVERYDAY!"

QUEENIE *(Jerking free)*: What the hell's gotten into you?

BURRS: I've been trying to get the two of 'em to a party of ours for years.

QUEENIE: So.

BURRS: Remember I told you they were getting rid of the vaudeville house down in the Bowery and moving uptown?

(Dolores positions herself so that she can overhear their conversation.)

The fact that they're here tonight means they're takin' me with 'em! 'N' if they're takin' me, they're takin' you.

(Queenie attempts to say something.)

Shut up! So go, be pretty, be nice. And don't do anything tonight to screw things up.

(As Burrs sends Queenie in the direction of Gold and Goldberg, lights reveal Eddie talking to the men Guests and Mae talking to the women Guests. Throughout the two conversations, they both drink incessantly.)

EDDIE: I usually go on just before the headliner and always right after Piergo's Trained Birds.

MAE: Of course I miss being one of the girls, dancing, the lights. But it's so much more rewarding touring with my champ.

EDDIE: Damn pigeons. Feathers and birdshit everywhere.

MAE: I knew I was married to a champ, but a hero!

EDDIE: And then it's: "Ladies and gentlemen—Eddie Mackrel. The Champ!" Course it ain't nothing like being in the ring. Ain't nothing like the real thing.

MAE: My Eddie's a hero just like Lindbergh, expect Lindbergh's white and flies a plane. My Eddie's colored and beats people up. *(Laughs)*

(Eddie sings:)

EDDIE:

So I'm there in the ring
And the crowd starts to shout.
I go in for the kill
And I knock the man out.
And the referee barks—
It's the end of the bout,
And that's the first time they called me:
"The Champ."

Yeah!

Those were the days
I ascended on high

Takin' on the Golden Boy O'Malley.
Oh my! Bye, bye, bye!
Those were the years and I
Gave 'em plenty of reasons
To call me "The Champ."
The women.
Anyone I wanted anyway.
Browns and blondes and women:
And then. Somehow. I was. One day . . .

Eddie and Mae.
Champ's gotta wife
Got settled down
Got a whole diff'rent life.
Can't take the Golden Boy
On anymore:
It's only onstage
I'm what I was before
Eddie and Mae
Eddie and Mae
Eddie and Mae—

MAE:

So he gave me a ring
In Buffalo.
Girls I'm glad I left the show—
I figure. One door opening is—
Uh? You know
Life is a dream since I married
"The Champ."
He plays the week and Saturdays
Three a night
Plus matinees.
In Detroit the theater ran out of A's.
So the marquee read:
"The Chomp."
And women?
They flock around him like hungry birds.
Jealous jealous women—
'Cuz my future lies in three little words:

EDDIE AND MAE!
TALK ABOUT BLISS!
NOBODY HERE'S GOT
IT BETTER THAN THIS.
SO WHAT IF I GAVE UP
MY PLACE ON THE LINE?
AT LEAST I GOT SOMETHING
I CALL MINE ALL MINE.

EDDIE:	MAE:
DUCK—	EDDIE AND MAE—
JAB—	EDDIE AND MAE—
FAKE—	EDDIE AND MAE—
LEFT—	EDDIE AND MAE—
HE'S OUT!	EDDIE AND MAE—
THOSE WERE THE YEARS	EDDIE AND MAE!
OF HIGH HOLY FAME	AIN'T WE A TEAM!
KING OF THE HILL	HAPPY AS CLAMS!
AT THE TOP OF MY GAME.	LIFE IS A DREAM!

EDDIE:

THE CROWD GOING WILD
AT THE SOUND OF MY NAME!
BEFORE—

MAE:

EVERYTHING SEEMS POSSIBLE
SINCE—

EDDIE & MAE:

I BECAME
EDDIE AND MAE—
EDDIE AND MAE—
EDDIE AND MAE—
EDDIE AND MAE—
EDDIE AND MAE—
EDDIE AND MAE!

(Dolores pulls Burrs aside.)

DOLORES: Shame on you Burrs, for being sooo hush-hush. And after all we have meant to each other.

BURRS: Now why would I do that?

DOLORES: Why indeed when you know so much about me and I know oh so much more about you.

(They share a generous, deadly laugh.)

BURRS: You found out about Mr. Gold and Goldberg moving uptown.

DOLORES: Umhm.

BURRS: And you want me to—

DOLORES: Play the overture and leave the rest of the score to me. Secrets?

BURRS: Secrets.

(Lights reveal Queenie smiling and pretending to listen as Gold and Goldberg laugh and rattle on.)

GOLD: Queenie, you gotta picture the—the thing.

QUEENIE: What thing?

GOLD: The thing! The thing! The sign.

GOLDBERG *(Translating)*: The marquee.

GOLD: The marquee! Millions of millions of lights.

GOLDBERG: In actuality, I'd say more like forty, fifty.

GOLD: To hell with actuality. We're talking Broadway, millions of millions of lights spelling out words: "Gold and Golden Presents:"

GOLDBERG *(Reassuringly to Queenie)*: —Gold and Goldberg.

GOLD *(Insistent)*: Gold and Golden.

GOLDBERG: Gold and Goldberg.

(The two men sing:)

GOLD:

GOLD AND GOLDEN
WE'RE GONNA BE ON BROADWAY.

GOLDBERG:

GOLD AND GOLDBERG
FIRST WE NEED A HIT.

GOLD:

HOW DID HAMMERSTEIN GET TO BE HAMMERSTEIN?

GOLDBERG:

HE MOVED UPTOWN.

GOLD:

HOW DID ALBEE GET TO BE ALBEE?

GOLDBERG:

He dumped the animal acts.

GOLD:

How did Ziegfeld get to be Ziegfeld?

GOLDBERG:

He fired the fat chorines.

GOLD:

How did Billy Rose get to be Billy Rose?

GOLDBERG:

He changed his name.

GOLD:

And we gotta do the same.
Forget the old routines—
If we want a shot at fame
We gotta do

GOLDBERG:

Hot

GOLD:

Slick

GOLDBERG:

Black

GOLD:

And blue.

GOLD & GOLDBERG:

Out with the old
And in with the new.

We're Gold and Golden (Goldberg)
We wanna be on Broadway.
Gold and Golden (Goldberg)
We gonna be legit.
And we'll do what it takes
To play canasta with the Shuberts—
We're Gold and Golden (Gold and Goldberg)
Hungry for a, hungry for a, hungry for a, hungry for a hit!
Hungry hungry hungry hungry hungry for a hit!
Hungry hungry hungry hungry—

GOLD: Hungry?

GOLDBERG: Hungry.

(Dolores and Burrs join Gold, Goldberg and Queenie.)

DOLORES *(Really turning on the routine)*: Oh Burrs, did I ever tell you about my last performance as Salome? Fourteen curtain calls, hundreds of roses strewn at my feet and the entire audience chanting: "More! More!" as I removed my final . . .

(As if seeing Gold and Goldberg for the first time.)

Oh hello.

(Dolores gestures for Burrs to begin speaking.)

BURRS: Messrs. Gold and Goldberg, meet the legendary Dolores Montoya. From Vienna to Vancouver, from Rio to Rajasthan, she has electrified the stages of the world with her élan. Having just returned from her acclaimed world tour, she is anxious to reappear on Broadway—

QUEENIE: Where she first appeared over forty-n—

DOLORES *(Interrupting)*: Many years ago.

(She sings:)

Gentlemen,

You are looking at the woman
Who invented "The Walk."
You know "The Walk."
I invented that.
You are looking at a female
Who has driven men to homicide.
How? Must you ask?
Look at these beautiful legs.
These legs were built to drive men mad—
Would you like to dance?

But first—

I hear you're moving uptown.
I'll move with you.

I HEAR YOU'RE TAKING TALENT.
TALENT I DO. I DO.

I'VE HEADLINED WITH THE BEST:
I CAN STILL PACK THEM IN—
I HEAR YOU'RE MOVING UPTOWN.
I KNOW THE WAY
'CUZ I'VE ALREADY BEEN . . .

WHEN YOU LOOK AROUND THE ROOM—LOOK:
TELL ME WHAT DO YOU SEE?
IMITATIONS OF IMITATIONS—
I INVENTED MYSELF.
I AM A CREATURE
WHO SACRIFICES LOVE FOR HER ART.
WHY? YOU MAY ASK—
WHAT WITH THESE SMOLDERING LIPS;
DO YOU KNOW WHAT IT'S LIKE TO KISS
SUCH SMOLDERING LIPS?
WOULD YOU LIKE TO FIND OUT?

But first—

I HEAR YOU'RE MOVING UPTOWN.
I'LL GO, YOU LEAD.
I'M READY FOR THE BIG TIME.
THAT'S WHAT I NEED, I NEED
I NEED TO RETURN TO THE PLACE
WHERE I USED TO BELONG.
I HEAR YOU'RE MOVING UPTOWN.

GOLD: Miss Montoya—
DOLORES: Dolores.
GOLD: Dolores. It's still early in the game. Who can tell?
GOLDBERG: Can you tell?
GOLD: I can't tell. Still lots of details to be worked out.
GOLDBERG: Lots.
GOLD: Lots.

(They nervously turn to go, acutely aware that Dolores is still watching them.)

(Confidentially to Goldberg) Which is exactly what I feel like. Lot's wife. And she is Sodom and Gomorrah incarnate.

GOLDBERG: Then don't turn around. Don't look back.

(They can't control themselves. They both slowly turn to see Dolores burning holes in them with her intensity.)

DOLORES:

I HEAR YOU'RE TAKING ME ALONG.
I HEAR YOU'RE TAKING ME
YOU'RE TAKING ME, YOU'RE TAKING ME, YOU'RE TAKING ME
ALONG!

(All of a sudden Queenie releases a violent scream—and faints. Burrs and everyone else rush to her.)

BURRS: What's wrong? What happened?

JACKIE: She was just standing there and all of a sudden—

BURRS: Outta my way. Queenie, what's wrong?

(Burrs takes her in his arms. She begins slowly to come to.)

QUEENIE: Burrsie? I need . . . I need . . .

BURRS: What? Tell me?

QUEENIE *(As if her dying words)*: I need to do the Black Bottom.

(Queenie squeals and begins to shake and dance with total glee. Everyone laughs except Burrs.)

BURRS: One of these days . . .

QUEENIE: Gotcha! Come on Nadine it's time to get nasty.

THE PARTY

Queenie grabs Nadine and begins to dance. She is reckless and wild. Her energy and abandon ignite the rest of the room.

She sings:

QUEENIE:

SAME OLD FACES SAME OLD NAMES
SAME ROUTINES AND SAME OLD GAMES.
QUEENIE NEEDS A NEWER KICK
NEEDS IT NOW AND NEEDS IT QUICK—
EVERYBODY WATCH QUEENIE GO
WILD!

(Queenie dances, throwing herself at everyone, downing drinks, but nothing seems to lift her as high as she wants to go.)

QUEENIE NEEDS SOME NEWER SKIN
NEWER SEX AND NEWER SIN.
DON'T NEED BURRSIE PAWIN' ME.
GOTTA GOTTA GOTTA GOTTA SHAKE IT FREE.
EVERYBODY WATCH QUEENIE GO
WILD!

GOTTA GET HIGH.
GOTTA GET THRILLED.
GOTTA GET FIZZED GOTTA GET FILLED.

EVERYBODY WATCH
EVERYBODY WATCH
EVERYBODY WATCH
EVERYBODY WATCH QUEENIE GO . . .

(The Guests and the room seem to take off flying as Queenie looks on, completely lost and left behind.)

DRY . . .
BURRSIE, I'M DRY . . .
DRY . . .

(And then in the middle of it all Black appears: handsome, strikingly so; suave, cool, direct; of unknown origin; something vaguely innocent about him, but a sense of weariness as well. Queenie and Black regard each other. She is about to cross to him when she sees that Kate is on his arm. Kate, Queenie's best friend, is a red-headed, dagger-tongued panther—a former chorine now would-be star. She grandly enters the party, arm and arm with Black.)

KATE: I'm here! I'm here! I'm here!
MAE *(Squealing)*: Kate!

(Everyone envelops Kate.)

We've seen your posters all over town. And I tell everyone, "That's my friend Kate. We danced together. And now I'm fat and she's a star."
KATE: Eddie!
EDDIE: Kate! Lookin' good!
KATE: Man you lookin' pretty damn good yo' own self.
MAE *(A bit peeved)*: He sure is.
KATE: Everybody meet my friend Mr. Black. *(To Black)* How about getting me a drink? *(Kisses him)* You know what I like and how I like it.
PHIL: Honey you know you a star when the shoes, the dress and the man all match.
OSCAR: We hear the show's going to Paris.
ALL *(Ad-libs)*: Really! Congrats! Alright!
OSCAR: Move over Josephine.
PHIL: Get ready for "the fastest legs in lights!"

(Kate does a dazzling shimmy. Everyone applauds.)

QUEENIE *(From across the room)*: More like the cheapest slut.
KATE: The cheapest slut, huh? I guess everybody's already had you so why even bother to charge?

(The party Guests whoop it up, enjoying the war.)

By the way Queenie, I love the dress.
QUEENIE: Why thank you, Kate.
KATE: I loved it even more three parties ago.
QUEENIE: Of course it's nothing compared to yours. It's amazing. Money can buy anything . . . except taste and hips.
KATE: Hers have filled out. Age tends to do that.
QUEENIE: Bitch!
KATE: Tramp!
QUEENIE: Whore!
KATE: Chorus girl!
PHIL: Now that's low.

(The room erupts into laughter.)

QUEENIE: Come here!

(Queenie and Kate hug like best friends.)

How ya been ya bum? You never call. You never come visit.

KATE: Now that I'm "a star," I can't be seen with just anyone. How's Burrsie been treatin' ya?

QUEENIE: Don't start. Nadine, come meet the glamorous, the wicked, the seductive yet deadly Miss Kate.

NADINE: You're beautiful.

KATE: Kid's got good eyesight.

QUEENIE: Lesson number two: hold your friends close but your enemies even closer.

NADINE: Which is Kate?

(Queenie and Kate sing:)

QUEENIE:

SHE'S A LITTLE BIT PAL.

KATE:

SHE'S A LITTLE BIT FOE.

QUEENIE:

SHE'S A LITTLE BIT SLICK.

KATE:

SHE'S A LITTLE BIT SLOW.

QUEENIE:

WHO'S GORGEOUS TO THE CUTICLE?

KATE:

WHOSE LOOKS AIN'T PHARMACEUTICAL?

QUEENIE:

I'M ALL THIS AND SHE'S ALL THAT.

KATE:

SHE'S ALL DOG AND I'M ALL CAT.

QUEENIE & KATE:

BUT UNDERNEATH THE FUR AND FAT
YOU'RE LOOKIN' AT
MY BEST FRIEND.

KATE:

SHE'S A LITTLE BIT STALE.

QUEENIE:

SHE'S A LITTLE BIT FRESH.

KATE:

SHE'S A LOTTA BIT ICE.

QUEENIE:

SHE'S A LOTTA BIT FLESH.

KATE:

I ALWAYS DO THE MOTHERING.

QUEENIE:

YEAH, SOME MIGHT CALL IT SMOTHERING.
DIFFERENT AS THE DAY AND NIGHT

KATE:

OPPOSITE AS WRONG AND RIGHT

QUEENIE & KATE:

TOGETHER WE MAKE DYNAMITE.
HOLD ON TIGHT
FOR MY BEST FRIEND.

QUEENIE: Let's see if you remember the old routine—
KATE: No thank you.
QUEENIE: What's a-matter? Can't move those thighs anymore?
KATE: Sugar, I don't have to.

(They re-create an old dance routine from their days on the chorus line together.)

QUEENIE & KATE:

*"WE SHARE
EVERYTHING—
STEAK AND EGGS
DIETING.
WE SHARE
EVERYTHING
AND LOVE!*

*WE SHARE
EVENING WRAPS
VASELINE
GARTER SNAPS.
WE SHARE
EVERYTHING
AND*

Luvva luvva luvva luvva luvva . . .
Love!"

(Queenie breaks away and flirts with Black. Kate interrupts.)

QUEENIE: Hello.
BLACK: Hello.
KATE: Have you two met?
BLACK: I haven't had the pleasure.
KATE: Well, honey you're one of the few who hasn't. Queenie, Black. Black, Queenie. *(To Queenie)* So you're still shakin' it down in the Bowery. Ain't they retired you yet?
QUEENIE: Too bad that all of that money you earn, you gotta spend on the love you can't get.

(Queenie and Kate sing.)

KATE:
WHAT'LL BE TONIGHT'S SPECIAL? LET ME GUESS—
"QUEENIE IN DISTRESS" AGAIN?
QUEENIE:
"KATE THE ICEBOX" IS JEALOUS OF ME
AND MY NAT'RAL SUCCESS WITH MEN.
KATE:
I CALLS IT LIKE I SEES IT.
QUEENIE:
SHE NEVER TELLS THE TRUTH.
KATE:
SHE'S A LITTLE BIT DUMB.
QUEENIE:
SHE'S A LITTLE BIT COLD.
KATE:
SHE'S A LITTLE BIT CHEAP.
QUEENIE:
SHE'S A LITTLE BIT OLD.
KATE:
SHE'S A LITTLE SOFT.
QUEENIE:
SHE'S A LITTLE HARD.

QUEENIE & KATE:

SHE'S A LOTTA LOTTA LUV LUVVA LUVVA LOVE—
SHE'S GOOD FOR THE BAIL.
I'M GREAT FOR A LAUGH.
SHE'S MY EVIL TWIN.
I'M HER BETTER HALF.

QUEENIE:

SHE CUTS THROUGH ALL THE GIN AND JIVE.

KATE:

SHE ALWAYS MAKES ME FEEL ALIVE.

QUEENIE & KATE:

STICKIN' THROUGH THE BLOOD AND GORE
CALL IT LOVE OR CIVIL WAR.
WHAT WE GOT IS SOMETHING MORE.
THANK HEAVEN AND HELL FOR
MY BEST FRIEND!—

(As the number comes to a dazzling end, everyone applauds. Burrs crosses to Kate.)

BURRS *(Taking her in his arms)*: Kate! Ya still got it in ya!

KATE: Burrs. The sound of your name makes me think of some roughed-up and hungry, ugly alley cat. It starts out licking you and ends up eating you alive.

BURRS: Oooo! The pot's calling the kettle black.

KATE: Roughed-up maybe. But hungry and ugly, never. So how are you and Queenie doing?

BURRS: Happy as clams.

KATE *(Toasting)*: Here's to not getting shucked.

(The Brothers D'Armano begin to play.)

BURRS: You're up to something. Tell me.

(He grabs at Kate. She gets away.)

KATE: And spoil all the fun? *(With a wink)* Hot-chitza-dee!

BROTHERS D'ARMANO *(Singing)*:

"IF I'M UP IN HARLEM
WHERE THE PLAYBOYS PLAY

AND YOU'RE OUT SLUMMING
TILL THE BREAK OF DAY
WHO CARES IF WE MISBEHAVE?
JUST AS LONG AS WE KNOW TO SAVE
A LITTLE MMMM
A LOTTA YUMMY YUM
FOR EACH OTHER . . ."

KATE: So Queenie, what do you think of Black?

QUEENIE: Who?

KATE: Queenie, you and I both know if any man who looked even half as good as Black knocked on your door, you'd be there with your undies at your ankles sayin', "Come on in."

(Kate and Queenie laugh. Eddie swoops down and grabs Kate. They dance.)

MAE: Lovin' Eddie is like lovin' Niagara Falls. The first time you see it, you're amazed by just how big it is.

MADELAINE & JACKIE: Ooooooo!

MAE *(Giggling)*: Stop! I'm talking about the Falls, not Eddie's whatever. And you think, "Wow, it can't get any better," yet each time it does. Doesn't it Eddie?

(She turns around to see Eddie dancing with and hanging on Kate.)

BROTHERS D'ARMANO:

"IF I COOK SOME CUTIE
AT THE COTTON CLUB
WHILE YOU SHOOT SOME SHANK
WITH MISTER OIL-AND-RUB
WE DON'T HAVE A JEALOUS BONE;
'CUZ WE'LL MANAGE WHEN WE'RE ALONE
A LITTLE MMMMMM
A LOTTA YUMMY YUM
MMMM . . . YUMMY YUM!"

(As Gold and Goldberg talk, Dolores enters. She listens in.)

GOLD: How old do you think Miss Montoya is?

GOLDBERG: Old. But not too old.

GOLD: Especially if all the stage lights are on.
GOLDBERG: And all the bedroom lights are off!

(Dolores assaults them, with a laugh.)

JACKIE: Brothers!
BROTHERS D'ARMANO: Jackie!
JACKIE: Don't you two ever get tired of each other?

(They all laugh.)

But seriously. Day in and day out, the same gestures, the same routines.
PHIL: We're happiest as a team.
JACKIE: How about you, Oscar? Ever long to tickle someone else's ivories? Ever long to take a spin on someone else's spinet? *(With a wink)* Gotta run.

BROTHERS D'ARMANO:
"I'M NO JACK HORNER
AND YOU'RE NO MISS MUFFETT.
CAN'T SIT IN A CORNER.
WE TWO LOVE TO ROUGH IT.
BUT WE'LL BOTH BE BACK IN EACH OTHER'S ARMS
COME MORN . . ."

KATE: Having fun?
BLACK: Interesting crowd. Your friend Queenie and that guy Burrs, they married or something?
KATE: More something than married. You sound like you wanna go play.
BLACK: Nah.
KATE: Go play. Go on. Besides, I got some playing of my own I wanna do.
BLACK: I see.

(He turns to go. She stops him.)

KATE: No matter what, we leave together.

(Kate pulls him back and kisses him, marking her territory. As Queenie eyes them kissing, Burrs crosses to her.)

BURRS: I just want you to know, I can see you.

QUEENIE: That's nice Burrs. I like to be seen.

(Dolores crosses to Burrs.)

DOLORES: Burrs, my pet.
BURRS: Dolores.
DOLORES: Gold and Goldberg are two little insects and I am the Venus flytrap. As soon as they have tasted my succulent fragrance, Dolores Montoya shall bloom once again. *(A toast)* Here's to no turning back.

(Burrs sees Queenie and Black eyeing each other.)

BURRS *(A toast)*: No turning back.
JACKIE *(As he eyes Oscar, a toast)*: No turning back.
KATE *(To Black, a toast)*: No turning back.

BROTHERS D'ARMANO:

"If I'm sprung and spanky
On a cocaine hum
While you're weird and wanky
Puffing opium.
Whatever our cravings need
We'll both have (aside from weed)
A little mmmmmm
A lotta yummy yum
For each other!"

(As the number ends, lights reveal Madelaine applying makeup to Nadine—making her look many years older—the first of a series of transformations Nadine will go through during the course of the evening.
As Madelaine sings, Dolores corners Queenie.)

MADELAINE:

Everyone has their secrets.

DOLORES: Queenie dear, in my day discretion was the rule.

MADELAINE:

Who we are is what we ain't.

QUEENIE: In your day, Dolores, they hadn't even invented electricity.

MADELAINE:

CHANGE YOUR NAME AND PUT THAT MASK ON;

DOLORES: You'll learn, but I'm afraid it will be too little too late.

MADELAINE:

THEN YOU JUST PRETEND
TILL YOU RUN OUT OF PAINT . . .

(Nadine sings:)

NADINE: Ahhh . . .

(She flirts with Black.)

I ALWAYS WANTED TO SEE THE LIGHTS OF BROADWAY.
I ALWAYS WANTED TO HEAR THE TRAFFIC ROAR.
I ALWAYS WANTED TO BE A PART
OF NEW YORK CITY'S GREAT BIG HEART
AND NOW I AM, I COULDN'T ASK FOR MORE.
I ALWAYS—I ALWAYS—I ALWAYS—

QUEENIE: Enough already.

NADINE:

I ALWAYS WANTED TO JINGLE WITH THE RIGHT CROWD:
I ALWAYS WANTED TO FEEL LIKE I BELONG.
I WANNA FEEL . . .

QUEENIE: Lesson number three. Get lost.

(Nadine backs away. Queenie starts up the Victrola. As Black crosses to her:)

Hello Mr. Black

BLACK: No "Mr." No nothing. Just Black.

QUEENIE: Ooooh. A man with a secret. A man with something to hide.

BLACK: Most people, once they see all I got to show, are satisfied.

QUEENIE: I'm not most people.

BLACK: Guess what?

QUEENIE: What?

BLACK: Neither am I.

(Oscar sings accompanied by the Victrola:)

OSCAR:

"TABU!
WHEN YOU'RE FORBIDDEN YOUR DESIRE."

BLACK: Kate tells me you're a dancer.
QUEENIE *(Simultaneously with Oscar below)*: Really? What else does Kate tell you?

OSCAR *(Simultaneously with Queenie above)*:

"TABU
YOU LEARN TO PLAY WITH FIRE."

BLACK: That you two go way back.
QUEENIE: To the Ice Age and beyond. And what do you do for a living?
BLACK: I smile a lot, dress well and look good.
QUEENIE: And you get paid for that?
BLACK: I do all right.

OSCAR:

"TABU!
WHEN YOU'RE DENIED WHAT YOU ADORE.
TABU!
YOU WANT IT ALL THE MORE . . ."

QUEENIE: So, show me.
BLACK: Show you what?
QUEENIE: The game, the hustle. Or is this it?
BLACK: Believe me, if Black was running the mooch, you'd be in his arms begging him to never leave you.
QUEENIE: Oh really? Well then, let's pretend it's late at night and you're at some fancy club and I'm drunk and rich. And I first see you or you see me. No, let's say, we see . . .
QUEENIE & BLACK: . . . each other.
QUEENIE: So go on, mooch me.
BLACK: Right here? Right now?
QUEENIE: Right now.
BLACK: You sure you're ready?

QUEENIE: Oh I can handle anything you got. Trust me.
BLACK: 'Cause if you melt or swoon, or—
QUEENIE: The mooch?

(Black sings:)

BLACK:

BLACK LIKES THE WAY THAT YOU
LOOK TONIGHT:
ELEGANT, SLEEK AND COOL.
BLACK LIKES THE WAY THAT YOU
SHAKE THE MOVES:
SO BEAUTIFUL BUT WATCH IT—
A PANTHER'S TRAPPED INSIDE.
TELL ME—WHO ROLLS YOUR CIGARETTES
AND KEEPS YOU SATISFIED?

TAKING CARE OF THE LADIES
I TAKE CARE OF MYSELF.
BLACK'S GLAD TO SEND YOU
WHERE YOU WANNA GO
AND BABY IT'S YOUR PARTY.
WHAT MORE YOU WANNA KNOW?
WHAT MORE YOU WANNA KNOW?
WHAT MORE?

QUEENIE: I can see how that might work on some women—desperate, lonely.
BLACK: But not you.
QUEENIE: Nope.
BLACK: OK. Here's another mooch. It's Sunday night, and this woman I know, let's call her Kate, an acquaintance . . .
QUEENIE *(Overlapping)*: Interesting choice of words . . .
BLACK *(Overlapping)*: . . . is invited to this party and she drags me along . . .
QUEENIE *(Overlapping)*: Drags you?
BLACK: . . . and the second I walk in I see this other woman.
QUEENIE: Who happens to be the best friend of your acquaintance—
BLACK *(Overlapping)*: Too many details can spoil a good mooch. And this woman is blonde, beautiful, and the way she holds her cigarette, the way her hand folds on her hip . . .

Black likes the way that
She burns tonight:
Ginger and smoke and sex.
Black likes the way that
She likes him back.

Everything about her
Says: "Danger—run away."
But something in her eyes seems to
Be begging me to stay . . .

Taking care of the ladies
I take care of myself.
Everything about you says:
"Danger—stay away."
But danger and a woman
What more I gotta say?
What more?
What more?

For a guy I talk a lot . . .
We oughta just listen to the music,
We oughta just dance . . .

OSCAR:

"Tabu!
Forbidden fruit upon the vine.
Tabu!
I'll never rest until you're mine . . ."

(Time seems to suspend itself. Black and Queenie dance to their own music which swells magnificently. Black and Queenie lock eyes, the music decrescendos.)

"It's whatcha wanna do but whatchaknowya shouldn't do—
Like what I wanna do with you:
You say you wanna do it, too?
That's Tabu! . . ."

BURRS *(To Kate)*: So, who's the third-rate Valentino?

KATE: Just some guy.

BURRS: What do ya mean, "Just some guy"? You picked him up climbing the stairs? Said, "Hey, I'm going to this party. Wanna come?"

KATE: He and Queenie seem to be getting along real well.

BURRS: Yeah, well, what can I say? My Queenie, she's a friendly kinda gal.

QUEENIE *(Sings)*:

AH . . . OUR FIRST DANCE . . . NOW THAT'S A MOOCH.

(Sally screams as Burrs goes charging at Queenie. He lifts his hand as if to strike her, but then the gesture turns into a Jolson-esque pose. He performs for the Guests.)

BURRS:

"FIDELITY IS A VIRTUE
TOO MANY, MANY, MANY OF YOU LACK;
MONOGAMY CAN EXERT YOU
KEEPING TRACK OF WHAT GOES ON
BEHIND YOUR BACK.
WOULD THAT YOUR SUGAR COULD BE TRUSTED;
INSTEAD OF BUSTED SCRUBBING
SOMEONE ELSE'S TUB;
IS IT TOO MUCH TO ASK—
IS IT SUCH AN AWFUL TASK—
TO BE FAITHFUL?
AH! THERE'S THE RUB . . .

WOULDN'T IT BE NICE
WOULDN'T IT BE GRAND
TO KNOW YOUR SWEETIE
WASN'T SQUEEZIN'
SOMEONE ELSE'S . . . HAND?
WOULDN'T IT BE NICE
WOULDN'T IT BE GOOD
TO KNOW YOUR LOVE
HAD NOT MADE LOVE
WITH HALF THE NEIGHBORHOOD?
OH!
HASN'T IT BEEN HELL

Having no success?
You wish your baby
Knew more words than:
'Open up'
And 'Yes!'
You can warn her once,
But then she'll go and do it twice;
She's everybody's cherry pie—
But you don't get a slice;
Makes you wanna chain her up
And pack her down in ice—
That wouldn't be nice
But wouldn't it be nice?"

(Music. Burrs's energy becomes more manic as he playfully assaults his Guests.)

Oscar and Phil—It's a thrill.
But while Jackie's fillin' Oscar,
How does po' Phil feel?

(Music.)

Sally, Sally, Sally, she's all mine.
I haven't heard her say, "I love Ma-du-line."

(Music.)

Eddie and Mae, ain't love great?
Ya better watch out, he's messin' with Kate.

"Don't it break your heart?
Ain'tcha got it rough?
You give your tootsie everything
But still it's not enough—
All the same you know
She's gonna come around one day.
She'll vow to love and honor and obey
And never stray.
You may be dead and buried by that time

But what the hey?
Hold out for paradise
Stock up on wedding rice.
You gotta make her love ya—
No matter what the price—
Couldn't it be—
Shouldn't it be—
Wouldn't it be—
Nice!—"

Hot-chitza-dee!

(He goes into an "encore"; the Guests join in.)

"Oh—
Hold out for paradise
Stock up on wedding rice.
You gotta make her love ya—
No matter what the price—"

(The lights fade on Burrs and the Guests. Black and Queenie are discovered in a quiet corner of the room.)

BLACK *(Indicating Burrs)*: Where'd you find that?

QUEENIE: Burrsie? He found me. Queenie on the skids and along comes Burrs trying to rescue what don't want to be saved. Trying to love what— *(A pause)* Well, hey . . .

(She sings:)

Some are born for higher things
Like hitchin' up to uptown kings:
I was born for iron beds and bums.
Well awrighty then,
That's the lowdown-down.

Swim with sharks in shallow pools
You get bit and them's the rules.
I got bit and almost eaten whole.

But I liked it, yeah.
That's the lowdown-down.

Some get good at trafficking in souls.
I got good at rollin' with the rolls.
Some get given everything they need.
Well, that's a lucky break:
I steal what I take and I roll.
And I plead and I duck—oh hey,
And I bleed.

Some are born to rise above
Sleepless nights and sloe-gin love-love-love;
I was born to ask, "Why was I born?"
And the answer is:

Get me some more ice, will ya?

(She holds out her glass. Black doesn't take it. Feeling naked and vulnerable, Queenie sits.)

Small town girl she comes to town;
Tin of rouge and strapless gown;
Dies a lot before she gets to die.
But with a smile she'll say:
"That's the lowdown-down . . ."

(As Burrs looks on, Black crosses in to kiss Queenie. Just as they are about to kiss, Black and Queenie look up. Kate is standing over them.)

BURRS *(To audience)*: You can warn her once but then she'll go and do it twice.

(To Guests) Take out the lights! Pffft!

(The lights go out. The Guests squeal with delight and gather around Burrs. Queenie crosses away and Black follows after, leaving Kate alone.)

Let's get this party going. No I mean really get things going. Unsnap those garters and starched lapels. It's time to get wicked and wild. It's time to get low. It's time for gin!

(Burrs presents a bottle of gin. The Guests whoop and holler, like possessed, mad animals.
Burrs sings:)

BURRS:
IF I GO MEAN—
IF I GO MAD—
BLAME IT ON THE GIN.

GUEST *(Overlapping "Blame it on the gin")*:
TIME FOR GIN

BURRS:
IF I GO (FLBFLBFLB)
IF I GO (EYYEYYEYY)
BLAME IT ON THE GIN.

GUEST *(Overlapping "Blame it on the gin")*:
TIME FOR GIN
TIME FOR GIN
TIME FOR . . .

BURRS, EDDIE & MAE:
DON'T GIMME NO WHISKEY
'CUZ I NEED MORE THAN BOOZE.

BURRS, JACKIE & BROTHERS D'ARMANO:
JUST POUR ME THE REAL STUFF
SO I CAN TASTE MY BLUES.

BURRS & GUESTS:
I NEED MY PARTY TO BEGIN
MY PARTY TO BEGIN
MY PARTY! MY! MY!

BURRS *(Simultaneously with Guests below)*:
IF YOU GO SOFT
AND TELL THE TRUTH
BLAME IT ON THE GIN.

IF YOU GO HARD AND GOTTA BLOW
BLAME IT ON THE (*YOU KNOW*)

GUESTS *(Simultaneously with Burrs above)*:
TIME FOR
TRUTH
TIME FOR GIN
TIME FOR

BLAME IT ON THE . . .

BURRS:

IF YOU FIND YOURSELF
IN SOME PRECARIOUS SITUATION
WONDERING WHO THE HELL'S HALLUCINATION
AM I IN?
DON'T LOOK AT ME—

BURRS & GUESTS:

BLAME IT ON THE—
BLAME IT ON THE—
GIN GIN GIN GIN
GIN GIN GIN!

(As the Guests continue to guzzle gin, Jackie grabs Oscar and pulls him into the bathroom.)

DON'TCHA MESS WITH MY PARTY.
YOU CAN'T TAKE AWAY WHAT'S MINE.
DON'TCHA KNOW IT'S MY PARTY?
TIME FOR THE DEVIL TO RISE AND SHINE.
DON'TCHA MAKE MY NIGHT SOBER.
DON'TCHA TELL ME I CAN'T GET HIGH.
DON'TCHA LEMME GO DRY.
DON'TCHA KNOW THAT I
GOTTA KEEP MY MY MY MY MY
PARTY
(WILD!)
WA-WA-WA-WA-WILD! . . .

(Lights reveal Queenie and Dolores.)

DOLORES: Queenie dear, I feel I must warn you.
QUEENIE: You don't like me and I don't like you so let's cut the crap.
DOLORES: Did you know Burrs was married?

(Though Queenie tries to pretend it doesn't, Dolores's information stops her cold.)

Beautiful and blonde, just like you. He beat her. With the heel of his shoe. "Till her lips turned blue." Honey, don't you know, the minute you think you know it all, is when life goes and takes a big bite outta your ass. And I've got the scars to prove it.

BURRS & GUESTS:

DON'TCHA QUEER UP MY PARTY.
IF YOU DO THERE'S HELL TO PAY.
DON'TCHA KNOW IT'S MY PARTY?
TIME FOR THE DEVIL IN ME TO PLAY—

(Continuing under the following scene:)

(WILD!)

(Lights reveal Queenie powdering her face. Burrs sneaks up behind her.)

BURRS: Hot-chitza-dee!
QUEENIE: Damnit, Burrs, you scared me.

GUESTS:

(DON'TCHA MESS UP—)

BURRS: You seem to be having fun.
QUEENIE: Isn't that supposed to be what you do at a party? Have fun?

GUESTS:

(DON'TCHA QUEER UP—)

BURRS: Missed a spot. What's the story with Kate's friend Black?
QUEENIE: You want Black's story, ask Black.
BURRS: I'm asking you.
QUEENIE: I don't have time for this.

(She turns to go. Burrs violently grabs her.)

BURRS: Don't ever think about leaving me. I love you. I love you. Don't you ever think about not loving me.

(Burrs kisses her hard—a desperate, angry kiss. Kate appears in time to see Queenie breaking away from Burrs.)

GUESTS:

(DON'TCHA EVER—)

KATE: What's going on here. Queenie?
BURRS: Nothing for you to worry about.

(He gently pulls up the fallen strap of Queenie's dress, pats her on the cheek. Romantic coon inflections.)

We's jes happy as clams . . .

(Jackie bolts out of the bathroom.)

GUESTS:

(DON'TCHA EVER—)

BURRS: Jackie!
JACKIE: Burrs!
BURRS: Debonair as ever!

JACKIE:

DON'T GIMME NO
DON'T GIMME NO
DON'T GIMME NO
DON'T GIMME NO!

BURRS & GUESTS:

DON'T GIVE ME NO ROOT BEER
'CUZ I NEED MORE THAN FOAM.
DON'T GIVE ME NO JELL-O
I'D RATHER DIE AT HOME.
GIMME GIMME GIMME GIN

GIMME GIN GIN GIN
GIMME GIMME GIMME WILD
GIMME GIMME GIMME
(MORE!)

KATE: Damnit Queenie, what's it gonna take for you to realize—

QUEENIE: Hey—a coupla aspirin and a gulp of gin and I'll be like brand new.
MAE: Everybody! The brothers are about to perform. Where's Oscar! Oscar!!!
EDDIE: Mae, shut up!
MAE: Here's Jackie! Can Oscar be far behind?
EDDIE: Damnit woman! I said shut up and stop making a fool of me!—

(Oscar bolts out of the bathroom.)

BURRS & GUESTS:
(GIMME MORE!)

PHIL *(Sotto voce)*: Well, well, well. I guess we should inform our fans that Phil D'Armano will be signing autographs outside the stage door and Oscar outside the bathroom door.
OSCAR *(Sotto voce)*: Don't start.
PHIL: It's a tad late for: "Don't start." No, I'd say things are pretty goddamn well underway.

BROTHERS D'ARMANO *(Performing for the Guests)*:
DON'TCHA LOVE A GREAT PARTY?
AND THE NIGHT IS JUST BEGUN!
DON'TCHA KNOW IT'S MY PARTY?

PHIL: Son of a bitch!!
OSCAR: Everybody's watching. Be professional.
PHIL *(Simultaneously with Oscar below)*: You show up late and I smile. You forget your harmonies and I smile. I press, powder and perfume this act into perfection and I smile, smile, smile—Well fuck you . . . fuck you!

OSCAR *(Scatting, simultaneously with Phil above)*:
WHA-WHA-WHA!

(Then, overlapping "fuck you":)

Fuck you!

BROTHERS D'ARMANO:
DON'TCHA STEP ON MY
TAILBONE.
TAKE A POWDER AND CUT ME FREE.
BURRS & GUESTS *(Overlapping "Don'tcha step")*:
WAA-WAA WILD!
WAA-WAA-WILD!
BROTHERS D'ARMANO & GUESTS:
AND THERE HAS TO BE
A CATASTROPHE
IF YOU DON'T GIMME-ME-ME-ME
MY PARTY
(Now!)

(Kate corners Queenie.)

KATE: You know, Queenie, you've never been none too bright. But do you gotta go be all the way there dumb?

QUEENIE: Get my life outta your mouth, Kate. It's none of your goddamn business.

BURRS & GUESTS:
(IF I GO MEAN
IF I GO MAD—
IF I GO HARD
AND GOTTA BLOW—
IF I GO SOFT
AND TELL THE TRUTH—
TRUTH)

(Continues under following scene:)

KATE: When is it gonna be my business? When he smashes your face in or throws you out some window and they call me to identify the body? And don't try to tell me Burrs ain't dangerous 'cause honey—the cemetery is full of women singing: "The My-Man-Wouldn't-Hurt-Me-Blues."

QUEENIE: I don't care how many lies Dolores spreads about Burrs. I know it's not true!

KATE: What lies?

MAE: Come on, Daddy Eddie. Let's dance.

EDDIE *(Simultaneously with Queenie)*: Get away from me!

QUEENIE *(Simultaneously with Eddie)*: Get away from me!

MAE: Eddie has no time to dance with Mae because he's too busy throwing himself at Kate.

KATE: Talk to me. Tell me what lies?

MAE: You don't know what I gave up for you.

KATE: What lies?

MAE *(Simultaneously with Queenie)*: You don't KNOW!

QUEENIE *(Simultaneously with Mae)*: NO! I'm sick of people telling me what to do!

(Queenie breaks free of Kate.)

MAE:

YOU'LL BE OUT ON THE STAGE
AND I'M OFF IN THE WINGS
AND I START TO THINK AND
THE THINKIN' STINGS
'CAUSE I THINK I'M MISSIN'
A LOT OF THINGS
BEING THE WHITE TROPHY BLONDE
OF "THE CHAMP."
YOU'RE OUT IN THE CLUBS
PARADIN' YOUR MEAT
SPENDING ALL YOUR ADVANCE
ON SNATCH OFF THE STREET.
YOU SEEN MORE ASS
THAN A TOILET SEAT.

GUESTS *(Overlapping "The Champ")*:

EDDIE AND MAE, EDDIE AND MAE
EDDIE AND MAE
EDDIE AND MAE, EDDIE AND MAE
EDDIE AND MAE.

MAE:

AND I BET YOU MAKE 'EM ALL
CALL YOU "THE CHAMP"
BUT TONIGHT IT'S MY PARTY

GUESTS *(Overlapping "my party")*:

MY PARTY

MAE:

AND MAE IS GETTIN'
GOOD AND JUICED.
DON'TCHA KNOW IT'S MY PARTY?

GUESTS *(Overlapping "my party")*:

MY PARTY!

MAE:

THE DEVIL IN ME'S
GONNA FLY THE ROOST!

KATE:

WHAT'S GONNA BE YOUR EPITAPH?
"PO' L'IL QUEENIE, SHE LUVVA-LUVVA LOVED
HER MAN?"
BETTER WAKE UP AND START
GETTIN' ALL THE WAY SMART.
IF YOU WANNA DIE, FINE THEN
YOU DO IT ALONE
'CUZ I AIN'T GONNA HELP YOU, SISTER
YOU'RE ON YOUR OWN—
YEAH—I GOT BETTER THINGS TO DO
THAN WRITE YOUR EPITAPH FOR YOU—
KATE IS GETTIN' WILD TONIGHT
KATE IS GETTIN' WILD
WILD!
WILD!

EDDIE *(Overlapping first "Wild!")*:

I GAVE UP MOST OF MY DREAMS FOR YOU
I GAVE UP HALF OF MY PAYCHECK, TOO.

GUESTS:

EDDIE AND MAE
EDDIE AND MAE
EDDIE AND MAE

EDDIE *(Overlapping first "Eddie and Mae")*:

I'D GIVE UP DRINKIN'
BUT WHAT GOOD WOULD IT DO?
THE WHOLE WORLD KNOWS YOU
BROUGHT DOWN THE CHAMP.

KATE:

KATE IS GETTIN'
WILD TONIGHT.
I DON'T PLAY BY
NO RULES—

EDDIE *(Overlapping "Kate")*:

SO TONIGHT IT'S MY PARTY.
YOU DON'T WANNA MAKE ME MEAN.
DON'TCHA KNOW IT'S MY PARTY?
THE DEVIL IN ME NEEDS
A NEW ROUTINE—

BURRS & GUESTS *(Overlapping "wanna make me mean")*:

DON'TCHA KNOW IT'S MY PARTY?

KATE:

NO MORE—

MAE *(Overlapping "No more—")*:

I GAVE UP MY LEGS AND
MY PLACE ON THE LINE.

KATE:

NO MORE—

EDDIE *(Overlapping "No more—")*:

I GAVE UP THE RING AND THE
CROWN AND THE GLOVE.

EDDIE & MAE:

I GAVE IT ALL UP FOR WHAT I THOUGHT WAS—

BURRS:	BROTHERS D'ARMANO:	JACKIE:	EDDIE & MAE:	GUESTS:
DON'TCHA EVER THINK ABOUT NOT LOVIN' ME	LUVVA LUVVA LUVVA—	S'LONG AS I GOT A FREE HAND	EDDIE AND MAE! EDDIE AND MAE! EDDIE AND MAE!	WILD— WILD— WILD— WILD!

(Mae slaps Eddie. Eddie strikes her back. Lights reveal Gold and Goldberg, drunk.)

GOLDBERG: What a night!

GOLD: What a night!
DOLORES: What a night, indeed. Come with me.

(Dolores seductively grabs them.)

GUESTS:	KATE:	BURRS:
DON'TCHA FUCK WITH MY PARTY!	YOU'RE ON YOUR OWN—	DON'TCHA EVER
YOU CAN'T TAKE AWAY WHAT'S MINE!	KATE IS GETTIN'	THINK ABOUT
DON'TCHA KNOW IT'S MY PARTY!	WILD TONIGHT!	NOT LOVIN' ME—
TIME FOR THE DEVIL TO RISE AND SHINE!	NO RULES!	TIME FOR THE DEVIL TO RISE AND SHINE!
DON'TCHA MAKE MY NIGHT SOBER!		SHE'LL GET A HUGE SHE-BANG
DON'T TELL ME I CAN'T GET HIGH!		
DON'TCHA LEMME GO DRY!		
DON'TCHA KNOW THAT I		
GOTTA KEEP MY PARTY—	KEEP MY PARTY—	KEEP MY PARTY—
WILD!	WILD!	WILD!
WILD!	WILD!	WILD!
WILD!	WILD!	WILD!

(As the cacophony of music and emotion reaches its peak, Black grabs Queenie and they exit.)

The intensity of the gin high gives way to desire. Bodies scattered throughout the room begin to reach out for one another.)

MADELAINE: Sally? Sally?

(Lights up on Madelaine, looking for Sally.)

Sally! Sallee! Sally-Sally-Saaaaaal . . . lee! SAL-LEE!

(Sally stands atop a chair. She has Mr. Goldberg's tie around her neck and is holding it aloft as if it were a noose. Madelaine sees her and smiles.)

I get drunk just saying your name. Now it's your turn. Say: "Ma-de-laine. Ma-de-laine, Maaaa-duh-laine!"

(Madelaine sings:)

I NEED TO FEEL YOUR TOUCH.
I KNOW YOU NEED THE SAME.
I CRAVE I WANT I BEG I NEED
TO HEAR YOU SAY MY NAME.
I'M SOMEONE YOU DESIRE.
I'M SOMEONE YOU CAN TRUST.

OSCAR & JACKIE *(Overlapping "desire")*:
(DESIRE)

(Overlapping "trust":)

(TRUST)

ALL:
I NEED I NEED I NEED I NEED

MADALAINE:
I NEED TO FEEL YOUR LUST.

ALL:
(HUNGRY HUNGRY HUNGRY)
I NEED I NEED—
(HUNGRY HUNGRY HUNGRY)
I NEED I NEED—

KATE:
I NEED I NEED—
I NEED I NEED—

(Lights reveal Kate and Burrs.)

BURRS: Forgotten what it's like to play with Burrs?

KATE *(As if coming on to him)*: I remember. A sloppy kiss in the beginning, and an even sloppier one at the end. And in between a whole lotta motion, but not much of a ride.

BURRS: And this Black is the answer to all you're looking for?

KATE: Burrsie, if some man is the answer, then I'm asking all the wrong questions. But the thing about Black . . . what Black has . . .

(She sings:)

KATE:

Black is a moocher
And I like it like that.
Three-pocket poocher
And I like it like that.
I like him the way that he is . . .
He is no . . . innocent
And Christ, he's guilty where it counts.
I use him daily in increasin' amounts
And I like it like that.
Un-huh un-huh . . .

I like it like—that.
Mmmhmmmhm . . .
I like it like—
In the morning light, when he rubs his beard
Then he touches me.
In the afternoon. When he draws my bath
Then undresses me.
Come 'round curtain time; when he spends my dough
Then he cheats on me;
Come the quarter-moon; when he drinks too much
Then he cries for me.
Breaking a stray in ain't so hard;
Hadta teach him to play in my backyard.

Black is a liar
And I like it like that.
Thinks with his wire
And I like it like that.
I'm in for the thrill of the kill . . .
If I can't have him—
Then nobody will.

ALL:

I need I need—

KATE:

I need to feel his touch—

ALL:

I NEED I NEED—

KATE:

I NEED TO FEEL HIS SEX—

ALL:

I NEED TO FEEL YOUR SEX.
I NEED TO HEAR MY NAME.
I NEED YOUR FIRE.
I NEED YOUR BREATH.
I NEED YOUR BLOOD.
I NEED YOUR . . . LUST.
LUST!
LUST!

(By number's end, the various naked torsos and limbs of the Guests lie all intertwined as lights reveal Queenie and Black standing on the fire escape to the apartment. They each have a glass.)

QUEENIE: I guess your mooch must be working. Kate, Burrs and everybody else is inside doing god knows what, and you got me out here all alone.

BLACK: Wait a minute. You think I do this kind of thing all the time, begin the evening with one woman and end with another?

QUEENIE: Yeah.

BLACK: Well, okay, maybe I do. But this is different. It is. Or maybe I need to believe it is. Every piece of me has learned to lie and tonight I need to try and not lie and see if I can still feel. See if I can still . . . Then again, maybe it's the gin.

QUEENIE: I haven't had any.

BLACK: Neither have I.

QUEENIE: This city. So many lights you can actually pretend one of 'em's shining on you.

(She sings:)

ALWAYS WANTED TO SEE THE LIGHTS OF BROADWAY.
I ALWAYS WANTED TO HEAR THE TRAFFIC ROAR.
I ALWAYS WANTED TO BE A PART
OF NEW YORK CITY'S GREAT BIG HEART.
AND NOW I AM. I COULDN'T ASK FOR . . .

I was that girl. I'm all of them. Trapped in a room full of shadows and not enough light. And soon we will fade away, into the walls, into nothingness. The end.

(Black sings:)

BLACK:

People like us: we get though the day
Surviving the city way better than most.
We go through the motions
From nightcap to nightcap:
We're here but not here.
With the heart of a ghost.

People like us: we meet up some night
In a room full of strangers who call themselves "friends":
It feels like a dream
But it's too hard to tell
Where the dream begins
And the real world ends—
And where—where do we belong?
We might have to ask ourselves:
Where do we belong?
People like us:
Private stock.
Where?

QUEENIE:

People like us. We take lovers like pills.
Just hoping to cure what we know we can't fix.
And we'll lay in their arms
And we'll say pretty things:
We'll be there but not there
But we'll still get our kicks—
People like us: we sure get our kicks:

And we heal awful fast and we don't even scar:
We are here but not here
In a room full of friends

We could join in the fray
Or stay here where we are—

BUT WHERE—WHERE DO WE BELONG?
DO WE NEED TO ASK OURSELVES
WHERE DO WE BELONG?
PEOPLE LIKE US.
FRAGILE GOODS.
WHERE?

BLACK:
WHERE?

BLACK:
WE DANCE ALONE ON A CROWDED FLOOR.

QUEENIE:
WE WEREN'T GIVEN MUCH.

BLACK:
AND WE DON'T EXPECT MUCH MORE . . .

QUEENIE:
—"MORE" IS NOT A WORD WE USE.
"MORE" WOULD NEVER BE ENOUGH.

QUEENIE & BLACK:
PEOPLE LIKE US: WE SLIP THROUGH THE CRACKS
WE'LL NEVER BE FAMOUS. AND WHO'S GONNA CARE?
NOBODY NEEDS US
AND EVERYONE'S HAD US—
WE'RE HERE BUT NOT HERE:
WE'VE BEEN THERE BUT NOT THERE—
AND WHERE—WHERE DO WE BELONG?
WE ONLY HAVE OURSELVES.
WHERE DO WE BELONG?
PEOPLE LIKE US.

QUEENIE:
LOST.

BLACK:
AND FOUND.

QUEENIE & BLACK:
WHERE . . . ?
WHERE . . . ?

(Black gently kisses her.

Lights come up to reveal the aftermath of the orgy—"limp arms lay flung in all directions/legs make fantastic intersections." Slowly, Sally, naked from the waist up, emerges from the sea of bodies, and, for the first time all evening, actually sees where she is.)

AFTER MIDNIGHT DIES

Sally sings:

SALLY:

Down goes the wall.
Down goes the guard.
After midnight dies
It ain't so hard
To see the truth.
No need for lies.
What we are is all we are
After midnight dies . . .

(Sally wanders around the party until she comes upon Mae, who sits alone, cigarette in hand. A disheveled Eddie crosses to her. On the other side of the room, Oscar crosses to Phil, who's asleep at the piano. Oscar shakes him awake.)

OSCAR: Hey.
MAE: Hey.
PHIL: What time is it?
EDDIE: Late.
MAE: Too late.

(Mae begins to cry. Phil plays the piano, Eddie sings, Sally looks on.)

EDDIE:

When the Golden Boy goes down
Hell, the crowd they get mean,
Can't believe what they seen,
Can't be true.
When the Golden Boy goes down
Fame steps up with a crunch
Lands a dirty left punch
And you're lunch for the newspapers—
Give us a smile boy!
You're the pride of your race!—
Hey wait, use the back door.
Remember your place.

YOU CAN LOOK AT THE WHITE GIRLS, SURE;
BUT, CHAMP, DON'T YOU TOUCH.
WHEN THE GOLDEN BOY WENT DOWN,
DID I FEEL LIKE A HERO?
NOT MUCH . . .

(The Brothers D'Armano intone a vocalise, emotionally fueled by resignation, forgiveness and regret.)

PHIL:
MMMM . . .

OSCAR:
MMM . . . WHO CARES IF WE MISBEHAVE?

PHIL:
M-M-M

OSCAR:
M-M-M

PHIL:
WE WON'T HAVE A JEALOUS BONE

OSCAR:
M-M-M

BROTHERS D'ARMANO:
AND WE'LL BOTH BE BACK IN EACH OTHER'S ARMS
COME MORN.
M-M-M-M-M-M

EDDIE:
WHEN THE GOLDEN BOY WENT DOWN
DID I FEEL LIKE A HERO?
NOT MUCH . . .
NOT MUCH . . .

(As Eddie and Mae, and Phil and Oscar kiss, Sally wanders until she finds Gold and Goldberg sitting at the kitchen table, in partial states of undress, very drunk and very lost.)

GOLD: What do you remember?

GOLDBERG: I remember walking through the front door and saying, "Great party." Next thing I know *ich stehte in mein gatkes und mein tookas stecht und dreussen*. And I can't find my pants. I have no idea who or what I am anymore.

GOLD: You are Goldoff. No, no I was Goldoff and now I'm Golden. No, no, you're . . .

(They sing:)

GOLDBERG:

Can't find my shoes
Ain't seein' straight.

GOLD:

Don't know the time
But I think it's too late.

GOLDBERG:

Don't know how I got here.
Don't know where I am.

GOLD:

Forgot my name.

GOLDBERG:

Must be the booze.

GOLD:

If I hadta name what I feel right now
I'd call it
"The movin' uptown blues."

GOLDBERG:

We did too much too soon, so what?
Everybody does.
The city's full of guys like us
Forgetting who they was.

GOLD:

I think I ran a deli once.

GOLDBERG:

I think I had a wife.

GOLD & GOLDBERG:

Walked in that door tonight and wham—
I'm living someone else's life—
Don't got a past.
Don't got a name.
Can't go back to
From wherever I came.
Whole room's spinning crazy.
Someone make it stop!

(Dolores appears.)

DOLORES: A promise made in the throes of passion is a promise to be kept. Violate that promise and terrible things can happen. Hell hath no fury like a woman . . . performer . . . legend scorned. *(She exits)*

GOLDBERG *(Sings)*:
I NEED MY PANTS.
GOLD *(Sings)*:
I NEED MY SHOES.
TOMORROW WE'LL BE SOBER MEN.
GOLDBERG:
AND JEW-LESS JEWS

GOLD: Gold and Golden?
GOLDBERG: Gold and Golden.

GOLD AND GOLDBERG *(Sings)*:
TONIGHT WE'RE LOST IN
"THE MOVIN' UPTOWN BLUES."

(Sally wanders until she finds Jackie and Nadine sitting on the bed. Dressed in one of Queenie's outfits, Nadine, under Jackie's tutelage, has just done her first line of cocaine.
Nadine sings:)

NADINE:
I ALWAYS WANTED TO SEE THE LIGHTS OF BROADWAY.
I ALWAYS WANTED TO HEAR THE TRAFFIC ROAR.
I ALWAYS WANTED TO BE A PART
OF NEW YORK CITY'S GREAT BIG HEART
AND NOW I AM—I COULDN'T ASK FOR MORE!—
CAN I HAVE SOME MORE?

(Jackie obliges.)

I ALWAYS WANTED TO JINGLE WITH THE RIGHT CROWD.
I ALWAYS WANTED TO FEEL LIKE I BELONG.
I WANNA FEEL LIKE ALL THE BIG GIRLS DO;
ALL BRIGHT AND FIZZED AND SPECIAL TO—

THERE'S NOTHING WRONG WITH THAT—
THERE'S NOTHING WRONG—THERE'S NOTHING WRONG—
THERE'S NOTHING WRONG WITH POUGHKEEPSIE
THAT LIVING IN MANHATTAN WOULDN'T FIX.
I'M JUST A KID IN POUGHKEEPSIE
BUT HERE A KID CAN GET HER GROWN-UP KICKS!

(She laughs.)

I ALWAYS WANTED TO SEE THE LIGHTS OF BROADWAY;
AND I WAS TOLD THAT IF I LOOKED TOO CLOSE
I JUST MIGHT GO BLIND.
BUT LITTLE SISTER'S LOOSE
AND WANTS HER SHARE OF JUICE;
IF THE LIGHTS OF BROADWAY BLIND ME
I DON'T MIND!—

Gimme some more.

JACKIE: What did you just say?
NADINE *(Throaty; determined)*: I want some more.

(Jackie sings:)

JACKIE: Ahhhhhhh.
I COULD LAP UP ALL THE CHAMPAGNE IN PARIS.
I COULD SLURP UP ALL THE OYSTERS ON CAPRI.
I COULD EAT AND DRINK AND SNORT AND SWILL
AND NEVER FEEL I'VE HAD MY FILL.
(IT REALLY ISN'T EASY BEING ME.)
TO SATIATE ME IS A CHORE:
OTHERS KNOW WHEN TO SAY ENOUGH'S ENOUGH.
LITTLE JACKIE CAN ONLY SAY:

I COULD KISS A DOZEN LIPS AND LOCK 'EM TIGHT.
I COULD KISS A HUNDRED MORE TOMORROW NIGHT.
I COULD KISS AND KISS AND KISS AND KISS
AND NEVER FEEL A SECOND OF DELIGHT—
BUT IN THE MORNING I'LL BE SORE.

OTHERS KNOW WHEN IT'S TIME TO CALL IT QUITS:
OTHERS KNOW WHEN THEIR CUPS ARE OVERFILLED:
OTHERS KNOW HOW TO SAY: "I'LL TAKE THIS OR THAT"
OR "EITHER/OR" OR "NEITHER/NOR."
LITTLE JACKIE CAN ONLY SAY:

MORE DANCING!
MORE SHEBANG!
MORE PARTY!
MORE VARIETY!
MORE MOTION!
MORE PIZZAZZ!
MORE DANGER!
MORE TOXICITY!
ALL I WANT IS

I don't know what it is I want.

ALL I WANT IS—
MORE—

(Forcing himself sexually onto Nadine.)

NADINE: No! Stop!

JACKIE:
MORE—MORE! . . .

(Sally watches as Nadine struggles, tries to scream, but Jackie covers her mouth, overpowers her. Lights reveal Eddie lying in Mae's arms.)

MAE: Nadine? *(Suddenly panicked)* Eddie wake up. Baby, something's wrong with Nadine. Eddie!

(A very drunk Eddie leaps up and goes charging into the room. He pulls Jackie off of Nadine and bashes his face. Just as he is doing this, the rest of the party Guests come rushing into the room, including Queenie, Black, Kate and Burrs. Eddie continues punching and swinging, threatening everyone.)

EDDIE: Who's next? Come on! Come on! Scared to take on The Champ? I'll take on all you muthafuckers. Right here! Right now! Come on!

(Eddie goes charging at Queenie and the others. Party erupts into pandemonium as Black grabs Eddie, whirls him around and clobbers him cold. Eddie goes down. During the above, Nadine desperately clings to Madelaine.)

QUEENIE: Nadine, baby, what's wrong?
JACKIE *(Playfully)*: Nothing's wrong.
MAE *(With an edge)*: What did you do to her?
JACKIE: Nothing! We were just playing and—and—and—well you saw him—drunk, out of control. He charges in, like some beast. She's screaming and he's swinging.
MAE: Liar! What did you do to my sister?

(Mae attacks Jackie. Burrs restrains her. Nadine clings to Madelaine.)

QUEENIE: Nadine, sweetie, tell Queenie what happened?

(Nadine is silent.)

Jackie said you two were just playing. Is that true?
JACKIE: Of course it's true. I'm a drunk and a bum, but I'm not—
MADELAINE *(Overlapping)*: Jackie, shut up!
QUEENIE: Did Jackie hurt you?

(Nadine shakes her head no.)

Did anyone hurt you?

(Nadine shakes her head no.)

You just kinda got a little scared, huh?

(Nadine nods; half smiles)

JACKIE *(Instantly buoyed)*: There, you see. The night is still young. Oscar and Phil, how 'bout a song?

*"Uptown
Is looking more like
Downtown
Which is looking more like
Uptown—"*

Come on, Queenie. Let's dance.

*"Bessie Smith is lusting for
A dish of Dorothy Parker
While Carl Van Vechten, naughty boy
Just wants his chocolate darker."*

(Jackie takes out his case of cocaine. Sally steps forward.)

MADELAINE: Sally! Let's go.

(Sally looks at Madelaine as if she's never seen her before and then calmly takes Jackie's arm and they start to walk away.)

(With an edge) Sally! *(And then desperate)* Sally!

(Sally stops and looks back at Madelaine.)

SALLY: Who's Sally?
EDDIE: Mae . . .
MAE: I'm here, Daddy Eddie. I'm here.
BURRS: Will everybody please go home.

(Music underscore as Eddie and Mae, Jackie and Sally, Gold and Goldberg, Oscar and Phil, and Madelaine fade into the night. Kate crosses to Black.)

KATE: So where were you?
BLACK: Catching some air.
KATE: Here's to hoping that's all you were catching.
BLACK: You're the one who brought me here, told me to go play.
KATE: Play, yes. Not fall in love.
BLACK: What?!
KATE: You're falling in love with her.

BLACK: Why do you care? As long as I "look good and deliver." As long as I play by your rules—

KATE: Last time I checked, Black, you were doing pretty damn good playing by my rules, spending my money.

BLACK: Yeah, well, maybe that's no longer enough.

(Kate sings:)

KATE: Well, well, well . . .

LOVERMAN'S IN LOVE?
GO ON—BE "IN LOVE"—AIN'T IT SWEET?
COME MORNING SHE'LL BE BACK
IN THE ARMS OF THAT CLOWN
AND LOVERMAN, YOUR ASS WILL BE
OUT IN THE STREET
AND THEN WHAT?
BACK TO PEDDLING THAT OLD MOOCH?
"BLACK LIKE THE WAY THAT YOU
LOOK TONIGHT:
ELEGANT, SLEEK AND COOL."
IT'S GETTING OLD. YOU'RE GETTING OLD—
THERE ARE YOUNGER MEN
OUT THERE NOW. MISTER BLACK.
I'M GONNA TELL YOU SOMETHING:
SOMETHING I LEARNED TOO LONG AGO:
LOVE AIN'T NOTHIN' BUT A WHOLE LOTTA NOTHIN'
AND YOU KNOW WHAT IT'S REALLY ABOUT?
IT'S ABOUT COMFORT, NOT LOVE, LOVERMAN.
IT'S ABOUT COMFORT
AND KEEPIN' HOLD OF IT, HANGIN' ONTO IT
AND DOIN' WHATEVER IT TAKES
TO GET MORE.
LOVE AIN'T NOTHIN' BUT A WHOLE LOTTA NOTHIN'
A WHOLE LOTTA NOTHIN'!

BLACK: That's you, Kate. That ain't me.

(He walks away from Kate.)

KATE:

DON'T YOU MESS MY PARTY.
DON'T YOU MESS WITH ME—
DON'T YOU FUCK WITH ME!

(Lights reveal, in another corner of the apartment, Queenie and Burrs.)

BURRS: Party's over, Queenie.
QUEENIE: Maybe yours, Burrs, but not mine. My party's just gettin' goin'.

(She turns to go. He grabs her.)

BURRS: I'm gonna—
QUEENIE: What? Beat me with the heel of your shoe, till my lips turn blue?

(There is a deadly intensity between them which is only broken when they both realize Kate and Black are standing there, watching.
Burrs sings:)

BURRS: Queenie's feelin' hot to-night! Yes she is.

WELCOME TO HER PARTY.
HOW YA LIKE THE DRESS?
WELCOME TO HER PARTY.
"BABY WHERE'S MY ICE?"
WHO HERE'S UP FOR ACTION?
WHO HERE'S NEW?
WELCOME TO HER PARTY.

(To Black) Who the hell invited you? And Blackie, my boy, since you're plannin' on throwin' a torpedo into the S.S. *Queenie,* I better warn you, don't touch the face.
QUEENIE *(Seething)*: Shut up, Burrs.
BURRS *(Coon inflections)*: 'Cuz nuthin' gets da little lady soooo riled up as gettin' caught wit' her face minus all of dat paint.
QUEENIE: I said shut up!
BURRS: 'Cuz like the cheap whore she is, everything's gots to be all perfumed and painted so's you don't smell the stink that's justa festerin' underneath.

QUEENIE *(Simultaneously with Burrs below)*: The stink I got on me is from living with you, lying next to you. You have seeped into the pores of my skin, into my blood until everything I own smells like you. And the only thing that'll wash me clean . . . is seeing you dead.

BURRS *(Simultaneously with Queenie above)*:
WELCOME TO HER PARTY,
"BURRSIE WHERE'S MY ICE?"
QUEENIE'S UP FOR DANCIN'.
QUEENIE'S UP FOR ANYTHING.

(Queenie throws herself at him, swinging and hitting him. Black pulls her into the bedroom and slams the door. Inside the bedroom, Queenie's energy is manic, out of control.)

QUEENIE: I gotta go. I gotta . . . I can't breathe, I can't . . . I can't . . .
BLACK: What do you want?
QUEENIE: I want . . . I want . . .
BLACK: Just say it. Tell me. Anything.

(Queenie sings:)

QUEENIE:
I DON'T WANT NO FIGHTIN'.
I DON'T WANT NO BOOZE OR BROKEN GLASS.
I DON'T WANT NO HONKY-TONK.
OR USED-UP MOOCH.

I DON'T WANT SHADOWS.
I CAN FEEL 'EM PRESSIN' DOWN ON ME.
I DON'T WANT THE NIGHT—
I DON'T WANT THE DARK—

THE "WAZZA-WAZZA-BLONDE"
THE GIN-AND-SCREW-IT EYES
THE TINTED MASK OF SNOW AND LIES

WHAT I WISH—
WHAT I WANT—
WHAT I NEED—
I NEED—

(Queenie collapses into Black's arms. Lights up on Kate. Burrs crosses to her.)

BURRS: You wanted this to happen. In fact, you planned the whole goddamn thing. Bringing Black here. Seducing me.

KATE: Seducing you?

BURRS: So that your boyfriend could move in on my wife.

KATE: It's one of the things I love most about you Burrs—despite evidence to the contrary, you're the innocent. You strike the match, the house burns down and you blame everybody else. *(Factual; direct)* Queenie ran into the arms of Black just to get the hell away from you.

BURRS: You don't know a goddamn thing about Queenie and me 'cause you don't know a goddamn thing about love.

KATE: She cheats on you and you suffocate her. If I were you, Burrs, I'd patent that love of yours, 'cause everybody I know is gonna wanna buy a bottle and swallow it whole.

(As Kate stalks away, Burrs turns to the audience.)

BURRS:

How many women in the world?
How many women? Take your pick.
So how come I hook into that one?
She knows my every trick. Yeah.
She knows what makes me tick-tick-tick—
Too late now. The damage is done:
How many women in the world
Know how to push that magic button—boom.
How many many many many many many many women?
One.

How many women on the earth?
How many women could I bear?
How come I put up with that one
Who's tangled in my hair?
She's got in everywhere—
In my skin
In my blood.
All I hear and see—
How many women on the earth

GET IN SO DEEP THEY KILL MY SLEEP—
HOW MANY MANY MANY MANY MANY MANY MANY WOMEN?
SHE . . .

(Burrs turns to find Gold and Goldberg, speaking to each other from opposite sides of the proscenium.)

GOLD: No, you tell him.
GOLDBERG: Why should I?
GOLD: Because we agreed before the night was over that one of us would let that clown know he was not gonna be a part of our uptown show. Now we have come to the man's house, drunk his liquor, and done god knows what with god knows whom . . .

(They see Burrs, standing, listening.)

Burrs we were just . . .

(Burrs turns away from them. To the audience:)

BURRS:

WHAT OTHER WOMAN CAN TAKE THE PUNCHES? Pow!
WHAT OTHER WOMAN WOULD LIKE THE PUNCHES? Pow! Pow! Pow!
WHAT OTHER WOMAN CAN LOOK AT ME AND SAY:
"OKAY. IT'LL DO."
"OKAY. IT'LL DO."
"OKAY. IT'LL DO." —"OKAY. IT'LL DO."

(Launching into his act:)

"MARIE WAS TRICKY
SLY AND STICKY.
BRUDDA, YOU WATCH OUT FOR DAT GAL:
SHE GWINA LUB-YA LIKE DERE'S NO TOMORR-AH
BUT COME TOMORR-AH YA GOTS PLENTY OF SORR-AH . . ."
OKAY. IT'LL DO . . .
OKAY. IT'LL DO . . .

(In isolated light:)

How many women in the world?
How many women can I take?
How much more of that one
Can I take before I break?
But I'm not gonna break
'Cause when I break
Nasty things occur . . .
How many women in the world
Make me weak—
Break me down—
Chew me up. Spit me out.
Make me yowwwwwl!
How many many many many many many many
Women?

(Burrs crosses to his theatrical trunk and slowly begins to put on blackface makeup.)

Her.
Her.
Her.

(Dolores is seen, wandering around the party, the darkened room now lit only by a few remaining candles.)

DOLORES: Okay—okay—who turned off all the lights? Go on, live in the dark, die in the dark, for all I care. When I was younger, youngish, whatever, I flourished in the light, naked to the world. As I got older, I loved the magic, the illusion of just one romantic light caressing the face, the rest of me cloistered in a shroud of darkness. But now I want the light stark and unforgiving. The kind of light that reveals all and spares none. 'Cause that's the real magic. Seeing who's got the stuff and who has not.

(She sings:)

So you think the party's gonna last forever
And you'll always fly this high—but that depends.
The higher the high, the harder you're gonna
Crash back down
When it ends.

YOU CAN MAKE A FORTUNE DOING NEXT TO NOTHING:
YOU CAN SIT THERE ON YOUR ASS AND SCREW YOUR FRIENDS:
BUT YOU BETTER KNOW HOW TO KICK—KICK—KICK YOUR WAY
OUTTA THE BURNING ROOM
WHEN IT ENDS.
YOU CAN SELL YOUR BODY TO THE HIGHEST BIDDER:
YOU CAN CALL IT "LOVE" AND CASH THE DIVIDENDS:
YOU CAN TAKE A MILLION LOVERS
BUT YOU'RE ON YOUR OWN
WHEN IT ENDS.

BEAUTY WON'T MATTER
AND BRAINS WON'T MATTER
WHEN THE WORLD FALLS APART
ONE COLD AND STARVING NIGHT.
MONEY WON'T MATTER
AND LOVE WON'T MATTER
IF YOU AIN'T GOT THE BALLS
FOR THAT ONE LAST FIGHT—

I CAN'T TELL YOU THAT NO PARTY LASTS FOREVER.
I BEEN THERE AND THERE AND THERE AND SEEN ENOUGH
SO YOU BETTER HOPE TO JESUS OR MOHAMMED
OR WHATEVER
THAT YOU GOT THE RIGHT STUFF
WHEN IT ENDS
WHEN IT ENDS
WHEN IT ENDS.

FINALE

Lights reveal Black asleep in bed, and Queenie standing alone, her face bathed in the pre-dawn light.

Queenie sings:

QUEENIE:

THE STARS ARE GONE
SLIPPED OUTTA SIGHT.
I OUGHTA FOLLOW THEM
INTO THE NIGHT.

But here is good
Feels almost right.
Don't call it love, yet
Just call it:
Light.

This is what it is
To wake up, yeah.
This is what it is
To feel warm, yeah.
This is what it is
To be filled, sure.
This is what it is
To be lost—help!
This is what it is
To be scared—God!
This is what it is—
This is what it is—
To know the day
And meet the sun
And find that I am not
The only one.
I am not the only one
Afraid of a world too big
And bright.

This is what it is
To live in . . .

(Black wakes up.)

BLACK: Hey.
QUEENIE: Hey.
BLACK: It's almost day.
QUEENIE: Yeah. I heard a rumor that six o'clock happens twice a day. I guess it must be true. You were asleep.
BLACK: Yeah. I was dreaming.

(Queenie crosses to the bed. They kiss. He pulls back.)

QUEENIE: 'Bout what?
BLACK: Cornfields.
QUEENIE: Cornfields?

(Black nods.)

Don't sound like a dream. Sounds more like a nightmare.
BLACK: No, no, it was nice. Quiet. I remember feeling a breeze. Maybe we ought to go see one.
QUEENIE: One what?
BLACK: A cornfield.
QUEENIE: At four thirty in the morning?

BLACK: No, not now. Tomorrow. Maybe the next day. There's gotta be one somewhere nearby. Pennsylvania maybe. Virginia, hell, I don't know.

QUEENIE: Oh sure, let's hop the Harlem El and say, "Mr. Conductor! Next stop, a cornfield!"

QUEENIE: Look, let's not want more, okay? Let's not even move. Let's not spoil this by wanting too much. Let's just be right here, right now, for as long as it lasts. For as long as we feel what we are feeling. Let's not even breathe. Okay?
BLACK: Okay.

(Queenie relaxes into Black's arms.)

When I was little, the only thing around me that seemed clean was the sky, but you couldn't touch that. Everything else felt like a broken-down version of what used to be. And that woulda been okay if I didn't know there were people, worlds where everything in 'em looked like it had just been taken out of a box three seconds before they'd put it on. And so I started changing everything about myself, the way I talked, how I walked into a room, even how I felt, just so I could be a part of that world where everything felt clean and new. But once I got there I realized just 'cause something's expensive and new, don't mean it's clean. As a matter of fact I've been sort of regretting ever even looking in the first place. Until tonight. When I touch you, I feel like I'm touching parts of you, no one has ever touched before. And in doing so, it's making me feel for the first time ever, clean.

(Black takes a handkerchief and goes to wipe her face. She stops him.)

QUEENIE: What are you doing?
BLACK: Trying to—
QUEENIE: No . . . stop . . . stop.
BLACK: Your face. Beautiful. I just want to see more.

(She looks at him.)

Please . . .

(She nods that it's okay. As he begins to wipe her face, she closes her eyes and lets him. The quiet moment is interrupted by the sound of the Victrola, distant in the background, playing a scratchy old recording of Burrs singing:)

VICTROLA:

"MARIE IS TRICKY
SLY AND STICKY.
BRUDDA, YOU WATCH OUT FOR DAT GAL:
SHE GWINA LUB-YA LIKE DERE'S NO TOMORR-AH—"

(The door to the bedroom slowly opens. The figure in the doorway casts a shadow over the entire room, then steps in. It's Burrs. In blackface. Queenie and Black stand, motionless.)

BURRS *(Sings)*:

"BUT COME TOMORR-AH YA GOTS
PLENTY OF SORR-AH . . ."

Hot-chitza-dee! *(As if his vaudeville act)* Hey Oscar and Phil, do you know "Good Coons Take It in the Rear"? No? Jackie'll teach you. His father taught him. Hey, Madelaine, show us your empty box . . . Of chocolates. Dolores, I've got secrets / Well so do you / I hear you're somewhat Negro / And a great deal Jew? In this corner, de Champ! And in this corner, his wife. *(Mimes punching himself)* "I'm fat! Pow! I'm fat! Pow! I'm fat! Pow!" *(On the last "Pow!" he pulls out a gun)*
QUEENIE: Burrs, what are you doing? Burrs, put the gun down.

(Black makes a move toward Burrs. Burrs points the gun directly at him.)

BURRS: Hey Gold and Goldberg, I hear you're doing a new musical called "Yikes! Let's Hear It for the Kikes!" *(To Queenie, crying out)* You whore. You fuckin' whore. You . . . I loved you! I loved—

How many women in the world
Say: "Okay—it'll do"?
How many many many many many many women?

(Burrs focuses all of his energy on Queenie, completely oblivious to Black, to anything else in the entire world.)

You!

QUEENIE: Burrs, please.

BURRS:
You!

QUEENIE: Please don't do this.

BURRS:
You!

QUEENIE: Burrs, please.

(Black charges at Burrs. They struggle, the gun between them.)

Black—

QUEENIE, BURRS & BLACK:
NOOOOO!

(Gunshot. Burrs staggers away from Black and falls onto the bed. Suddenly, the entire Company envelops the stage and performs the opening vaudeville number, during which Kate enters and hurries Black to safety. Alone, Queenie watches the vaudeville—which tries to lure her into its revelry.)

COMPANY:
Queenie wazza blonde and her age stood still
And she danced twice a day in the vaudeville.

So.
So.
Now you know.

A fascinating woman
As they go . . .
Queenie wazza wazza wazza
Queenie wazza wazza wazza
Queenie wazza wazza wazza
Queenie wazza wazza wazza
Queenie . . . !

(At the vaudeville number's climax, the Company turns to Queenie demanding her to join them.)

QUEENIE:

Queenie wazza . . .
Blonde
In a vaudeville show . . .
And she hid what she was
With a mask of snow . . .

This is what it is to be lost.
This is what it is to be scared.
This is what it is—
This is what it is—

(As Queenie begins to remove her makeup, the Company slowly drops their vaudeville persona and sings:)

COMPANY:

To lose what was
And long for more
And grasp at love
And breathe in hurt
And leave the night
And say good-bye
And say good-bye
And say good-bye
And say . . .

QUEENIE:

THIS IS WHAT IT IS
TO LIVE IN LIGHT . . .

(Queenie is bathed in morning light. Scared, unsure but hopeful, she smiles at the dawn.)

THE END

DATE OF SCRIPT

April 2000
(Black's monologue on page 440 was cut from the text during previews of the original production, but reinstated by the authors for this publication.)

COPYRIGHT

PERFORMING RIGHTS

The stock and amateur rights to *The Wild Party* are controlled exclusively by The Rodgers & Hammerstein Theatre Library, 229 West 28th Street, 11th Floor, New York, NY 10001, without whose permission no performance of it may be made. Website: http://www.rnh.com.

All other inquiries should be addressed to the authors' representatives as follows:

For Michael John LaChiusa: Douglas & Kopelman Artists, Inc., 393 West 49th Street, Suite 5G, New York, NY 10019. Attn: Charles Kopelman. Phone: 212-445-0160. Fax: 212-246-7138.

For George C. Wolfe: Loeb & Loeb LLP, 345 Park Avenue, 18th Floor, New York, NY 10154. Attn: Seth Gelblum, Esq. Phone: 212-407-4931. Fax: 212-407-4990.

ORIGINAL PRODUCTION

The Wild Party was commissioned and developed by The Joseph Papp Public Theater/New York Shakespeare Festival. It received its world premiere on Broadway at the Virginia Theatre on March 10, 2000, opening to critics on April 13. It closed on June 11, 2000, after playing thirty-six previews and sixty-eight regular performances.

The Wild Party was produced by The Joseph Papp Public Theater/New York Shakespeare Festival (George C. Wolfe, Producer) and Scott Rudin/Paramount Pictures, Roger Berlind, Williams/Waxman. It was directed by George C. Wolfe. The set was designed by Robin Wagner, costumes by Toni-Leslie James, lighting by Jules Fisher and Peggy Eisenhauer, sound by Tony Meola, orchestrations by Bruce Coughlin, choreography by Joey McKneely, hair design by Jeffrey Frank; the music director was Todd Ellison, the music coordinator was Seymour Red Press, the technical supervisor was David Benken, the production stage manager was Gwendolyn M. Gilliam, artistic producer (NYSF) was Rosemarie Tichler, senior director, external affairs (NYSF) was Margaret M. Lioi, the managing director (NYSF) was Mark Litvin, the general manager (NYSF) was Michael Hurst, the associate producer (NYSF)/dramaturg was Wiley Hausam, casting was by Jordan Thaler and Heidi Griffiths, the press representative (NYSF) was Carol R. Fineman and Thomas V. Naro, general management was by 101 Productions, Ltd., marketing was provided by The Karpel Group, and the press representative was Barlow/Hartman Public Relations. Production photographs were taken by Carol Rosegg; illustration was by Miguel Covarrubbias; graphic design was by Paula Scher/Pentagram.

The original cast (in order of appearance) was as follows:

QUEENIE .... Toni Collette
BURRS .... Mandy Patinkin
JACKIE .... Marc Kudisch
MISS MADELAINE TRUE .... Jane Summerhays
SALLY .... Sally Murphy
EDDIE MACKREL .... Norm Lewis
MAE .... Leah Hocking
NADINE .... Brooke Sunny Moriber
PHIL D'ARMANO .... Nathan Lee Graham
OSCAR D'ARMANO .... Michael McElroy
DOLORES .... Eartha Kitt
GOLD .... Adam Grupper

GOLDBERG .... Stuart Zagnit
BLACK .... Yancey Arias
KATE .... Tonya Pinkins

UNDERSTUDIES .... Nicole Van Giesen, Dominique Plaisant, David Masenheimer, Jeff Gardner, Jennifer Frankel, Ching Valdes-Aran, Adrian Bailey, Jennifer Hall

AWARDS

The Wild Party was nominated for seven Tony Awards, including Best Musical, Best Original Score, Best Book, Best Actress in a Musical (Toni Collette), Best Actor in a Musical (Mandy Patinkin), Best Featured Actress in a Musical (Eartha Kitt) and Best Lighting Design (Jules Fisher and Peggy Eisenhauer).

It received three Drama Desk nominations: Outstanding Actor in a Musical (Mandy Patinkin), Outstanding Actress in a Musical (Toni Collette) and Outstanding Featured Actress in a Musical (Eartha Kitt). Other nominations included the Outer Critics Circle Award for Outstanding Actress (Toni Collette) and The Drama League Award for Distinguished Production of a Musical. Toni Collette won a Theatre World Award.

The original cast recording of *The Wild Party* received a Grammy nomination for Best Original Cast Album.

AUDIORECORDING, VIDEORECORDING AND MUSIC PUBLISHING

Original Cast Recording: Decca Broadway 012 159 003-2. Produced by Phil Ramone.

Videotaped by the New York Public Library's Theatre on Film and Tape Archive at the Virginia Theatre on Broadway on May 18, 2000. 117 minutes. Format: 3/4" SP Color. Catalog Number: NCOV 2428. Restricted to qualified researchers. Contact: New York Public Library for the Performing Arts, 40 Lincoln Center Plaza, New York, NY 10023-7498; telephone: 212-870-1642; website: www.nypl.org/research/lpa/lpa.html

Vocal Selections: Warner Brothers Publications.

ORCHESTRA INSTRUMENTATION

Piano
Woodwinds (4—all double or triple)
Trumpets (2)
Trombone
Violins (3)
Bass/Tuba
Drums
Percussion
Guitar/Banjo

BIOGRAPHIES

Warren Abbott

Michael John LaChiusa

MICHAEL JOHN LACHIUSA (Composer/Lyricist, Co-Librettist), born in 1962, was represented on Broadway during the 1999–2000 season by *Marie Christine* and *The Wild Party*, receiving Tony nominations for Best Score and Best Book for both shows. His other work includes *Little Fish, Hello Again, First Lady Suite, The Petrified Prince, Break/Agnes/Eulogy for Mister Hamm* and *Chronicle of a Death Foretold*, for which he received a Tony nomination for Best Book (with Graciela Daniele and Jim Lewis). He was the 1998–1999 Composer-in-Residence at the Lyric Opera of Chicago where his new musical *Lovers and Friends* (*Chautauqua Variations*) was presented in June 2001. Mr. LaChiusa is a member of The Dramatists Guild. His numerous awards include the 1995 Gilman & Gonzalez-Falla Musical Theatre Award and the 1999 Ed Kleban Award. Recordings include the Grammy-nominated cast album of *The Wild Party* (Decca Broadway), *Marie Christine* and *Hello Again* (both on RCA Victor) and *First Lady Suite* (PS Classics).

GEORGE C. WOLFE (Co-Librettist, Director) won the Tony Award in 1993 for his direction of *Angels in America: Millenium Approaches* and in 1996 for his direction of *Bring in 'Da Noise, Bring in 'Da Funk*. His other directing credits on Broadway include *On the Town*; *The Tempest*; *Twilight: Los Angeles 1992*; *Angels in America: Perestroika*; *Jelly's Last Jam* (of which he is also an author); *Topdog/Underdog*; and *At Liberty!*, starring Elaine Stritch.

For The Joseph Papp Public Theater/New York Shakespeare Festival, where Mr. Wolfe has served as Producer since 1993, he has directed Shakespeare's *Macbeth, Blade to the Heat*, Brecht's *The Caucasian Chalk Circle* and *Spunk*, which he adapted from Zora Neale Hurston stories. For Harlem's famed Apollo Theatre he wrote and directed *Harlem Song*. Wolfe also directed *Amistad* at the Lyric Opera of Chicago and is the author of *The Colored Museum*. In addition to Drama Desk, Outer Critics Circle, Drama-Logue and OBIE awards, he was named a "living landmark" by the New York Landmarks Conservancy, and he was honored as a "Library Lion" by the New York Public Library.

Julia Maloof

George C. Wolfe

THE JOSEPH PAPP PUBLIC THEATER/NEW YORK SHAKESPEARE FESTIVAL (Producer) Founded by Joseph Papp in 1954 and now one of the nation's preeminent cultural institutions, The Joseph Papp Public Theater/New York Shakespeare Festival is a theater where all the country's voices, rhythms and cultures converge and which serves as a forum for ideas. In 1962, the Delacorte Theater in Central Park was erected to provide the Festival with a permanent summertime home in which to present free Shakespeare in Central Park, which continues to this day. Since 1967, the Festival has made its year-round home at the former Astor Library, renamed The Public Theater, which was rededicated as The Joseph Papp Public Theater in 1992. The building opened with the musical *Hair* and was followed by such plays and musicals as *No Place to Be Somebody; The Basic Training of Pavlo Hummel; That Championship Season; Short Eyes; A Chorus Line; For Colored Girls Who Have Considered Suicide When the Rainbow is Enuf; The Pirates of Penzance; The Normal Heart; The Colored Museum; Fires in the Mirror; The Tempest,* starring Patrick Stewart; *The Seagull,* starring Meryl Streep; *Bring in 'Da Noise, Bring in 'Da Funk; Topdog/Underdog;* and *At Liberty!*, starring Elaine Stritch. The Public Theater/NYSF productions have collectively won thirty-three Tony Awards, 128 OBIEs, thirty-four Drama Desk Awards, six New York Drama Critics Circle Awards and four Pulitzer Prizes. Twenty-five shows have transferred to Broadway.

WILEY HAUSAM is the executive director of the Jack H. Skirball Center for the Performing Arts at New York University, which will open in fall 2003. From 1993–2000, he was an associate producer at The Joseph Papp Public Theater/New York Shakespeare Festival, supervising musical theater. During that time, he worked closely with Michael John LaChiusa, George C. Wolfe, Adam Guettel, Tina Landau, Savion Glover and Jason Robert Brown. He was the artistic director of the acclaimed Songbook Series at Joe's Pub from 1998–2002, when the series ended (*Backstage* Bistro Award 2001, *New York* magazine's Best of New York 2001). He produced Faith Prince's solo concert show *Leap of Faith* (DRG Records). Hausam founded the New Lyric Festival in Northampton, Massachusetts, a summer musical theater festival in 1996 and 1997. He has consulted for the Lyric Opera of Chicago and the Center for Contemporary Opera in New York City, and teaches in the Graduate Musical Theater Writing Program at New York University. Prior to 1993, he was an artists' representative at International Creative Management.

Carol Rosegg

Wiley Hausam